The Wycliffite Heresy
Authority and the Interpretation of Texts

Kantik Ghosh argues that one of the main reasons for Lollardy's sensational resonance for its times, and for its immediate posterity, was its exposure of fundamental
problems in late medieval academic engagement with the Bible, its authority and
its polemical uses. Examining Latin and English sources, Ghosh shows how the
same debates over biblical hermeneutics and associated methodologies were from
the 1380s onwards conducted both within and outside the traditional university
framework, and how, by eliding boundaries between Latinate biblical speculation
and vernacular religiosity, Lollardy changed the cultural and political positioning
of both. Covering a wide range of texts – scholastic and extramural, in Latin and
in English, written over half a century from Wyclif to Thomas Netter – Ghosh
concludes that by the first decades of the fifteenth century Lollardy had partly won
the day. Whatever its fate as a religious movement, it had successfully changed the
intellectual landscape of England.

KANTIK GHOSH is Darby Fellow and Tutor in English Literature at Lincoln College,
Oxford. He has contributed articles to *Poetica*, *New Medieval Literatures*, and the
Scottish Literary Journal. This is his first book.

CAMBRIDGE STUDIES IN MEDIEVAL LITERATURE 45

The Wycliffite Heresy

Authority and the
Interpretation of Texts

CAMBRIDGE STUDIES IN MEDIEVAL LITERATURE

General editor
Alastair Minnis, *University of York*

Editorial board
Patrick Boyde, *University of Cambridge*
John Burrow, *University of Bristol*
Rita Copeland, *University of Pennsylvania*
Alan Deyermond, *University of London*
Peter Dronke, *University of Cambridge*
Simon Gaunt, *King's College, London*
Nigel Palmer, *University of Oxford*
Winthrop Wetherbee, *Cornell University*

This series of critical books seeks to cover the whole area of literature written in the major medieval languages – the main European vernaculars, and medieval Latin and Greek – during the period c. 1100–1500. Its chief aim is to publish and stimulate fresh scholarship and criticism on medieval literature, special emphasis being placed on understanding major works of poetry, prose, and drama in relation to the contemporary culture and learning which fostered them.

Recent titles in the series

Christopher Cannon *The Making of Chaucer's English:
A Study of Words*
Rosalind Brown-Grant *Christine de Pizan and the Moral Defence
of Women: Reading Beyond Gender*
Richard Newhauser *The Early History of Greed: The Sin of Avarice in Early
Medieval Thought and Literature*
Margaret Clunies Ross *Old Icelandic Literature and Society*
Donald Maddox *Fictions of Identity in Medieval France*
Rita Copeland *Pedagogy, Intellectuals and Dissent in the Later Middle Ages:
Lollardy and Ideas of Learning*

A complete list of titles in the series can be found at the end of the volume.

The Wycliffite Heresy

Authority and the Interpretation of Texts

KANTIK GHOSH

Lincoln College, Oxford

PUBLISHED BY THE PRESS SYNDICATE OF THE UNIVERSITY OF CAMBRIDGE
The Pitt Building, Trumpington Street, Cambridge, United Kingdom

CAMBRIDGE UNIVERSITY PRESS
The Edinburgh Building, Cambridge CB2 2RU, UK
40 West 20th Street, New York, NY 10011-4211, USA
10 Stamford Road, Oakleigh, VIC 3166, Australia
Ruiz de Alarcón 13, 28014 Madrid, Spain
Dock House, The Waterfront, Cape Town 8001, South Africa

http://www.cambridge.org

First published 2002

Printed in the United Kingdom at the University Press, Cambridge

Typeface Adobe Garamond 11.5/14 pt.   *System* LATEX 2$_\varepsilon$ [TB]

A catalogue record for this book is available from the British Library.

Library of Congress Cataloguing in Publication data
Ghosh, Kantik, 1967–
The Wycliffite heresy: authority and the interpretation of texts / Kantik Ghosh.
p.   cm. – (Cambridge studies in medieval literature; 45)
Includes bibliographical references and index.
ISBN 0-521-80720-4
1. Bible – Evidences, authority, etc. – History of doctrines.   2. Bible – Criticism,
interpretation, etc. – History – Middle Ages, 600–1500.   3. Wycliffe, John, d. 1384 – Views
on authority of Bible.   4. Lollards.   I. Title.   II. Series.
BS480 .G48   2001
273'.6 – dc21   2001025958

ISBN 0 521 80720 4 hardback

To Anouk and Ingmar, for inspiration

Contents

Acknowledgements

My first debt of gratitude must be twin: to my doctoral supervisor at Cambridge, Richard Beadle, for his advice, guidance and encouragement, and to Anne Hudson, for her immense generosity with her time and expertise, and her abiding patience with my numberless importunities. It is an equal pleasure to thank those who, over the years, have helped with criticisms, suggestions, references or general encouragement: in particular I must mention Helen Cooper, Douglas Gray, Sally Mapstone, Suzanne Reynolds, Michael Sargent, Wendy Scase and Fiona Somerset. Rita Copeland, Eamon Duffy, Alastair Minnis, James Simpson and an anonymous reader for Cambridge University Press have been invaluable commentators: to them I remain deeply indebted. Jeremy Catto and Maarten Hoenen kindly read and commented on Chapter 1, and Sir Anthony Kenny generously made time to discuss aspects of Wyclif's thought amidst many pressing demands. The munificent award of a post-doctoral fellowship from the Japan Society for the Promotion of Sciences enabled a crucial visit to Tokyo to examine manuscripts in Japanese collections. Toshiyuki Takamiya kindly provided access to relevant manuscripts in his personal collection, for which I remain very grateful. Nigel Wilson generously clarified some of the knottier points of scholastic Latin, while Andreas Janousch did the same for the finer points of academic German; I am much indebted to them for sparing the time from their own research. My fellow English tutors at Lincoln College, Oxford, Stephen Gill and Peter McCullough, have been unfailingly supportive: it is a pleasure to acknowledge their kindness and understanding. I must also thank Oxford University Press and the Editorial Board of *Poetica* for granting permission to reprint sections from two articles: 'Eliding the Interpreter: John Wyclif and

Scriptural Truth', which appeared in *New Medieval Literatures* 2 (1998), and 'Contingency and the Christian Faith: William Woodford's Anti-Wycliffite Hermeneutics', which appeared in *Poetica* 49 (1998). I am grateful to the various libraries whose manuscripts collections I have consulted; particular thanks must go to the staff of Duke Humfrey's in the Bodleian and of the Manuscripts Room in Cambridge University Library. Warm thanks are also given to the authorities of the Prague National Library for permission to use the photograph of one of the manuscripts in their collection on the cover. Finally, it is an especial pleasure to be able to thank St John's College and Jesus College, Cambridge, and Lincoln College, Oxford, for their many and varied generosities; this book could not have been written without their financial and other support.

Abbreviations

AHDLMA	*Archives d'histoire doctrinale et littéraire du moyen âge*
BGPTM	Beiträge zur Geschichte der Philosophie und Theologie des Mittelalters
BRUO	A. B. Emden, *A Biographical Register of the University of Oxford to AD 1500*, 3 vols. (Oxford, 1957–9)
CCCM	*Corpus Christianorum (Continuatio Mediaeualis)*
CIVICIMA	Comité International du vocabulaire des institutions et de la communication intellectuelles au moyen âge
CHLGEMP	*The Cambridge History of Later Greek and Early Medieval Philosophy*, ed. A. H. Armstrong (Cambridge, 1967)
CHLMP	*The Cambridge History of Later Medieval Philosophy*, ed. Norman Kretzmann, Anthony Kenny and Jan Pinborg (Cambridge, 1982)
HLW	Richard Sharpe, *A Handlist of the Latin Writers of Great Britain and Ireland before 1540* (Turnhout, 1997)
MED	*The Middle English Dictionary* (Ann Arbor, MI, 1954–)
MLD	*Dictionary of Medieval Latin from British Sources* (Oxford, 1975–)
MM	Miscellanea Mediaevalia (Berlin, 1962–)
PL	*Patrologia Latina*, ed. J.-P. Migne
RTAM	*Recherches de théologie ancienne et médiévale*
SCH	Studies in Church History
WBK	G. A. Benrath, *Wyclifs Bibelkommentar* (Berlin, 1966)

Introduction

'Non est finis potencie sic glosantis' ('There is no end to the power of glossing so'), says John Wyclif disapprovingly in his *De Apostasia* of a particular interpretation of a biblical passage relating to the Eucharist.[1] His statement invokes the twin counters of the following study: 'power' and 'glossing', 'authority' and 'interpretation'. The 'text' to be glossed or interpreted is of course the Bible. Wyclif, and the heresy which arose from his dissident thought, placed the notion of an unglossed, indeed *deglossed* biblical text at the centre of both academic and popular politics.[2] Such a gesture both was premissed on and implied various startling radicalisms. Preeminently, it involved the notion of reclamation: the Bible had to be reclaimed from the discourse of glossing. For Wyclif, this primarily signified a reclamation from contemporary academia and Church and the hermeneutic practices institutionalised therein. Equally importantly, such a reclamation would only be the prelude to the liberation of the deglossed text into discourses other than those traditionally empowered to deal with the Bible, discourses outside the institutionally demarcated ones of Church and University with their attendant mechanisms of control and security. Such a liberation is simultaneously also a reclamation: this was what Christianity had been like 'originally', the *fides antiqua scripture* referred to in *De Apostasia*.[3]

Indeed, the three elements I have just pointed to are central to the thought of Wyclif and his later followers: a Bible liberated from a corrupt academia and its associated intellectual practices, as well as its perceived values and norms; a Bible self-consciously made accessible to a readership considered – at least theoretically – to be 'simple' and unlearned; the above processes seen as culminating in, indeed constituting, a return to the lost truths of Christ, of the apostles, and of the *ecclesia primitiva*. Wyclif's dissidence therefore has its roots in his alienation from what he perceived to be the contemporary academic world, and the place of the Bible in it, and as a result, is in its nature not merely theological, but also methodological. The hermeneutics arising out of his methodological revisionism forms in its turn the basis for a radical politics and ecclesiology, and accounts for the dense, if often confused and self-contradictory, intellectual content of what became a popular heresy.

However, though Wyclif rebelled against the interpretative practices that he felt characterised the academic milieu of his times, he remained sufficiently embedded within that milieu to invoke its hermeneutic categories and use its intellectual tools. Indeed, his rebellion is not predicated on a simple and facile rejection of the premises and the superstructures of contemporary academic study of the Bible. What he instead attempts is a transformation, a reclamation of even academia from its present corrupt state into what it ideally should be: a devoted handmaiden serving the Word. As a result, Wyclif's thought involves major redefinitions of inherited intellectual discourses; these, he feels, must be realigned in correct ways. Lollardy is therefore not just an anti-intellectual heresy advocating a fundamentalist return to the Bible, though anti-intellectualism does form one of its major facets; it is equally an *intellectual* heresy struggling to come to terms with some of the most crucial late-medieval issues relating to the place of the intellect in the domain of faith,[4] issues most problematically highlighted in the context of the logical study of God.[5]

One therefore recognises in the often exhilarating novelties of Wyclif's thought, and of that of his followers, some conceptual polarities of the most venerable Christian pedigree: reason and authority, *scientia* and *sapientia*, Aristotle and Augustine, Scripture and Tradition, philosophy and theology, logic and rhetoric, learning and revelation. These binaries come to the surface recurrently, and are subjected, in Lollard writings, to almost ceaseless redefinitions and reconfigurations in response to polemical and philosophical exigencies. In the works of those arguing against Lollardy – and these are given equal attention in the pages that follow – the reconfigurations are undertaken preeminently to confront the unprecedented Lollard achievement of converting into popular vernacular currency ideas traditionally confined to an academic Latinate mint.[6] It is in such reconfigurations and in the context – intellectual, political, ecclesiological – underlying them that much of the interest of the Wycliffite heresy lies. The following study accordingly finds its focus in a primarily synchronic vision of political and intellectual interaction, in which the importance of texts and ideas lies more in their engagement with one another, than in their individual diachronic histories. Indeed, it is one of my major contentions that the works produced in and around the Lollard heresy can be most illuminatingly studied when one gives conceptual centrality to the ongoing dialogue in which they participate. Instead of tracing intellectual genealogies – which in any case must necessarily remain dubious, given the state of our present knowledge of fourteenth-century hermeneutics after Ockham and before Wyclif – I have traced the outlines of a dialogue and its underlying ideological motivations. A history of textual interpretation cannot be isolated from a history of interpreters and their extra-textual aims, and the institutional and cultural contexts within which they operate.

For the purposes of a study of the Lollard heresy in its hermeneutic aspects, the central institutional context is provided by medieval academia in general, and more specifically, by Oxford University and its intellectual practices. One must of course begin with an acknowledgement of the immense diversity – in terms both of contents and of methodologies – of what we describe as late scholasticism, and of the consequent danger of hasty if attractive generalisations. Phillipe Buc has recently argued for an awareness of the polysemy of medieval clerical discourse, and its internal tensions and contradictions: 'La polysémie des éléments du discours clérical rend possible une propagande politique présentant à chacun ce qu'il voulait entendre... Fonction d'un réel manque d'unanimité, la polysémie pouvait toujours se résoudre en ses éléments affrontés' ('The polysemy of the elements of clerical discourse made possible political propaganda allowing each to think what he wished... The effect of a genuine absence of unanimity, such polysemy could always resolve itself into its conflicting elements').[7] Buc also argues against the notion of a monolithic clerical discourse providing absolutist ideological control.[8] The Lollard heresy needs to be placed against such a background of richly conflicting discursive traditions, as one of its primary polemical – one might even say existential – emphases was directed precisely against this perceived conflictual nature of contemporary academia. Indeed, it is a perception of fragmentation and ideological conflict which forms the core of Lollardy's own generalising vision of the medieval university and its discursive practices. The implications of such fragmentation and conflict for the study and, more importantly, for the *uses* of the Bible, are felt to be profoundly negative and constitutive of an effective eclipse of all that the Word of God should stand for. It is therefore no surprise that one of the major thrusts of Lollard anti-academic polemic should be directed against those medieval intellectual traditions which are inseparable from conflict: preeminently, those relating to dialectic, rhetoric and the associated uses of the Bible.

Dialectic had always been a problematic methodology. St Augustine saw in it 'une arme victorieuse contre toutes les cavillations des hérétiques' ('a victorious weapon against all heretical sophistries'), but it turned out to be a two-edged weapon, and as early as the eleventh century there were protests against its indiscriminate and impertinent use.[9] Though in theory dialectic, and the disputational methodologies accompanying it, were meant to lead to the establishment and elucidation of 'truth', in practice it had assumed a rather different form:

> the disputations . . . became more and more an exercise of dialectical skill for its own sake and less and less a method of presenting and reconciling diverse opinions on a topic of substantial import . . . There is a certain tension between the medieval ideal of 'demonstrative' science as a system of proofs deducing conclusions by ordered steps from first principles, and the actual forms of doctrinal disputation. The arguments adduced in a disputation have an almost fortuitous character and are certainly not always demonstrative. Their aim is principally to persuade the opponent.[10]

The interpenetration of the discourse of 'truth' (theoretically the province of dialectic) and of that of persuasion (theoretically the province of rhetoric) signalled in the above quotation was recognised and built into the disputative structures of medieval academia,[11] and occasioned the running criticism of 'sophistry'[12] (a criticism, we may note, which is almost a refrain in Lollard writings). Palémon Glorieux describes the background to this rhetorical quality of medieval disputation in a passage which bears quotation at length:

> Dans ces disputes quodlibétiques en effet l'homme entier se trouvait intéressé: il y venait avec son tempérament, ses ambitions, ses travers, ses qualités; il y apportait sa personnalité scientifique avec ses animosités, ses décisions, ses préventions. Les débats . . . ne demeuraient

pas . . . dans les hautes sphères de la spéculation; ils abordaient presque infailliblement les questions d'actualité, provoquant par le fait toute une série d'actions et de réactions chez ces hommes qui vivent avidement la vie de leur milieu . . . le polémiste en particulier se laissera très vite entrevoir; la rapidité de pensée, la précision des idées présentées, la netteté dans les positions adoptées trahiront l'entraînement intellectuel et les qualités d'exposition.[13]

The entire man was involved in these quodlibetic disputes: with his temperament, his ambitions, his failings as well as his qualities. He brought to them his scientific personality with its animosities, its determinations and its prejudices. The debates were not confined to high spheres of speculation; they dealt, almost unfailingly, with questions of current interest, thereby provoking a succession of actions and reactions among men who lived the life of their milieu avidly. In particular, the polemicist would reveal himself most quickly [in such debates]; the rapidity of thought, the precision of the ideas presented and the clarity of the positions adopted would betray intellectual training and qualities of exposition.

As we shall see in the following chapters, for Wyclif and the Lollards, contemporary scholastic endeavour is reduced to a sterile game of vanity and power premissed on the methodologies described above by Kenny and Glorieux. Most disturbing for them was the extent to which the Bible was implicated in such an academic milieu with its self-conscious accommodation of interested readings and 'distortions' of the sacred text.[14] In attempting to confront such received uses of the Bible, Lollardy was of course taking on not just the disputative practices of medieval academia and the place of the Bible within such practices, but more generally, received notions of textual *auctoritas* and of accepted uses of biblical exegesis.

Marie-Dominique Chenu has acutely pointed out that 'la "scolastique" commence dans la manipulation des dossiers que le théologien a rassemblés' ('"scholasticism" began with the manipulation of dossiers assembled by the theologian').[15] Textual *auctoritas* is above all a question of manipulation: biblical and other 'authoritative' passages provide an occasion for an interested, reinventive hermeneutics which can be rhetorical (when affective or persuasive) or dialectical (when argumentative, confrontational or ludic), or both.[16] Roland Barthes describes this hermeneutics as a process wherein the 'authoritative' text is 'used, and in a sense *managed*, like reinvested capital',[17] a modern version of Alan of Lille's celebrated *aperçu* that 'an authority has a wax nose, which means it can be bent into taking on different meanings'.[18] A culturally central text which also happens to be the product of ancient, and very different, milieux must necessarily be reinvented to accommodate later needs; however, what is extraordinary about medieval academic discourses is the extent to which this process of reinvention is acknowledged and worked into the very fabric of highly self-conscious exegetical *mentalités*.[19] Such an acknowledgement gives rise to its own peculiar tensions: sceptical awarenesses of various orders coexist with equally varied rationalisations of biblical reinvention in liaisons of greater or lesser happiness. But one must stress the happiness, and if one allows oneself a single generalisation about 'medieval scholasticism', it would be one that would stress the working accommodation of contradiction and conflict within an intellectual framework which is at ease with, and indeed valorises – one might almost say finds its *raison d'être* in – the notion of dialogue. Alain de Libera underlines its importance; after a discussion of humanist mockery of the perceived medieval predilection for disputation, he adds: 'la charge humaniste touche juste sur un point proprement médiéval: la pensée 'universitaire' est une pensée agonistique, la loi de la discussion s'impose à tous' ('the humanist accusation precisely touched on one properly medieval point: "university-thought" was agonistic, for the discursive imperative imposed itself on all').[20]

The *agon* of medieval academia finds its institutionally sanctioned expression not only in the disputative methodologies so central to its functioning,[21] but also, as I pointed out above, in one of its most important intellectual tools: the exegesis of 'authoritative' texts, preeminently that of the Bible. Textual 'authority' exists in a relationship of dialogue with the interpreter: a source-'authority', seen as the repository of value, is ceaselessly reinvented through a process of hermeneutic supplementation.[22] The medieval vocabulary for this process is varied: the verbs commonly used are *adaptare, applicare, supplere*.[23] Such supplementary readings are theoretically acceptable when the text in question is the Bible, because of its status as the Word of God, infinite in signification.[24] In practical terms, such hermeneutic strategies began with early Christian apologetics, and therefore retained, for later ages, patristic sanction.[25]

The basic tension in Christianity as the evolving religion of a (constantly reinterpreted) text – a tension between source and supplement, between the divine Word and human glossing – assumes overt prominence in self-conscious academic textual discourses which are centred around reading and exegesis. In particular, 'correct' modes of the study of the Bible came to be a charged area of debate in the fourteenth century, with a perceived falling-off from dedicated, properly oriented biblical studies, into extraneous vanities.[26] Lollardy therefore seeks to restore the Bible to the position of centrality that is its due, and finds one of its primary concerns in the notion of 'right' reading. As a result, its fundamental anxiety is, in general terms, about the threat of discourses based on biblical studies suffocating the text they are in theory meant to elucidate, and specifically, about the threat of the realm of 'glossing' taking over the realm of the 'text'. Evidently, such a disjunction implies a positivistic, essentialist notion of the 'text' and its possible meanings. An important conceptual polarity in Wycliffite writing – one that I choose as a governing paradigm for the following study – therefore opposes a dialogic, interested and, by implication, corrupt 'glossatorial' hermeneutics institutionalised in Church and University, to a (in theory) monologic apprehension of the divine mind through a transparent 'open' text. Such a vision is necessarily a chimera, but that is beside the point. What is important is that Lollardy finds its self-definition in the notion of disinterested reading, which in Lollard theory is identified with reading in accordance with God's intention. One of its central polemical thrusts is therefore in the direction of a denial of the inevitable dialogism of hermeneutics; indeed, as we shall see, much of Wyclif's own thought and that of his followers is actively uneasy with the very notion of a systematic textual hermeneutics, and all that it implies.

Wycliffism's theoretical postulation of an 'open' biblical text which offers meanings to readers both within and without sanctioned discourses of Church and University, meanings which are *essentially* those informing Christ's teachings and the *ecclesia primitiva*, necessitates an engagement with some of the inherited Gordian knots of the academic study of the Bible.[27] For Lollardy, as I pointed out earlier, is not predicated on an outright rejection of the academic superstructures of the study of the Bible. Instead, its affinity to a theoretical monologism results in a tormented involvement with received intellectual categories and methodological dichotomies.

One of the most important of these relates to the traditional polarisation of the two kinds of knowledge of the Bible: *scientia* and *sapientia*. As Tullio Gregory has pointed out, the terms are subject to a variety of conflicting uses, in a manner going back to Augustine.[28] In this study, however, I will be using *scientia* to designate the academic, philological study of the Bible, involving, roughly, the following elements: a knowledge or at least an awareness of the importance of Greek and Hebrew, close rationalist attention to the text, a reliance on context to clarify dubious points of interpretation, an awareness of the centrality of textual criticism, an acknowledgement of the different cultural circumstances in which the Bible was written and compiled. *Sapientia* involves a non- or supra-rational apprehension of divine meaning, perhaps as a result of direct inspiration from the Holy Ghost, and aligns itself with tradition and authority rather than with reason.[29] While *scientia* stresses the intellectually accessible aspects of biblical language, *sapientia* emphasises its abiding opacity and mystery. Though Wyclif and the Lollards use the actual terms in a variety of ways, the polarisation I have sought to underline is central to their thought. I will therefore use the words in the rather schematised senses outlined above as a convenient conceptual tool to clarify certain recurring motifs in the writings of the Lollards and their antagonists.

Sapientia, as I pointed out above, aligns itself with authority and tradition. In this scheme of things, relevant textual meaning is the product of much more than the text. The exegete must take into account what Heiko Oberman calls Tradition I: Tradition as the history of scriptural interpretation.[30] A crux of Lollard polemic therefore consists in the determination of the extent to which 'Tradition' is acceptable as a valid means of determining biblical meaning. As with the Lollard treatment of the *scientia-sapientia* dichotomy, there is much variety in their handling of the notion of 'Tradition'. One comes across the entire range of opinions from Wyclif, who had a stated predilection for early tradition and biblical commentaries from the first millennium after Christ, to later followers such as Anne Hudson describes, who considered even the exegesis of the four major Fathers as 'glossatorial' and corrupt.[31] However, though there is much difference of opinion within the Lollard camp regarding the precise limits of acceptable early exegetical tradition, there is a general emphasis on the rejection of contemporary glossing, and on the need to go back to the *originalia* of the Fathers. The positivist historiography underlying such a 'back to the *fons religionis*' approach, and the implied vision of the 'essence' of Christianity is only another aspect of what I have described as Lollard monologism. The contrasting dialogic approach to tradition is well described by Joseph de Ghellinck in the course of his explanation of why, despite the availability of the works of the early Fathers, 'on voit la grande majorité des auteurs, S. Thomas excepté et quelques autres, se contenter habituellement des textes patristiques fournis par ces trois séries de recueils, les *Quatuor Libri Sententiarum* de Pierre Lombard, la *Concordia* de Gratien . . . et la *Glossa Ordinaria*' ('the great majority of authors, excepting St Thomas and some others, is seen habitually to be satisfied with patristic texts provided by these three anthologies, Peter Lombard's *Quatuor Libri Sententiarum*, Gratian's *Concordia* . . . and the *Glossa Ordinaria*).[32] De Ghellinck proceeds to explain 'cette espèce d'insouciance' ('this kind of carelessness'), this avoidance of 'la question du passé' ('the question of the past') in the tranquil possession of tradition:

> Cela est dû à la manière dont on concevait l'argument de tradition ou d'autorité. Car, sans être nullement synonymes en théorie, les deux genres d'arguments se confondaient concrètement. C'est là croyons-nous que réside le vrai motif de cette apparente pénurie de l'argument patristique. Comme on l'a fait remarquer plus haut, l'on avait conscience de vivre de la tradition. Mais ce n'était pas directement à la tradition qu'en appelait l'argumentation technique, mais plutôt à une 'auctoritas', prise sans doute à un représentant de cette tradition . . . il [the authoritative author] est envisagé comme dépositaire des mêmes prérogatives que les autres auteurs admis au rang d'auctoritates.[33]

> It was due to the way in which arguments from tradition or from authority were conceived of. For, without being at all synonymous in theory, the two kinds of argument became mixed in actuality. It is here that the true reason behind the evident poverty of patristic argument lies. As we have noted earlier, one was conscious of living from tradition. But technical argumentation did not directly invoke 'tradition' but rather an 'authority', taken doubtless from a representative of this tradition . . . [The authoritative author] was envisaged as

a repository of the same prerogatives as the other authors admitted to the rank of 'authorities'.

De Ghellinck clarifies the intimacy of arguments from authority and arguments from tradition: both are seen to be changing and developing through time, and not historically resident at one particular moment which must therefore be recovered without adulteration or indeed interpretation. 'Authority' and 'Tradition' are dialogic – waxen-nosed, if one demands a sceptical formulation – and adapt themselves to changing circumstances and requirements.[34] This received approach to 'Tradition' implies an acknowledgement of the dependence of relevant biblical meanings on extra-textual imperatives operating within time and historical processes. Lollard thought categorically denies this dependence. As we shall see, the idea of a supernal Bible which is independent of the temporal and yet incorporates all that is spiritually relevant to the temporal, necessitates a troubled and recurrent Lollard engagement with the authority of 'Tradition'.

A fundamental problematic underlying Lollardy's ambiguous response to 'Tradition' is its Augustinianism. The role played by the works of St Augustine in late-medieval thought is still imperfectly studied, but there can be no doubt that it was a major one.[35] Augustine's hermeneutic writings were peculiarly problematic. They had been written at a time when the very nature of the new faith was being defined against various opponents, and as a result, apologetics or polemics is central to their significance.[36] Augustine's exegesis therefore incorporates various, often conflicting elements; most important for our purposes is his equal emphasis on the study of the biblical text for a proper understanding of it (and the associated valorisation of rhetoric and dialectic), and on the importance of a correct ordering of one's inner life for the right apprehension of biblical meanings. The biblical text, in Augustinian hermeneutics, is both centrally important and displaced. As Brian Stock has pointed out, 'The final lesson of Augustine's education as a reader is that nothing is learnt from reading itself'.[37] One of the most important conceptual loci of Augustine is therefore not scripture but *caritas*. Readings are right only in so far as they lead to *caritas*, and indeed, if one possesses *caritas*, one does not even need the scriptural text.[38] The definition of *caritas*, which is both extra-textual and crucially important, is assumed to be understood. Significantly, it can and does accommodate, throughout the Middle Ages, various extra-textual imperatives: the individual's inspired (and 'charitable') understanding of the Bible, as also the authority of an exegetical tradition encompassing 'charitable' readings which may not be evident in the actual biblical text. The potential for contradiction and self-contradiction arising out of the profound late-medieval devotion to Augustine, and the general failure to acknowledge the importance of the fact that Augustine wrote in very different cultural circumstances, was immense. As Karlfried Froelich has pointed out of late-medieval disputes over Augustinian hermeneutics:

> this was a fight over the words of St Augustine that once, in a world of religious fervor, of spiritual enthusiasm, of optimism and of oneness of purpose, had made eminent sense but now failed to do so . . . Students of Augustine in the early fifteenth century had no choice but to end up in a dilemma.[39]

As we shall see, some of the most important hermeneutic tangles of Wycliffism – revelation and inner inspiration as opposed to scriptural study, 'authority' as opposed to 'reason' – have roots in a troubled engagement with Augustine.

It is now time to point to the basic hermeneutic emphases of the Lollards. The most immediately noticeable is their theoretical celebration of the 'literal sense' of the Bible as the source of relevant hermeneutic discourse. In its engagement with the nature of the 'literal sense', Lollard thought is particularly indebted to Wyclif, who in turn drew on varied intellectual traditions. The 'background' to Wyclif's thought is vast and one suspects often unstated; it would therefore be foolish to attempt to chart definitive hermeneutic genealogies. However, in the matter of the 'literal sense', Wyclif's thought can be productively placed in relation to that of some of his major scholastic predecessors, preeminent among whom are Thomas Aquinas, Nicholas of Lyra and Richard Fitzralph. Here I will provide a rough intellectual trajectory of late-medieval involvement with the 'literal sense'. For the student of Lollardy, such a trajectory must necessarily be somewhat tentative, as Oxford thought in the decades immediately preceding Wyclif's remains imperfectly known.[40]

Beryl Smalley pointed out in her magisterial study that there was, over the thirteenth and fourteenth centuries, a growing emphasis in exegesis on the 'literal' sense of the Bible.[41] Aquinas and others were concerned with the superior value of the 'literal' sense (as opposed to the 'allegorical' or 'spiritual' senses), and Smalley suggests that this was a stepping '"through the looking-glass" out of their world of reflections into everyday life'.[42] However, Smalley's radiant formulation demands qualifications so large that it scarcely stands any more. The late-medieval involvement with the 'literal' sense shows clearly the unsolvable problems raised by the academic study of the interpretative bases of a religion grounded on centuries of the exegetical reinvention of a text. The work of Aquinas, Lyra and their successors betrays, first, a deep unease with inherited modes of textual reinvention as encapsulated in the traditional four-fold exegetical model; second, an attempt to address this unease by advocating a reliance on the 'literal' sense as the desired hermeneutic norm; and third, a resultant attempt at the redefinition of the 'literal' which does not substantially alter the prevailing exegetical situation.

Thomas Aquinas devotes much attention to the 'literal' sense in his *Summa Theologica* and in his *Questiones quodlibetales*. The details of his thought on the issue have been extensively studied;[43] here I will only point to what is immediately relevant to Wyclif's own theorisations. According to Aquinas, the words of scripture necessarily pertain to the domain of the 'literal'; 'even rhetorical figures – metaphor, fictive similitude, and parable or rhetorical allegory – as linguistic phenomena, are assimilated to the literal sense'.[44] For it is not the figure which constitutes the 'literal' sense, but that which is figured; in his classic example, when scripture speaks of the 'arm of God', the 'literal' sense is not that God has an arm, but that God has the power generally attributed to an arm.[45] The underlying principle is that of intentionality: it is the intention lying behind a figure which is its 'proper' sense. As a result, as Gilbert Dahan points out, the christological interpretation of Psalm 29.4 (*Domine eduxisti ab inferno animam meam*) can be defended as the 'literal' sense.[46]

The problem at the heart of Aquinas's redefinition of the 'literal' is well-stated by Dahan: 'la théologie est une science, mais le texte sur lequel elle se fonde n'est pas un texte "scientifique"' ('theology is a science, but the text upon which it is founded is not a "scientific" text').[47] As a result, the proponent of a 'scientific' biblical hermeneutics has also to accommodate the 'non-scientific' needs of those reading the Bible; in other words, the advocate of a 'literalist' hermeneutics has to make space for the extra-literal. A similar tension informs the work of Nicholas of Lyra. In his celebrated prefaces to the *Postilla literalis*, Lyra simultaneously complains of the suffocation of the 'literal' by proliferating allegories, and redefines the 'literal' so that it incorporates much that would formerly be classed as 'spiritual'. As Spicq points out, 'Il insiste fortement sur la nécessité de faire reposer le sens spirituel sur le sens littéral; et il reconnaît qu'on ne peut argumenter à partir du sens allégorique . . . Par ailleurs, dans le Prologue *De intentione auctoris et modo procedendi*, Nicolas de Lyre, commentant la troisième règle de Tychonius, admet explicitement deux sens littéraux' ('He insists strongly on the necessity of basing the spiritual sense on the literal sense; and he recognises that one cannot argue from the allegorical sense . . . Furthermore in the Prologue *De intentione auctoris et modo procedendi*, Nicholas of Lyra, in commenting on the third rule of Tychonius, explicitly allows for two literal senses').[48] Lyra emphasises what William of Nottingham had called the *duplex sensus literalis*, the 'two-fold literal sense'. Such a 'literal' sense encompasses both the surface, immediate meaning of the scriptural words as well as the figurative or christological meanings. As part of the intention informing the words, these other senses are also 'literal'.[49] As Spicq points out, Lyra attributes the double literal sense to passages from the Old Testament cited in the New to counter Jewish allegations that Christian readings distort the original sense of Old Testament passages. Once again, we see the recuperation – here for Christian apologetic purposes – of the domain of what would have been traditionally called 'spiritual' through a redefinition of the 'literal'.

Richard Fitzralph[50] continued in the direction of this semantic reclassification of the various senses of the Bible. He may have been exposed 'to the foremost biblicist of the day, Nicholas of Lyra'.[51] His political career and his role in the Armenian disputes led him to compose his 'most important and influential contribution to medieval theological literature', the *Summa de Questionibus Armenorum*.[52] According to Walsh, 'Fitzralph took as his guideline the literal interpretation of Scripture, both Old and New Testament, as the one source of authority which would be accepted without question by all parties',[53] for arguments based on the 'literal sense' would persuade those who would not accept the traditional spiritual superstructure of the Western Catholic Church. But as with Aquinas and Lyra, Fitzralph's exegetical theory identifies the 'literal' sense with meanings intended authorially:

> Sweeping aside all objections to the definition of the 'sensus litteralis', Fitzralph maintained that the main clue to the interpretation of the Scriptures was to know the mind of the author: 'non refert quis sensus proprie dici debeat litteralis alicuius scripture, dum tamen scias mentem auctoris', and then stated the guiding principle of his *Summa*, namely that the literal interpretation of scriptural passages would be determined by the obvious meaning of the author.[54]

The polemical potential of what Walsh calls 'the subjective manner in which [Fitzralph] chose to interpret the literal sense'[55] would later, as we shall go on to see, be exploited fully by Wyclif.

What emerges from the work of Aquinas, Nicholas of Lyra and Fitzralph is, as I said before, a redefinition of the 'literal' which does not substantially alter but instead 'repackages' inherited exegetical norms. The older distinction between the 'literal' and the 'spiritual' is recast as a distinction between two aspects of the 'literal'. This species of casuistry was in a sense inevitable. Christianity was a religion which had developed through varied and incessant exegeses of its central text; abiding by what its words seemed to suggest 'literally' as both a theoretical and a practical imperative was not feasible. The Bible being 'Jewish scripture in Greek guise reflecting a much older culture and state of consciousness',[56] the recovery of the 'literal' (in the sense of a hypothetical original meaning intended by the author(s) of scripture), even if possible, would be at best irrelevant and at worst harmful to the faith as actually practised and believed. Moreover, one had always to guard against 'judaising'.[57] Above all, biblical exegesis did not take place in an isolated realm of the 'spiritual', but existed in relation to contemporary theological, political and doctrinal needs. Verger stresses the fact that 'l'exégèse des grands docteurs dominicains et franciscains n'a rien de la paraphrase pieuse – *Scriptura sola* – à quoi aurait pu mener par elle-même la pratique de la vie apostolique' ('the exegesis of the great Dominican and Franciscan doctors is quite unlike the kind of pious paraphrase – *sola scriptura* – to which the practice of the apostolic life could have led by itself').[58]

The problems thus inherent from the beginning in the redefinition of the 'literal' sense came to the surface in a particularly troubling fashion with the Lollards. Interested – and to us, highly 'arbitrary' – interpretations of the Bible are adduced and defended by both the heretics and their opponents as part of the divine intention and therefore 'literal'. The details of this process will emerge in the course of the individual chapters, and tell a fascinating story of a hermeneutic deadlock. However, what transforms a learned hermeneutic crisis into a cultural crisis on a much larger scale, and what makes Lollardy unique for its times, is its combination of university training and (successful) popularising aims. What needs to be kept in mind always, therefore, is the academic nature of the Lollard heresy, and its embeddedness in traditions of self-conscious intellectual endeavour. By its unprecedented placing, at the centre of a scrutiny which was both academic and popular, of learned discourses of hermeneutic engagement with the most important text of medieval culture, it radically problematised issues fundamental to the very definition of Christianity, and to the perceived validity of the social, political and intellectual discourses traditionally enjoying its sanction. In the intellectual sphere in particular, Lollardy problematised, by throwing into uncomfortable and uncompromising relief, all that Damasus Trapp has described as characteristic of fourteenth-century thought: 'historical and logical criticism, interest in language, in liberty of conscience, and liberty of research'.[59] For the purposes of this study, one of the most important aspects of this process of problematisation consists in the radical enlargement of the range of those empowered and equipped to deal with matters of philosophical theology. A criticism of perceived intellectual degeneracies, however sharply articulated, would by no means have had an impact comparable to that of Lollardy, had it been confined to the Latinate club of academics and churchmen. Though my study will not examine the transformation of academic dissent into popular heresy – for that the reader is referred to Anne Hudson's oeuvre, in particular to her *Premature Reformation* – an abiding awareness of the implications of such a transformation informs the following chapters.

This study looks at a range of texts, Lollard and anti-Lollard, in Latin and in English, academic and extra-mural. These texts, written over a period of half a century and often addressing one another, are examined as they engage in a dialogue in which certain contested ideas and emphases surface repeatedly: the 'literal sense', God's intention, the normativity or otherwise of the *ecclesia primitiva*, the exegetical role of the Fathers, the limitations and definitions of 'Tradition', the uses of *scientia* and indeed of the whole range of academic discourses, the nature and reliability of *sapientia*, the uses of revelation, the rewards and dangers of biblical textual criticism. The focus of my study, as I have stated before, is less the diachronic histories of the ideas pointed to above than the understanding of how they form part of a synchronic interaction of ideologies. It is the twists and turns given to the waxen noses of received authorities and inherited paradigms that interest me, as these are deployed in a specific warfare over hermeneutics. Part of the fascination of Lollardy lies in the extent to which both the propagators and opponents of the heresy are explicitly aware of, utilise, and indeed lay bare the ideological motivations of religious and intellectual discourses. A synchronic study highlights the confrontation of discourses, and thereby throws into relief their internal structures and interrelations. Of course, any historical narrative inevitably suggests its own diachronic perspectives, and mine, as I will now explicate, is no exception, but the reader needs to bear in mind that the overarching *histoires* which do emerge in the course of the following study must be regarded, in the light of the significant lacunae in our knowledge of late-medieval intellectualities, as provisional, more correctly seen as helpful conceptual frameworks which enable us to 'place' some of the varied riches of the time, than as definitive accounts of 'intellectual history'.

The diachronic narrative of the following study I see as emerging from the juxtaposition of three distinct temporal frames within my chosen fifty-odd years. The first consists in the Latinate scholastic debates from the 1370s and 1380s of John Wyclif and his Oxford contemporaries, preeminently William Woodford. The second moves on to the 1390s and the 1400s, when vernacular Lollardy had already become a recognised and threatening presence. I examine scholastic debates at Oxford over the desirability or otherwise of biblical translations, Lollard vernacular hermeneutical discourses as exemplified in the English Wycliffite Sermons, and Nicholas Love's *Mirror of the Blessed Life of Jesus Christ*, an orthodox vernacular meditative text the contents of which are explicitly and pervasively anti-Lollard. The third frame focuses on the 1420s and later, when Lollardy had already been subjected to massive civil and ecclesiastical repression, and when the liberties of academia had been substantially curtailed. Thomas Netter of Walden is at the centre of this terminal frame.

Wyclif's major theoretical tract on biblical hermeneutics, *De Veritate Sacre Scripture*, forms the starting-point for the following enquiry. While I do not ignore the more important of Wyclif's debts to his scholastic and patristic mentors, I pay primary attention to his ideological and methodological emphases. My study therefore chooses as one of its governing themes Wyclif's use of the *idea* of scripture. For Wyclif, the Bible is above all an ideologically empowering concept, a 'text' which, as occasion demands, is shorn of all textuality. Such a vision offers its own freedoms and necessitates its own evasions: freedoms relating to the 'Bible' as a transparent means of access to God's mind, evasions which seek to ignore the 'Bible' as a text in language(s) and on parchment. Corollaries to this approach are many: a profound unease with problems of language, particularly metaphor, an equal unease with the traditional hermeneutic sanctions which build on and utilise creatively such linguistic problems, an indecisive theorisation of the importance of textual criticism, a correspondingly tormented engagement with the 'scientific' study of the Bible and its accompanying institutionalisations, a highly selective and schematised vision of the growth and development of Christianity, and underlying all this, an epistemological rejection of dialogism. *De Veritate* thus operates in terms of many of the polarisations around which the Lollard debate would revolve.

Wyclif's hermeneutic and other theorisations were taken up by William Woodford, an Oxford contemporary who was also one of his most prolific opponents. Woodford belonged to a generation of Oxford scholars who wrote and argued in an academic milieu not yet put on the defensive by Lollardy: his tracts studied here – the *Quattuor determinationes in materia de religione* – therefore show an extraordinary liberty of thought, well in keeping with Trapp's description of the fourteenth century as one in which 'a breath-taking freedom prevails in the intellectual field'.[60] Woodford chooses, in response to Wyclif's monologic idealism, a pronouncedly dialogic, contingent, relativist framework of analysis, within which, in a tone of urbane, often playful scepticism, he dismantles the very bases of the heresiarch's ideology of the Bible. In response to those aspects of Wyclif's vision of the Bible which are ahistorical and 'detextualising', Woodford points to the known historical circumstances of the growth and development of Christianity, the textual contingencies underlying the formation of the present canon of the Bible, and the necessary and inevitable relativisms of interpretation. His work, apart from the intrinsic interest of its intellectual daring and robustness, demands our attention as an instance of what Wyclif was rebelling against: an academic freedom of thought which had come to flirt with outright scepticism[61] while retaining, as an institution, privileges theoretically premissed on a quite different religio-intellectual endeavour.[62]

If Woodford's work responds to Wyclif's thought from a benign sceptical vantage-point with its own attendant freedoms, that of the Oxford men who devoted much attention to the rights and wrongs of biblical translation chooses a conservative, not to say reactionary, focus. The tracts of William Butler and Thomas Palmer – *determinationes* on the subject of a vernacular Bible – are defensive of the prerogatives of the academic establishment, and unapologetically clear that such prerogatives, in order to exist at all, must be exclusive to that establishment. While Woodford's sceptical hermeneutics is premissed on an unanxious sense of institutional security, and thereby can afford its own liberalisms, Butler's and Palmer's equally sceptical hermeneutics is accompanied on their part by a pronounced sense of being members of a threatened tribe, and a concomitant ruthlessness. Richard Ullerston, the other polemicist on the issue of translation studied here, is more of an enigma; he tries to argue simultaneously, and in a necessarily self-contradictory fashion, for accessible biblical meanings and the power of the ecclesiastical hierarchy to dictate such meanings. The three *determinationes* thus point towards a rigidification of the orthodox line on hermeneutics and its relation to Latinate power, and my study of them forms the first section of the second frame of my narrative, relating to the years when Lollardy had already begun to elicit responses vastly different from the intellectually open-ended critiques of Woodford.

The English Wycliffite Sermons show us why the orthodox line should have hardened. They are a demonstration of the effects of an appropriation of learned exegetical discourse by the vernacular, and clearly show the dangers envisioned in such a process by Palmer and Butler. The sermons interpret passages from the Bible and base polemical arguments on their interpretations. Their primary conceptual tussle – inherited

:ral sense' and its uses, and they demon-
extending Wyclif's intentionalist dictates
⊃ offer crucial insights into the varied and
Lollard theorisations, and warn us against
e intellectual convictions and the exegeti-
Lollardy. The sermons show a 'vernacular
'vernacular philosophy') in development
e radical potential of making intellectual
communities outside the regulatory power
institutions. They help us to understand
ismay at such a development, and the as-
orthodox line on issues of vernacularity
and lay intellection, embodied in terms of legislation with the passing
of *De heretico comburendo* (1401), and the severe censorship laws of
Archbishop Thomas Arundel, the *Constitutions* (1407–9).[63] The sermons also explicate the motivation underlying Arundel's categorical
prohibition of intellectual endeavour outside strictly regulated and supervised institutional frameworks, and throw light on the developing
establishment emphasis on non-rational modes of spirituality, and the
active promotion of affective devotion: prayer and meditation, though
they have their own threatening potential, seem to be less unmanageable
than the informed polemic of the sermons.

Nicholas Love's *Mirror* is an instance of the self-conscious polemical deployment of inherited affective modes of devotion against the
Lollards. A loose translation (with numerous polemical additions) of
the pseudo-Bonaventuran *Meditationes vitae Christi*, Love's meditative
text received official endorsement of its anti-Lollard endeavour from
Archbishop Arundel. The *Mirror* counters Lollardy not only through
its very form – a series of emotive 'imaginations' on the life of Christ
as different as possible from the kind of scriptural argumentation evidenced in the Wycliffite sermons – but also through explicit doctrinal
arguments as well as implicit hermeneutic strategies. It is these strategies, as also the *Mirror's* deployment against the Lollards of elements of
their favoured vocabulary, that form the focus of my study.

Nicholas Love brings us to the end of the second stage of my diachronic *histoire*. The vernacular sermons, the Oxford debates on biblical translation and Love's polemical affectivity are part of a world already

significantly different from that of Wyclif's and Woodford's scholastic *agon*. Intellectual issues have been popularised and have thereby become politicised on an altogether different scale. The relationships of systems of power and systems of biblical interpretation are overtly recognised and contested. The establishment response is largely one of paranoia and repression, as evidenced in *De heretico comburendo* and Arundel's *Constitutiones*. In the decades following these repressive measures, there is a growing recognition on the part of orthodoxy that the problems raised by Lollardy are too potent to be contained by force alone.[64] We witness a third stage in my *histoire*: one in which orthodox writers attempt to confront Lollardy through a systematic examination of its intellectual premisses.

Thomas Netter of Walden was one of the most encyclopaedic of these later orthodox writers. His *Doctrinale antiquitatum fidei ecclesiae catholicae*, written in the 1420s, attempts a comprehensive rebuttal of Wycliffite thought in its doctrinal and hermeneutic aspects. Netter's anti-Wycliffism, while once again in the nature of a genuine intellectual engagement, is however qualitatively different from that of Woodford. This difference, which is both methodological and epistemological, suggests the transformations that intellectual orthodoxy had undergone in the course of its battle with an academic heresy turned popular. Indeed, the very fact that one can use the phrase 'intellectual orthodoxy' meaningfully suggests the changes which have taken place. Netter's work, unlike that of Woodford, does not imply a secure academic milieu in which discourses of varying degrees of scepticism can flourish. In its anxious and tormented attempts at forging a vision of Christian meaning which can offer, in the manner of Wyclif's own vision, unambiguous and monologic certitudes, the *Doctrinale* suggests a collapse of what I have been describing as hermeneutic dialogism. As such, Netter's work points to one of the major characteristics of orthodox anti-Wycliffite writings of this 'post-Lollard' age: some of the main emphases of Lollardy have had to be rationalised and incorporated *within* the intellectual structures of a redefined orthodox order.

Lollardy therefore is not just an 'English heresy',[65] but also, and equally importantly, 'an academic heresy'. What it problematises uncompromisingly and irrevocably, through criticism, participation and resistance, is what Alain Boureau has called the 'essential and fleeting phenomenon of medieval history: the radical intellectualisation of the world under the effects of Christianity'.[66] This aspect of the heresy was recognised and responded to contemporaneously: Arundel's censorship laws are a remarkable document in that they attempt to address the whole range of intellectual discourses from elementary instruction in the schools to advanced disputations within Oxford as well as lay engagement with any doctrinal or religious issue. It is a testimony to Lollardy's success in its popularising aims that the same set of laws should simultaneously seek to control and ideally to exterminate academic freedom within Oxford University, and intellectual endeavour in an extra-mural world of lay disputation. The achieved Lollard coalescence of hitherto disparate discourses in an Englished biblical *scientia* upset in a unique and unprecedented way that scholastic balance finely described by Boureau as premissed on 'foundations of revelation and reason, in a fertile relationship of tension and congruence'.[67]

John Wyclif and the truth
of sacred scripture

De Veritate Sacrae Scripturae[1] constitutes Wyclif's most extended theoretical engagement with the nature of biblical meaning and the interpretative problems posed by biblical language. A part of his so-called *Summa Theologiae*,[2] it forms one of the corner-stones of his increasingly radical conceptualisation of a Church guided by an ideal *lex Christi* abstracted from scripture.[3] It was written around 1377–78,[4] after the first, and cataclysmic, volume of *De Civili Dominio*,[5] his revisionist tract on the nature of *dominium* and its dependence on grace.[6] *De Civili Dominio I* resulted in Wyclif's being summoned to St Paul's in 1377 to answer charges of heresy; moreover, eighteen propositions from his book were condemned by Pope Gregory XI in a series of bulls dated 22 May 1377. William Woodford OFM wrote his *Determinatio de Civili Dominio*, and Nicholas Radcliffe OSB his *Dialogi* in refutation of Wyclif's views; a host of other monks and seculars joined in the fray.[7] Thus beleaguered, Wyclif spent most of 1377–78 answering his critics.

De Veritate, though primarily a theoretical treatise on hermeneutics, is therefore also in the nature of a polemical tract, always aware of, and often addressing directly, the contemporary disputes. As the work progresses, its tone acquires a heightened stridency, from a more or less focussed study of scriptural signification in the first fifteen chapters, to an increasingly polemical engagement with issues of heresy, ideal priesthood, papal authority and dominion in the later sections. The present chapter will concentrate on Wyclif's hermeneutic principles and arguments, though it will not lose sight of the centrality of his polemics to his theories of right reading.

Indeed, a fundamental aspect of Wyclif's hermeneutics is intimately related to contemporary political and ecclesiological conflict. Because of *De Veritate*'s embeddedness in a wide-ranging and developing dispute over dominion, Wyclif treats scripture above all as an ideologically empowering concept. His hermeneutic theory is therefore global in its vision of scripture, and attempts to exclude any troubling consciousness of the Bible as an anthology of texts written in varying modes, in different times by different people.[8] Prior to *De Veritate*, Wyclif had completed a commentary on the whole of scripture – the *Postilla super totam bibliam*;[9] he was therefore undoubtedly aware of the numerous complexities in and discrepancies between the various parts of scripture. A major polemical point of *De Veritate*, however, is that scripture is a unity of ideas in God's mind, and that all its parts lead to the same unchanging *veritas*: 'tota scriptura sacra est unum dei verbum' ('the whole of sacred scripture is one word of God', II.I I 2/4).[10] This has its practical effects on Wyclif's procedure, so that what his work offers is a combination of general statements about biblical meaning and statements of peculiar specificity based on readings of particular passages, often selected, according to local needs and exigencies, from a range of very different scriptural texts. The methodological, and tonal, complexity of the work is, as a result, immense; and the conflict of differing modes of interpretation which I have sought to underline in this chapter demands that the reader bear in mind the developing polemical context of Wyclif's scriptural *lectio*.

The following account will proceed thus: an analysis of Wyclif's discussion of Judges 9 will be succeeded by individual treatments of some of the major theoretical nexus of the tract. These include, preeminently, the issues of metaphor and 'improper' language, 'authorial intention', contextual reading, the role of 'reason' in the interpretation of scripture, 'scriptural logic', and problems of textual criticism. As suggested earlier in my Introduction (p. 8), my analytical framework will utilise the conceptual polarity of *scientia-sapientia* to clarify the two major approaches to scripture embraced by Wyclif's polemic. The first of these is broadly Aristotelian, and sets out to examine the Bible as a complex textual object which offers to its devoted, rationalist student a growing body of information about the way it works.[11] The other, broadly Augustinian, looks instead to illumination: the truths of sacred scripture are vouchsafed through prayer and divine grace to him who lives a life of virtue and rectitude.[12] One should stress that this working distinction of 'approaches' is to an extent artificial, as in practice, the two align themselves in various relationships, of mutual reinforcement as well as of conflict and contradiction.

One of the problems lying at the heart of Wyclif's engagement with scriptural language is that of its metaphoricity or 'improperness'. 'Metaphor', in its foregrounding of the constructedness of linguistic meaning, underlines the determining importance of the perceiving agent or culture.[13] Wyclif, in his universalising attempt at limiting the cognitive role of the individual – thereby discounting the inevitability of hermeneutic variation – seeks instead to stress the fixity, stability and determinateness of biblical meaning. In this scheme of things, the Bible becomes a coherent system of signifiers informed by an accessible and clarifying divine will. The complexities of biblical language therefore assume a highly problematic status: they must be both acknowledged and transcended.

Towards the beginning of the second chapter of *De Veritate*, Wyclif cites Gregory's remark that the words of the Bible are as leaves to its sentential fruit:

> voces enim verborum scripture non sunt nisi ut folia ad fructum sensus proficiencia. unde si obumbrant sensum, si confundunt, si distrahunt vel quomodocunque impediunt, sunt extirpanda, figuranda vel aliter aptanda. (1.21/8–11)

> For the sounds of the words of scripture are nothing unless as leaves making way for the fruit of sense. Therefore, if they obstruct, confuse, alienate or in any way impede the sense, they are to be plucked out, fashioned ('figured') or otherwise adjusted / made suitable.

If the words obstruct the sense in any way, they are to be rooted out, fashioned (with also the suggestion of 'understood figuratively'), or otherwise adapted, made fit. This clear Gregorian dichotomy of sense and words, with its exhortation to dismiss what is verbally problematic by resorting to a 'sense' already possessed, leads Wyclif to refer yearningly to the state of the blessed who apprehend divine sense supra-linguistically: 'melius foret, ut patet in beatis, capere sentenciam sine verbis, si nostra inferioritas non obesset' ('it were better, as appears in [the case of] the blessed, to apprehend the *sentence* without words, if [only] our inferiority did not hinder [us]') (1.21/12–14).[14]

JUDGES 9

The passage just cited in the last section needs to be borne in mind when one examines Wyclif's tussles within and with the realm of language. A key passage in the fourth chapter of *De Veritate* begins with an extended citation of Judges 9:8–15, dealing with the 'parable' of the trees. 'Quid ergo foret ista scriptura nisi fabula vel poema?' ('What therefore would this [piece of] scripture be unless a fable or a poem?'), asks Wyclif (1.63/24). Aristotle is cited as saying that poets lie; Augustine that Jesus's parables are not lies, but, properly understood – 'si bene intelligatur' – 'mysteries'. According to Augustine, from whose *Contra Mendacium* the point is taken, though the narrations be fictive, the significations thereof are true (1.64). Aquinas makes the same point in *De Potencia*: scriptural locutions are metaphorically true (1.65/6).

Having cited his *auctores*, Wyclif proceeds to point out that figurative locutions, which are either metaphorical or similitudinal, are of three kinds: allegorical, parabolical and feigned or fictional (1.65/13–16). The realm of allegory concerns true historical facts which yet signify that which is to be believed in the later church, as for example, the paschal lamb in the Old Testament signifies Christ. 'Allegory' always implies that the narrated events did in fact happen and were recorded in scripture; Gal. 4:22–4 is cited in confirmation (1.65/16–66/14). In parabolic locutions, the scriptural *sentence* is narrated according to some similitude, though the narrated events are not recorded as actual events [*historizata*] in scripture. This is the case with Christ's own parables (1.66/16–19). The third category of figurative language is fictive: when the events narrated are not true literally so that they may signify the truth mystically (1.66/22–4). Wyclif then returns to Judges 9, collecting Augustine as authority on the way. The three trees in the relevant verses from Judges (the olive, the fig and the vine) are three historical figures. 'Per olivam intelligunt Hebrei Othoniel' ('By the olive the Jews understand Othoniel'); Jer. 11:16 is offered as justification of this interpretation, as the tribe of Judah, of which Othoniel was a member, is therein described as an olive tree. By the fig is understood Deborah; and by the vine, Gideon, a member of the tribe of Joseph which is described as a fruitful bough in Gen. 49:22. Further references, to the context of the parable in Judges 9, and to 1 Sam. 8:5, bolster Wyclif's defence of the biblical verses from the charge of 'falsity' (1.67/1–68/2).

Such a 'contextual' interpretation in terms of the *circumstancia litterae* is however immediately followed by Wyclif's own moralisation:

> ex ultima parte fictitie videtur michi notari, quod sacerdotes Cristi, qui debent esse vicarii vitis vere, non debent civiliter dominari, cum conficiunt corpus eius et sangwinem, que letificant deum et homines, sed celebrantes debent memorari eum, qui non potuit civiliter dominari ... si enim tempore ante legem sine exemplo Cristi persona laica deseruit civilitatem propter devocionem, multo magis sacerdotes Cristi sic facerent exemplo sui magistri. (1.68/3–13)

> In the last part, it seems to me to be signified in a fictional manner that the priests of Christ, who must be vicars of the true vine, must not [undertake civil dominion], since they produce his body and blood which delight God and men. Instead, celebrating [the Eucharist], they must remember him who could not [undertake civil dominion] ... For if in the time before the [New] Law, without the example of Christ, a lay person renounced civil authority for devotion, the priests of Christ should do so much more [according to] the example of their Master.

Note how this reading of the parable as an *exemplum* for priests – they are to renounce all civil dominion – hovers indecisively between the suggestion that the 'fiction' 'intrinsically' carries this meaning, and a more historically aware reading drawing a relevant moral from a quite different cultural circumstance.

Wyclif then returns to the earlier biblical-historical scheme in which the bramble of Judges 9:14 'significat mistice Abymalec' ('signifies Abymalec in a mystical fashion', 1.68/14). The bramble, according to Isidore, is a small shrub which emits fire; therefore it corresponds mystically to the evil act of Abymalec who killed his seventy brothers. The cedars of Judges 9:15 are Abymalec's terrified nobles, for it is often the case in the Bible that noble men are called cedars (1.68/15–22). Wyclif next proceeds to his own individual interpretation. The *doctor* who goes deeper into the scriptural text beyond the particular signified sense will find that its apparent sterility gives way before a hidden mystical sense:

> unde preter sensum particularem signatum quidam doctor fodiens profundius scripturam, que videtur tam sterilis, invenit in ea latentem

sensum misticum de statu universalis ecclesie, sic quod per ligna in-
telliguntur rudes humani generis, qui ex servitute bestiali appetunt
in affectu habere hominem seculariter imperantem, et tales ierunt,
quia recesserunt a religione status innocencie et cristi, cum abierunt
in concilio impiorum. (1.68/23–69/5)

Therefore, the doctor delving deeper into [this passage of] scripture
will find in it, beyond the particular signified sense, which seems so
sterile, a hidden mystical sense [pertaining to] the state of the universal
Church. Thus by the trees are understood the ignorant / simple of
human kind, who, because of their bestial sevitude, desire emotionally
[in their *affect*] to have a man ruling [over them] in a worldly manner,
and such [men] came into being, because they receded from the [form
of] religion of the state of innocence and of Christ when they passed
into the council of the impious.

For the reader seeking profundities beyond the immediate, therefore,
Judges 9 becomes a parable of the human condition: of fallen man's
appetite for power which results in a rejection of Christ himself. The
reference to the 'council of the impious' is probably an additional jibe
at the ecclesiastical politics of the day: the biblical text is here offering
adverse comment on the fallen state of the present-day Church.

The suggestion is drawn out in the passage which follows. The three
trees 'are' the three ages of the Church: before the (Old) Law, under
the Law and the Church of Christ. Priests of the latter must bear spiritual fruit by rejecting secular dominion and turn instead to matters
celestial (1.69/6–21). John 15:1 ('I am the true vine'), and other biblical references to olives, figs and vines[15] are cited in more or less forced
confirmation of such an interpretation. By the bramble is understood
the antichrist; and this identification leads on to a long passage on those
who desire mundane glory. When Wyclif returns to the bramble, the
antichrist is compared to the bramble 'racionabiliter': the evil, through
their love of wealth, are divided among themselves like the spines of
the bramble (Luke 8:14 is cited – Christ comparing thorns to riches
and pleasures); the bramble is sterile like the antichrist; third, just as
the bramble causes the light of the sun to be obstructed, similarly,
those belonging to the antichrist obscure the similitude of God in their
souls (1.71/13–72/1). Wyclif concludes with saying that this sense is the
catholic sense intended by the Holy Ghost: 'concluditur esse catholicus

et a spiritu sancto intentus' (1.72/2–3). The following passage returns to the theme of the clergy's ideal renunciation of civil dominion.

I have discussed Wyclif's treatment of Judges 9 at some length because it is fairly representative of his general procedure in *De Veritate*. There is a discernible interest in supporting 'mystical' interpretations of any scriptural passage with references (often unconvincing, forced and demanding equally 'mystical' readings) to other passages; there is almost always a consolidatory theoretical gesture in the direction of divine intention; there are tormented attempts at showing the substantive rightness of scriptural comparisons, their 'essential' groundedness in 'real' points of similarity between vehicle and tenor; and there is ample scope for Wyclif's own, often idiosyncratic and highly polemical interpretations. What we witness is a practical utilisation of all the hermeneutic liberties offered by a 'parabolic' language, and at the same time a theoretical striving towards a 'sciential' codification of the problems thereof.

It will be useful now to examine Wyclif's theoretical pronouncements on various issues in hermeneutics: 'parabolic' language and the 'literal' sense; authorial intention; the importance of contextual interpretation; scriptural logic and the role of 'reason'; and problems of text and textual criticism.

'IMPROPER' LANGUAGE

The major thrust behind Wyclif's discussion of improper significations is a desire to deny their inevitable ambiguity. His philosophical realism[16] has an important role to play in this, for metaphorical language habitually links together, or has the potential to link together, things not immediately or obviously similar. The main emphasis in Wyclif's theory of predication in *De Universalibus* lies on the transference of predication from the domain of language to that of reality. As Alessandro Conti has pointed out, 'Wyclif hypostatizes the notion of being and considers equivocity, analogy and univocity as real relations between things, and not as semantical relations between terms and things.'[17] In the words of Jesse Gellrich, 'his project was to decentralize language as the matrix for studying the universal: rather than seeking it *post rem* in linguistic events, he sought a return to the classical *universalia ante rem*'.[18] Wyclif therefore introduces, in his *De Universalibus*, a new, enigmatic category of predication called 'essential predication'. The concept of 'essential predication' in all its metaphysical complexity has been clarified recently by Conti;[19] what needs to be underlined here, however, is the extent of Wyclif's commitment to realism which necessitates the postulation of a new category of predication. Logical conflicts which were traditionally solved by resorting to purely linguistic predication demand, in Wyclif's realist world, new explicatory mechanisms.[20] Given such a realist philosophical thrust against the constitutive role of language in our perception of the 'external' world,[21] it is easier to understand Wyclif's profound unease with metaphor, and indeed, with any figurative language.

Towards the beginning of *De Veritate*, Wyclif takes up Jesus's words in John 10:9 – 'I am the door' – and uses them as a launching pad for a discussion of the equivocity of scriptural language (1.9). 'Equivocal' words vary in meaning according to context, for it is not just names with which we are concerned but also with things. Hence the 'famoso principio logico: in equivocis non est contradiccio, cum non sit nominis tantum, sed rei et nominis' ('the famous logical principle: there is no contradiction in equivocation, since it is not just [a matter] of the part of speech, but of the thing as well as of the part of speech') (1.9/8–10).[22] Augustine's explanation of the phrase 'manibus ligwe' from Prov. 18:21 is discussed next. We well know that the tongue has no hands, but the scriptural passage makes sense because what is being referred to is the power of the tongue: 'que sunt manus ligwe? potestates ligwe' (1.10/15–16).

A few passages later, Wyclif comes to discuss the theory of such interpretations: 'ulterius restat videre, ad quem sensus locuciones huiusmodi figurative debent intelligi' ('it further remains to be seen, how [to what senses] figurative locutions of this kind must be understood', 1.14/14–15). Figurative passages must be understood according to the 'mystical', 'spiritual', 'symbolic' and 'proportional' senses. A proposition in mystical theology attributes the name of a creature to God. The conditions of analogy make possible the attribution of the imperfect – the properties according to kind in the creature – to God in an equivocal sense. And this is also true of the names of creatures of one genus being attributed to a creature of another in commendation or vituperation (1.14/16–15/3). The discussion proceeds to examine the status of the word 'lion' in the Bible, which signifies to the rude grammarian

a roaring four-footed beast, but to the theologian, God or the devil
(1.15/7–9). There follows a long passage demonstrating how the nature
of the beast is indeed a proper, 'real' analogy for Christ: 'consideremus
itaque naturam illius bestie et videamus, si in Christo possumus reperire
analogum' ('let us consider the nature of this beast and see if we are able
to find an analogy in Christ', 1.16/4–5). Various aspects of the lion – its
regal status, its roaring, its strength and its peculiar way of bringing
its infants to life – are all shown to have parallels in Christ's being and
life (1.16/6–17/28). The passages which follow undertake a similar
demonstration in relation to the lion and the devil (1.18/1–19/16).
The section is rounded off with the assertion that all the various names
attributed to God in the scriptures can be justified thus: 'ex quotlibet
talibus proprietatibus leonis colari potest analogum, propter quod deus
analogice foret leo. et ita de quibuscunque nominibus, que scriptura
sibi attribuit' ('an analogy can be derived from any such property
of the lion, on account of which God analogically would be a lion.
The [same can be said] of any name that scripture attributes to him',
1.19/17–20).

What emerges from Wyclif's discussion of Christ as lion is a desire to
smooth out the problematic ambiguity of figurative language, to anchor
figures not in the realm of language but in the realm of things: both
Christ and the lion participate by virtue of their distinct but related,
'analogous' natures in real universals.[23] Wyclif's realist use of the notion
of analogy has been commented on by Conti: 'Those things are analogical which have the same name and are subordinated to a single concept,
but according to different ways. Analogical things *therefore share the nature* signified by that name according to various degrees of intensity.'[24]
The resemblance of analogous things is not a matter of linguistic convention but of shared natures; in other words, judgments of likeness are
perceptions of universals.[25]

Wyclif returns to the issue of figurative language in the fifth chapter:
'figurativas locuciones ad sensum misticum debemus defendere a falsitate, cum sint predicabiles ad sensum plus preciosum' ('we must defend
from falsity figurative locutions in the mystical sense, since they are
predicable in a more precious sense', 1.92/5–7). The critic of figures, according to him, objects that the confusion of things of one species with
things of another would result in the death of all systematic thought:

all definitions and distinctions of universals would perish (1.92/11–15). Wyclif goes on to point out, however, that such misgivings arise 'ex ignorancia sophismatum et logice' ('out of ignorance of sophismata and logic').

> conceditur igitur, quod homo est leo, serpens, vermis etc., et sic in qualibet specie tamquam eius principium, ut patet de Cristo, qui est omnia in omnibus et principium cuiuslibet predicati secundum deitatem. verumptamen non est fera vel alia creatura qua homo, et patet, quod non pereunt diffiniciones vel distincciones universalium. (1.92/21–6)
>
> It is conceded therefore that man is a lion, a serpent, a worm etc., and thus [is present] in any species just as if [he were] its principle, as appears in Christ, who is all in everything and, according to [his] deity, the principle of whatever is predicated [of him]. Nevertheless, a wild creature or any other creature is not as man, and it is evident that definitions or distinctions of universals do not perish.

In this new justification of human-animal figures, man is held to be related to all other species just as if he were their principle. He is thus similar in this respect to Christ himself who is the principle of whatever is predicated of him. The issue becomes clearer when Wyclif cites Aristotle as *auctor*: God did not create any creature wiser than man and did not collect in any other animal what he collected in man. Therefore, there is no custom or quality which is not found in man but is found in some other animal; and man is, in other words, a 'minor mundus' (1.95/3–96/5).[26] Thus, there is no contradiction in such equivocal uses of language according to essential and figural predication: 'et ista philosophia naturalis [Aristotle's] est utilis pro intellectu scripture nec est contradiccio in sensibus equivocis secundum predicacionem essencialem et figuralem' ('And this natural philosophy is useful for the understanding of scripture; and there is no contradiction in equivocal senses according to essential and figural predication', 1.96/5–8). The passage is summed up by the citation of yet another *auctoritas*, this time Boethius's *Consolation of Philosophy*: a passage from Book IV, Prose 3, on the bestialisation of the vicious man, which for Wyclif constitutes yet another recognition of the 'essential' validity of comparisons between man and animal. The 'real' resemblance lies not indeed in a shared corporeal species but in shared 'qualities': 'ecce, quomodo homo, medius inter angelos et bestias, virtutibus deificatur, sic viciis bestiatur morum qualitate, non corporis specie' ('see, how man, intermediate between angels and beasts, deified by virtues, is thus bestialised by vices [in terms of] the quality of [his] morals, [though] not [in terms of his] corporeal nature', 1.97/8–10). Otherwise scriptural verses such as John 10:35 ('deus illos dixit deos'); Ps. 22:16 ('circumdederunt me canes multi'); Matt. 7:6 ('neque mittatis margaritas vestras ante porcos'); and Rev. 22:15 ('foris canes et venefici et inpudici et homicidae') would all be nullified (1.97/10–18). A few passages later, Ps. 22 is taken up again, this time to discuss verse 6: 'I am a worm and no man'. Such passages, it is alleged, 'non possunt excusari a falsitate de virtute sermonis' ('cannot be excused from falsity by the force of the word', 1.101/12–13).[27] But scriptural logic hides profound truths; and in this case the reference is to Christ who was, as Augustine points out, 'sine concubitu instar vermium procreatus' ('begotten without sexual contact in the manner of worms'), and who was not a man 'formaliter' because of his divinity (1.105/27–107/5).

The above passages underline Wyclif's obsessive interest in justifying the domain of figurative language by pointing to 'real' and not merely 'perceived' correspondences between vehicle and tenor. As he points out, there is no contradiction, according to 'essential predication', in this category of scriptural equivocation.

PARABLES

Wyclif's justification of the next form of equivocation – parables – is more complex. The section begins, as usual, with a discussion of the literal sense. It is asserted that 'sensus . . . literalis est utrobique verus, cum non asseritur a recte intelligentibus' ('the literal sense is everywhere true, [even] when it is not affirmed by those understanding [it] rightly', 1.73/5–6). The literal sense is the primary truth ordained by the Holy Ghost to bring forth the other senses. As Aquinas points out, the parabolic sense is contained in the literal. Words signify both properly and figuratively, and the literal sense is not the figure but what is figured. So, when scripture speaks of the arm of God, the literal sense is not that God has a corporeal arm but that he has the power generally associated with an arm (1.73/12–22). 'Ecce', says Wyclif, 'quante sancti doctores laborarunt ad excusandum scripturam sacram a falsitate' ('how much holy doctors labour to excuse sacred scripture from falsity', 1.73/24–5), and plunges immediately into an extraordinary defence of the 'truth' of parables.

The argument, such as it is, is convoluted. The main point seems to be Wyclif's dissatisfaction with Augustine's apparent acquiescence in the non-literalness of parables:

> [According to Augustine] 'parabola dicitur, quando datur similitudo de aliquo'. ex quibus colligitur, quod omnes locuciones parabolice ewangelii sunt vere ad sensum, quem debent habere, ut dicit Augustinus. sed difficultas est, si locuciones parabolice sint vere ad literam. et videtur Augustinum sentire, quod sint ficte. (1.74/10–15)

> '[A text] is said to be a parable, when a similitude to something is given.' From which it is inferred, as Augustine says, that all parabolic locutions of the gospel are true according to the sense they must have. But the difficulty is whether parabolic locutions are true literally. And Augustine seems to consider that they are feigned.

Wyclif confesses to have speculated often on this conclusion of Augustine's; and it seems to him that neither a parable nor a similitude can exist without a 'solid basis' ('solidum fundamentum'). The similitude cannot be one between truth and the non-existent, that which is not. Indeed, the parable of the prodigal son sounds probable enough, and it seems that Augustine did not consider it false. This is specially the case since the God of truth possesses many truths unknown to us, and by means of these, he can parabolically express truth (1.74/16–75/5). Wyclif therefore concludes that when Augustine says that the parable is not about 'res gesta' – things which actually happened – he perhaps intended to say that they are not about events which are explicitly chronicled elsewhere in scripture: 'et quando Augustinus dicit, quod non sit res gesta, forte intelligit, quod non sit res in scriptura sacra alibi chronicata' (1.75/18–20). Hebrews 7:3, in which Paul describes Melchisedec as 'without father, without mother, without descent', is cited in confirmation: the Apostle obviously intended us to 'supply' the qualification that his words meant that Melchisedec's genealogy was not *expresse*[28] chronicled in scripture, though it might have been available apocryphally (1.75/22–23). The argument then takes a slight turn, and Augustine

is cited as explaining that some passages of scripture are purely historical, some mystical and some mixed (1.76/21–5). Augustine's queries
about the literal truth of the 'res gestae' narrated in the parable of
the prodigal son are next cited. What is undeniably true, according to
Augustine, is that the lord indeed said these words, but it is not necessary
that 'ad literam facta monstrentur' ('that they should be shown to [have
happened] literally', 1.77/9). 'Ecce', says Wyclif in yet another of his 'supplementing' readings of the saint: 'videtur [Augustine] dicere quod non
exigitur, ut ad literam monstrentur facte parabole, suple, ut inserantur
alibi historiace in scriptura sacra' ('Augustine seems to be saying that it is
not necessary that parables should be shown to have happened literally,
[i.e., it is not necessary] that they should have been inserted as actual
events elsewhere in sacred scripture', 1.77/13–15). The same argument,
says Wyclif, is offered by Grosseteste, when the latter wonders why Jesus
first appeared to Mary Magdalen. Grosseteste explains that because of
the stringent editorial practices of the compilers of the gospels, nothing was written down unless noted by all. Hence John's qualification
in 20:30: 'multa fecit Jesus, que non sunt scripta in libro hoc'. There
follows a list of the twelve appearances of Christ between his resurrection and his ascension (the first two, pre-Magdalenic, on apocryphal
authority) (1.77/22–79/2). Wyclif concludes:

> ecce, quam multa vera non sunt expressata in scriptura sacra, que sepe
> restringit loquelam ad illa, que ibi asseruntur. quando ergo scriptura
> dicit, quod primo apparuit Marie Magdalene, intelligitur, quantum
> ad apparicionem in scriptura expressatam, et sic credo, quod loquitur
> Augustinus. (1.79/3–8)

> See, how many truths are not [expressly stated] in sacred scripture,
> which often restricts the discourse to [those things] which are asserted
> at that point. Therefore, when scripture says that [Jesus] first appeared
> to Mary Magdalen, it is understood that [the statement pertains to]
> apparitions expressly stated in scripture; and thus, I believe, Augustine
> speaks.

Wyclif returns to the prodigal son a few pages later, once again making the point that the 'history' was true, though narrated by Christ as
a parable or a piece of apocrypha (i.e. not expressly present in scripture). The story is also parabolically true according to Jesus's own sense,

which – rather than the historical sense, which nevertheless the parable possesses – is literal in this case (1.82/16–83/5).

The implications of this remarkable piece of parabolic theory are to be noted. The major, and unexpected, point which emerges is the profound 'realist' gulf which separates Wyclif from two of his most important *auctores*: Augustine and Aquinas. Augustine has many justifications for figurative language in *De Doctrina Christiana*: exercising the devout mind, concealing truths from the unworthy and so on,[29] but underlying all these, as emerges in that classic passage of his, is the rhetorician's delight – hesitant, faintly apologetic, but nevertheless impressively and movingly articulated – in non-literal uses of language.[30] Aquinas, despite his deep unease with figurative language, nevertheless justifies it, in an Aristotelian fashion: 'human knowledge begins in corporeal sense, and poetic metaphors constitute sensory modes of representation which give us access to the higher "world of intelligence through the world of sense"'.[31] What informs Wyclif's discussion of the parable is, however, an extraordinary reluctance to admit that spiritual truths can be communicated by means of 'fictions'; hence his decision here entirely to ignore the substantial body of medieval discussion about the rhetorical usefulness (or otherwise) of parables.[32] Indeed, his discomfort with the notion of fictive truth is such that he actually cites, in an uncharacteristic fashion, apocryphal material as authoritative in his bid to 'literalise' or rather 'realise' – 'make real' – parables.

THE FOUR SENSES OF SCRIPTURE

Wyclif returns to the issue of figurative language later in *De Veritate* in an extended discussion of the traditional four-fold senses of scripture. In one of his key statements in relation to this, he seems to dismiss centuries of debate about the relation between the literal sense and authorial intention. He cites the mnemonic verses 'litera gesta docet . . . ', and proceeds to state that although whichever sense is possessed by the letter can be called literal *de virtute sermonis*, it is learned custom to describe the literal sense as that which the Holy Ghost first imparted to lead the faithful to God:

> quamvis autem quilibet sensus, quem habet litera, possit de virtute ser-
> monis dici congrue literalis, doctores tamen comuniter vocant sensum

literalem scripture sensum, quem spiritus sanctus primo indidit, ut animus fidelis ascendat in deum. (1.119/18–120/3)

Although whichever sense the letter has could accordingly, by the force of the word, be said to be literal, nevertheless doctors customarily describe as the literal sense of scripture that sense which the Holy Ghost first imparted so that the faithful soul might ascend to God.

This calm assumption of an identity of the 'literal' sense and divine intention as normative in learned discourse is startling. The interrelationship of the 'literal' sense and various kinds of intention, both human and divine, had indeed exercised past scholars – Aquinas, Lyra and Fitzralph, as we have seen in my Introduction (pp. 11–14), are the most immediately relevant – but such an untroubled definition is not quite so simply endorsed in their work. However, the discussion continues: the [literal] sense is sometimes historical, when talking of the *gesta cristi* and the *gesta patrum*; it is sometimes moral or tropological, as for instance in Deut. 6:5 and Matt. 22:37 (both straightforward exhortations to love God); it is allegorical in verses such as 1 Cor. 10:2 (Paul here describes how '[our fathers] were all baptised unto Moses'); and it is anagogical in passages such as Luke 20:35–6 (Christ's words about the state of the blessed after resurrection) (1.120). And the four senses, though distinguished from each other, are not opposed, for the literal sense teaches truth, while the allegorical goes beyond history to teach that which is elsewhere present *ad literam* (1.121/4–9). As example, we are offered Gen. 17 and Gal. 4:22–4: the former narrates the story of Abraham's sons, while the latter draws out *ad literam* the meaning inherent in the history. Abraham thus signifies God the Father and his two sons the two testaments. Reading scripture according to the first sense without the second elicits only the historical meaning; when the second sense is superadded, one gets the allegorical significance (1.121/16–20). The *Doctor Subtilis* is next quoted: whatever is not literal in one part of scripture is literally present in another; and therefore, though some passages may have many senses, scripture in its entirety has all these senses for the literal sense (1.122/2–6). Wyclif then asserts that he has come across no relevant *doctor* who would dissent from such an analysis, though some of the more misguided ones might believe that the senses are nowhere mixed. Raban Maur is next cited as *auctor*: the advantage of simultaneous history and allegory lies in their separate uses: the slow are fed by history and the quick by allegory (1.1 22/6–1 2). Returning to Gen. 1 7, Wyclif proceeds to point out that if one of the faithful were to understand *pure* ('simply') the mystical sense of the passage, without discrediting the history, the allegorical sense would be to this reader literal. And thus, since the sense of scripture is the truth ordained therein by the Holy Ghost, it seems that the literal and allegorical senses are the same. In passages without a historical sense, the literal and allegorical senses are identical. In other words, the first 'orthodox' sense conceived by the reader of a particular scriptural passage is the literal (1.1 22/1 4–25).

Wyclif goes on to emphasise the point that the literal sense is to be sought after everywhere, even though its precise nature varies: 'utrobique enim tenendus est sensus literalis, qui quandoque est nude historicus, quandoque allegoricus, et quandoque mixtim' ('for the literal sense is to be sought after everywhere, which sometimes is nakedly historical, sometimes allegorical and sometimes mixed', 1.1 23/6–8). The moral or tropological sense sometimes has a prior historical sense, and sometimes is, *inmediate*, the literal sense. The three senses are ultimately summed up thus: the allegorical teaches *mediate* or *inmediate* what is to be believed; the anagogical what is to be hoped, and the tropological what is to be done meritoriously. They thus correspond to faith, hope and charity. The three senses are 'literal' when elicited *inmediate* from scripture and either allegorical, tropological or anagogical when elicited *mediate*.[33]

The important point here is Wyclif's vacillation between a revolutionary concept of the 'literal' as that sense intended by God in all its 'spiritual' fullness, and a second, more traditional concept of the 'literal' as the surface or historical sense which is the basis for deeper, 'mediately elicited' significances. The problem, unnoticed or at least unacknowledged by Wyclif, is that the first concept – the 'literal' sense as God's spiritual plenitude – makes all the traditional categories of hermeneutic analysis, to which he nevertheless subscribes, redundant. It is perhaps worthwhile to point out here that the vocabulary of *mediate* and *inmediate* had a long prehistory in medieval epistemological discourse,[34] and, most relevantly for our purposes, in the debates of Aquinas, Giles of Rome and others about the knowability and intelligibility of the divine nature, and the role of the human mind in conceiving God. As Hester Gelber explains, there was substantial disagreement among thinkers over whether human concepts of God had an 'immediate'[35] foundation in the divine essence, or whether such concepts were 'mediate', i.e., having their foundation primarily in human modes of understanding.[36] Wyclif's use of the terms here I find problematic and self-contradictory, a point to which I will return, but the epistemological concerns underlying their use come to the fore clearly in the passages which follow.

The tormented attempt at codifying scriptural signification that I have been charting is succeeded by a remarkable passage in which Wyclif denies the constitutive role played by the perceiving intellect in the creation of meaning. He speaks of a past stage in his career when he tried to distinguish between the four senses 'ex opposito', defining the 'true' sense of scripture as not only the one intended by its author, but 'agregatum' from that and the mode of our understanding:

> quandoque autem contendebam distingwendo hos quatuor sensus ex opposito per rangas inutiles, vocando sensum non solum veritatem, quam autor asserit de scriptura, sed agregatum ex illo et modo intelligendi nostro.[37] (1.124/3–7)

> But at one time, I strove to distinguish these four senses in the opposite way / through opposition by useless lines of division, describing as the sense [of scripture] not only the truth which the author of scripture asserts, but aggregated from it [the sense] and the mode of our understanding.

Later, it seemed to him that such a conceptualisation was unacceptable: 'infundabilem et superflue onerosum' ('ungroundable and unnecessarily burdensome'). The true sense is one on which the eyes of God are fixed eternally, for he himself is the sense which we seek in scripture. Moreover, the distinction of the senses would not apply to such an 'aggregated' sense, since the latter would be neither historical nor mystical nor signified by scripture, but would vary according to the modes of human understanding (1.125/8–16). Taking the act of conceiving for what is conceived (i.e. the sense of scripture), whether that act be erroneous or catholic, is irrational and ungrounded (1.125/17–20). Only that sense which God and the blessed read in the book of life is always true and invariable. If any apparent errors are found in scripture, they are those of the reader, of the 'wrongly conceiving' – 'error male concipientis'. Scripture must be understood 'pure catholice' ('exclusively in a catholic sense'), and extraneous fallen senses should not be mixed with the catholic sense (1.1 27/18–21). The intellect should be brought back from the realm of 'impossible senses' to that of 'catholic contemplation'. The blessed do not elicit wavering senses from scripture. False interpretations rip the creator apart in the text of scripture; 'carnal' and 'noxious' cogitations must therefore be put to death against the stone of justice (this from the Gloss on Psalm 137) (1.1 27/23–129/1).

I have outlined Wyclif's 'argument' in so extended a fashion because it is important to realise the multidirectional quality of his thought and its dizzying, often contradictory movements. Wyclif is in these passages very much struggling to articulate what is in effect a new hermeneutic discourse while being caught in inherited categories of analysis. This emerges most clearly in his discussion of the traditional four-fold scheme of interpretation. There is a major dichotomy in his argument: if the literal sense is synonymous with the divine authorial intention, which intention naturally informs the whole of the Bible, the postulation of meanings elicited *mediate* and *inmediate* becomes problematic. Either one accesses the divine intention – through whatever means – and achieves what by definition ought to be the *inmediate* meaning, or one does not get God's meaning at all. The notion of meanings elicited *mediate* is based on a fundamental recognition of the constitutive role played by the perceiving intellect and its analytical categories in the construction of relevant 'meaning'. The sphere of 'mediate' meanings encompasses intellectual discourses – some of which I will be examining – which would play an important role in the Lollard heresy: interpretative or ecclesiastical traditions (as in William Woodford); hierarchy (as in William Butler); hermeneutic desire in the disputant or in the contemplative reader (Nicholas Love); inventive exegesis and 'adapted meanings' used for homiletic and polemical purposes. But what all of these categories foreground is the interactive, dialogic nature of scriptural meaning. Wyclif's profound but uneasy commitment to a non-discursive and monologic apprehension of divine truth emerges with a remarkable clarity in the passage which we have been examining; and it is no accident that the discussion of the four-fold exegetical model leads seamlessly into a discussion of perception, and an affirmation of the independence of known object from knowing subject.

It is worthwhile to chart the larger argumentative movement in the section I have been outlining: from a recognition of the multiple significances of a figurative scriptural language and an attempt to contain the fluidity of these significances while accommodating the traditional schema of analysis which was based on irreconcilable cognitive premisses, Wyclif moves to a dismissal of these premisses which postulate the necessary dependence of significance on the perceiving mind. Finally, he arrives at a categorical disjunction of a transcendent realm of an ideal catholic sense from that of a wavering fallen earthly hermeneutics.

It is no surprise, therefore, that Wyclif does go on to postulate a Fall which is above all hermeneutic: 'exhinc enim cecidit genus humanum a statu innocencie temptacione diaboli, qui fuit primus questionista scriptura falsificans' ('for mankind fell as a result of this from the state of innocence through the temptation of the devil, who was the first questionist[38] falsifying scripture', 1.1 29/20–2). Eve, we are told, was seduced because the devil perceived how she did not hesitate to adulterate God's words:

> serpens callidus quesivit racionem huius scripture [the divine prohibition in Gen. 2:16–17], cui suffecisset allegasse autoritatem mandantis, cum fides scripture sit principium propinquius primo principio quam principio vel [*sic*] maxime sciencie doctrinalis. sed mulier ex sinistro conceptu scripture non ipsam falsificavit, sed dubitavit dicens, quod 'de fructu ligni, quod est in medio paradisi, precepit deus, nec comederent ne tangerent, ne forte moriantur', et statim diabolus videns hominem in fide scripture titubantem et ex alio latere ad scripturam sacram prohibicionem tactus ligni monstruose addentem, ac si mandatum domini vellet corrigere vel gravare, statim mentitus est, scripture domini contradicens: 'nequaquam', inquid, 'moriemini' et sic seductum est genus humanum ex defectu sensus scripture.[39]
> (1.1 29/27–30/13)

The sly serpent questioned the reason of this piece of scripture. It would have sufficed to have alleged to him the authority of the lawgiver, since the faith of scripture is a principle closer to the First Principle than to that of the highest doctrinal science. But the woman, out of her perverse concept of scripture, did not indeed falsify it, but doubted, saying: 'Of the fruit of the tree which is in the midst of the garden, God hath said, Ye shall not eat of it, neither shall ye touch it, lest ye die'. And the devil, instantly seeing that man was wavering in the faith of scripture, and monstrously adding to holy scripture from elsewhere the prohibition relating to touching the tree, as if he wished to correct or burden the divine mandate, immediately lied, and contradicting the scripture of the Lord, said: 'Ye shall not surely die.' And thus mankind was seduced because of forsaking the sense of scripture.

Eve altered the specific words of the divine prohibition and added a gratuitous reference to 'touching' the forbidden tree (Gen. 3:3), as if she wished to correct or 'burden' the divine mandate, thereby making it clear to the devil that she was wavering in the faith and therefore ripe for seduction. The postulation of such a Fall, brought about as a result of hermeneutic perversity,[40] seems almost inevitable in Wyclif's vision of scripture with its all-important *décalage* between biblical certitude – synonymous with the original ideas in God's mind – and the wavering and disabled realm of the human apprehension of meaning (the domain of hermeneutics).

The self-conflicted analysis of the nature of the 'literal sense' arising from such a vision of scripture characterises Wyclif's discussion of the four senses not only in *De Veritate* but also in his commentary on Gal. 4:24. We find the standard statements about the 'literal' sense: it is the basis for the superstructure of the other senses,[41] like the foundation of a building; it is the only sense on which arguments can be based.[42] Almost in the same breath – and this is the key move – the 'literal' sense is identified with the divine authorial intention; and a new category of 'sensum litteralem multiplicem' is postulated. The multiplex literal sense is evidenced in passages such as 2 Sam. 7:14 ('I will be his father') which applies *ad litteram* to both Christ and Solomon, insofar as the latter prefigures the former. Otherwise the Pauline use of the verse in Hebrews 1:5 as applying to Christ would be unauthorised. That the verse also applies to Solomon is evident from 1 Kings 5:5. When therefore an apostle or some other scriptural writer expresses a particular scriptural sense, that sense is as authentic as the literal, since there are no grades of authorisation of senses in scripture (i.e. the whole of scripture, as God's Word, is of equal authority). The apostle knows the 'full' sense of the passage from the Old Testament as authentically as Moses, Solomon, and so on.[43] Therefore, from the same passage of scripture, four men might have four distinct senses, all of which are 'literal': these are the *duplex, triplex,* and *quadruplex sensus litteralis.*[44] Having achieved this crucial redefinition of the 'literal', as, in effect, the originary full sense of a passage in God's mind, Wyclif returns unexpectedly to the traditional classification: in this scheme, the literal sense corresponds to the *scientia* which every theologian must have even before faith, while the other three, like fruit hidden in cortex, correspond to faith, charity and hope.[45]

It is in the context of this significant uncertainty in Wyclif's visions of the 'literal' that certain crucial aspects of his hermeneutics must be placed. For this hermeneutics is of a peculiar nature: repeatedly, Wyclif seems to be laying down coherent intellectual, 'sciential', strategies to make sense of the biblical text, only to leave this academic discourse behind suddenly, without warning, and launch into full, revelatory flight into the mind of God. This disconcerting treatment of scripture has its roots, as we shall see, in Wyclif's notion of scripture itself: it is both a text and a supra-text. Apparently sciential analytical categories – 'authorial intention', 'logic', 'text' – are thus both invoked and left behind through a complete transformation of these categories.

INTENTIO AUCTORIS

We have been examining Wyclif's troubled attempt to codify and contain the uncertainties of figurative signification within the domain of a lucid and stable literal sense – explicitly associated with a non-fideistic *scientia* in his commentary on Galatians 4:24 – endowed with all the appeal of an 'objective' certitude. This ideological thrust in the direction of clarity and unambiguity is lent further substance by Wyclif's extreme intentionalism. 'Intention' is normally handled in a positivist fashion – as productive of hermeneutic certainty – and questions which might legitimately be asked as to the exact means of accessing the divine intention are generally ignored.

In a revealing passage in the third chapter, we are exhorted to understand the Bible according to God's intention: 'debemus ergo intelligendo scripturam sacram sensum puerilem abicere ac sensum, quem deus docet, accipere' ('therefore, in understanding sacred scripture, we must reject the childish sense, and accept the sense which God teaches', 1.42/13–15).[46] As authority, Wyclif cites 1 Cor. 13:11 ('When I was a child, I spake as a child, I understood as a child, I thought as a child: but when I became a man, I put away childish things'). Dionysius is next cited: it is irrational and stupid not to attend to the force of the intention [*virtus intentionis*] and instead to focus on the words or the naked sounds [*diccionibus*; *sonos nudos*]. Grosseteste is quoted on the vulgar misinterpretation of the word 'eros' as unchaste love; and Dionysius yet again on the fallacy of interpreting according to vulgar use rather than the intention of the words and the author (1.42/15–43/18). Thus, says Wyclif, did the old theologians labour to know the sense of scripture and reject 'alios sensus infidelium seu puerorum' ('other senses of the unfaithful or the immature'). Just as the child first learns the alphabet, then to make syllables [*sillabicare*], thirdly to read and lastly to understand, similarly, the theologian passes through the stages of grammar, scriptural grammar, authorial intention, 'quousque quarto viderit sine velamine librum vite' ('until, fourth, he may see without any veil the Book of Life'). In each successive stage, the imperfections of the stage preceding are transcended (1.44/5–19). And since the intention of the Holy Ghost is the ultimately desired fruit, the leaves and husk of the words are to be disregarded. And that is why Christ and the saints wrote above all in the tablets of the heart, since that is the most perfect (1.44/20–7).

What such passages clarify is the all-important ideological force of Wyclif's intentionalism. Though the passage begins with the suggestion of almost a coherent pedagogic scheme to lead the reader to subtler senses of scripture, it ends with a gesture in the direction of the 'tabula cordis' of the faithful in which the truths of Christianity are written.[47] In such a framework, textual hermeneutics, paradoxically, is ignored: the Bible is here no longer a verbal text demanding interpretation but the discourse of true belief originating in God and existing in the hearts of the faithful. The passage thus highlights the tension at the heart of Wyclif's argument. One seems to ground oneself on the text of scripture through an attempt to learn its own special grammar according to its *intentio auctoris*; one ends, however, in a realm transcending the text, where the book to be read is the Book of Life.[48]

This almost camouflaged movement from a system of textual interpretation to a direct apprehension of God's mind, a movement which relies on an unsignalled and unacknowledged change in the premisses of discussion, is characteristic of Wyclif's thought in *De Veritate*.

One apparently anchors oneself in the realm of *scientia*, thereby re-taining for one's polemic all the 'scientific' attractiveness of such a view-point,[49] only to shift suddenly one's argumentative premisses into the quite distinct realm of *sapientia*. The hermeneutic method-ologies which are brought together here in one single argumentative flow are philosophically removed. What they do have in common is a shared polemic of accessibility: the scriptural text dictates its own meanings to its devoted student – thus, by implication, discounting the necessity of specialised clerkly training in other disciplines; at the same time, by in effect displacing the scriptural text with the book of life and the *tabula cordis*, the inspired *fidelis* attains to an unques-tionable autonomy. The anti-institutional thrust of this polemic be-comes explicit a few pages later: 'non enim est dominus iste invidus, si alii habeant modum[50] suum, sed hoc precipiendo amat comunica-cionem et odit proprietatem superbam. unde in tanta humilitate tradidit logicam suam, quod potest competere cuicunque' ('for God is not envi-ous if others should attain to his discourse [have the mode of his logic], but teaching this, he loves participation and hates proud possession. On account of this he gave his logic in such humility that it can be appropri-ate for/ belong to all', 1.48/1 9–23). Wyclif's expansion of the sphere of those who can be capable of understanding divine 'logic' is to be noted; its extreme radicalism emerges when placed in the context of standard medieval theorisation of the intellectual limits of the non-clerical laity such as discussed by Ruedi Imbach.[51]

Such an ideological emphasis on a 'direct' communication between God and man leads to numerous charged references to God as 'imme-diate' *auctor* whose meanings should ideally inform human discourse while themselves, of course, remaining inviolate and supernal. Whatever is 'right' in our reading of scripture is God's, not ours: '[deus] est autor inmediatus cuiuscunque sensus recti nostrorum codicum' ('God is the immediate author of every correct sense of our books', 1.48/7–8). All 'verbal contention' about the meaning of scripture is therefore useless, 'since the author is to be investigated humbly': 'verbalis contencio est in doctrina scripture inutilis, cum sensus autoris sit humiliter indagan-dus'; and all 'contrary' senses should be dismissed: 'ideo sepe consulunt doctores, ut sensui autoris intendatur dimisso sensu contrario' ('there-fore the doctors often advise that the sense of the author be striven for, contrary senses being rejected'). What is important is to attempt to understand scripture according to God's way of speaking, not ours: 'quid igitur valet verbose contendere, quod veritas cristiane fidei non dependet super virtute sermonis nostri? . . . ideo soleo dicere, quod quelibet pars scripture sacre est vera de virtute sermonis divini' ('therefore, is it worthwhile to debate verbosely, since the truth of the Christian faith does not depend on the power of our [discourse]? . . . Therefore I am accustomed to say that each part of sacred scripture is true by the power of the divine Word', 1.103/11–21). Sacred scripture should be understood 'catholice, pure ad sensum autoris' ('in the catholic fashion, purely according to the sense of the author', 1.183/15).

CONTEXT

In practice, the emphasis on authorial intention does have one tangible result. There is in Wyclif a pronounced awareness of the importance of scriptural context in matters of interpretation. There is an oft-repeated stress on taking scripture in its integrity, and on the dangers of the traditional medieval predilection for citing single-verse authorities which are then glossed without any regard to possible meanings suggested by the context.[52] Those who 'truncant scripturam ad imponendum ei calumpniam' ('those who mutilate scripture to impose sophistries on it', 1.79/10–11) are criticised. What is important is to gather the sense of the whole: 'oportet enim secundum Augustinum grossare minucias fractas et laceratas in sua integra, ex quibus sensus scripture colligitur' ('According to Augustine, it is necessary to gather the broken and torn fragments into wholes, from which the sense of scripture is [then] elicited', 1.79/17–80/2). Context and authorial intention go together: 'oportet capere scripturam in sua integritate pertinenter ad sensum autoris' ('it is necessary to understand scripture in its integrity according to the sense of the author', 1.80/7–8). Distinguishing heretics from true Christians, Wyclif points out that heretics mangle scripture, and not accepting it as an integral text, instead extract what they need to misinterpret: 'heretici enim lacerando negant, scripturam sacram esse veram, et non concedendo eam ex integro capiunt eis placitum, quod extorquent ad sensum sinistrum' ('for heretics deny sacred scripture to be true by tearing it apart, and not accepting it in its unity,

take what is pleasing to them, which they distort to make evil senses',
1.136/21–4).[53]

Indeed, the emphasis on 'integral words' results in a fascinating interpretation of a passage from Book IV of Augustine's *De Doctrina
Christiana*. As we have had occasion to note already, Wyclif was not entirely in sympathy with Augustine's attempt to rehabilitate the rhetoric
of scripture within the discourse of classical rhetoric; for Wyclif, with his
basic distrust of the postlapsarian realm of language, it is – as we shall
see later – scriptural 'logic' rather than eloquence which forms the more
relevant ideological *bonum*. While the saint underlines the superiority of
scriptural rhetoric to all other kinds, he retains the classical dichotomy
between wisdom and eloquence. In the passage which Wyclif discusses
from *De Doctrina* Book IV, ch. 5, Augustine refers to three categories of
the devout: those who remember the words of scripture but are careless
about the sense; a second, higher category of those who do not care for
the words but see into the heart of their meaning; and the highest, third
category of those who are faithful to both meaning and words. The entire passage occurs in the context of discussing the relative importance
of wisdom and eloquence, Augustine's point being that wisdom is better
than eloquence, though a combination of the two is best. For Wyclif,
the Augustinian 'eloquence' becomes 'textual fidelity' to the exact words
of scripture:

> 'sunt', inquid [Augustine] 'qui eas [the words] legunt et negligunt,
> legunt, ut teneant, negligunt, ne intelligant. quibus longe sine dubio
> preferendi sunt, qui verba earum minus tenent et cor earum sui cordis
> oculis vident. sed utrisque ille melior est, qui et cum wlt, eas dicit,
> et sicut oportet, intelligit'. ecce, quod ille, qui tenet verba et sensus
> scripturarum est melior quam ille, qui tenet sensum non tento tenere
> verborum ex integro. (1.149/11–14)

> 'For there are', says [Augustine], 'who read and yet neglect them;
> they read to remember the words, but are careless about knowing the
> meaning. It is plain we must set far above these the men who are not
> so retentive of the words, but see with the eyes of the heart into the
> heart of Scripture. Better than either of these, however, is the man
> who, when he wishes, can repeat the words, and at the same time
> correctly apprehends their meaning.' See [how Augustine says] that
> he who remembers the words [as well as] the sense of scripture is better

than he who remembers the sense without attempting to remember the words in their wholeness.

In the passage which follows, however, he recognises that Augustine is praising scriptural eloquence, and since eloquence often ornaments doctrine, we must imitate that quality of the sacred writings (1.1 49/20–2). But Wyclif's unease with rhetoric is such that he quickly moves on to, for him, the much safer category of scriptural 'logic':

> si ergo debemus sequi eloquentes nostre legis in eloquencia, que sequitur eorum sapienciam inseparabili famulatu, ut dicit Augustinus sexto capitulo [of *De Doctrina* Book IV], multo magis in logica, que est necessarior et pertinencior veritati. (1.1 50/2–6)

> Therefore, if we must follow in eloquence those eloquent in our law, [an eloquence] which follows their wisdom as an inseparable servant, as Augustine says in the sixth chapter, [we should do the same] much more in logic, which is more necessary and more pertinent to the truth.

Indeed, it is tempting to suggest that Wyclif's postulation of scriptural 'logic' as the exemplary *modus loquendi* of scripture owes a great deal to the traditional, and especially Aquinian, association of logic with the domain of *scientia*,[54] and his own distrust of rhetoric as a suspect manipulation of the ambiguities of a fallen human language.[55]

'LOGIC' AND 'REASON'

An abiding theme in Wyclif's praise of logic is its 'unity'. Scriptural logic is the highest of its kind, and functions as the yardstick for all other logics (1.48/24–49/8). The 'unity and conformity' of discourse is as desirable in the postlapsarian world as it was in the prelapsarian. The confusion of tongues was inflicted on man in punishment of pride; the deviation from 'logic' into divisions and disputes is therefore a sin. Peter and Paul exhorted all to speak as one the word of God; it is thus desirable to communicate harmoniously (1.49/23–5 0/5). In the passage which follows, it becomes clear that for Wyclif, 'logic' is almost synonymous with the various ways in which scripture handles language. He speaks of the various 'modes' of scriptural logic:

> scriptura sacra habet multas manieres logicarum . . . [The Christian] nunc debet uti [the logic of scripture] uno modo logice et nunc alio,

secundum quod docetur ex spiritu consilii et regulis caritatis, ut exponendo theologiam misticam debet uti logica plana scripture. et quando loquitur cum eis, quibus celandum est misterium fidei, debet uti logica scripture mistica. (1.50/14–19)

Sacred scripture has many kinds of logic . . . [The Christian] must use [the logic of scripture] now in one mode of logic and now in another, according as he is taught by the counsel of the Holy Ghost and by the rules of charity, as in explaining mystical theology he must use the plain logic of scripture. And when he speaks to them, from whom the mysteries of the faith are to be hidden, he must use the mystical logic of scripture.

The exegete must use the scriptural 'plain' logic when explicating mystical theology, while the 'mystical' logic is to be used when speaking to those from whom truths are to be hidden. 'Mystical' logic thus serves the same function as Augustine's 'figurative' language. It can also defend the faithful from persecution, as 'equivocating' to the unworthy is endorsed by the example of Christ himself (1.50/20–51/1).

Wyclif goes on to refer to Matt. 5:37 as the epitome of the logical clarity of scripture ('But let your communication be, Yea, yea: nay, nay'). Christ's dictum suffices 'pro omni communicacione logica necessaria viatori' ('for all logical communication necessary to the wayfarer'). All that is external to such an all-encompassing scriptural logic, 'gracia cuius est omnis sciencia vel doctrina' ('by the grace of which all learning and doctrine exist'), is not necessary for salvation but is rather a function of fallen *curiositas* as it finds expression in dialectical method (1.51/11–25). A corollary to this dismissal of all that is beyond scripture is that scripture dictates its own meanings, according to which the Christian must speak: 'cristianus debet loqui sub autoritate scripture verba scripture secundum formam, qua scriptura ipsa explicat' ('the Christian must speak the words of scripture under the authority of scripture according to its form, which scripture itself explicates'). This 'form of words' is then identified, as we by now have come to expect, with scriptural logic: 'logica scripture stat in forma verborum et modo loquendi' ('the logic of scripture inheres in the form of words and the mode of speaking') (1.51/26–52/10).[56]

The lines which follow criticise the 'turbata' 'sciencia tradicionis humane' ('confused learning of human tradition', 1.53/3–4). Wyclif then returns to the words of Christ already cited to emphasise their message of 'logical' unidirection and unambiguity, and the coalescence of words and intention they imply (1.53/18–25). He sums up this section on 'logic' by a firm avowal of its affinity to Christian certitude: this logic leads 'recte' ('directly') to the ultimate end 'sine tumultuosis ambagibus' ('without stormy obscurities'), and is the most certain. Other 'logics', as for instance those of Oxford, are variable, ephemeral and a matter of transient fashions (1.54/6–14).

What emerges from this fairly extended account of scriptural 'logic'? Most important, one feels, is the virtual subsumption of all matters of scriptural language within the category of 'logic', while in theory opposing it, or at least suggesting its marked superiority, to rhetoric. Equally important is the ideological thrust in the direction of unity and clarity, resulting in the kind of generalising movement that is fairly common in Wyclif: scriptural 'logic' informs not just the text we possess but also Christ's life and teachings. As Wyclif emphasises, Christ gave this 'logic' not only in niggardly *sententiae*, but also, simultaneously, informed the Church fully as much by his own example (in the broadest sense: 'moribus') as by the logic of his verbal communication. The opening out of this particular logical discourse to include the divinity itself also enables the typical Wycliffite polarisation of this highest *scientia* and fallen human discourses. School logic, in particular, is the realm of uncertainty, disputation and dialogue. Divine 'logic' is above all monologic: one can only apprehend, but not interact with it.

Wyclif's complex – and I will go on to argue, ideological – treatment of the notion of 'logic' needs to be examined further. On one level, he in effect rehabilitates, indeed 'recuperates' 'logic', by means of important redefinitions, into his philosophy of scripture. On another level, he rejects contemporary academic logical discourses as sublunar and curious. The category of 'scriptural logic' thereby becomes a polemical weapon which can be deployed against any academic hermeneutics Wyclif wishes to disavow. Wyclif's own logical works – as opposed to his *theorisation* of logic – seem to have been largely perceived as uncontentious; hence the frequent, and to all appearance, uncontroversial, incorporation of his logical writings into late-medieval collections of logical teaching.[57] His theory of scriptural logic, however, is entirely ideological – such 'logic' can encompass any aspect of scriptural signification, and, indeed, can be understood properly only through faith.

What then is the rationale for Wyclif's notion of 'scriptural logic'? Interesting insights emerge if one places Wyclif's involvement with logic in the context of thirteenth and fourteenth century scholastic speculation about the role of logic in faith. As Hester Gelber's and Michael Shank's work shows, there was a variety of responses offered by scholars to the perceived discrepancy of Aristotelian logic and Trinitarian theology (as enunciated dogmatically in the Fourth Lateran Council of 1215). While some thinkers sought to reconcile the two, others, such as Ockham and Robert Holcot, came close to a radical separation of the domains of faith and logical reasoning. Holcot paid particular attention to the relationship of logic and theology; as he said in his *Quodlibeta*:

> In conceding or denying either propositions or consequences, the Catholic needs to use no logic but the determination of the Church, nor other rules discovered by man such that these rules be "necessitive" of his concessions or negations in matters of faith. This is evident since in such matters natural logic is deficient.[58]

I would suggest that at least part of the impulse behind Wyclif's peculiar accommodation of a redefined 'logic' within his hermeneutics is his consciousness of the possible fideistic implications of a total renunciation. Fideism is, as Holcot's work shows, only a step away from an acceptance of ecclesiastical dogma as determinant. Wyclif however has a strong investment in retaining individual hermeneutic independence based on what I have been calling 'scientia'. Hence his acceptance of a rationalist intellectuality: the Bible as a 'text' open to hermeneutic systematisation must be kept in the foreground to keep the claims of Church traditions at bay. As Maarten Hoenen has pointed out:

> The language of theology was not only that of logic, but also that of the tradition of the Church. When [theories] departed from or clashed with it, it was not logic but tradition that eventually decided what was true and what was untrue. The standard for theology was tradition rather than philosophy.[59]

So far one has been looking at the ideological role played by celestial 'logic' in Wyclif's thought. It is equally important to see what he does with such a logical category in practice. In an important passage, Wyclif postulates two kinds of divine logic and urges us repeatedly to abide by it, both when it is 'express' and when it is 'hidden': 'teneamus ergo illam nunc secundum partem eius expressam et planam et nunc secundum partem eius enigmaticam atque absconditam . . . semper autem sub autoritate magistri Cristi finaliter propter ipsum' ('let us abide by [that logic], now according to its express and plain part, and now according to its enigmatic and hidden part . . . but always under the authority of [our] lord, Christ, and ultimately, because of him', 1.55/6–10). He then proceeds to discuss some instances of 'enigmatic' scriptural logic. Taken up first are Christ's words in Luke 11:26 ('and from him that hath not, even that he hath shall be taken away from him'). The apparent contradiction is resolved by a reference to Augustine: only he who knows how to use gold can be held to 'have gold'; he who does not, is possessed by gold rather than being himself the possessor. Hence, when this saint speaks of the possession of the unjust, it is equivocally 'subunderstood' to signify 'unjust occupation' and 'pretended possession' (1.56/17–57/2). It is this insight – that those who have also do not have – which is communicated by the apparent self-contradiction of Jesus's words. A related issue – the possession of the just – is next considered. Augustine is cited on Song of Solomon 2:6 to redefine that true possession. But the 'carnal' seek to deny the import of such passages by misinterpreting scriptural logic and by insisting that there is no having of temporalia unless 'sensibly', no right nor possession unless 'politicum'. Moreover, since Christ promised a hundredfold to those who renounced for him, surely one would be entitled, in place of one wife, to a hundred (1.58/3–8). Believers of such arguments, says Wyclif, have a heart blind and indisposed to the comprehension of celestial logic (1.58/18–21). Such a logic necessitates spiritual intellections, not carnal ones: it can be conceded that one will have a hundred brothers or sisters as long as these are 'spiritualiter intellectis', not 'carnaliter' (1.59/1–5).[60]

In practice too, therefore, the study of scriptural 'logic' is hardly to be distinguished, in terms of methodology, from Wyclif's hermeneutical concerns[61] and his engagement with the Bible's enigmatic and non-literal uses of language. 'Logic' is thus often coupled with 'grammar': 'nec oportet timere offensionem logicorum et gramaticorum, quos oportet submittere se ad discendum in scriptura tam novam gramaticam quam logicam' ('it is not necessary to fear the attack of logicians and grammarians, who must [instead] submit themselves to learning in scripture

a new grammar as much as a new logic', 1.86/24–27). All the various
parts of scripture, though they may each have multiple senses, lead ultimately to one final verity: 'quelibet pars caracteris scripture sacre est
vera habens per ordinem multos sensus, cum deus sit primus et ultimus
sensus cuiuslibet creature et particulatim habent alie partes scripture
pro sensibus veritates ducentes in veritatem illam finalem, ad quam
concurrunt veritates singule ut ad centrum' ('every part of every letter
of sacred scripture is true, having, according to [divine] arrangement,
many senses, since God is the first and last sense of every creature, and,
individually, every part of scripture has for its senses truths leading to
that final truth to which all individual truths run as to the centre',
1.87/4–9). The theologian does not need to discuss the distinctions
of the parts of speech or of propositions, as grammarians and logicians do, since he has a 'superior and more right metaphysics' than the
introductory disciplines for children (1.87/12–88/1).[62] Contemporary
academic logic, in Wyclif's vision, is therefore generally dismissed as
'sophistry',[63] and as such, polarised against the 'true' logic of Christ's
Word. The Saviour, the 'subtilissimus logicus non verecundabatur in-
sophistice dicere verba' ('most subtle logician was not ashamed to say
words in a non-sophistic manner'), unlike academic theologians, who
ostentatiously revel in 'subtilitate logice, in habundancia argumentorum' ('in logical subtlety, in an abundance of arguments'), and who are
motivated by their 'libido rixandi' ('desire to dispute'). The true logic is
one which must transcend the false: 'decet habitum philosophi integrari
ex arte sophismatum, ne a sophistis capiatur in verbis' ('the *habitus*/cloak
of the philosopher should be repaired by the art of sophismata, and not
be seized by sophists in words').[64]

Scriptural 'grammar' and 'logic' are thus assimilated into a transcendent godly discourse, these apparently sciential categories almost 'tran-
substantiated', retaining merely the accidents of their roles in the trivium. A similar fate befalls 'reason',[65] an intellectual faculty that Wyclif
considers essential to a proper understanding of the Word, and one
which would have in the years to come a long history in the writings of
his followers and opponents. In the discourse of Wyclif and that of his
followers, 'reason' is 'rationality', and as such it supports a philological
approach to the Bible; it is also, simultaneously, a supra-rational faculty
which can be identified with God himself.

The emphasis on 'reason', along with that on 'logic' and the 'literal' sense, seems at first glance indisputably to point to an Aquinian hermeneutic model. Aquinas's own endorsement of 'reason' is clear-sighted in its recognition of its limited validity and usefulness in matters of divinity. The end destined for all of us by God 'exceeds the comprehension of reason', though in our attempts at achieving that end, 'reason' can clarify and explicate what has been revealed by God. In his *Commentary* on Boethius's *De Trinitate*, 'reason' is given the function of demonstrating truths that are the preambles of faith, of clarifying truths by employing comparisons from the teaching of the philosophers, and of vanquishing in argument those who speak against the faith.[66] In the *Summa Theologiae*, the rational treatment of matters divine is justified thus: 'there is nothing to stop the same things from being treated by the philosophical sciences when they can be looked at in the light of natural reason and by another science when they are looked at in the light of divine revelation.'[67] There is no contradiction between the light of faith and the light of reason, since both are the gifts of God: 'rather, since in imperfect things there is found some imitation of the perfect, though the image is deficient, in those things known by natural reason there are certain similitudes of the truths revealed by faith.'[68] In Chenu's succinct formulation, the Aquinian *ratio* illustrates, elaborates and promotes in the domain of human truth the principles of theology.[69]

Aquinas's definitive and careful rehabilitation of reason in the discourse of faith is undeniably attractive to those interested in postulating an accessible biblical text, for the thrust of his synthesis is towards the possibility of attaining to some limited but nevertheless valid understanding of the faith through rational clarification and explication. It is therefore not surprising that Wyclif should invoke the power of rational reading, though, as we shall now see, with significant modifications.

Wyclif brings up the issue in the context of a discussion of the exegetical principles to be borne in mind by the student of scripture: textual correction, study of biblical logic, and submission to biblical authority, to reason, to the Fathers, and to the Holy Ghost (1.1 94–201). He begins the section on reason by citing Augustine's dictum from *De Doctrina Christiana*, that whatever in scripture seems to be leading to the criminal or the vicious must be understood figuratively, until it harmonises with charity. He continues: 'ex quo patet, quod utrobique in scriptura

sacra est conformitas racioni et per consequens racio est testis neces-
sarius ad habendum sentenciam scripturarum' ('From which it appears,
that sacred scripture is everywhere in conformity with reason, and therefore reason is a necessary witness to gather the sense of the scriptures',
1.200/13–16). A few lines later, Wyclif cites *De Doctrina* again, this time
to make the qualification that the authority of scripture is nevertheless
to be preferred to 'racioni humane' ('human reason'), since sacred scripture is the same as the Word of God, which is of the highest authority
(1.200/22–5).

The ambiguities of the passage are significant. First, Augustine is interpreted in such a way that 'reason' becomes synonymous with charity:
all true scriptural readings must lead to charity, 'from which it appears',
that scripture is always in accordance with 'reason'. 'Reason' here becomes not an interpretative faculty brought to bear on the Bible from
outside, but, as an aspect of *caritas*, a quality defined by, informing and
commensurate with the Bible. This is of course a far cry from Augustine
himself, whose reliance on 'reason' is entirely tentative and conditional,
and to whose vision of 'reason' Wyclif returns: 'reason' and 'scripture'
are two not necessarily harmonious sources of authority, with scripture
naturally occupying much the superior position.[70] Once again, Wyclif's
use of an important concept is characterised by a polemically significant
ambiguity: an ambiguity which enables him simultaneously to exploit
the resources, and, when necessary, transcend the shortcomings of a
rationalist intellectuality.

TEXTUAL CRITICISM

The duality in Wyclif's thought that I have been pointing to, a duality
consisting in a theoretical adherence to a *scientia* which repeatedly ex-
pands to encompass within itself various sapiential liberties, goes some
way towards explaining his extraordinary lack of interest in textual criticism. As has been pointed out,[71] Wyclif's Bible is ultimately an idea in
the mind of God independent of local and temporal contingencies. The
codices, words and other 'artificials' are merely an aid to memory and in
no sense constitutive of scripture; as such, they form the fifth and least
of the five scriptural 'grades' (1.108/15–109/3). Scripture can be taken
for the signs 'quomodocunque signaverint' ('howsoever they signify') or

'ut signant sensum dei' ('as they signify God's sense'). Wyclif naturally abides by the latter conceptualisation (1.1 09/6–7). Hence Christ's words in John 10:35: 'non potest solvi scriptura, quem pater sanctificavit et misit in mundum'. In these words, Wyclif suggests, truth seems to be hinting at itself [*se ipsam innuere*], since Christ was endowed with sacred humanity and sent to the world to save it (1.1 09/11–15). The implied identification of the Book of Life and Christ is taken up in the dense passage which follows discussing the use of 'quem' [i.e. Christ] and not 'quam' [i.e. scripture] in the above verse:

> iste liber non potest solvi, cum deitas ac humanitas septiformi gracia copulantur insolubiliter in eadem persona . . . unde ut doceamur in hoc dicto intelligere illum librum et non opera hominum, ordinavit spiritus sanctus in correctis codicibus hoc relativum 'quem' et non 'quam'.[72] (1.1 09/21 –1 1 0/2)

> This book cannot be destroyed, since deity and humanity are joined indivisibly in the same person through sevenfold grace . . . Therefore, so that we may learn to understand in this statement that book [i.e. Christ] and not the works of men, the Holy Ghost ordained in correct codices this relative 'quem' and not 'quam'.

There follows the important passage, cited by Minnis,[73] describing 'sensible scripture' as akin to the picture of a man: just as we refer to the picture as the man 'propter similitudinem' ('because of a similitude'), we use 'sensible scripture' to refer to the real thing. If indeed scripture were to be identified with its material embodiments, it would be encumbered with all kinds of vulnerabilities and would consequently be of no authority:

> nam sic esset omnis scriptura sacra viciabilis a sutore, autorizabilis a scriba, ymmo a cane solubilis et corrigibilis a scurra sicut maculabilis, et omnis scriptura foret a quotlibet hominibus hereticabilis, dampnabilis et adversabilis, nullius virtutis directive vel honoris et per consequens nullius autoritatis. (1.1 1 1 /1 4–1 9)

> For if in this manner all sacred scripture were [subject to] corruption by a cobbler, to authorisation by a scribe, even to destruction by a dog and to correction as well as pollution by a buffoon, all scripture would be [subject to] being made heretical, damnable or [to being made] open to opposition by anyone, and [would be] of no guiding virtue or honour and therefore of no authority.

Mark 13:31, Luke 16:17, Matt. 5:18 and John 10:35 are then cited in confirmation of the absolute invulnerability of scripture (1.112–13). This scripture was fulfilled in Christ; once again the relevant passages from the gospels are enumerated. And since the deeds of Christ are not *finaliter* dependent on the works of man or skins or words, codices and other *artificilia*, it would be heedless to neglect the superior scripture to attend to its mere semblances (1.113/5–9). And this scripture, in its true sense, is the one explicated by Christ to his apostles in Luke 24:25 ff (1.113/16–19).

Wyclif proceeds to confess that when he was young, he tried to understand and defend scripture according to its sense since it was obvious that it could not be verified according to the 'skins of beasts' (i.e. material codices), until God directed him to understand the equivocation involved in the use of the word 'scripture'. Sometimes the Bible speaks of 'scripture' in the first mode (i.e. Book of Life), sometimes in the second and third modes (i.e. intelligible and 'effective' or 'existential' being of truths) (1.114/1–9). Similar is the case with its use of 'liber': books of soul and conscience (Apoc. 20:12; Daniel 7:10); codices as in the book given to Christ in Luke 4:17; and the Book of Life (1.114/11–14). Scripture makes little or no mention of the fourth and fifth modes, those of truths written naturally in the soul of man, and material books respectively. The generation seeking signs is only interested in these lowest modes (1.114/20–24). And these can be called sacred only in so far as they lead the faithful to the celestial scripture, just as sacerdotal vestments and other ornaments are called sacred. Therefore the material forms of scripture can be called sacred only to the extent that they lead to a perception of the will and the ordination of God, which constitute the most sacred scripture. Understanding scripture wrongly is not a function of sacred scripture at all, since the effect, whence it is said to be sacred (i.e. leading to the will of God) is absent. Therefore the faithful Christian, and specially the theologian, works hard so that scripture is indeed sacred to him through a correct *intellectus* and *affectus* (1.115/24–116/5). Note the characteristic vertical movement of Wyclif's thought: 'scripture' is identical with Christ and the will of God. Therefore, either one possesses *sapientia* in one's correctly ordered intellect and affect or one has nothing to do with scripture at all: the book itself is quite irrelevant.

The eleventh chapter contains a substantial section on textual matters, drawing largely on Jerome's work on textual criticism and medieval responses to it.[74] It begins with a discussion of the authority of the Old Testament, and objections raised against it. Authorities of the New Testament confirm only particular *dicta* of the authors of the Old; are therefore all our Old Testament codices authentic? Moreover, though in the beginning the Hebrew scripture was 'indefectibiliter data' ('given without possibility of corruption'), Esra himself collected the Hebrew writings badly. Jerome's translation is often wrong, and modern scribes have not ensured that the books which we have are properly emended (1.232/13–23).

It is interesting that in answer to these problems, Wyclif comes up with what appears to be a thoroughly traditional assertion of the ever-presence of God in his Church: 'ecce, ego vobiscum sum omnibus diebus usque ad consumacionem seculi' (Matt. 28:20). Hence, codices must be corrected according to the sense and authority of the Church; and the *sentence* of such codices taken from the head of the Church, Christ (1.233/9–11). Luke 24:27 suggests that the Christian, like Christ, must accept the whole of the Hebrew witness. The 22 books of the Old Testament, as Jerome says in his Prologue to Galatians, are authentic and should be accepted along with the New Testament. The dispersion of the Jews with their Hebrew books is beneficial: we can have recourse to their Hebrew codices;[75] second, individual Jews instructed by God can give effective witness; and third, truths prophesied and fulfilled of them can give credence to the rest of scripture (1.233/25–234/7).

The translation of Jerome is approved by the sanctity of his life, his skill in Hebrew, and the concordance of his translation with Hebrew and Greek codices. The New Testament cites many passages from the Old which differ from the septuagintal version, because the latter hid many mysteries from the Egyptians. (The implication is that we have the correct readings in the New Testament quotations, and the Old Testament as preserved is defective.) And this accounts for the calumnies directed against Jerome by the envious (1.234/23–235/6). As for modern codices, they can be defective in part from the sin of the Church. Codices are required only temporally and 'by supposition'; what is always required is the sense. God often punishes sin by surrendering the sinful into 'reprobate' senses; but of course he can never corrupt his own law, even though those capable of understanding or abiding by his law might be lacking (1.235/10–25).

The following passage discusses the Manicheans, who, though they questioned scriptural truth, did not ascribe the falsity to the apostolic scribes, but to the corruptors of codices (1.236/1–16). Wyclif then moves on to a new issue: that of the validity of the writings of pagan authors and of apocrypha. Once again he speaks as a traditionalist: the writings of Homer and Virgil contain many truths, and if we accept the authority of the Old Testament because parts of it are alleged as 'catholic' in the new, we must also accept the authority of the poets. Paul after all quoted 'Eumenides' in Tit. 1:12 (1.236/17–237/9). Similarly, many apart from the four evangelists wrote evangels, as for instance Nicodemus. A crucial passage from Augustine (*De Civitate Dei*, Book 18, ch. 38) on the formation of the canon is next cited: many writings, because of their excessive antiquity, are of suspect authority and therefore not included in the canon (1.237/10–21). Wyclif then changes direction once again, and after briefly referring to the superiority of scriptural sense over mere codices, goes on to justify the use of pagan poets in argumentation: poets and philosophers such as Plato cannot be drawn upon to 'prove' faith but can certainly be alleged as *auctores* in persuasive debate (1.238/20–25). Since one of the issues now is the conditional validity of the non-canonical text, i.e., it is acceptable if inspired by God, Wyclif proceeds to lay down principles to judge whether or not a prophecy is true. Both the 'sentence' and the life of the prophet are to be noted: if there is a falling-off from living the Christlike life, the authenticity of such a person can legitimately be doubted (1.239/14–17). For the authority of members of the 'Church' lies in this, that they live 'conformiter ad Cristum' (1.240/25–6).

Wyclif then returns to his earlier theme of the valid authority of the Old Testament. We believe the Old Testament authors above all because their writings lead to charity (1.241/16–18). Their authority holds good only in so far as they proclaim the word of God. As for Nicodemus, there is no reason to discredit him or other apocryphal writers as false, though it is not necessary that the militant church believe them *explicite*; the Church has therefore neither damned nor canonised them. She has enough defence in the 22 books of the Old Testament and the 24 of the New: to add further books to the canon would seem to be unduly burdensome (1.242/9–15). Many apocryphal books are indeed written in the Book of Life and therefore to be believed explicitly or implicitly (1.242/16–23). In any case, it is useless to quarrel over apocrypha, for that is a form of paying attention only to the fifth grade of scripture while neglecting the more important prior grades (1.242/27–243/4). And if it is asked whether it is necessary to believe in codices or scripture in the fifth mode, it is replied that though it is necessary to believe in all scripture in common, it is not necessary to believe in each and every particular codex. Only 'correct' books are believed in as signs of authentic scripture (1.244/5–13).

The argument that I have been charting is more than usually fragmented, for it vacillates between a recognition of the importance of the textual problems of the Bible, and a desire to relegate all such problems to the irrelevant category of scripture 'quinto modo'. What is even more surprising is the apparent traditionalism of some of Wyclif's positions. The continuing presence of God in the Church used as justification for ecclesiastical textual authority is scarcely what one has come to expect of this strident critic of the spiritual corruption of the Church and its consequent non-authority. One gets the sense that Wyclif is indeed aware of the central relevance of textual matters to his ideology of authority, but refuses to acknowledge this relevance. My own suggestion would be that Wyclif, knowing as he did his Jerome and his Augustine (as well as his Nicholas of Lyra) so well, did not wish to enter into the extremely tricky question of the formation of the canon and related matters of textual authority. A genuine *theoretical* engagement with the history of the Bible would necessitate uncomfortable *aperçus* into the nature both of the biblical text and of the otherwise idealised *ecclesia primitiva*. Wyclif therefore takes the easy way out: what is all-important is scripture 'primo modo' which of course transcends all such textual detail. This also explains the unusual gentleness of his approach to apocryphal material: in the non-textual world of this particular discussion in *De Veritate*, such material is acceptable as long as it is 'true'. It would be left to William Woodford to recognise this basic weakness in the thought of his opponent and use it to dismantle the heresiarch's radical textual idealism.[76]

'FIDES EST SUMMA THEOLOGIA'

The aspects of Wyclif's hermeneutics we have been discussing hitherto can broadly be understood, despite their contradictions and complexities, as part of the 'sciential' discourse of *De Veritate*, which regards the scriptural text as an accessible and determinate body of meaning, the explicatory principles of which can be codified into a coherent system which can be studied and learnt.[77] There is, however, equally strongly present a quite different discourse: one which acknowledges and builds on a postulated incommensurability of scripture, which remains, despite all human attempts at clarification, an opaque, dark and problematic realm of signification, and which depends, for a proper understanding of itself, on a correct sapiential ordering of the perceiving intellect: 'fides autem est summa theologia' ('for faith is the highest theology', II.234/3–4). Just as lead cannot be converted into gold unless calcined properly, similarly, the student of the Bible cannot achieve *sapientia* unless humbled through contrition (1.60/12–15). Augustine is cited on scriptural obscurity: it is to exercise the faculties of the devout; and the interpretative difficulties are 'medicamenta dei' ('God's remedies', 1.60/20–23).[78] The truly faithful – clerk or lay, man or woman – submit themselves 'interiorly' to the logic and eloquence of the Bible (1.117/2–6).[79] The style of scripture, on Augustine's authority, is humble; the puerile and the proud are therefore equally incapable of understanding it. The profundity of scripture, again on Augustine's authority, is such that a life-time of devoted study is not enough to exhaust its significance. And paradoxically, scripture's 'impenetrable altitude' provides its *cultor* with the securest refuge (1.117–19).

The principles of interpretation of such a problematic text become correspondingly elusive. Hermeneutics is therefore, in this strand of thought, displaced by 'right living', which provides, indeed embodies, the most dependable access to scriptural significance. The argument, we may note, is circular: from scripture one elicits the principles of ideal humility, which principles in their turn underlie and dictate a correct hermeneutics. Wyclif therefore criticises the Pope for suggesting that concepts of right living can vary over time. The Pope maintains that his life should be the ideal to be imitated rather than the rules given in scripture by Christ. If it is objected that his life is different from that of Christ and his apostles, he answers that temporal changes require this, and that he can, out of the plenitude of his power, dispense with the obligation to imitate Christ and his apostles (1.152/27–30). But Wyclif disagrees, for he has elicited from scripture that priests must minister the sacraments humbly and live a life of Christ-like poverty. Neither temporal variation nor papal dispensation can modify this basic requirement, this debt to Christ. Luke 22:25–6 is next cited. 'I have confirmed', Wyclif goes on to say, 'secundum fidem scripture ex modo vivendi Cristi et suorum apostolorum conformiter ad hunc sensum, que vita est optimus interpres scripture' ('according to the faith of scripture from the mode of Christ's life and that of his apostles in conformity with this sense, that life is the best interpreter of scripture', 1.153/12–15). One is repeatedly exhorted, in Augustinian fashion, to avoid those senses of scripture which lead away from the right life (1.185/23–186/2). The devout must always guard against sublunar temptations (1.187/13–15); and he must, on the authority of Augustine, pray to be vouchsafed proper understandings: 'sed oret, ut intelligat' ('but let him pray, so that he may understand', 1.188/16–7). Augustine is again cited on the duty of the pious to honour scripture 'et opere et mente' ('in works and in the mind', 1.189/2).

CONCLUSION

The tension in Wyclif's thought that I have been seeking to clarify, a tension between a sciential attempt at scriptural codification, and a sapiential, *caritative* reliance on a celestial scripture occasionally finds explicit expression in *De Veritate*. In the second chapter, Christ's equivocal words in John 7:8 are discussed. Christ says that he will not ascend to the feast; yet, a few verses later, he does so, secretly (John 7:10). Wyclif maintains that Christ's words should be 'subunderstood' in such a way that there is no contradiction. Just as we say 'non comedi' or 'non celebravi', implying a certain time-period pertinent to the sense being communicated, Christ too intended his words to be understood in a certain way. When interrogated by his brothers about the hour of his ascension into Jerusalem, 'verissime asseruit, quod non ascenderet, suple: publice pro hac hora' ('he asserted most truly that he would not ascend; supply: in public, for this hour', 1.24/3–6). Augustine is cited on the meaning of

Christ's secret ascension (1.24–25); and Wyclif underlines the mystical mnemonics of Christ's words and actions: 'ut memoraret nobis allegorice, tropologice et anagogice cursum presentis temporis ad futurum' ('in order to bring to mind for us allegorically, tropologically and anagogically, the course of present time leading towards the future', 1.26/6–8). We must remember that the feast in question was in memory of the Israelites' habitation in the desert; when fleeing from the Egyptians, they communed with God and were commanded to keep three feasts every year (Exod. 1 9; 23:1 4). 1 Cor. 1 0:1 1 ('Now all these things happened unto them [the Israelites] for ensamples..') is next cited; therefore Christ's own actions are mystical: 'dignatus est Cristus aperire nobis in facto suo sensum misticum huius historie' ('Christ thought fit to show to us in his deed the mystical sense of this *historia*', 1.26/1 6–7). For the faithful are liberated by Christ from Egyptian servitude, a state in which we serve the devil pharaoh in the darkness of sin (1.26/1 7–20).

Wyclif thus explicates the multiple significances of Christ's apparently contradictory words and actions:

> ecce, quot misteria parturit festum cristi et verbum, quod videtur nobis incultum et contradiccionem sapiens eo, quod ignoramus equivocacionem et causam, propter quam scriptura sic equivocat. si, inquam, hec debite nosceremus, diceremus, quod nec in verbis domini nec in eorum sequela sit redargutio, sed multiplex informacio. (1.27/22–27)

> See, how many mysteries the feast of Christ, and his words, which seem to us trivial [uncultivated] and to savour of contradiction in him, bring forth. This is because we are ignorant of equivocation and the cause for which scripture equivocates thus. If, I say, we were to know this as we ought to, we would say that neither in the words of the Lord nor in what follows them is there any contradiction. Instead, there is manifold teaching [in them].

However, he remains uneasily aware that mystical readings of scriptural passages can be, and indeed are subject to 'misuse'. He summarises the contrary argument that in such a linguistic framework all doctrinal disputation would be confounded, since anyone would be able to invent such equivocations at will and contradict himself. All Aristotelian philosophy, and all certitude of faith through discourse would perish (1.28/8–1 2). Wyclif's answer is that though man can misuse scriptural logic [*abuti sciencia logice scripture*], the Christian must not invent equivocations unless 'pertinenter fundabiles' ('suitably capable of being grounded') in scripture.[80] Having thus begged all questions he set out to answer, he proceeds to damn all contemporary disputation for not leading *caritative* to the elucidation of scripture and the utility of the Church. What is necessary as antidote to such vainglory is the humility of scriptural logic; doctrinal disputation would then be saved by celestial logic (1.28/25–29/4). Once again, though in this instance with almost schematic clarity, Wyclif's attempted reliance on a coherent sciential apparatus of exegesis gives way, because of his absolute refusal to admit the dialogic nature of any discourse, before a hermeneutics of humility and *caritas*, which at the same time defines and is defined by scripture. One is more than ready to be a 'supplementing' reader, yet one's supplements are not theoretically constitutive of meaning: the 'source', which is in this case scripture, remains inviolate. 'Exposition', in this scheme of things, is only a handmaid clarifying the words of her *domina*, the scriptural text: 'exposicio quidem non est scriptura sacra, sed eius preco vel ancilla, non negans dominam suam, sed ex verbis propriis, que mutuatur de domina, ipsam reverenter detegens and explanans' ('exposition is not sacred scripture but [as it were] her herald or handmaid. She does not contradict her lady, but by means of special words borrowed from her, reveals and explains her respectfully', 1.386/15–18). 'False' expositions are correspondingly dismissed as belonging to the realm of perverse 'glossing'.

The complexities – and simplicities – in Wyclif's vision of scripture are captured pregnantly in one of the rare 'figures' which he himself uses. In describing the unity of the truth which informs each and every part of scripture, he speaks of a group of people dragging a ship along: 'sicut enim, multis trahentibus navem, quilibet eorum trahit navem . . . sic quelibet pars scripture significat ipsam bene intelligentibus fidem, spem et caritatem' ('For just as when many people drag a ship along, each of them drags the ship . . . similarly, each part of scripture signifies the same faith, hope and charity to those understanding rightly', 1.86/15–19). The image is fascinating, for its comparison (of the parts of scripture offering truth, to men dragging a ship) locates the agency of meaning firmly in the text: the various parts of scripture are bearing along the ship of divine truth. But the image collapses almost immediately, for the brief vision that we get of scriptural words and scriptural sentence forming an independent entity removed from all the contingencies of the perceptual – the men will be dragging the ship even if there is no one to watch them – is brief indeed, and the phrase 'bene intelligentibus' introduces the whole world of hermeneutics that Wyclif has taken such paradoxical pains to deny.

Wyclif's theorisations thus bring to the surface in a cumulative fashion the ambiguous positioning of textual hermeneutics in his vision of Christian meaning. The Bible is a text which demands explication; more importantly, though, it is a discourse of truth – a discourse encompassing God's mind and the life of virtue and rectitude – which is essentially independent of the text. Wyclif therefore simultaneously establishes a hermeneutics and denies its significance; rather, the hermeneutics of text and the 'hermeneutics' of life are collapsed into each other. This tension between the two hermeneutics would prove to be one of the focal dichotomies of Lollardy: are interpretations to be judged in terms of intellectual, academic categories, however defined ('text', context, authorial intention, the 'literal sense', 'logic'), or are they to be judged in terms of the life of the interpreter, and the possible validity of his claims to revelation? Such a dichotomy goes some way towards explaining the presence in Lollardy of an extraordinary critical interest in matters of text and interpretation, and a tendency to valorise 'revelation'. The former is self-consciously open to critiques and academic discussion; the latter is by its very nature beyond the domain of any intellectual engagement.[81]

De Veritate thus situates itself on an uneasy interface between the academic and the revelatory. It does not place these two approaches to Christian meaning in any rigorous hierarchy, traditional or otherwise: an academic hermeneutics is not consistently described, as one might have expected, as a propaedeutic leading to a sapiential apprehension, and enactment, of God's truth in a virtuous life. Wyclif has his own reasons to avoid a straightforward acceptance of the sapiential approach. Such an approach is unsuited to his purposes – which include a rejection of ecclesiastical authority, and involve a desire for sciential certitude – because the 'sapiential' scheme in effect emphasises the dialogic, indeterminate and ever-developing nature of meaning, and by implication, the centrality of the knowing subject and the interpretative traditions informing him. Alexander of Hales, for instance, made a firm distinction between biblical science, which has to do with the disposition of the individual,

and other human sciences, which educate the intellect through rationalist tools.[82] One mode seeks to arrive at speculative certitude through
'divisiones, definitiones and ratiocinationes' while the other mode seeks
to achieve a love of God through precepts, examples, exhortations, revelations, prayers, 'quia ii modi competunt affectum pietatis' ('because
those methods are appropriate to a pious disposition'). Alexander associated scripture with 'hidden' significations: 'sicut proprium est scientiae
humanae tradi per sermones manifestos, ita proprium divinae sapien-
tiae ut sit per sermones occultos' ('just as it is appropriate for human
knowledge to be transmitted by means of statements that are clearly
understandable, so it is appropriate for divine wisdom to be transmitted through statements which have a hidden meaning'). In general,
scientia was associated with (natural) reason, while *sapientia* had closer
affinities to 'authority' as embodied in a long tradition of inspired biblical study.[83] The sapiential framework thus foregrounds the knowing
subject, the authority of the Church and its interpretative traditions,
and (biblical) linguistic complexity. Wyclif rejects the straightforward
sapiential model because of his ideological investment in postulating
an originary, unchanging and accessible biblical meaning, the principles of which are open to codification, and towards which the faithful
should direct themselves, a meaning which is not only independent of
the contingencies of ecclesiastical traditions but indeed of the mundane
realm altogether, a meaning which is not dependent on a dialogic interaction with the realm of the human and the historical. At the same
time, he is distrustful of the purely sciential, not only because of its
vulnerability to rationalist criticism, but also because of its associations
for him with a fallen rhetoric and a fallen logic, and above all, with
the *institutionalised* discourses of these disciplines, directed, according
to him, towards earthly vanity rather than celestial knowledge. What he
does – to describe it in a schematic fashion with all the attendant dangers
of over-simplification – is to accept apparently a sciential hermeneutics
which is then opened out to incorporate all the interpretative freedoms
that the traditional sapiential model enabled. His uneasy recuperation of
scientia, though theoretically suspect, is nevertheless ideal for polemics:
ecclesiastical authority can be denied on the basis of a scriptural *lectio*
which is both academic-rationalist and a mode of life. Ideologically,
though not in terms of theoretical coherence, such a 'hermeneutics' is

near-unassailable. The combination of an academic study of the Bible and an inspirational access to the divine mind was a remarkably potent one, as future anti-Lollard thinkers would realise; philosophically, Lollardy would have to be fought in terms of both detailed textual studies and an examination of the ethics of revelation.

However, it would be unjust to Wyclif to suggest that he was a mere polemicist, interested only in his local victories. What *De Veritate* enacts, in its troubled formulations and reformulations of the nature of scriptural significance and ways of achieving that significance, is the thwarted emergence of a 'positivist'[84] discourse from within the analytical categories of a very different discourse, one with strong affinities for the sceptical and the rhetorical, and one which emphasises the dependence of relevant 'meaning' on power as it finds institutionalised expression in the Church and in the universities. Indeed, *De Veritate* points the way towards a hermeneutic cul-de-sac. The problems always inherent in scholastic exegesis of the Bible – in the academic study of a theoretically divine text constantly reinvented through interested hermeneutic practices – attain a peculiarly stark clarity in Wyclif's treatise. *De Veritate* seems to suggest an apparent collapse, in the final decades of the fourteenth century, of the scholastic dialogic model of scriptural interpretation, a model which accommodates the reinvention of scripture through an implicit or explicit foregrounding of the problematic natures of language and interpretation and their interaction with the various local powers and investments of religious and political institutions. The baffled idealism of Wyclif's tract and its profound unease with inherited hermeneutics which can neither be accepted nor be rejected out of hand, given the nature of Christianity as an evolving religion of the book, arise from an increasingly threatened perception of the extent to which the theoretical source of all transcendent certitude, the Bible, is implicated in rhetoric through institutionalised and variable interpretative practices. It is to a recognition and indeed a defence of such institutionalisation of hermeneutics that I will turn in the next two chapters. The first studies a set of tracts by William Woodford, one of Wyclif's ablest opponents, and the second analyses the hermeneutic conflicts informing the Oxford debate over translating the Bible into the vernacular.

2

William Woodford's anti-Wycliffite hermeneutics

One of John Wyclif's important and abiding generalisations about the nature of the Christian faith was that all 'truths' necessary to faith are found 'expressly' in the Bible, and the more necessary, the more expressly: 'omnis veritas est ex scriptura, et ut necessarior est expressior'.[1] The word 'express', with its implicit denial of a readerly or institutionally ordained hermeneutics in the construction of meaning, brings to a focus one of the key issues raised by the Lollard heresy: that of the role of interpretation in establishing what is 'authoritative'.[2] In William Woodford's *Quattuor Determinationes in Materia de Religione*, a set of four anti-Wycliffite tracts investigating the nature of 'authority', the 'expressness' or otherwise of biblical meanings forms one of the crucial points of debate.

William Woodford,[3] Vicar to the Franciscan Minister Provincial of England in 1390, was a polemicist who wrote voluminously against Wyclif from around 1376 (*De dominio civili clericorum*) till 1397 (*De causis condemnacionis articulorum 18 damnatorum Joannis Wyclif*). He wrote primarily in defence of the mendicant orders, but, as Anne Hudson points out, he 'was regarded by his contemporaries as a spokesman for a less sectarian position as well'.[4] In particular, his *Causis condemnacionis* was written to the commission of Archbishop Arundel. The *Quattuor Determinationes*, written in the Oxford Schools in 1389–90 after Wyclif's death, is a defence of the so-called 'private' religions and a demonstration that they are 'authoritative'.[5] The first determination refutes Wyclif's assertion that the Early Church, before Pope Sylvester, was not endowed; the second deals with Wyclif's belief that all truths necessary to salvation are contained in scripture, and the more necessary, the more 'expressly'; the third and fourth are a defence of the validity of private religions in particular, and more generally, of human institutions and laws. In the process, a variety of issues is raised, including the vexed ones of ecclesiastical tradition, acceptable *modi legendi* of scripture, the status of *lex humana* and whether or not it can indeed be considered as a category altogether separate from the *lex divina*, and the nature or natures of 'authority'.

In this chapter, I will be considering primarily those sections of the tracts which are of immediate relevance to questions of text, interpretation and authority. I will endeavour to show how Woodford's thought encompasses frameworks of analysis which to Wyclif were irreconcilably opposed. For the *QD* share, unexpectedly, in many of Wyclif's own 'historicist' perceptions of the growth and development of Christianity,[6] while retaining a predilection for modes of argumentation which Wyclif repeatedly disavowed as facile scholastic wordmongering. This methodological difference between Wyclif and Woodford can be traced to the radically different implications of the separate consciousnesses of history in the two authors: in Wyclif, it leads to an idealised vision of an absolute access to and recoverability of the past and the *fons religionis*; in Woodford, on the contrary, the past and the authorities of the past – including the Bible – are considered outside of any such absolute framework, as part of a continuing process of development and change inevitably embedded in the uncertainties of human perception. Woodford's work is informed by a deep awareness of the necessary contingency of human judgment,[7] and its consequent reliance on fallible traditions and institutions.

The role of tradition in the interpretation of the faith and the scriptures therefore occupies an important position in Woodford's polemic.[8] He shows himself to be aware of Wyclif's faith in the possibility of textual meanings arising independently of the interpreting reader. The second determination begins with a firm distinction being made between what is contained in scripture 'explicite vel implicite in sensu suo historico vel litterali' ('explicitly or implicitly in its historical or literal sense') and what is contained 'secundum sensum anagogicum, allegoricum [vel] tropologicum' ('according to the anagogical, allegorical or tropological sense', p. 42; fol. 76r). Arguments with any pretensions to having the Bible as authority must be based on the former, but not on the latter: 'quia per sic contineri in ea non ostenditur veritas esse catholica nec heresis esse heresis' ('because by being thus contained in it, a truth is not shown to be catholic, nor a heresy to be a heresy', p. 42; fols 76r-v). The basic (Augustinian) idea had been variously espoused by Hugh of St. Victor, Aquinas and Nicholas of Lyra[9] in their attempt to privilege the literal sense but it assumed special prominence in the Lollard heresy. The Prologue to the Wycliffite Bible cites the same topos;[10] it obviously fitted in with Lollard distrust of human ingenuity in perverting or negating biblical meanings and its postulation of a final truth accessible through a rational, literalist, 'inspired' reading of the Bible. What is interesting about Woodford's formulation is his suggestion that 'catholic' truths cannot be proved by the 'spiritual' senses. As we shall see later, Woodford makes an important distinction between the fundamental tenets of the faith as articulated by Christ ('catholic truths') and the faith itself, which includes many lesser but nevertheless indispensable verities.

Woodford resumes the subject of the various senses and their 'explicit' or 'implicit' meanings in an extended passage in the 4th determination. He cites Ockham's distinction – from the *Dialogus* – between the two classes of meanings. According to the Venerable Inceptor, an 'explicit' meaning is one which 'patenter in eadem [sacred scripture] apparet vel in sua forma vel deduccione manifesta' ('appears openly in scripture either in its form or through open deduction'); while an 'implicit' meaning is one which occurs

> nec in sua forma nec deduccione manifesta, sed subtili deduccione inferri potest ex contentis explicite in eadem, a viris sapientibus et scientificis. (p. 174; fol. 99r)

> neither in its form nor through open deduction, but can be inferred from contents explicitly [present] in scripture through subtle deduction by wise and learned men.

Woodford goes on to cite Wyclif, the 'doctor venerabilis huius universitatis solempnis' ('the venerable doctor of this great university'), who argues that the 'explicit' sense can only be deduced from the historic or the literal sense intended by the author, while the 'implicit' is the 'mystical' sense. Woodford indicates his awareness that these terms are subject to a variety of uses, but states that his preference is for the Ockhamite version, 'quia sic sumitur communiter et secundum modum famosiorem' ('for such is the customary and more well-known usage').[11] It is a significant preference, for Woodford's vision of 'authoritative' meaning owes less to the postulation of an accessible authorial intention than to a more comprehensive vision of relevant textual meaning as the product of a complex interaction between the scriptural words and the various prerogatives of individuals, institutions and traditions. Though he does often refer to the unquestionable assumption that the first authors of scripture wrote through divine inspiration, he never makes the Wycliffite claim to the possession of absolute meanings on the part of the reader through 'inspired' or 'rational' access to the *intentio auctoris.*[12] On the whole, he tends to avoid formulations of meaning which involve the invocation of authorial intention, preferring instead to cite interpretative traditions. For instance, Woodford criticises Faustus's heresy – that neither Moses nor the prophets are acceptable to Christians because Christ said that all who came before him were thieves and robbers – based on a 'literal' reading of John 10:8, not from an intentionalist but from a traditionalist point of view:

> Faustus incidit in illam heresim quod non sunt recipiendi Moyses et prophete a catholicis, quia Christus dixit in euangelio, fures fuisse et latrones omnes venientes ante se, et sic quia noluit intelligere verba euangelii secundum interpretacionem virorum apostolicorum sed secundum quod prima facie sonabant. (p. 66; fol. 80v)

> Faustus fell into the heresy that Moses and the prophets are not to be accepted by believers, because Christ said in the gospel that all who came before him were thieves and robbers. And Faustus did so because he did not wish to understand the words of the gospel according to the interpretation of apostolic men but according to their superficial sense.

Again, speaking of Hewydius's heresy, that Mary had children other than Jesus (based on 'literal' readings of Matt. 1:18, 25; John 2:12), he says:

> Et sic quia intellexit verba scripture secundum quod sonant prima facie, nolens recipere interpretacionem virorum apostolicorum. Ideo incidit in hanc haeresim. Ieronimus autem recepit interpretacionem predescessorum suorum et confutavit hanc heresim per tales interpretationes. (pp. 66–7; fol. 80v)

> And [he said these things] because, not wishing to accept the interpretation of apostolic men, he understood the words of scripture according to their superficial sense. Therefore he fell into this heresy.

> But Jerome accepted the interpretation of his predecessors and con-
> futed this heresy by means of such interpretations.

Tradition remains centrally important.

Indeed, Woodford is keenly aware that the postulation of absolute meanings independent of the network of 'authorities' which constitute 'tradition' must presuppose the postulation of an absolute text. This was one area in which Wyclif laid himself abundantly open to criticism, though the same was not true of his followers. Though he does address the issue in *De Veritate Sacrae Scripturae*, his main emphasis, as we have seen, lies on scripture as the 'Book of Life', and to that extent as indepen-dent of material books.[13] Of the 'quinque gradus sacre scripture' ('the five grades of scripture'), only the fifth and least important consists in 'codi-cibus, vocibus aut aliis artificialibus' ('books, words and other signs').[14] Such a stance is understandable as an expression of Wyclif's faith in the inviolability of 'true' scripture. However, for a polemic which bases itself on the exact words of scripture to be understood according to its own logic, the necessity of having reliable texts would seem to be paramount.

To return to our passage from the 4th determination, Woodford sug-gestively moves on to discuss the actual textual condition of the Bible. He points out that 'ille biblie textus quem nos communiter habemus' ('the biblical text which we generally have') is 'corruptus et falsatus' ('corrupt and falsified', p. 174; fol. 99r). This is not of course to ques-tion sacred scripture as the Word of God as transmitted by its first authors.[15] He goes on to cite *De victoria contra Judeos* which criticizes Jerome's translation for being based on a corrupt text; he also suggests that Jeremiah prophesied such corruption in Jer. 8:8 ('the pen of the scribes is in vain') and 23:36 ('for ye have perverted the words of the living God'). Woodford rounds off this particular section by stating quite baldly that not only is the text which the Church has in general altogether corrupt, but even the text derived from Jerome's translation is corrupt and false, as Jerome translated a corrupt and false text: 'sed eciam textus quem habet et habere deberet ex translacione Ieronimi, est cor-ruptus et falsus, quia textum corruptum et falsum Ieronimus transtulit' (p. 175; fol. 99r).

What is interesting to note is that Wyclif's followers would have agreed. The Prologue to the Wycliffite Bible laments the state of the scriptural texts and states categorically the need to establish a Bible 'somdel trewe'.[16] Woodford's response to the perception of textual flux and 'corruption', is, however, and quite characteristically, not one of textual anxiety. Instead of postulating the need for textual studies with the ultimate aim of arriving at some version close to a hypothetical 'original', Woodford presents textual uncertainty as an argument against Wyclif's assertion that scripture is all-sufficient because all relevant truths are contained in it. For Woodford, the absence of a fixed, incontrovertible scriptural text on which to construct faith only deepens his partiality for ecclesiastical tradition and the sacred meanings formulated by it.

Indeed, he shows a remarkable awareness of the textual uncertainty of scripture. The 25th 'veritas' in the 2nd determination begins with the statement that the Bible is corrupt: 'Ille biblie textus quem nos communiter habemus, multos et diuersos patitur defectus, et diuersa sunt in illa contenta quibus non oportet fidem indubiam adhibere' ('that biblical text which we have in general suffers from many and diverse defects; and there are contained in it diverse things to which it is not necessary to bring certain faith', p. 93; fol. 85r). He then proceeds, on the authority of Jerome, to point to factual contradictions in the Gospels,[17] textual variations,[18] the inevitable errors in the scribal transmission of so complicated and disputed a document as the Bible.[19] St Augustine's *De Doctrina Christiana*, Book II, c. 15, where the saint speaks of the relative authorities of the Greek and Latin versions, is cited; so is Nicholas of Lyra on the variation of the Latin and Greek versions from the Hebrew.[20] The complexities and contingencies in the formation of the canon are also pointed to: St. Paul's lost 'Epistola ad Laodicenses' is not part of the canon, although 'auctentice vera' ('authentically true'), yet the uncertainly authored 'Epistola ad Hebreos' is included because considered authoritative now by the Church.[21] The Bible refers to many other books no longer extant and therefore outside the present canon, thereby verifying their 'authority'.[22]

The scriptural text in isolation gradually emerges as an uncertain conglomeration of uncertain authorities, assuming different meanings, different degrees of profundity and significance for different readers.[23] It is therefore almost impossible – outside the domain of the 'explicit' or the 'express' basics – to state firmly what is or is not scriptural. 'Nescio hoc fundare in sacra scriptura' ('I do not know how to found /'ground' this in sacred scripture') is not, Woodford asserts, sufficient ground for claiming that 'ergo hoc non est fundabile in sacra scriptura' ('therefore this cannot be based / 'grounded' in sacred scripture') (p. 175; fol. 99r).[24] The perceptions of 'pueri, layci [et] illiterati' ('children, laypeople and the unlearned'), for instance, would be severely limited. As for the great Fathers and doctors:

> Verumtamen quando maiores doctores, qui fuerunt in ecclesia et in scrutinio sacre scripture, vt Augustinus et Ieronimus, asserunt quod consuetudo aliqua vel lex non est contenta in sacra scriptura, quamvis doctor modernus magni nominis et valoris asserat quod lex vel consuetudo est in sacra scriptura contenta, quousque sciat fundare vbi sit in sacra scriptura contenta, non oportet quod in hoc sit igitur credendum, quia in casu tali pocius credendum est Augustino ut Ieronimo et aliis maioribus. (p. 176; fol. 99r)

> Nevertheless, when the doctors who were greater in the Church and in the study of sacred scripture, such as Augustine and Jerome, assert that a custom or a law is not contained in sacred scripture, while a modern doctor of great name and worth asserts that the law or custom is contained in sacred scripture, until such time as he [the modern *doctor*] may know to ground where it [the contested law or custom] may be contained in sacred scripture, it is not necessary that he is to be believed in this, because in such a case, Augustine and Jerome and the other greats are rather to be believed.

The *modernus* may assert that a particular law or custom is to be found in scripture against the opinion of the earlier scholars, but until he knows how to 'found' it in scripture, the greater authorities are to be believed in preference to him. The enigmatic relevance of scripture abides,[25] and the curious phrasing of 'quousque sciat fundare ubi sit in sacra scriptura contenta' suggests the developing shifting significances of scriptural words.

To an extent, Wyclif himself was sufficiently embedded in this tradition of conceptualising scripture to use it for his own ends, though he would not, of course, have given it theoretical sanction. In an intriguing passage in *De Apostasia*, a work strident in its distrust of 'glossing', fables, 'ymaginacio',[26] Hildegard of Bingen's prophecies and other such 'perversions' of scriptural meaning,[27] and one to which Woodford repeatedly addresses his remarks, Wyclif shows himself to be standing, to borrow Edward Harris's image, 'with one foot in the Scholastic age, [while] the other is seeking a resting place elsewhere'.[28] On the one hand, there is the desire to achieve a finality of meaning in terms of access to the (divine) *intentio auctoris*; on the other, there is an awareness of the enigmatic polyvalence of the scriptural words by reason of the unfathomability of God's will and the inadequacy of man's. In an uncharacteristic moment of doubting his own interpretation of Prov. 6:12–14, as outlining the signs of the sevenfold apostasy of the friars, Wyclif says that perhaps it will be objected that his reading is a distortion:

> Sed obicitur quod dicta sentencia de apostasia septemplici non est sentencia de fide scripture spiritus sancti, sed heretice ficta pocius et extorta. Hic dicitur, quod sive fratres, sive papa vel angelus de celo perfecerit opus nefandum, in ista scriptura septemplici prefatum, tunc spiritus sanctus ordinavit in ea ad tutelam fidelium istum sensum; ideo non restat eius inprobacio nisi probando efficaciter, quod dicte apostasie non conveniunt sectis fratrum. Quo facto concedam cum eis, quod spiritus sanctus non illos intenderat in hoc loco.

> But it is objected that the above mentioned statement concerning seven-fold apostasy is not a statement derived from the faith of scripture of the Holy Spirit, but is rather invented and distorted in a heretical fashion. This is said [in reply]: if the friars or the Pope or an angel from heaven should have committed the sinful deed foretold in this sevenfold scripture, then the Holy Spirit ordained this sense [i.e. that detected by Wyclif] in scripture for the instruction of the faithful. Therefore [Wyclif's interpretation] is not disproved unless by proving efficaciously that the said apostasies do not fit the sects of the friars. Which when done, I will concede with them [Wyclif's detractors] that the Holy Spirit did not intend them [the friars] in this place.[29]

It is fascinating to note how for Wyclif the *locus* of meaning is firmly situated in authorial intention, even to the extent of saying that if his argument is proved wrong, then he would concede that the Holy Spirit intended differently. This is really having the best of both worlds: the finality that a theoretically accessible authorial intention can be made to endow an interpretation with, and the flexibility that a reader- or situation-oriented hermeneutics so emphatically has.[30] The passage from *De Apostasia* shows clearly the problems inherent in the citation of *intentio auctoris* as the defining criterion of meaning: 'authorial intention' is merely another site of hermeneutic warfare.[31]

Woodford shows himself to be acutely aware of the dubiety of any attempt at fixing scriptural meaning. A member of the high clerical orthodoxy, he was more than conscious of the way scripture was and had been habitually used in disputation and the *quodlibeta*. Speaking of those who assert that all truths necessary to salvation are to be found in scripture, he points out that they are probably not speaking of the 'sensu historico vel litterali precise' ('historical or literal sense in a precise fashion', p. 176; fol. 99r). He proceeds to say that many such truths are included in sacred scripture in so far as it is the 'Book of Life', and not in so far as it signifies the canon of the Bible, both in 'text and sense', as transmitted by the first authors of scripture.[32] The passage which follows further clarifies his argument; many 'truths' are contained in scripture not 'properly'[33] but 'largely':

> Vlterius dico, quod multe tales auctoritates intelliguntur non de contineri proprie, sed large, pro quadam similitudine vel diriuatiue. Vnde non est aliqua veritas, quin secundum aliquam similitudinem misticam, consimilis contineatur in scriptura, licet ipsa in se vel in suo auctore non contineatur proprie in eadem. (p. 177; fol. 99v)

> Furthermore, I say that many such authorities are understood to be contained [in scripture] not properly, but largely, by means of some similitude or in a derivative manner. Whence there is no truth but that it may similarly be contained in scripture by means of some mystical similitude, although in itself or in [terms of the intention of] the [scriptural] author it may not be contained properly in scripture.

Such a recognition of the fundamental instability of linguistic meaning the moment one leaves the elementary realm of the 'explicit' or the 'express' informs the puzzling passage which follows. Woodford is still arguing against the assumption that all necessary truths are contained in the literal-historical sense of the Bible. He points out that in the natural sciences, as distinct from theology, things as well as words are signifiers:

> Dico 7°, quod in aliis scienciis a sacra theologia significant non solum voces sed et res ipse a vocibus distincte. Patet hac in sciencia medecine, et in qua non solum isti termine 'vrina' et 'pulsus'

significant, sed res ipse multo magis significant disposicionem malam vel bonam corporis humani. Et in sciencia naturalis philosophie, maxime in libro de animalibus et in libro metheororum, in quibus non solum [voces] significant philosophis terminum, sed et res ipse . . . Et theologus . . . quando allegorizat et tropologizat vel anagorizat textum scripture, respicit ad res quas considerat; philosophus naturalis et ad proprietates earum et secundum quod res naturales secundum diuersas proprietates significant. Secundum hoc diversimode anagorizat et allegorizat. (p. 177; fol. 99v)

Seventh, I say that in sciences other than sacred theology, not only words but things themselves as distinct from words signify. This appears in the science of medicine, in which not only the terms 'urine' and 'pulse' signify, but the things themselves signify to a much greater extent the good or evil disposition of the human body. [Similar is the case] with the science of natural philosophy, especially in [Aristotle's] *Libro de animalibus* and *Libro Metheororum*, in which not only the words signify the term[34] to philosophers but the things themselves [do so] . . . The theologian . . . when allegorising, tropologising or anagogising the text of scripture, looks to the things which [the text] considers; the natural philosopher looks at their properties, according to which natural things have meaning, in accordance with [their] diverse properties. The natural philosopher then anagosises and allegorises [i.e. interprets] in diverse ways according to this [i.e. the mode in which the actual properties of natural things signify].

It appears that Woodford is saying that while the theologian interprets words which signify things, the natural philosopher interprets the properties of things directly, without a comparable dependence on words. Woodford is here drawing upon the complex medieval debate over the nature of scientific knowledge: is such knowledge of a 'thing' or of a 'sign'? Here he seems to decide in favour of scientific certitude: the natural philosopher interprets the properties of *things* rather than those of words.[35] Woodford goes on to say, in a remarkable passage, that it is not the custom of the philosopher to allegorise the philosophical text, though it would be possible to do so and find in it truths as in sacred scripture:

Non est autem consuetudinis philosophorum allegorizare vel tropologizare textum naturalis philosophie. Possibile tamen esset allegorizare et tropologizare textum philosophie, et in illo secundum sensus misticos reperire veritates qua in scriptura sacra. (pp. 177–178; fol. 99v)

> But it is not the custom of the philosophers to allegorise or tropologise the text of natural philosophy. Nevertheless, it would be possible to allegorise and tropologise the text of philosophy, and to find in it, according to the mystical senses, truths as in sacred scripture.

This is a markedly explicit formulation of the slippery, unreferential nature of what is purely linguistic, and the overwhelming power of interpretative customs in 'textual communities'. The hinterland to this discussion of hermeneutic custom is provided by the vast body of early and mid fourteenth-century debate over the modes of interpretation and language-use appropriate to different disciplines.[36] Such debate achieved its greatest notoriety in the Parisian disputes of 1340 centering around Ockham and Ockhamist hermeneutics, in the course of which the importance, in matters of interpretation, of the *materia subiecta* (topic of a discussion) was often underlined. As Kaluza says in his discussion of the 1340 Paris Faculty of Arts Statute against 'Ockhamists', and its attempted definition of *virtus sermonis* (force of the word/meaning), 'il y a une *virtus sermonis* tout court, et une autre *virtus sermonis* réservée à chaque *materia subiecta*' ('there is a *virtus sermonis*, period; and another *virtus sermonis* specific to each *materia subiecta*').[37] Woodford's formulation of the different conventions of textual interpretation in different disciplines is given a sceptical inflection here and is used to support his defence of senses other than the literal:

> Non tamen est intencionis mee dicere quod sensui literali sacre scripture est solummodo intendendum, quod sensus aliquando multum faciunt ad edificacionem. (p. 178; fol. 99v)

> Nevertheless, it is not my intention to say that only the literal sense of sacred scripture is to be striven for, because [the other] senses from time to time do much for edification.

The argument here is rhetorical: the non-literal senses, though unfit for proper argumentation, are vital for edification. The train of Woodford's thought is to be noted: in case his formulation of the contingencies of language and interpretation is read as a capitulation to Wycliffite criticism of senses other than the literal, he makes it clear that he regards the 'mystical' senses as equally though differently relevant to the faith.

For the establishment of 'catholic' truths, they are not sufficient, but for the affective deepening of the faith, they are essential.

We must remember that Woodford is arguing against the position that all truths necessary to salvation are contained in the literal-historical senses of scripture. For Woodford, with his holistic vision of faith and the truths of faith as encompassing scripture, tradition, traditional interpretations and the spiritual superstructure of the 'mystical' senses, it is unacceptable, if the 'literal' sense is to retain any genuine autonomy, to claim that 'faith' is delimited by it. 'Truth', as he says, is in a state of continuous flux, whereas scripture is not:

> Dico 8°, quod sumendo sacram scripturam pro multitudine veritatum in canone biblie contentarum vel per textum secundum intencionem auctoris, et simul ponendo quod in illa sacra scriptura omnis veritas continetur tamquam pars in toto, oportet concedere illam sacram scripturam infinicies in hoc instanti variatam et mutatam, et quod infinicies mutabitur in omni instanti futuro. Nam in hoc instanti infinite veritates incipiunt esse et infinite desiuiunt esse, et numquam pars auferri potest a toto sine ipsius mutacione, nec noua adquiri toto sine eius mutacione. (p. 178; fol. 99v)

> Eighth, I say that in taking sacred scripture for the multitude of truths contained in the biblical canon or in the text according to the intention of the author, and in simultaneously postulating that all truth, both in part and in whole, is contained in that sacred scripture, it is necessary to concede that sacred scripture to be in this instant varied and changed to an infinite extent, and [also to concede] that it will be infinitely changed in every future instant. For in this instant infinite truths begin to be and infinite truths cease to be, and a part cannot be deducted from, or new things added to, the whole without its changing.

In the *Quattuor Determinationes*, at this relatively early stage of the Lollard heresy, the 'literal' sense has not been allowed to subsume the rhetorical dimension of exegesis.[38] As a result, he cannot but point out that attempting to confine the Christian faith to the literal sense of scripture is misguided. Woodford in many ways has too profound a sense of the contingent nature of much of the faith and its development through the centuries to postulate the ideal of an unmediated, pure faith capable of being constructed only out of the explicit literal meanings of scripture.[39]

The consciousness of contingency and variation within a larger framework of unquestioned belief finds repeated expression in Woodford's involvement with the canon and its 'authority'. Junilius' *Instituta regularia divinae legis* are quoted on the subject of varying authorities:

> [Junilius] dicit quod apud orientales de Apocolipsi Iohannis admodum dubitatur, ita quod liber Apocalipsis apud orientales non est tante auctoritatis quante sunt alii libri prophetici sacre scripture. Ponit eciam ibi aliquos libros perfecte esse auctoritatis, aliquos medie auctoritatis. (p. 75; fol. 82r)

> Junilius says that [the authority of] the Apocalyse of John is somewhat doubted in the Eastern Church, so that Apocalypse is not, in the Eastern Church, of such authority as are the other prophetic books of sacred scripture. Therefore he says here that some books are of perfect authority, whereas others are of moderate authority.

An important passage from Book II, chapter 8 of Augustine's *De Doctrina Christiana* outlining the dependence of canonicity on ecclesiastical authority is also cited.[40]

The definition of 'authority' is one of Woodford's key concerns. Wyclif, in the *De Apostasia*, had associated the qualities of scriptural 'explicitness' or 'expressness' with 'authoritativeness'.[41] Woodford argues that, first, 'implicit' truths in the Bible are often more necessary for salvation than the 'explicit', and second, if one looks at the history of the Christian faith, major disputes have arisen over what is merely 'implicit' but centrally important:

> magis necessarium est ad salutem credere quod Spiritus Sanctus procedit a Patre e Filio, quam quod Thare fuit pater Habrae, quia est articulus fidei positus in symbolo ecclesie, quem omnem sacerdotem oportet explicite credere; non sic autem quod Thare fuit pater Habrae; et cum explicite conuenitur in scriptura quod Thare fuit pater Habrae [Gen. 11:26] et solum implicite habetur in scriptura quod Spiritus Sanctus procedit a Patre e Filio. Vnde de isto articulo fuit aliquando in ecclesia magnum dubium et propter istum articulum sunt Greci diuisi ab ecclesia. (p. 48; fols 77r–v)

> It is more necessary for salvation to believe that the Holy Spirit proceeds from the Father and the Son, rather than that Terah was the father of Abram, for the former is an article of faith placed in the Creed of the Church which every priest must explicitly believe; such

is not the case with Terah being the father of Abram, although it is explicitly agreed in scripture that Terah was the father of Abram, and only implicitly that the Holy Spirit proceeds from the Father and the Son. Whence from this article there sometimes arose great debate in the Church, and it was because of this article that the Greeks separated from the Church.

The 'authenticity' of truths is dependent on institutionalised forms of interpretation which are ultimately extra-scriptural.

It is in this context that Woodford's uneasy and quite topical interest in conciliar authority should be placed.[42] He outlines the conditions in which a council's ruling can be absolutely binding, but prefaces his discussion with a historical demonstration of the importance of conciliar rulings in cultures other than Christian. He cites the example of the Romans who habitually consulted 320 men 'curam habentes de multitudine' ('who were in charge of the multitude'), and also that of the Jews and the Saracens (p. 88; fol. 84v).[43] Woodford proceeds to describe the charcteristics of an ideal council:

> Si maior multitudo illorum qui consenciunt in determinacionem sit legitime congregata [this of course begs a number of questions as to the definition of 'legitimacy'] et reguletur in materia fidei ambigua per peritos in theologia et philosophia sancte vite, qui non sunt affectati amore inordinato vel odio inordinato ad illam materiam de qua fit determinacio, nec sunt tales qui timeant racione mali infligendi dicere veritatem, nec ratione ambitionis vel cupiditatis recedere velint. (p. 89; fol. 84v)

> If the major part of those who agree in a decision is legitimately congregated, and is guided in ambiguous matters of faith by those skilled in theology and philosophy [and of] holy life, is [constituted of those] not affected by inordinate love or inordinate hate [in their judgment of] the matter being determined, is [not constituted of those] who fear to speak the truth because of evils to be inflicted, or those who would retreat because of ambition or greed.

Apart from such criteria defined by the moral integrity of the participants in a council, the authority of conciliar rulings is also dependent on the church's *continued* acceptance of the determinations: 'si ecclesia diu persistit in tali determinacione sine reuocacione et sine impugnacione peritorum in sacra theologia' ('if the Church persists for a long while in such a determination without revocation and without criticism from those skilled in sacred theology'). These signs being present and recognised, the council can be judged to have had the blessing of God: 'habent catholici iudicare concilium illud esse congregatum in nomine Christi, et quod Christus fuit in medio eorum et quod determinacio eorum processit ex instinctu Spiritus Sancti' ('the faithful must deem the Council to have been assembled in the name of Christ, and that Christ was in their midst, and that their decision proceeded from the inspiration of the Holy Spirit', p. 89; fol. 84v).

Woodford then goes on to introduce the concept of conciliar error. He thus almost lands himself in the Wycliffite double-bind of *De Apostasia*: if a decision has been regarded as right for an unspecified but long period of time, then the Holy Spirit must have endorsed or inspired it, in which case there can be no question of revocation or error. But by virtue of his fundamentally historical, relativist vision of Christianity, Woodford suggests, though he by no means makes it explicit, a way out from the dilemma. Earlier, he had made a distinction between 'catholic truth' (unchanged, fundamental tenets of the faith dictated by Christ and the apostles), and 'ecclesiastical truth', contingent truths formulated by various churches as articles of faith according to local needs and exigencies.[44] Theoretically, a 'catholic truth' can be incorporated by the Pope and Council into the realm of 'ecclesiastical truth', but an 'ecclesiastical truth' cannot be elevated by anyone to the status of 'catholic truth'. Woodford reinvokes this distinction in the context of his discussion of conciliar error[45] though he does not make the connection explicit. It remains a suggestion, but a rather clever one, for getting round the problem of having an authority enjoying divine (absolute) endorsement which nevertheless is obviously subject to some vicissitude in certain areas of its jurisdiction.

Indeed, Woodford places himself within a framework of thought which lays much more stress on the contingent and changeable nature of 'authority', whether that authority be hermeneutic or institutional, than on the theory of an absolute faith independent of local and temporal variation, based on a text which is a 'speculum in quo veritates eterne relucent' ('a mirror in which eternal truths shine').[46] In his work, there is a prominent historical consciousness of a certain kind,[47] a sense of the diversity of customs and traditions and their embeddedness in time. In Wyclif, history occupies an indeterminate place; it is undoubtedly there, particularly when it is necessary to chart the decline of the Church from its putative days of innocence,[48] but its main function is to postulate an original *fons* of religion towards which the faithful should direct themselves.[49] For Woodford, there is no such early state of perfection, for even the religion which Christ practised, tainted as it was with Judaic customs, is no longer appropriate for us.

> Et constat quod talis religio commixta et Iudaica et Christiana, non est illa communis, ad quam omnis fidelis de necessitate salutis astringitur, cum nullus fidelis tenetur iudaizare (p. 137; fol. 92v)

> It is certain that such a mixed Judaico-Christian religion is not that common [religion] to which all the faithful are bound by the necessity of salvation, because no faithful person is obliged to 'judaise'

For Christ to 'judaise' then was perfect, but times have changed:

> Illa completa regula quam Christus tunc obseruauit, commixta fuit ex regula Iudaica et lege Christiana, quia Christus iudaizauit vsque ad diem mortis sue, et licet iudaizare tunc fuit valde perfectum, tamen iudaizare nunc est valde pestiferum. Et ideo illa completa regula quam Christus obseruauit, fuit perfectissima tunc, non est perfectissima nec perfecta nunc.[50] (p. 138; fol. 92v)

> That complete rule which Christ then followed was a mixture of the Judaic and Christian laws, since Christ 'judaised' until the day of his death. And though to 'judaise' then was absolutely perfect, to 'judaise' now is absolutely unacceptable. And therefore the complete rule which Christ observed was the most perfect then, [but] is now neither the most perfect, nor even perfect.

In Woodford's vision, the variable nature of the faith and its 'authorities' exists not in any conflict with the divine and the absolute but in a relationship of reciprocity. Even Christ obeyed human laws when he was man, and this is not to arrogate to man the prerogatives of the divine, or to suggest that man is the architect and God the mere craftsman.[51] As Catto points out, Woodford understood the 'necessity for a hierarchy of perfections', for [human] counsels as well as [divine] precepts.[52] If such were not the case, if all civil dominion were evil, then the very extent of what would have to be condemned makes the proposition absurd.[53]

Woodford thus ultimately did not plumb the full implications of Wyclif's innovations. At this relatively early stage of the heresy, the programme of the Lollards had not emerged in all its extreme and successfully popular radicalism. As a result, in spite of his acute grasp over some aspects of Wyclif's thought and their deficiencies, Woodford remains embedded in a traditional world of learning and disputation, with its still largely unquestioned acceptance of the inherited sites of *auctoritas*.[54] This emerges most provocatively in his handling of logical argumentation. Woodford's polemical rhetoric often takes the form of extending the implications of Wyclif's arguments to the point of absurdity. The desire here is not so much the establishment of 'truth', as the playing of logical games and the display of agonistic ingenuity – what Peter von Moos calls 'Spielernst' ('serious game')[55] – within a larger framework of political-academic security.[56] Here the tradition of quodlibetic disputations, as also disputations in the field of canon law, is central. In the latter, arguments are frankly rhetorical; the only aim is to subvert one's opponent's point of view, and almost anything goes.[57] In the former, as I have emphasised in the Introduction (pp. 4–5), the disputations tend to become an exercise of dialectical skill at the expense of their theoretical investment in the establishment of truth through demonstration.

Woodford's *Quattuor Determinationes* must be read in this context. Though Hudson's judgment that his work is like a stately warship which never comes within sight of its target[58] is to an extent valid, it is too harsh. Woodford does tackle intelligently many of Wyclif's myopic criticisms of tradition, but often insists on arguing from within the conventions of scholastic disputation. Wyclif and he had known each other at Oxford, and had frequently and by all accounts disputed without acrimony.[59] Wyclif himself, in his early career, had lauded dialectics as central to the pursuit of truth,[60] as indeed in theory it was.[61] Given both their origins in the Schools, it is unsurprising, if imperceptive on his part, that his arguments often take the form of showing how Wyclif's statements are self-contradictory or logically absurd. I will provide a few of the more colourful instances of such 'flyting'.

Wyclif's argument that the ephemerality of 'private' religions is a symptom of their imperfection is countered thus:

> Patet illud 3°, quia primo religio ordinata homini pro statu innocencie valde citio defecit: non enim durauit per medietatem diei naturalis. Ergo religio illa prima pure innocencie fuit imperfecta moraliter loquendo, consequens absurdum. (p. 127; fol. 91 r)

Third, it appears that the first religion ordained to man in the state of innocence came to an end exceedingly quickly: it did not even last half a natural day. Therefore, that first religion of pure innocence was imperfect, morally speaking, which is an absurd consequence.

Again, Wyclif is cited as saying that the 'private' religions should be dissolved: 'vt totum genus humanum fieret magis vniforme et simile' ('so that the whole of humankind might be more uniform and similar', p. 129; fol. 91 v). One of the arguments advanced against this takes the form of suggesting that if Wyclif's premiss were to be accepted, then, ideally, all Christians should be either men or women, old men or young boys, soldiers or farmers and so on (p. 130; fol. 91 v). However, it would be unfair to Woodford to suggest that such arguments form the bulk of his criticism of Wyclif, even though he is often carried away by his own verve. Even within the discussion of the 'absurdity' just cited, he goes on to offer more serious stuff as justification of variety: the topos of Christ's mystical body (1 Cor. 12:4ff), which was one of the major texts used in the context of hierarchy, is invoked.[62]

Woodford's logic often takes the form of demonstrating how Wyclif's arguments 'peccant in forma' ('are erroneous in form'):

> Asserit [Wyclif, in *De Apostasia*] quod licet omnis apostasia sit grauis in homine, tamen apostasia in religiosis et specialiter exproprietarie viuentibus est Deo et ecclesie magis odibilis, et per consequens peior. Ex quo ergo, vt dicit, apostasia a religione priuata religionis exproprietarie est quacumque alia apostasia peior. Ergo est peior apostasia a religione communi. Cum ergo apostasia a religione sit illius religionis ablacio, in sic apostatante, sequitur quod posicio religionis exproprietarie sit melior posicione religionis communis, quod negat et cuius oppositum hic intendit. (p. 147; fols 94r–v)

> Wyclif asserts that although all human apostasy is grievous, nevertheless, apostasy in the religious [i.e. those belonging to religious orders], and specially in those living without property, is more hateful to God and the Church, and therefore worse. From which it follows, as he says, that apostasy from a private religious order without property is worse than any other apostasy. Therefore, such apostasy is worse than that from the common religion. However, since apostasy from a religious order is the withdrawal from that order in the act of apostasy, it follows that the position of an order without property is a better one

than that of the common religion, which contradicts [Wyclif], and the opposite of which [conclusion] he here intends.

There are several other occasions on which Woodford underlines the fallaciousness of Wyclif's logic and his arguments by logical demonstrations.[63] What emerges from these criticisms is his quite signal failure to address Wyclif's repeated disavowals of such usage of scholastic logic in his later works. Wyclif's emphasis on a distinct scriptural 'forma' and 'logic', an understanding of which is essential to any serious attempt at interpreting the Bible, is also ignored.[64] This is related to Woodford's inability to realise that 'reason' plays a role in Wycliffite exegesis very different from the role it plays in school logic. Of one of his arguments, he says that its premises 'non potest racionabiliter Magister negare' ('the Master cannot reasonably deny', p. 142; fol. 92v). Woodford does not address the virtual redefinition of the hermeneutic role of 'opyn reson', to borrow the ubiquitous Lollard phrase, that Wyclif brought about,[65] nor does he tackle the redefinition of 'valid' logic.

To a certain extent therefore, Woodford remains an unselfconscious part of the older academic world of agonistic logical disputation which so often shades into sceptical play, a world which Alain de Libera has described as one of 'dialectisation absolue'.[66] However, as I attempted to show in the earlier half of my discussion, Woodford's critique of the Wycliffite idealism in matters of faith, which in its own way is no less ahistorical than the logic-chopping of the schoolmen, is often very acute. The problem with Wyclif's historical analysis of 'authority' is that it is both exhilarating and myopic; the implications of history for the definition of valid authority are recognised only up to a point and no further.[67] What is formidable about Wyclif's achievement is that he forced the academic-political establishment to formulate its own historicist counter-polemic, to enter the realm of 'the same kind of historical-moral arguments which would beset sixteenth-century scholars'.[68] What is disheartening is the almost immediately-achieved loss of the kind of scholarship which makes Woodford's tract so attractive: broadly sceptical and essentially humane.[69] The established Church would soon crystallise in an authoritarianism as extreme as the fanatical idealism of the later Wyclif.

3

Vernacular translations of the
Bible and 'authority'

An emphatic recognition of the power of interpretation – 'glossing' – in determining the 'meaning' of authoritative texts, particularly the scriptures, and perhaps 'perverting' or 'negating' them, formed the basis of Wyclif's programme of reform. The dependence of what is understood by 'faith' on an ultimately arbitrary hermeneutic dictated by a political-ecclesiastical authority the exact status of which had been always open to question[1] led him and his followers to postulate an unmediated absolute faith as an achievable ideal. A crucial factor in such a faith would obviously be the availability of an unmediated, 'naked', Biblical text in an accessible language. This formed the matrix of the Lollard involvement with translation.[2]

Wyclif's theoretical disjunction of human authority and scriptural interpretation provides the context for many of the contemporary disputes relating to issues raised by the Lollard heresy. One of the most significant of these was centred on the validity or otherwise of Biblical translations into the vernacular. Important insights are afforded when one compares a cluster of similar texts written at around the turn of the fourteenth century, before Archbishop Arundel's censorship laws – the *Constitutions*[3] – drafted in 1407, and promulgated in 1409, categorically prohibited all disputation on this issue. The texts are in the form of academic *determinationes*; and at least two of them were written at Oxford. The first is by Master Richard Ullerston[4] possibly written c. 1401; the second by William Butler[5] written in the same year; the third perhaps by Thomas Palmer probably written at around 1400, and certainly before 1407.[6] It is important to recognise at the outset – as Anne Hudson points out[7] – that debating or even defending Biblical translations at this time was by no means an indication of heresy.

Ullerston was himself very much a member of the clerical orthodoxy – he wrote a *Defensorium Dotacionis Ecclesiae* against the Lollard attack on endowments, and compiled a set of sixteen *Petitiones* for the Council of Pisa in 1408.[8] His consideration of the issue at hand acquires an important charge when studied as evidence of the views of a section at least of the unpolemical orthodoxy. Ullerston is not a polemicist in same way as Butler and Palmer: his is, it appears, a genuinely disinterested attempt at exploring the implications of vernacular translation. His work shows considerable linguistic insight, offers sophisticated critiques of certain oft-bandied ideas, and suggests an impressive acquaintance with patristic and later academic writing; but it also betrays tantalising failures of perception. For Ullerston never seriously addresses the central Lollard involvement with the definition of valid religious authority. This curious myopia on the part of an otherwise obviously intelligent and learned man suggests the extent to which Wyclif's radical thought brought to the forefront issues of 'authority' in a novel fashion.

Ullerston's tract[9] is cast in the form of a debate between two *doctores*, one against and one in favour of translation, with Ullerston's own, implied, sympathies being with the latter.[10] Thirty numbered arguments opposing translation are listed; a section discussing the meanings of the words *transferre* and *interpretari* follows; detailed arguments overturning the ones already cited form the ensuing bulk of the tract; and at the end, there is attached a series of nine propositions in favour of translation. I will begin by examining those points in the debate which relate most directly to the issue of authority.

Of the arguments advanced by the first doctor against biblical translation, only a handful tackle the associated problems of interpretation and authority. Points 13 and 14 suggest that an easy accessibility to the sacred text would prompt women, rustics and similar other *indocti* to usurp the office and thereby detract from the dignity of the preacher:

> si scriptura sacra in ligwam uulgi esset translata, tunc... quelibet uetula docendi officium vsurparet... quilibet rusticus docere presumeret. Et sic duplex honor bonis presbiteris debitus qui uerbo laborant et doctrina ut uult apostolus I Thimotheum 5 a probabili tolleretur, ergo etc. (fol. 195v cols. a-b)

> If sacred scripture were to be translated into the vulgar tongue, then
> any old woman might usurp the office of teaching . . . [and] any peas-
> ant might presume to teach. And thus the double honour owed to
> good priests, who work with the Word and doctrine as the Apostle
> wishes in 1 Tim. 5 [: 17] would be probably annulled, therefore etc.

The fifteenth point begins with the topos of the Church as Christ's
mystical body which would be dissolved if its various members did
not maintain a strict hierarchy. If the laity and the simple presumed
to teach and violate the *arcana fidei*, faith would be threatened and
the church would collapse. A knowledge of Latin is sufficient for such
dangers to arise; how much more so would be the case if vernacular
Bibles were available.[11] A passage from Jerome's *Ad Paulinum* is quoted
which laments the desecration of scripture by 'garula anus . . . delirus
senex . . . sophista verbosus' ('garrulous old woman . . . doting old
man . . . verbose sophist') who attempt to explain to others what they
do not understand themselves. Moreover, not understanding what the
prophets and the apostles mean, they adapt the biblical witness to their
own incongruous sense:

> nec scire dignantur, quid prophete aut apostoli senserint; sed ad sen-
> sum suum incongrua adaptant testimonia, quasi grande sit et non
> viciossimum dicendi genus deprauare sententias, et ad uoluntatem
> suam sensum trahere repugnantem. Hec Ieronimus. (fol. 195v col. b)

> They do not deign to notice what Prophets and Apostles have intended
> but they adapt conflicting passages to suit their own meaning, as if it
> were a grand way of speaking – and not rather the faultiest of all – to
> misrepresent a writer's views and to force the scriptures reluctantly to
> do their will. Thus Jerome.[12]

The reply to this last argument only obliquely addresses the question
of hierarchy and neglects to answer Jerome's criticism of those who
'deprave' the sense of scripture. It is first pointed out that the desire to
usurp the office of teaching has more to do with 'malicia uoluntatis'
('malice of will') rather than with a knowledge of languages; for true
faith can never lead men to err: 'nullus ex fide infusa credo errat' ('I
believe that no one infused with faith errs', fol. 202v col. b). This is
followed by a reference to the episode of Medad and Eldad (Numbers
11:26ff.) who were inspired by the spirit to prophesy. Num. 11:29 is

quoted: '[Moses] inquit . . . Quis tribuat ut omnis populus prophetet, et det eis deus spiritum sensum' (fol. 203r col. a).[13] Deuteronomy 4:6, a passage about the greatness of a wise and understanding people, follows; allusions to Jerome's *Contra Jovinian* – all cannot be virgins but those who attempt to be so are to be lauded – and Luke 19:20, the episode of the servant who did not invest his lord's money, occur next;[14] and the passage ends with a gesture in the direction of priestly authority: excessive zeal, though pious, should be restrained, and 'moderate uero incedentibus laxent habenas' ('and let them relax the reins in a moderate fashion to those marching', fol. 203r col. a).

The preceding argument had been slightly more specific in its response to the issue of lay preaching and disputation. Within certain limits – husband to wife (I Cor. 14:35), parents to children (the examples of Tobias, Tob. 1:9–10, and 'Zuzanne', Dan. 13:1 ff. are cited), older women to younger (Tit. 2.3–4) – lay predication is acceptable.[15] Each must do his duty according to his measure; indeed, the duty of the paterfamilias in relation to 'suos omnes' forms a parallel to that of the priest:

> Eciam uos pro modulo uestro ministrate Christo, bene viuendo, elemosinas faciendo, nomen doctrinamque eius quibus potueritis predicando, vt vnusquisque paterfamilias in hoc nomine agnoscat paternum affectum sue familie se debere. Pro Christo, et pro vita eterna, suos omnes moneat, doceat et hortetur, corripiat, impendat beniuolenciam, exerceat disciplinam, ita in domo ecclesiasticum et quodammodo episcopale implebit officium, ministrans Christo, ut in eternum sit cum ipso. Hec Augustinus.[16] (fol. 202v col. b)

> But you yourselves also in your own way serve Christ, by good lives, by giving alms, by preaching his name and doctrine as you can; and let every father of a family acknowledge in this name the affection he owes as a parent to his family. For Christ's sake, and for the sake of life eternal, let him warn, and teach, and exhort and rebuke all his household; let him show kindliness, and exercise discipline; and so in his own house he will be filling an ecclesiastical and kind of episcopal office, and serving Christ, that he may be with him for ever. Thus Augustine.[17]

Each of us has his duty according to his status in life; and the unlawful usurpation of sacerdotal powers (as opposed to the merely catechetical) is condemned as anathema. The dissemination of scripture, containing as it does exhortations to humility and dissuasions from presumption, would be beneficial to the hierarchy of clergy and laity rather than contrary to it (fol. 202v col. b). It is interesting to note that very little is made of the quotation from scripture with which Augustine begins the passage from *Super Johannem Omelia* 51 cited above: 'Vbi ego sum, illic minister meus erit.' The potential for making a case for the validity of inspired lay preaching seems not to be recognised.[18]

The reply to the thirteenth argument is the most perfunctory of the group. It merely states that, first, women had not taken to preaching in the primitive church even though, according to Lyra, 'benedicciones et cetera omnia fiebant in uulgari' ('blessings etc. were all made in the vulgar'), and second, the fact that good customs are subject to abuse is no reason for abandoning them (fol. 202v col. a).

Argument 18 against translation suggests that the availability of the sacred canon and the missal 'cum toto servicio ecclesio' ('with the entire Church service') in the vulgar would result in the ruin of the clergy, the Christian worship and the sacraments: 'tunc enim uilesceret totus clerus, uilesceret cultus diuinus, uilescerentque omnia ecclesie sacramenta. Tunc enim laici reputarent clericos inutiles' ('For then the whole of clergy would become worthless, as would divine worship and all the sacraments of the Church. For then lay people would consider clerks to be useless', fol. 196r col. a). The response to this rather grim vision of disorder merely reasserts, with some biblical and classical colouring, the principle of decorum. Some tasks, such as the ministering of sacraments, are appropriate only to the clergy and 'in nullo casu laicis' ('and in no case to lay persons'), these local suitabilities forming part of a grand 'congruencia ordinis naturalis' ('harmony of the natural order'). The sexes, for instance, have each their appropriate functions: one does not, unless there is an emergency, yoke cows to carts, as in 1 Samuel 6:7. Women do not normally go into battle, though there was the exceptional instance of Penthesilea and her Amazons. It is not entirely clear whether the duties assigned to priests 'non solum regulariter verum eciam vniuersaliter' ('not only according to the [specific] rules of ecclesiastical discipline but indeed generally and universally') would be subject to such exceptional reassignments.[19] Anyway, the author goes on to point out, having the life and doctrine of Christ in the vulgar is a different matter altogether from ministering the sacraments. The former would merely excite the simple to devotion; indeed, such, according to Lyra, was the case with the primitive church.[20] The argument then moves on to the validity of administering the sacraments in languages other than Latin – the examples of Hebrew, Greek and Italian are cited.[21] It is further pointed out that the *Liber de questionibus Armenorum* of Ardmachan (Archbishop Fitzralph, one of Wyclif's few contemporary *auctoritates*), from which the above point is taken, was 'edited' in the Roman curia and approved by God (fol. 203v cols. a-b).

The 24th point argues that translations would result in every lay person becoming an 'impromptu predicator' ('impromptu / unprepared preacher') which would imply a disrespect for 'omnes ordines omnesque religiones' ('all orders and all religious orders', fol. 196r col. a). The countering argument once more cites the example of the primitive church where 'benedicciones et cetera fiebant in wulgari' ('blessings etc. were made in the vulgar'). It goes on to refer to the times of Bede when in spite of the Bible being available in the vernacular, clerks and monks were held in veneration. The disrespect to which they are often subjected in present times is identified as the result of their appalling deficiencies. And if the laity is indeed wise and knowledgeable, so much the better. The friars can then set about converting the multitude of infidels (fol. 205r col. a). The argument takes a slightly different turn as Bacon's *Opus Tertium* is cited as saying that children ought first to be instructed in morals – hence Boethius's veneration for Seneca. Instead of studying the fables of Ovid and other poets, and versified Bibles which cut out everything and are worth nothing, it would be much better if they were to listen to and construe the gospel in prose (fol. 205r col. b).[22] As for the criticism of the clergy which lay people might offer if they were to possess a knowledge of scripture and the monastic regulae, it would be either deserved or irrelevant: 'Si enim puri essemus profecto calumpnias hominum nequaquam metueremus' ('For, certainly, if we were pure, we would never fear the calumnies of men'). A quotation from Seneca about good and bad consciences follows. And if the laity were to ask humbly questions pertinent to salvation, divine scripture has ordained a remedy for them: Deut. 32:7, 'Interroga patres tuos et annunciabunt tibi, maiores tuos et dicent tibi' (fol. 205 v col. a).

What emerges from this survey of some of the crucial points of debate touched upon in Ullerston's *determinatio* is its quite remarkable failure to address the fundamental issue of the relationship of *auctoritas* and interpretation. The important Wycliffite disjunction of biblical text and human hermeneutics is ignored; the extent to which the Christian faith is a construct of the Church goes either unrecognized or is assumed as axiomatic; and as a result, the ideal proposed seems to be the utopian one which consists in the laity having access to the text of vernacular scriptures, the interpretation of which is nevertheless dictated by an unquestioned ecclesiastical hierarchy. The deficiencies of the establishment are noted without the possible effect of these on the official teaching of the Church being taken into account. An almost naïve – by the standards of turn-of-the-century Oxford – vision of meaning informs Ullerston's tract; for a man who was well acquainted with at least a part of Wyclif's writings,[23] and presumably familiar with the sophisticated hermeneutic debates going on at Oxford, such an apparent unawareness of the questions he is begging is startling. It may indicate the extent to which Wyclif would virtually have had to create, for large sections of his 'audience', the framework of thought in terms of which he sought to argue, a framework constituted by a rigorous disjunction of the authority of the text, accessible to the individual *fidelis* through reason and inspiration, and the authority of the Church. It would also underline the remarkable Lollard achievement of converting into popular currency ideas not always immediately comprehensible even to those familiar with the abstruser academic mint. It is unfortunate that one knows so little about contemporary perceptions of Ullerston's tract. Vienna, Österreischische Nationalbibliothek MS 4133, the only near-complete text extant, offers few clues. The tract may have reached Bohemia 'along with the multitude of writings by Wyclif himself and his followers';[24] or, given Ullerston's prominence in the Conciliar movement, it may have reached central Europe through orthodox channels (just as Thomas Netter's and William Woodford's anti-Wycliffite materials were circulated later).[25] Whatever be the case, the other material in the manuscript is unintriguingly orthodox: Jerome's commentary on Jeremiah, Lamentations and

Daniel, and Honorius Augustodunensis's commentary on Canticles, here ascribed to Orosius.

The manuscript in which William Butler's *determinatio* is found, MS K.2.2 of Merton College, Oxford,[26] is more revealing. The thrust in the direction of polemical orthodoxy is prominent. Besides Butler's tract, the manuscript includes a defence of the order of preachers by Thomas de Sutton,[27] a Dominican friar and fellow of Merton in the late thirteenth century; Walter Hilton's defence of images,[28] here ascribed to Thomas Palmer; a tract on pilgrimage; a *determinatio* on the subject of the adoration of images by Robert Alyngton, Chancellor of the University *c.* 1393 and well-known logician who knew and wrote against Wyclif;[29] a selection of *quaestiones* from the commentary of William of Nottingham on Clement of Llanthony's *Unum ex Quattuor*;[30] selections from Giles of Rome, Grosseteste and Rolle; a tract on usury by John Eyton, canon of the Augustinian monastery at Repton;[31] the *Ecclesiastical Hierarchy* of the Pseudo-Dionysius; tracts by Augustine of Ancona;[32] and homilies by the popular sermon-writer John Waldby, relative of Robert Waldby who was Archbishop of York and a member of the famous anti-Wycliffite council of 1382.[33]

The compiler of Merton K.2.2 had obviously a strong polemical interest in his material. His decision to include Butler's tract in such a compilation is amply vindicated when one considers its strident orthodoxy. For Butler is much more to the point than Ullerston. His emphasis falls firmly on the socio-ecclesiastical hierarchy and the incontrovertibility of the meanings dictated by it. He quotes Augustine's *De Moribus Ecclesiae Catholicae*, where the saint says: 'Naturae ordinem habere se, ut, cum aliquid discimus, rationem praecedat auctoritas' ('The order of nature is such that, when we learn anything, authority precedes reason', p. 402). He proceeds to highlight the comparative safety of the 'melior, securior, atque expeditior' ('the better, more secure and more efficient') 'via audiendi' in which only supervised, mediated knowledge is offered (p. 403). In fact, towards the beginning of the determination, there is an explicit avowal of the necessity of supervised readings of scripture and the consequent advisability of having the texts in Latin. Replying to the argument that Latin texts can be as faulty and textually inaccurate as those in the vulgar (incidentally, this is one of Ullerston's points),[34]

Butler points out that there is a system of control over the former which the latter often escape: the texts can be corrected easily in the universities, which would not be possible once copies were multiplied among the people; moreover, even the Latin text should not be made available to whoever wishes to read the Bible, for experience shows that therein lies the cause of many heresies and errors:

> Huic dico, quod ecclesia ordinavit universitates in quibus docentur scripturae et scribuntur libri, qui si falsi sunt, facile possunt corrigi; quae politia non potest commode servari stante multiplicatione tanta populi; nec debent praelati hoc admittere, quod singuli ad libitum eorum legant scripturam in Latinum translatam; quia, sicut experientia satis docet, hoc fuit multis modis occasio incidendi in haereses et errores. Non est ergo politicum ut quicunque, ubicunque, quantumcunque voluerit se det ferventi studio scripturarum. (p. 401)

> To this I say, that the Church ordained universities in which scriptures are taught and books are written, which, if false, can be easily corrected, which strict rule cannot be observed as is due when such multiplication [of copies] exists among the people. Nor must priests allow this that individuals at their will read scripture translated into Latin, since, as experience teaches sufficiently, this was, in many ways, the cause of falling into heresies and errors. Therefore, it is not prudent that whoever [so wishes] should give himself to the fervent study of scriptures wherever and to whatever extent he may wish.

Indeed, unsupervised readings of scripture have their very real, hermeneutic dangers: 'Nam, dato quod populus legeret ad alium sensum qui non est scripturae, de scriptura non haberet tunc sententiam' ('for, given that the people may read [according] to another sense which is not that of scripture, they would not have [in that case] the *sentence* of scripture', p. 403). Unskilful readers of scripture are compared, after Augustine, to 'imperito chirurgico' ('an unskilled surgeon') who can kill instead of curing. The only valid doctors are ordained priests (p. 404).

This emphasis on regulated, supervised, mediated readings of scripture naturally shades into a questioning of the powers of reason. Postlapsarian reason is subject to severe limitations: 'adveniente corruptione intellectus iam non est nobis cognoscibilis effectus per causam in contingentibus, sed cognoscimus causam per effectum' ('The corruption of the intellect having come already, effect[s] are not knowable by us by cause[s] in [the matter of] contingents, but [instead], we know cause[s] by effect[s]').[35] It is especially inadequate in the context of interpreting a text which is full of ambiguities and obscurities:

> in ambiguo plurima se ostendunt, quorum quid potius accipiendum sit penitus ignoratur; sed in obscuris parum aut nihil quod attendatur apparet . . . Cum ergo populus sit difficilis intellectus et scriptura sacra sit plena ambiguis seu obscuris, immo, secundum Dionysium, sacris poeticis informationibus; quomodo, quaeso, foret eorum legere medium in via cognitionis sententiae scripturae sacrae? Relinquitur ergo, quod vulgarem populum in scriptura sacra legentem non est medium deducens eos [*sic*] in notitiam eiusdem scripturae.[36] (pp. 404–5)

> In [the case of] ambiguity, many [meanings] show themselves, of which the one preferably to be accepted may be utterly unknown; but in [the case of] obscurities, little or nothing of what is to be striven for appears . . . Therefore, since the people are reluctant of intellect, and since sacred scripture is full of ambiguities and obscurities, rather, according to Dionysius, [full of] sacred poetic teachings, how, I ask, would reading them be a way to the path of knowledge of the meaning of sacred scripture? We are therefore reduced to the conclusion that there is no means of bringing the common people, who read in the holy scriptures, to the knowledge of those same scriptures.

The dismissal of 'rational' readings which are accessible to all as a point of entry into the meanings of scripture is followed by a full-scale endorsement of the principle of hierarchy. The inferior orders of angels are illuminated by the superior; and since the earthly hierarchy must follow the pattern established by the heavenly, 'illuminatio passiva viantium de ordine inferiori dependere debet complete a volitiva viantium in ordine superiori' ('the passive illumination of the wayfarers of the inferior order must depend completely on the will of wayfarers of the superior order', p. 407). The inferior angels are not permitted

> speciales habere libros, in quibus per spiritualem lecturam sive specialem possent cognoscere talia inflammantia affectum [to religious piety] sine revelatione aliqua ordinis superioris. (p. 408)

> to have private books, in which, by spiritual or private reading, they may be able to know such stirrings of the emotion without revelation from some superior order.

It is therefore useless to grumble against the earthly authorities for not permitting a similar *lectio*. To be taught is sufficient:

> Et rogo multitudinem celestis patriae ut tales lecturas non permittant in ecclesia militante, quousque doceatur per aliquos sufficienter, quod sic est in ecclesia triumphante. (p. 408)

> And I ask the multitude of the celestial fatherland that they do not permit such readings in the militant Church, as long as [the lay Christian] is taught by others in an adequate manner, since that is the situation in the triumphant Church.

The clarity and explicitness of Butler's formulation bring into unusually sharp focus what is often glossed over or denied – the necessarily arbitrary yet absolute nature of authority, ecclesiastical, legal or otherwise. Butler's adherence to the pseudo-Dionysian framework of thought is certainly a rhetoric of justification; but more importantly, it assumes a covenantal view of the structure and operation of the created universe which was deeply antipathetic to Wyclif's own realist metaphysics. The Ockhamite tendency to replace 'innate or inherent virtue in things with assigned or ascribed value that can operate in nature as well as in the church'[37] informs Butler's vision of an absolute yet *ordained* hierarchy.

> The distinction between viewing divine power simply (*absoluta*) or according to God's created and revealed systems (*ordinata*) was used in thirteenth-century theology, became more prevalent in Scotus's thought, and became a principal tool in Ockham's theology, testing the degree of necessity involved in laws that operate in nature and in the process of salvation.[38]

Wyclif himself was of course strongly opposed to the concept of such a hierarchy. He pointed out in *De Ecclesia* that even within the angelic ranks, there was opposition, and justified opposition, against particular members of the higher orders. Michael led the good angels of the lowest order against Lucifer.[39] Wyclif characteristically replaced the traditional concept with his own internalised one: hierarchy defined in terms of purity, enlightenment and *recte vivendi* (qualities, it is assumed, not subject to hermeneutic variation) rather than any externally imposed order. In the late fourteenth century, according to David Luscombe, there was 'a readiness on the part of a number of polemicists to challenge those who relied on Dionysian notions of hierarchy to proclaim the immunities of priesthood'.[40] Butler's unquestioned ratification of the principle and his nostalgic vision of an antiquity in which the greatest princes bowed to their spiritual superiors (p. 408) need to be placed in this context. We may recall here that Wyclif's point of view on this issue was very different: the necessity of monarchic control over the Church had been forcefully underlined in *De Ecclesia*.[41] Butler's hierarchical vision thus emerges as a part of his reactionary ideology; it has very little to do with his actual perceptions of lay capacities for scriptural understanding. As Ruedi Imbach has emphasised, 'für ein angemessenes Verständnis der kirchlichen Hierarchie und ihrer Auswirkungen für die mittelalterliche Weltdeutung ist es indessen wichtig festzuhalten, dass die klerikale Würde... nicht bloss einen geistigen Sinn besitzt, sondern auch *politisch* verstanden sein will' ('it is important to note, for an adequate understanding of ecclesiastical hierarchy and its impact on the medieval interpretation of the world, that the dignity of the clerics did not merely have a spiritual meaning but also demands to be understood politically').[42] Hudson rightly points out that the Lollards, arguing in favour of translation, were more realistic about the specificities of the social situation and the actual needs of the laity: 'The Lollard texts are... more realistic about society at this stage of the medieval period. They point out that between the clergy and illiterate labourer there is large group of laymen who are relatively well-educated, who can read their native language and who have wealth to purchase books.'[43]

However, though the ideological thrust of Butler's argument may often be glossed over by larger topoi such as those of hierarchy or the mystical body of Christ, it does emerge, from time to time, in all its stark authoritarianism. Speaking of the ancient prohibition – alluded to by Maimonides, the great Jewish commentator – on discussing the literal meaning of scriptural words lest it lead the simple into error or despair, Butler says:

> non solum populo non est intimandum de revelationibus, [de originibus],[44] de attributis, vel de accidentibus eucharistiae, ut exemplificat assertor opinionis contrariae; immo quod non est licitum intimare populo per praedicationem multa plana legis; nam si scripturam haberent quam legere scirent, tunc in disputationem legis de facili possent prorumpere, quod summe prohibet ius civile. (p. 414)

Not only is the people not to be told of revelations, of origins, of attributes or of accidents of the Eucharist, as the holder of the contrary opinion adduces as example, it is not even lawful to tell the people many plain [things] of law through preaching, for if they have scripture which they [are able to] read, then they would be easily able to break into disputation[s] of law, which civil law prohibits above all.

The 'people' must be rigorously excluded from all possibility of participating in disputation on matters relevant to the law of Christ.[45] Butler proceeds to refer to a passage from a decretal stating 'quod laicus de fide disputans publice vel private excommunicandus' ('that a lay person disputing [matters] of faith in public or in private is to be excommunicated'). He concludes with stating that scripture – whether in its 'plain' or more 'obscure' parts, and whether or not accompanied by the glosses of approved doctors – is not to be read by the common people:

> [It follows] quod propter subtilitatem litteralis artificii ipsius sacrae scripturae, et haec per doctorum plana testimonia, quod sacra scriptura nec pro parte eius plana, nec pro parte eius obscura, nec cum doctorum approbatorum expositionibus quomodolibet a vulgari populo sit legenda. (p. 41 4)

> [It follows] that because of the subtlety of the learned artistry of this sacred scripture, and this by the plain testimony of doctors, sacred scripture neither in its plain nor in its obscure part[s], nor with the exposition of approved doctors, is to be read by the vulgar people howsover [they choose].

This explicit and, even by the standards of its day, extreme prohibition articulated, Butler moves on to another topos, that of the Church militant as the mystical body of Christ, of which each member has its proper function. Just as only digested and transformed food reaches organs of the body other than the stomach, similarly 'sacerdotes accipiant [sic] scientiam per scripturas de Deo, et meditantes apud se toto populo subministrant' ('priests receive knowledge of God through scriptures, and meditating by themselves subminister [this knowledge] to the whole populace', p. 41 6). All of which feeds quite naturally into that other popular topos: that of the milk of light doctrine and the meat of ghostly substance.[46] Milk, which is easy to digest, and does not demand dental labour, is the analogue of miracles, which offer an edification independent of intellectual labour:

> lac, [Chrysostom] inquit, sine labore et opere dentium manducatur, et manducantem sua suavitate delectat. Sic miraculum nec laborem videntibus imponit, sed videntes admiratione delectat et ad fidem nos molliter invitat. (p. 41 6)

> Milk, says [Chrysostom], is drunk [chewed] without exerting the teeth, and delights the drinker [chewer] with its sweetness. In a similar manner, a miracle does not impose work on those seeing [it], but delights them with wonderment and invites us gently to faith.

But the scriptures – 'perfectionis doctrina et iustitiae' ('the doctrine of perfection and justice') – require 'spiritualibus dentibus' ('spiritual teeth', pp. 41 6–1 7). Of course, it is the function of the ecclesiastical authority to use its spiritual teeth and determine which particular kind of predigested nutriment to supply to the laity.[47]

The emphasis on making bits and pieces of scripture available to the laity according to perceived appropriatenesses ties in with the generally rhetorical, audience-oriented thrust of Butler's argument. He refers to a passage from Origen's *Super Leviticum* where the different requirements of audiences of differing eruditions are underlined. The ultimate example of Christ is cited – he himself used and commanded his disciples to use parables to speak to the unlearned:[48]

> Vides ergo quomodo docuit ea ipse, aliis indumentis uti debere pontificem cum procedit ad turbas, et aliis cum perfectis et eruditis ministrat. (p. 41 2)

> You see therefore how he himself taught these things: the priest must use some [kinds of] covering when he goes before crowds, and other kinds when he serves the perfect and the learned.

The acts of devotion which the faithful should aim at are prayer and meditation and these can be achieved without reading translations: 'optimum medium ad cognoscendum Deum [est] de Deo cogitare et ipsum Deum suppliciter exorare' ('the best way of knowing God is to think of him and pray to him humbly'). What is important is the *intentio fidelis* and the aim of devotion, not the acquisition of inappropriate knowledge which is liable to be misinterpreted. The gulf between this concept of a mediated, rhetorically appropriate faith[49] which discourages any intellectual engagement with the Bible on the part of the laity, and Wyclif's idealised vision of meanings arising incontrovertibly through the inspired, rational understanding of an incontrovertible and 'democratic'[50] text hardly needs to be emphasised.

The interpenetration of the issues of biblical translation and authorised religion was at least partially recognised by the Dominican friar from Germany, Cornelius Oesterwik,[51] who compiled Cambridge Trinity College MS B.15.11[52] for an Oxford Dominican John Courteys[53] in 1430. The manuscript, neatly written and economically but functionally decorated, is in the same hand throughout. It includes, apart from a *determinatio* against translation which a contemporary hand ascribes to Palmer, Woodford's *Contra Trialogum Wiclevi*; a list of articles against the *Trialogus*; a number of tracts by Simon Boraston; and Vincent of Beauvais's *De Instructione Puerorum Nobilium*.[54]

1430 was of course a late enough post-*Constitutions* date for such a suggestive collection to be unsurprising; nevertheless it is interesting to note that following the tract on translation is a tract defending the absolute validity, rightfulness and unitariness of papal authority. Simon Boraston was a Dominican friar from the first half of the fourteenth century who was one of the earliest polemicists in the controversy between secular clergy and the mendicant friars;[55] his tracts *De Unitate et Ordine Ecclesiastice Potestatis* and *De Mutabilitate Mundi* (both written in 1337) were contributions to the debate and stressed the incontrovertibility of the single source of earthly power which informs, through successive mediations, the entire ecclesiastical hierarchy. William Woodford, the other major polemicist whose tract against the *Trialogus* forms the first section of B.15.11, we have already encountered. Vincent of Beauvais's *De Instructione Puerorum Nobilium*, a tract on 'education' – conceived in the broadest possible sense – written for the children of St Louis, is a highly traditional work embedded in established modes of scholarship, with copious citations from the pagan authors and the major patristic and scholastic writers, particularly Jerome and Hugh of Saint Victor.

The determination ascribed to Palmer is the only one of the three investigated here that identifies the proponents of Biblical translation with the Lollards.[56] Among much that is unremarkable and repetitive, Palmer has one crucial passage against translation. After making the standard arguments relating to the difficulty of rendering the arcane senses of scripture in an inferior language, Palmer proceeds to question the assumption that there is one easily accessible literal sense. He begins by alluding to the Ciceronian-Hieronymic cliché of translation being either 'de verbo ad verbum, aut de sententia ad sententiam' ('word for word, or sense for sense', p. 428).[57] He goes on to show that the vocabulary of the English language is not rich enough for a translation in the former mode to be possible: 'Non primo modo, quia multae dictiones Latinae non habent dictiones in Anglico correspondentes' ('Not in the first way, because many Latin words do not have corresponding words in English', p. 428). He then proceeds, acutely, to question the often theoretically or polemically accepted assumption that there is in fact one literal sense:

> Nec translatio debet fieri de sententia ad sententiam, quia sententia eiusdem litterae Latinae est apud diversos diversa; in quem igitur sensum transferri debet ignoratur. Dicit forte quis, quod habeat sensum litteralem, moralem, allegoricum et anagogicum: transferri tantum debet quoad sensum litteralem. Contra, sensus litterales sunt diversi secundum opinionem diversorum, et stat argumentum sicut prius. (pp. 428–9)

> Neither should translation be made sense for sense, since the sense of the same Latin word / text is diverse according to diverse people. Therefore, it is not known into which sense [a passage] must be translated. Suppose someone says that that [though] a passage may have literal, moral, allegorical and anagogical senses, it must nevertheless be translated [only] as far as the literal sense. But no, literal senses are diverse according to the opinion of diverse people, and the argument remains as [stated] earlier.

Palmer strikes at the heart of the theoretical Wycliffite assumption of an accessible unitary literal meaning; the inevitability of interpretation in translation is thus underlined.

It is significant that he should do so; for the 'literal meaning' was a way of cutting several Gordian knots. Wyclif himself was a believer in the importance of the literal sense, though his theory, as we have seen, was subtle and complicated, with intentionality playing an important role. Some of his followers were less abstrusely devoted to the literal sense. The Prologue to the Wycliffite Bible, for instance, cites Augustine as saying that 'oonly bi the literal vnderstonding a man may argue aȝens an aduersarie'. Anything in scripture that is apparently not in conformity with the dictates of *caritas* demands figurative explication; the rest 'owith not to be gessid a figuratijf speche'. 'Goostly vndirstondingis' are not 'autentik . . . of beleeue' unless

> groundid opynly in the text of holy scripture, in oo place other other, either in opin resoun that may not be distroied, either whanne the gospelris either other apostlis taken allegorie of the olde testament, and confeermyn it.[58]

Palmer himself, in a passage preceding the one already quoted, had devalued the importance of the literal sense. Gregory's exposition of Deut. 22:6–7[59] is cited:

> sensus litteralis, qui est quasi magister aliorum sensuum, dimitti debet, et pulli eius retineri, allegoriae et anagogiae, quia *littera occidit, spiritus autem vivificat.* Quomodo, igitur, simplices illiterati, vel sola grammatica instructi, illos pullos trium sensuum ignorantes, non errarent habentes magistrum, scilicet litteralem sensum, tamen de pullis non curantes? (p. 424)

> the literal sense, which is, as it were, the master of the other senses, must be put aside, and its young, of allegory and anagogy, retained, because *the letter killeth, but the spirit giveth life* [2 Cor. 3: 6]. How, therefore, would the simple who are illiterate or trained only in grammar, [who are] ignorant of the young of the three senses, not err, having the master, i.e. the literal sense, but not attending to the young?

It should be noted that the concept of 'literal sense' assumed in this instance is much simpler than that of Wyclif. As we have seen, Wyclif's literal sense, since it is defined by intentionality (another of his hermeneutic invariables) may include 'valid' figurative readings.

Ullerston's text, unlike Palmer's, assumes that a faithful translation according to the 'literal' sense is possible. The doctor who disputes against translation bases his third argument on the fact that translation can only render the 'literal' sense and is therefore unsuitable for rendering the primarily figurative Old Testament: 'vetus testamentum cessauit secundum sensum litteralem, sed interpretacio non est nisi secundum sensum litteralem, ergo etc' ('the Old Testament has ceased according to the literal sense, but translation cannot exist except according to the literal sense, therefore, etc', fol. 195r col. a). The answer to this tries to show that, first, the Old Testament, especially in its moral parts, does to some extent work non-figuratively; secondly, that the logic of the argument is fallacious, as, arguing on the same principle, one could demand that parts of the Old Testament be written in no language at all (fol. 199v col. b).

The doctor's sixth, and related, point, is based on Augustine's *De Doctrina Christiana*: 'Plerumque a sensu auctoris demus aberrat interpres si non sit doctissimus, sed talem non est facile invenire' ('Indeed, the translator wanders astray from the sense of the author many times unless he is very learned, but such [a man] is not easy to find' fol. 195r col. b). This objection is not really answered. It is merely stated that such exacting requirements would disqualify everyone from holding any office (including that of king or pope) ideally demanding perfection (fol. 201r col. b).

Ullerston does, however, from time to time, use phrases such as 'translatio fidelis' or 'transferre fideliter'. It soon emerges that by a faithful translation he means a faithful rendering of *sentence*. What is interesting is that he refers to Bacon's citation, in the *Opus Tertium*, of Jerome's concept of the non-equivalence of languages[60] without really taking into account its possible effect on translation, in so far as it would imply the inevitability of interpretation.

> Item, quod non potest fideliter transferri in uulgare non debet transferri in uulgare. Sed una lingwa non potest fideliter per aliam exponi propter diuersitatem proprietatum loquendi in diuersis lingwis. (fol. 195r col. b)

> Item, that what cannot faithfully be translated into the vulgar must not be translated into the vulgar. But one tongue cannot be faithfully expounded by another because of the diversity of the properties of speaking in diverse languages.

Augustine's *De Doctrina Christiana* is cited again as authority for the aperçu that certain words, such as interjections, cannot be translated into other languages (fol. 195v col. a). Ullerston's doctor associates with such failures of fidelity another related failure, that consisting in textual corruption. The old translations have been rendered corrupt over time; therefore it is dangerous to translate according to the texts we possess. Moreover, our knowledge of the ancient languages is imperfect:

> Preterea si ab olim translacio erat fidelis et modo corrupta periculo-
> sum est secundum illam transferre, sed sic est de translacione quam
> habemus, ergo etc. . . [Bacon] inquit que fuerunt bene translata sunt
> modo corrupta propter hoc quod lingwas ignoramus; sicut inquit
> patet per totam bibliam et philosophiam quia nec scimus scribere
> nec legere nec proferre et per consequens perit verus intellectus. Et
> hec causa inquit habet locum in corruptione textus sacri.[61] (fol. 195 v
> col. a)

> Besides, if formerly the translation was faithful and now corrupt, it
> is dangerous to translate according to it, but such is the case with
> the translation which we have, therefore etc . . . Bacon says that those
> [texts] which were well-translated are now corrupt because we do not
> know the languages; as, he says, appears across the whole of the Bible
> and in philosophy, since we know neither to write nor to read nor to
> expound. True understanding perishes as a result. And this condition,
> he says, has its source in the corruption of the sacred text.

The reply to these arguments fails to address any of the issues raised. Bacon's concept of the essential asymmetry of languages is dismissed with a naïve reference to the translative practices of students in 'scolis gramaticalibus' ('grammar schools'). The earlier doctor had pointed out that it is difficult to translate logical texts without inventing a new vocabulary. The counter-argument states that even if this is conceded, it by no means follows that scripture, especially those parts of it most necessary to salvation, cannot be translated, for there is a great difference between the express knowledge of scripture and the knowledge to be derived from the liberal arts (fol. 201 v col. a). Besides, inventing a new vocabulary is not as reprehensible as it is made out to be; almost all present day preachers do so:

> sic enim pene omnes predicatores in nostro uulgari anglico nomi-
> nando nomina Christi, beate virginis et aliorum sanctorum infini-
> torumque aliorum appocopant seu alio modo permutant. (fol. 201 v
> col. b)

> Thus almost all preachers in our vulgar English cut short or change in
> some other way in naming [them], the names of Christ, of the Blessed
> Virgin and of other saints, and of infinite others.

The doctor's second point is initially conceded: 'translaciones longius deriuate sunt imperfecciores' ('translations which are derived more distantly [from the original] are more imperfect'). One begins to expect the argument finally to get somewhere, when Ullerston plunges into a defence of Jerome, citing Augustine's *Epistola ad Fortunatum* as justification for rejecting Bacon's *auctoritas*. (Augustine's letter states that all human authorities can freely be contradicted.) This is followed by another endorsement of the importance of having a knowledge of things as opposed to words: though we do not write 'Jesus' or 'Israel' as the words are written in Hebrew or Greek, it would be wrong to say that this implies a failure in our knowledge of the things signified, for, despite the changes, 'verum intellectum de re signata habemus' ('we have a true understanding of the thing signified') (fol. 202r col. b).

There is, however, one point where Ullerston comes close to recognising the extent to which any definition of 'fidelity' would depend on the Church. Defending Jerome's translation from the criticism implied by Augustine when he speaks of the 'impericiam latinorum interpretum' ('the inadequacy of the Latin translators'), Ullerston outlines the probable rationale of Augustine's praise of the Septuagint above all other versions, and his criticism of Jerome for basing his translation on the original Hebrew.[62] Augustine, Ullerston points out, naturally preferred the Septuagintal translation because it had long been accepted and confirmed by the custom of the Church, which is equivalent to law. Jerome's translation, though better, was new and therefore not as immediately acceptable. Men judge of temporal laws when they institute them, but judge according to them once they are instituted and confirmed; Augustine, too, if he were to live now, would have chosen to concord with the Church in preferring Jerome's translation.[63] The dependence of law or the interpretation of it on custom was of course another knotty issue.[64] Ullerston gives a clear account of it by referring 'legality' entirely to ecclesiastical authority and tradition. In this scheme of things, it is enough for the Church to accept a translation for it to be acceptable: the distance from the thought of Wyclif, and the translators of the Wycliffite Bible, scarcely requires emphasis.

The (deliberate?) naïveté of Ullerston's tract is thus interrupted from time to time by flashes of genuine insight. Particularly impressive is his deconstruction of the topos relating to the hierarchy of languages.

First, the adjective 'barbarous', indiscriminately applied to the vernaculars, is shown to be arbitrary and subjective. Aquinas's Commentary on Aristotle's *Politics* is cited as explaining the term 'barbarus' thus: 'Quidam dicunt omnem hominem barbarum esse [ei] qui lingwam eius non intelligit' ('Some people say that every man is a barbarian for him who does not understand his language') (fol. 201 v col. b). This is followed by a reference to 1 Cor. 14:11, a passage endorsing such a definition. Moreover, Bede translated 'liberales artes' and 'liberales sciencias' into English; therefore it is a language quite capable of articulating sophisticated thought. It is pointed out that French, another such 'vulgar' tongue, has a long tradition of scholarship in it.

More interestingly, Ullerston questions the assumption that vernacular languages are not 'grammatical'. Indeed, this was one of Palmer's major arguments: English is a barbaric tongue and therefore incapable of articulating the arcane mysteries of the faith.[65] He speaks of the *incongruitas* and *falsitas* which would arise from rendering the scriptures in a language unregulated by grammar:

> Sacra scriptura in multis locis salvari non potest aliquando incongruitate et falsitate, nisi per figuras et regulas grammaticales, sicut ostensum est in quodam tractatu quem vidi, in quo erant omnes figurae grammaticales, et declaratae et quotatae, ubi per eas sacra scriptura in partibus suis ab errore servata et defensata. Igitur in nullam linguam quae non regulatur regulis et figuris grammaticalibus est ipsa transferenda. (p. 426)

> Sacred scripture sometimes cannot be defended in many places from [charges of] incongruity and falsity unless by [means of] grammatical rules and figures, as is shown in a certain tract I have seen, wherein all grammatical figures were enumerated and explained, in which sacred scripture [was] defended and saved from error in its parts by [means of] these. Therefore, it is not to be translated into any language which is not governed by grammatical figures and rules.

Even a language regulated by grammar would not provide an exact equivalent or preserve the 'proprietates'; the proper significances of Latin words, for instance, 'non possunt servari in Graeco linguagio' ('cannot be preserved in the Greek language'). It is obvious, therefore, how remote would be the possibility of being faithful to the original tongue in English or any other 'lingua barbarica' ('barbaric language') (pp. 427–8).

Ullerston denies the equivalence of 'vernacular' and 'ungrammatical': 'si per linguam non gramaticatam linguam uulgarium intelligamus, planum est quod falsum assumitur' ('if by "a language unregulated by grammar" we understand the "vulgar tongue", it is evident that the premise is false'). For a 'grammar' to exist, it is not necessary that it be written down. 'Grammar' consists in 'recte loquendi, racione pronunciandi, recteque scribendi' ('speaking, writing and pronouncing correctly'), even when the principles thereof are only retained memorially:

> ydioma fixum habet gramaticam sibi apropriatam, quamuis talis gramatica non sit in scripto tradita. Sufficit enim in minus famosis ydiomatibus, quod industria congrue loquendi et scribendi in illis sit tamen memorie comendata. (fol. 204r col. b)

> A fixed language has a grammar appropriate to itself, even though such grammar may not be handed down in writing. For it suffices in [the case of] the less famous languages that the zealous activity of speaking and writing in a harmonious fashion in these [languages] is nevertheless entrusted to memory.

Besides, there is authoritative precedent for the use of the vulgar. According to Fitzralph, Mark himself wrote in Italian; and if it is said that the Apostles did not write in vulgar Greek because the Greek of the Bible is different from the contemporary vulgar form, it must be pointed out that languages change over time:

> sic est in multis uulgaribus linguis quod pro processu temporis notabiliter permutantur. Sic patet de anglico nostri temporis et temporis sancti Bede. (fol. 204r col. a)

> This is the case with many vulgar tongues which change perceptibly over the course of time. This appears [if one compares] the English of our time with that of the time of St Bede.

Ullerston's *determinatio* thus occasionally achieves keen insights into the workings of language, translation and *auctoritas*. On the whole, however, his work is characterised by an apparent incomprehension of the fundamental issues involved in the debate over translation. The hermeneutic consequences of the free availability of scripture are never really taken into account. Ullerston is in this respect embedded in tradition: the disjunction of text and interpretation (especially that provided by the ecclesiastical hierarchy) that the Wycliffites emphasised seems inexplicably to pass him by. What is particularly revealing is his usage of certain key terms and phrases, among them, for instance, *nudum textum*. Speaking of preaching the gospel, Ullerston quotes Grosseteste:

> Si . . . aliquis dicat, quod nescit predicare, proprium remedium est, quod resignet beneficium suum. Tamen melius remedium dicam potest enim quelibet talis persona vel sacerdos repetere in septimana nudum textum ewangelij diei dominice, ut tunc sciat saltem historiam grossam subditis suis refferre. (fol. 198v col. a)

> If . . . someone says that he does not know [how to] preach, the proper remedy is to resign his benefice. Nevertheless, I will say that there can [be] a better remedy: for such a person or priest to revise[66] over the week the naked text of the gospel for Sunday, so that he may then at least know the whole story to tell his inferiors.

The phrase is used in the context of preaching, without any apparent awareness of the – by this time – dubious status of preaching the actual gospel text. Wyclif himself had accused the friars of suggesting that only pastoralia should be preached[67]; he of course advocated Gospel preaching. Helen Spencer points out that 'gospel preaching had become associated in people's minds with heresy and sedition', and the popularisation of academic matters by the Lollards.[68]

Ullerston, however, in a very un-Wycliffite manner, goes on to suggest that preaching of the naked text should be followed by that of the 'epistolas festorum' and the 'vitas sanctorum'.[69] He therefore uses the phrase *nudum textum* without any apparent awareness of its heretical resonances. Such usage goes hand in hand with his almost synonymous use of the words *predicare, exponere, transferre, conuertere, reserare sensum in uerbis latentem*, even *transmutare*. The passage devoted to distinguishing between *transferre* and *interpretari* ends with the implication that languages being equivalent, translation need not involve interpretation.[70] The only important distinction he makes is between these actions and *disputare*, which is condemned as anathema to be punished by excommunication (fol. 207r cols a-b).

The blurred outlines of such potentially disparate concepts fit in well with Ullerston's general classification of scripture with other 'authoritative' texts – works by Orosius, Bede, Gregory, Boethius, Rolle and so on. No distinction is made between having the sacred text by itself and having it with gloss: hence the 'sacra pagina cum doctoribus' ('the sacred page with [the expositions of] the *doctors*') in the vulgar is what is often aimed at. The one argument which comes closest to recognising that translation itself might be a form of 'glossing', of introducing 'prophanas vocum nouitates' ('profane novelties of words'), is answered in a characteristically short-sighted way:

> Non enim prohibet apostolus [I Tim. 6:20] vocum nouitates simpliciter, ut dicit glosa communis, sed prophanas scilicet que sunt contra religionem . . . alie inquit nouitates non sunt uitande, sunt enim doctrine religionis congruentes uerborum quedam nouitates. (fol. 206r col. a)

> For the apostle does not prohibit [new words] outright, as the common gloss says, but profane words, i.e. [those] which are against religion . . . Other novelties, [the apostle] says, are not to be avoided, for some [new words] are in harmony with religious doctrine.

Ullerston's tract forms an intriguing mixture of erudition and imperceptiveness. Potentially relevant issues are touched upon without their larger – and, with the benefit of hindsight, most central – implications being realised or addressed. Indeed, his *determinatio*, as opposed to those of Palmer and Butler, suggests an earlier world, an earlier framework of reference, before the issues brought by the Lollards into the centre of both popular and academic politics had become quite clear and indeed quite threatening. Had not the dates of Ullerston's career made such a hypothesis somewhat unlikely, it would have been tempting to suggest that the text was perhaps composed in the early 1390s, and revived in 1401, the word 'editus' in the fragment preserved in Gonville and Caius College Library, Cambridge,[71] in that case referring, with typical medieval imprecision, to 'publication' or 'promulgation' rather than 'composition'.[72] A gap of even ten years or so would have made all the difference. Margaret Aston shows how quickly official perceptions of the threat of vernacular texts developed and crystallised into dictatorial opposition; how initially it had been taken for granted that 'if people were learning false doctrine, they were learning it from preachers':

> [S]ince the authorities acted on their normal assumption that popular errors must stem from the spoken word, it was some years before

the textual bases of Lollardy began to be exposed. Vernacular theology . . . was quite new. It took churchmen by surprise.

Aston further points out that

by the end of the fourteenth century the English language had been injected with a range of new words, making it possible to do something that previously was as impossible as it had seemed undesirable: to discuss the doctrine of the eucharist in the vernacular.[73]

Ullerston still argues *for* the possibility of fashioning a vocabulary in the vernacular to compensate for its theological and logical deficiencies (fol. 201 v cols a-b). Indeed, his argument often takes the form of stating that (a) the Christian faith, which was preached by Jesus to the simple and the illiterate, does not require an arcane vocabulary to be communicated, in so far as it can be communicated in our essentially inadequate human tongues; and (b) whatever vocabulary is necessary for communicating the faith can be, and indeed often is, new-fashioned. There is none of the official paranoia about a vernacular theological vocabulary which became the norm at around the turn of the century;[74] in fact, there is no separately suspicious consciousness of any 'lay scholastic' speculation which would question the prerogatives of the clergy. It is this consciousness which informs the tracts of Butler and Palmer: hence their repeated emphasis, by the authority of Paul (2 Cor. 12:4), on the necessity of concealing the *arcana fidei* from the *simpliciter litterati*.

The gulf between the tract of Ullerston and those of Butler and Palmer is that between two different conceptual worlds. Ullerston's, whether or not it was chronologically anterior, is the older: the textual hermeneutic framework that it espouses still gives, or attempts to give, the impression of an orthodoxy largely at ease with itself, before its unexamined prerogative to dictate sacred meanings has been seriously threatened, and before the interpretative authority of the Church and the textual authority of the Bible have been uncoupled. Ullerston was one of the many who had some sympathy with parts of the Wycliffite programme:[75] is this tract an attempt to present an unpolemical and therefore unavoidably short-sighted case for certain Wycliffite demands without confronting their larger, more radical implications? Whatever be the answer, one point emerges clearly from the very composition of such a tract by a member of the high orthodoxy in the late fourteenth century: the vastness of the Lollard achievement that in the space of three decades was to transform the character of the medieval English Church. The watertight division between the worlds of academic speculation and popular observance – a division which Ullerston seems to assume as axiomatic – was suddenly breached; and assumptions about the relationship of 'meaning' and *auctoritas* began to be subjected to an unaccustomed vernacular scrutiny. It is to this domain of the vernacular that we proceed in the next two chapters: to the English Wycliffite Sermons, a vast body of writing perhaps meant for preaching, and incorporating much discussion of 'authority' and hermeneutics, and to Nicholas Love's *Mirror of the Blessed Life of Jesus Christ*, a sophisticated, orthodox reworking of an inherited devotional text explicitly battling Lollard interpretative and textual practices through a self-conscious, polemical appropriation of the traditional *mentalité* of affective meditation.

4

The English Wycliffite sermons: 'thinking in alternatives'?

The 294 Wycliffite sermons of the long English cycle[1] remain some-what of a mystery. That they were composed as parts of a single uni-fied whole seems, on the evidence supplied by Anne Hudson, beyond doubt.[2] Not only are they found in the extant manuscripts either in the form of the full cycle or in the form of selections based on com-prehensible liturgical patterns, but there is also no evidence that any part of the cycle was allowed to circulate before the whole was com-plete. The sheer volume of material would suggest a collaborative effort, but authorship, whether single or multiple, remains obscure.[3] What is even more puzzling is the intended purpose of the sermons. Some are in the nature of skeleton-pieces, providing only a basic gloss on the lection, with the implication that the speaker should build upon the framework provided; others offer extended passages of polemic and fuller exegeses. The tonal variation is great: occasionally, the sermons seem to assume a fairly learned audience and therefore include logical references and recondite academic jokes; at other times, the audience visualised seems to have been secular and lay, one which would sym-pathise with the denigration of academics and the mockery directed against clerical pretensions. Equally interesting is the presentation of the text in the manuscripts.[4] The amount of time and attention evi-dently devoted to matters of lay-out and textual correction, the general size of the volumes, and the scrupulous distinction made, by means of underlining, between the lection and the rest of the text would seem to suggest that the sermons were meant for reading.[5] A possi-ble hypothesis, advanced by Hudson, is that the 'sermons' were used for group study in Lollard schools.[6] Such a hypothesis would also ex-plain the occasional erudite reference: if the discussions were led by a

learned, possibly ex-Oxonian Lollard, such references could be eluci-
dated.

More important for the purposes of this chapter is the extent to which
the sermons are indebted to Wyclif's own sermons and other writings.
As should emerge from my discussion, the sermon-writers were certainly
well acquainted with Wyclif's ideas, both in their general emphases and
in their specificities. Many passages draw on related passages in Wyclif.
However, as Gradon and Hudson have pointed out, the sermons are
not straightforward translations of Wyclif's Latin *Sermones*, at least not
as the latter have been preserved in the extant manuscripts.[7] Rather,
they seem to be pieces of exegesis and polemic drawing on the corpus
of Wyclif's work according to their own needs. And it is primarily as
exegesis that this chapter considers the sermons, a decision which is
afforded some support by the layout of the text in the manuscripts:
the underlining of the lection on the first translation, but not of repeated words or of other biblical texts, is a convention followed in the
Wycliffite *Glossed Gospels* and in the Lollard revision of Rolle's Psalter
Commentary.[8] My analysis of the sermons considers them as a whole,
and discounts issues of single or multiple authorship, as well as problems
of intended audience or readership. I examine exegetical passages from
the sermons, and attempt to elucidate their underlying hermeneutic
principles, thereby seeking to underline the problems of interpretation
which come to the fore in vernacular writing in late-medieval England
rendering academic philosophy and theology in English. Such writing
elides, in a fashion of which William Butler would not have approved,
the crucial distinction between the (relatively) demarcated domain of
Latinate intellectual speculation and that of (at least potentially) 'popular' enquiry in the vernacular.[9]

A convenient point of departure is offered by the second sermon
on the Sunday Epistles, which begins with a citation of Romans 15:4.
Nicholas Love, as we shall see later, glosses the Pauline passage thus:
'all thynges þat ben written generaly in holi chirche ande specialy of
oure lorde Jesu cryste þei ben wryten to oure lore'.[10] The Lollard
preacher is significantly different: 'Poul bygynneþ at byleue, and seiþ
þat *alle þingus þat ben wryton* in oþer of Godys lawis *ben wryton to
oure lore*, for þo þingus ben byleue þat men shulden konne byfore
oþre'[11] (1.481/3–4). The passage points to an important hermeneutic

assumption underlying the vernacular Wycliffite sermons, an assumption inherited from Wyclif:[12] an extreme and categorical disjunction of God's Law and man's. The distinction between divine prescription and human adulteration and corruption thereof recurs constantly, the Woodfordian consciousness of the necessary interpenetration of the two in culture and politics being rigorously eschewed. The thrust of the sermons seems to be largely in the direction of a certain hermeneutic naïveté (or polemical shrewdness), an attempt to fix and define meaning theoretically while in practice retaining the creative prerogatives of traditional exegesis. This becomes clear in the continuation of the passage just quoted. God's Law is stated, as in *De Veritate*, to be independent of parchment and ink (thereby bypassing the complexities of textual criticism), since it consists in pure divine 'sentence'. Such 'sentence', however, is all-encompassing:

> We speke not of enke and parchemyn, but of þe sentence þat God seiþ . . . ȝif men taken more largely þes wordis þat Poule spekiþ heere for alle maner treuþis þat ben wryton in ony book, ȝet alle þese trewþus ben wryton in Godus lawe on som maner; as trewþus þat ben more nedfull ben wryton þere more expresly,[13] and trewþus not so nedfulle ben hydd þere in comun wordis. (1.481/5–16)

Augustine is cited as saying that even heresy and falsehood are contained in the comprehensiveness of the Word: 'And siþ falshede, as Austyn seiþ, is trewe in a maner, al falshede or heresye is wryton in Godus lawe. And so monye traueylon in veyn to wyte how heretykis schulden be knowone' (1.481/16–19). There is, however, a sudden change in direction: 'But schortly al þis falshede þat is vngrowndud in Godus lawe is heresye in a maner, and al heresye is such' (1.481/19–20). The category of 'groundedness in God's Law'[14] is suddenly invoked, a category which, when left as an undefined imperative, begs all problematic questions of interpretation.

In discussing Luke 15 and explaining why Jesus 'receyued frely þese synful men [publicans and sinners]', the sermon-writer explains that Christ wished to demonstrate his general lordship so that the false prelates might not deceive the populace: 'þese prelatys wolden fayn þat al Godys lawe were hangyng on hem, for to spuyle þe peple; for þanne wolde þey telle þis lawe and putte þerto false vndyrstondyng as þey myȝten hafe more wynnyng of þe peple' (1.233/28–31). This consciousness of a fallible and imposed hermeneutics often leads to exhortations to desist from 'curious' tamperings with God's word. Having related the story of the fishermen and their real and metaphorical catch from Luke 5:1–11, and explicated it literally and historically, the reader is warned:

> Hit is no nede to depen vs in this story more þan þe gospel tellith, as hit is no nede to busyen vs to wyte what hiȝte Tobies hownd;[15] hold we vs payed on þe mesure þat God hath ȝyuen vs and dreme we noht aboute newe poyntis þat þe gospel leuyth, for þis is synne of curiouste . . . (1.241/36–40)

The passage seems to be a warning against both academic speculation about perceived inadequacies or inconsistencies in the gospel narrative, and the tradition of a creative meditative exegesis filling in gaps in the biblical story such as Love's *Mirror* exemplifies. However, such dissuasions do not seem to affect the sermon-writer's own interpretative strategies, for the above passage is followed by a full-scale 'spiritual vndurstondyng', in which aspects of the fishermen's net are held to 'betoken' aspects of doctrine (1.242/49–53). The exegesis ends with: 'And mater of þis net and brekyng þerof ȝyuen men gret mater to speke Godis word, for vertuwes and vices and trewþes of þe gospel ben mater inow to preche to þe peple' (1.243/68–70). What the passages just examined underline is a theoretical disjunction of God's Law and man's, text and 'ungrounded' glossing, accompanied by, in practice, a creative or inventive hermeneutics identical to the traditional modes of interpretation.

It is this tension in the sermons, between a theoretically determinate scriptural meaning and a practical utilisation of scriptural polysemy for polemical and other purposes, that will form the focus of my analysis. The sermons certainly inherit many of Wyclif's own troubled formulations of the nature of biblical meaning. Very similar concepts are foregrounded – the 'literal' sense, *intentio auctoris*, 'reason' – to construct a coherent scheme of interpretation. At the same time the complexities in these concepts necessitate, as in Wyclif, a shift in ideological *locus* from interpretation to interpreter, a shift which I will begin by examining.

Instead of constructing a theory of 'correct' interpretation, the sermons therefore tend to focus on the 'correctness' of the interpreter's life.

The implication is that the interpreter who realises in his life the art of *recte vivendi* becomes in effect a transparent mediator of God's Word. Sermon 56 outlines the importance of deeds:

> And . . . traueleyde Powle in techyng of charyte, and teelde sixtene condicionys þat schulden folwe it; and as monye men seyn þat þei been hoole in body, monye men seyn þat þei ben in charyte . . . but ʒet þei gabben oponly as þer lyʒf schewiþ. þis lore þat Cristus scole axsuþ loueþ no gabbyngus, but þat þei don in deede as þer mowþ confessuþ. (11.7/40–8/57)

The Pope's party 'openly' fails to live the Christian life; therefore their claims to revelation must be a sham. The relevant passage bears quotation in full:

> Men schulden loke þat þei weron certeyn þat God wolde worche þus wiþ hem, byfor þei spak of þis power [to bind and to unbind] . . . for lying in such a cas smacchede a myche more synne þan was in þes disciples þat Crist reprouede so scharply . . . for þei ['prelatis'] for pruyde feynon falsely, and coueytise of worldly godys, to do þing þat þei may not do . . . For þis is fowl blasfemye þat is a fowl synne of alle oþre; as, ʒif a man put on God falsehede þat he myʒte not haue . . . It is no dreede alle þese popys þat seyn þat þei grawnton such pardowns, seyn oponly ynow þat God grawnteþ hem byfore; and ʒif God knowe hem vnworþi to haue such pardown of hym, þese popis blasfemen in God . . . And þus schulden prelatis ben war to graunte no þing in þe name of God but ʒif þei weron sykur byfore þat Godus iustise grauntede it. And þis myʒte þei not knowen but ʒif þei hadden reuelacion; and ʒif owre prelatis abyden euere such reuelacion, þei schulden disseyue fewe men or none in grauntyng of such pardownys. (11.34/100–122)

Note the movement of thought here. What is desirable is God's 'certain' approval; what is to be avoided is 'putting' or imposing on God 'falsehoods' he cannot intend; the only certain way of knowing that something is indeed granted by God's justice is 'revelation' (which of course can be claimed by anyone). 'Hypocrisy' therefore becomes the final negative criterion of judgment; for the absence of a proper inner ordering of the will in accordance with the will of God automatically implies an incapacity to receive revelation, failure in scriptural understanding and a devaluation of God's law.[16] Hence the false traditions of the Pope are the more perilous in their assumption of rightness: 'In þis laste pursewyng of owre modyr [by means of the 'new mennys lawes, as decretallys and decrees'], þat is greet and perelows, haþ anticrist muche part aȝenys Iesu Crist, and feyneþ by hypocrisye þat he haþ þe ryht part' (II.59/124–7).

In a passage in Sermon 66, the issues of right living and hermeneutics are brought to the fore. The passage begins with a recognition of the intentionalist fallacy; access to divine intention can be claimed by all interested parties.

> And as anemtis Cristus lawe þat men schuldon growndon hem inne, anticrist haþ fownde þis cautel, to seye þat it is muche false; and ȝif men seyn þat Godis lawe mut nedys be soþ to Godis entent, þei grawnton þat þis is soþ but þe entent lihȝ in hem. So, as princes of preestis, and pharisees ioynede wiþ hem, wole[n] interprete Godis lawe, aftur hem schal it be takon. (II.60/8–14)

The sermon recognises that in practice this merely means that *exposicio* is *domina* once again: 'And so þer exposicion is more in auctorite þan is text of Godis lawe' (II.60/14–15). This is followed by a direct confrontation with the power of institutionalised hermeneutics, which, to all purposes, dictates what the Bible means:

> And by þe cautel of þe feend þese ben maade myhty to þe world, and by ȝiftus þat þei ȝyuon to seculer men, and to somme clerkys, þei han monye comunes wiþ hem, and of alle maner of men; and cryon þat þus seiþ hooly chirche, to whiche we schuldon algatis trowe, and do worschipe to it . . . And þus is Cristis cause feld down for a tyme. (II.60/15–61/21)

The apparent *impasse* is then resolved by a gesture in the direction of *recte vivendi*:

> And þis rewle han monye men to iuge wel in þis mater: ȝif a man lyue riȝt lyf boþe to God and to man, and haue for hym text of Godis lawe, and wyt þat sowneþ to charyte, and symplenesse in lyuyng, wiþ forsakyng of worldly lyf, it is tokne þat þis mon haþ þe riȝt part of Iesu Crist; for anticrist draweþ euere to pruyde and coueytise. And herby may men knowe what man holdeþ wiþ anticrist. (II.61/22–28)

We seem to be given here a comprehensive catalogue of Lollard positives: right living, textual fidelity, an (Augustinian) predilection for 'charitable'

readings, simplicity of life, and a renunciation of worldly power. But as
is usual in the sermons, such principles of judgment are invoked only
to be collapsed almost immediately: 'But be war wiþ hypocrisye, for þat
bygyluþ monye men to trowe þat men ben Cristus childron, al ȝif þei ben
þe feendys lymes' (II.61 /28–30). We are back where we were: hypocrites
may display all the signs of rectitude and yet remain a deeply dissembling
'text'. Replacing the biblical text with the 'text' of the interpreter's 'real'
truth is merely substituting one unknowable for another.

This tendency of the sermons to shift the *locus* of hermeneutics from
the biblical text to the reader, means, in practical terms, a reliance on
the revelation vouchsafed to privileged Lollard readers (or, indeed, non-
readers): we enter here the realm of Lerner's 'ecstatic dissent'. In the
sermon we have been examining, one is exhorted to rely on God's kindness in one's hour of hermeneutic need:

> But algatis be we war þat we confesse not falshede, and denye not
> Cristus lawe, for no caas þat may falle. ȝif we vndirstonde not þe wyt,
> grawnte we þe forme of þe wordys, and confesse we þe trewþe of hem,
> al ȝif we wyte nat which it is. And þus fayle we not God in lif, and
> he wole not fayle vs in lore; for þus he byhotuþ þat we schal haue in
> syche howr what we schal speke. (II.62/56–61)

The above passage is informed by a hermeneutic abdication: the devout
reader merely 'believes' that the Word of God is 'true', and God does
not fail him when the need arises. The Bible is crucial to this process –
we have to 'grant' the 'form of words'; equally, by the emphasis on direct
divine inspiration, the textuality of scripture is transcended. The biblical
text is thus simultaneously given theoretical centrality and displaced
altogether.

This can result in a movement away from close analysis of text and
interpretations thereof to the detection of symptoms of hypocrisy or
(inner) right living, a movement often supporting overt polemics. In
Sermon 67, the denial of the authority of the friars becomes an outward
indication of a correct inner disposition:

> And so, by alle oþre sygnes þat þei feynon in religioun, aspye how þese
> frerus cam in, and by whois auctorite . . . And þis schulde alle men do
> in dede . . . And here may men wel assaye wher clerkis and knyȝtus,
> wiþ þer comunes, louon God as þei confesson, and doron stonde by

hys lawe; for he þat is necligent in so luytul þing for to do, wolde sone be neccligent in hardere þing of more charge. (ii.70/138–151)

There is a repeated attempt at correlating faith and deeds. Sermon 71 leaves some passages from Matt. 24 to be expounded by those chosen by God:

> for men þat ben chosone vnto blisse of heuene oþer men þat han tyme to expoune þis capitle and ben tawte of God and meuyde for to tellon it, and specially ȝif þei seen þe dede acorde wiþ þe speche, may telle more of Cristus wordis heere. (ii.93/132–6)

Sermon 121 emphasises the probability of the man living the good life being one of the blessed:

> For ȝif a man were eyr apparaunt of Englond or of Fraunce, monye men woldon do hym worschipe for þis worldly tytle; myche more ȝif a man be eir of þe blisse of heuene. And apparaunce of þis herytage is more licly to trewe men,[17] by good lif of men aftur þe lawe of Crist, þan apparaunce of worldly lordschipe by descense of heritage. (ii.314/106–11)

At the same time, there is a recognition of the ultimate unknowability of the truly righteous man. Sermon 55 acknowledges that vice and virtue are hidden: 'Al þis is hud þing, for ȝif suche men semon to doon yuele, and somme syche semon to do good, as ben many ipocrytis, neþeles þe ende is hyd of whyche þei schulden take þer name' (ii.4/81–4). Sermon 81 makes a similar point: 'And þerfore we schal vndurstande þat þer ben two goodnessis in werkys; goodnesse in kynde of werkys, and goodnesse in vertewys. þe furste may be wiþowte þe secounde...' (ii.152/71–75). Sermon 93 speaks of the dubious worth of the Church's canonisations: many of them are for 'lordschipe, or money, or fauour of partus':

> For þus may þe cowrt be blyndud in monye suche canonysyngus. Also false wytnessus proue not byfore God; why schulde we byleue þat þese wytnessus seyn soþ? Also monye syche signes þat ben holdone myraclis may be don by þe feend... what euydence is of þese, þat þis soule is in heuene? (ii.223/58–63)

Sermon 118 talks of the papal electors not knowing 'wher þei cheson a feend' (ii.306/23); and Sermon 70 speaks of sin being ever-hidden in the souls of hypocrites (II.84/52–3). Only at the day of doom will men be known in their proper colours: 'And at þe day of doom, whan bookis schal be opone, þe whiche bokis ben mennys sowlys, and conscience of hem, þanne schal boþe good and yuel knowe mennys werkys and þer þowtys' (II.43/6–8). The topos of man's soul as a book[18] here assumes an added charge: these books will achieve hermeneutic 'openness' only at the end of time.

The sermons' indecision with regard to the possibility of knowing certainly the extent of an individual's 'true' realisation of right-living is echoed in their extraordinarily protean hermeneutics. There are two major strands in the sermons' exegetical theory. One postulates an 'open' biblical text, the meaning of which is determinable in terms of an accessible authorial intention, an oft-invoked but imprecise community of belief – typically gestured towards in the phrase 'as men commonly say', and (sciential) biblical study. The other acknowledges that the scriptural text is infinite and polyvalent in signification – not 'open' but 'sutil'[19] – and will remain so from our necessarily inadequate human view-point.

The first theoretical angle finds expression in such sermons as 58. Referring to Luke 10:2 ('The harvest truly is great, but the labourers are few: pray ye therefore the Lord of the harvest, that he would send forth labourers into his harvest'), the sermon states: 'And here Crist techeþ oponly þat men schulde not buye þis offys, ne take no meede of þe puple to trauele þus in Cristus name' (II.18/50–2). Sermon 121, explaining Christ's words in John 17:14 ('I have given them thy word; and the world hath hated them, because they are not of the world, even as I am not of the world'), says: 'And þis men vndurstonden þus: þis world is alle þo men þat ben dampnyde for loue of þe world and þanne þis word of Crist is opon' (II.317/58–60).

Against this vision of an 'open' biblical language is posed the corrupt and mercenary homiletics of the friars: 'coueytise of wyckede preestis blemscheþ hem and þe puple, for comunly þei schapon þer wordis aftur þe eende þat þei coueyton' (II.19/84–6).[20] Grammarians are also to blame; along with the philosophers they are responsible for devaluing the intrinsic truth of Christ's words, suggesting instead that their glosses are to be honoured. Sermon 56 refers to Matt. 12:49–50 ('Behold my mother and my brethren' [Christ referring to his disciples]) the metaphoricity of which is mocked by corrupt literalists:

> þes wordis of Crist ben scornyde of grammaryens and dyuynus. Gramariens and philosofrus seyen þat Crist knew not his gendris, and bastard dyuynes seyen þat þes wordis of Crist ben false; and so no wordis of Crist bynden but to þe wyt þat glosours tellon. (II.280/13–17)

The sermon proceeds to dismiss such savants as heretics and fools, and instead offers 'som wyt þat God haþ 3ouen vs' (II.280/19). Christ's intention is explicated next:

> And þus telluþ Crist a sutylte þat is of gostly breþren in God; for be it man or be it womman, þat serueþ God trewly, he is on þes þre maners knyt to Crist... Furst he is Cristus broþer by his soule... siþ he is Cristus suster by hys flesch... and aftur he is Cristus modyr by þis hool kynde maad of hem two. (II.280/22–281/28)

The interpretative theory underlying such exegeses is best formulated in Sermon 67's description of the *modus operandi* of the Word: 'It is seyd ofte-tymes þat maner of speche of Godis lawe is to denye þe instrument, and to graunte þe pryncipal' (II.66/33–34).[21] The ideal interpreter is an instrument denied (and self-denied) – he is entirely transparent, mediating openly an open text: 'tellon oponly his [God's] trewþe, and susteynon his lawe to men' (II.85/73–4).

The postulation of an open text, and the theoretical devaluation of glossing, result in a stress on the sentential unity of the Bible (interpretation becomes conceptually central otherwise, if the text is self-contradictory and fissured). Sermon 78: 'And it may falle ful wel þat Crist in diuerse tymes seyde dyuerse parablus, þe whiche weron of lych sentences' (II.129/2–4); Sermon 87: 'but o þing we trowon as byleue, þat no gospel contraryeþ þe oþur, and no part of þe gospel is false, but yche part acorduþ to oþur' (II.187/20–22); Sermon 91: 'eche part of þis resoun [the Word] bytokneþ þe same trewþe' (II.215/33). The gospels are all of the same sentence despite factual variations (II.300/44–301/50).[22]

'False glosus' (II.130/22) are opposed to this essentialist vision of biblical truth. The implied assumption of God's-eye view in postulating a single, unified scriptural sentence outside the domain of glossing, finds explicit expression in Sermon 78:

> And þe story of þe gospel [Luke 19:28] telluþ how Crist, whanne he
> hadde seyd þese wordus, wente byfor oþur men and steyȝede into
> Ierusalem. And þis bytokneþ þat þis sentence, al ȝif it be scorned here
> in erþe, ȝeet it is kept saf in heuene, and is aboue mannys power.
> (II.134/126–30)

A non-literal reading of the scriptural passage is here used to underline
its transcendence of the realm of human interpretation. The 'truth' of
God's law is thus independent of the contingencies of human experience
and belief: 'For al ȝif anticrist haue browt a lawe þat lettuþ þe vse of
Godus lawe, ȝet þe trewþe of Godus lawe, and þe dette to vse it, lastuþ
euermore, and bynduþ men ful harde' (II.147/147–150).

The complexities of biblical language – typically, those of its metaphoricity – and of the textual transmission of the Bible are therefore
disregarded *sub specie aeternitatis*.

> And as we schulden haue byleue þat alle Cristus wordus mote nede
> be trewe, so we schulden haue byleue þat þis sentence [Luke 2:18: the
> shepherds' narration of their vision of the angel announcing Christ's
> birth] was seyd of Crist, whiche sentence is told to us by figurus and by
> mannys writyng. And þis is þe leeste byleue þat we schulden haue in
> al owre feiþ . . . We schulde not trowe in þis enke, ne in þese skynnys
> þat is clepud booc, but in þe sentence þat þei seyen, whiche sentence
> is þe booc of lyf; for al ȝif þer ben manye trewþus and diuerse resonys
> in þe gospelus, neþeles eche of þes trewþus is þe substaunce of God
> hymself.[23] (II.226/14–227/24)

Note the suggestive coupling of 'figures' (both 'signs' and 'metaphors')[24]
and 'man's writing', for the domains of the sign, especially the complex,
metaphorical sign, and that of textual transmission, are precisely those
which are most resistant to an essentialist vision of meaning. The sign
demands the agency of the human interpreter, and the physicality of
the biblical text is subject to worldly mutability. Metaphor is unfixed in
signification, demanding human completion of meaning; and the same
is true of the text as ink and parchment.

Opposed to the contingent vision of meaning based on uncertain significations and textualities is the sermons' reliance on 'expressness' and
intentionality. The parable of the Wedding Feast (Luke 14:8–11) does

not make perfect sense literally; therefore Christ is speaking here figuratively: 'Here we schal vndyrstonde þat Crist spekiþ not here of worldly feste, ne of place, for þanne his sentence were noht . . . And herfore schulde we vndyrstande þat þis feeste ys þe laste soper' (1.288/28–33). Again, introducing a reading of John 4:46–53 (the healing of the son of the nobleman from Capernaum) as a comment on 'mannys wit by synne slydon fro God', the sermon-writer refers to God's ordained meaning: 'þis story seiþ vs þis secownde wit þat God ӡyueþ to hooly writ' (1.306/33).

The emphasis on divine intentionality is one of the *foci* of the sermons' hermeneutics. The loaves and fishes of John 6 should be interpreted as the Pentateuch and the books of Wisdom and the Prophets, because 'þe goostly foode is purposyd of Crist for to be tooknyd by bodyly foode' (1.324/54–56). Again, the spiritual interpretation of Luke 21:25 is justified thus: 'But, for þat Crist haþ ordeynut hit, þes wordis of Crist may be vndurstanden goostly' (1.332/50–51). Christ's intention is referred to frequently. In Matthew 8:10, 'Crist mente not of his apostles, ne of his modyr, ne of his meyne' (1.366/58–59), and the travailing woman in John 16:21 is read as 'owre modir hooly chirche' in consonance, we are assured, 'to Cristus entent' (1.444/32–33). Associated with this is the sermons' attempt to localise and fix Christ's metaphorical meanings. Sermon 103: '*And Jesu seyde to hym: "I am weyӡe, trewþe and liӡf"* [John 14:6]; as ӡif he wolde mene to cristene men, knowe ӡe me and loue ӡe me, and ӡe knowen alle þes þingus' (II.260/50–261/52). Sermon 111 has: '"*May ӡe two drynke*", seiþ Crist, "*þe chalis þat I schal drynke*" [Matt. 20:22] and wiþoute drede Crist vudurstod by þis chalis his passion' (II.283/30–32). Sermon 117 has:

> But here [John 12:31] schal we vndurstonde þat al þat God haþ ordeyned to peyne mote nedis be dampnede in helle, but monye bygylude by þe feend weron ordeyned of God to turne to Crist . . . And to þis entent spekuþ Crist in þe word þat comeþ aftur; *þat ӡif he be hyӡed fro þe erþe he schal drawe alle þingus to hymself* [John 12:32]. No doute Crist spekuþ here of his passion of þe cros for þanne Crist is hyӡed from þe erþe to monye vudurstondyngus. (II.303/24–31)

It is indicative of the sermons' abiding hermeneutic self-consciousness that entirely commonplace interpretations of the biblical texts are here given such intentionalist and theoretical body: the consolidatory phrases 'no doubt' and 'to many understandings' are added when – one would have thought – a plain reference to John 12:33 ('This he said, signifying what death he should die'), which is provided a few lines later, would have been enough justification.[25]

The intentionalist thrust of such passages is legitimate within a theoretical framework which postulates that 'euery part of holy wryt telluþ Godus word, þe olde lawe in fygure, and þe gospel expressely' (II.167/18–19). This movement in the direction of hermeneutic certitude also finds what at first sight appears to be another, related mode of expression. However, as I will go on to argue, though rhetorically performing a similar function, this second constituent of the sermons' positivist hermeneutics is built on quite different premisses. Repeatedly through the sermons, reference is made, generally as a mode of hermeneutic consolidation, to an undefined body of 'men' or 'clerks' who, it is suggested though never specified, constitute a valid interpretative community.

Sermon 68, discussing Luke 6:17, says: 'And so men seyn comunly þat men sewedon Crist for fyue causys' (II.71/14–5); and Sermon 73, interpreting Matt. 24:2, says: 'And by þes wordus takon men þat Crist telde luytul by þe temple' (II.100/17–8). Other examples are provided by Sermon 71:

> [Interpreting Matt. 24:24- 'For there shall arise false clerks and false prophets'] And heere it semeþ to monye men þat Crist spac of þis tyme in whiche þese two popis fiȝton þus togydere; for siþ Crist is alwytty, and loueþ wel his chirche, and telluþ in Apocalipse of monye lasse perelus, why schulde he not tellon of þis, þat is so perelows? And clerkis han a rewle, þat a word seyd by hymself schulde be vndurstonden for þe more famous. (II.91/90–94)

Sermon 83:

> [Interpreting Matt. 10:5] þes wordus moton be wel vndurstondene to þe wyt þat God spekuþ hem; for Crist hymself wente ofte-times to gentiles and Samaritans ... And so men seyn comunly þat Crist here forbed goyng into þe weyȝe of gentile folc; but he forbed not to go to hem. (II.161/17–162/27)

The last two passages are particularly interesting: both start from the theoretical authority of the text, and of the divine intention, however interpreted; both end with the invocation of the authority of an extra-textual interpretative community. In itself, such invocation would not have been worthy of particular notice; it does stand out, however, in the context of a heresy so insistent on the denial of the hermeneutic authority of various traditional interpretative communities. Anne Hudson has pointed out how Lollards use the phrase 'many men think/say/feel' to introduce controversial beliefs; and Christina von Nolcken has emphasised Lollard reliance on generalising phrases to describe themselves.[26] However, as Hudson recognises, such references to the opinion of 'men' occur not just in controversial contexts.[27] My reading suggests that Lollard writers use these phrases not only to signal specific unorthodox beliefs but also as a more general gesture in the direction of an interpretative community, and its implied hermeneutic authority. Such a gesture does on occasion expose fundamental disjunctions in Lollard thought on the issue of the precise locus of textual authority: does it inhere in the biblical words, or in the interpretative authority of a reading community? For instance, when discussing the relevance and worth of celebrating the feasts of saints canonised by the Roman Church, a sermon says:

> But siþ þes seyntus be not expressud in þe lawe of holy writ, men be not holdene to trowe expressely þat þese ben seyntus in heuene; for aftur þat trewþe is in hooly wryt schulde men trowe þis trewþe.
>
> And so, as it is ofte seyd, holy wryt conteneþ alle trewþe; som trewþe expressely, and þat schilde men þus trowe; and som trewþe pryuely, and þat schulde men trowen in comun. (II.224/73–79)

There would seem to be here an invocation of a 'common' tradition of faith based on the non-express, 'pryue trewþes' of scripture perilously similar to the tradition endorsed by the Roman Church itself: a set of long-established and commonly held beliefs whose very commonality is a symptom of their truth, such truth being simultaneously granted an oblique grounding in the Bible. Rhetorically, such an invocation is acceptable – yet another argument in favour of whichever 'open' interpretation is being advanced. In terms of hermeneutics, however, such a gesture in the direction of 'tradition' opens the way to recognising the emphatically this-worldly constitution of what is in theory an other-worldly text. But we shall return to the issue later.

The third important strain in what I describe as the 'consolidatory' or 'positivist' aspect of Lollard hermeneutics (i.e. its emphasis on a non-problematic and accessible biblical meaning) relates to biblical scholarship, with an interest in 'circumstantial' readings. Sermon 18, discussing Matt. 10:34 ('I came not to send peace, but a sword') justifies its pacifist glossing of the passage thus: 'for comunly in holy wryt is swerd clepud "word"; and þis is a swerd scharp on boþe sydes, boþe to kerue awey synne, and to norsche vertewys' (ii.94/9–11). Again, in Sermon 166, the Lollard vision of the Eucharist is defended cleverly in terms of other biblical passages:

> It is seyd þat autour of alle seiþ þat his lore is not his, for it is not his principaly but it is Goddis þat sente hym [John 7:16]. And sumtyme Crist spekiþ by his manhed, and sum tyme he spekiþ in forme of his godhed. And wolde God þes heretikis in mater of þe sacrid oost conseyueden þis speche, and vndirstonden wel Ambrose þat þis oost is not bred aftir þat it is sacrid, for it is not aftir principaly bred but þe body of Crist by uertu of his wordis, and þanne shulden þey shame of þer feyned accidentis.[28] (iii.131/8–16)

Again, discussing John 15:26–7, verses interpreted by the Greeks to 'trowe þat þe Hooly Goost comeþ not forþ but of þe Fadur, and not of Crist þat is his Sone; for þe ton seiþ Crist and in þis gospel leueþ þe toþur...' (i.460/21–3), the sermon-writer refers to John 8:28:

> And to þis þat Grekys seyn þat Crist leueþ þis word, certis so doþ he manye oþre for certeyn cause, and ȝeet we trowon hem. As Crist seiþ þat his lore is not his, for hit is principally his Fadris, and ȝeet we trowon þat hit is hys, but þe welle is in his Fadur. (i.460/38–461/42)

Such an interest in reading one biblical passage in terms of another is not merely polemical. In Sermon 113, the word 'castle' in Luke 10:38 is explained as a 'walled town': 'for ofte-tymes þe gospel clepuþ siche wallude townys castelus' (ii.289/5–6).

There is, moreover, a heightened consciousness of 'text', and a desire to present the more abstruse interpretations as 'according' to the text: 'þe secownde vndurstondyng of þis parable of Crist is more sutyl and trauelows, and acordyng wiþ þe tixt' (ii.125/49–50). Interpreting John 1:27, Sermon 29 says:

> And herfore seiþ Iohn þat *he is not worþi to lowse þe þwong of Cristes scho*, and þis men vndyrstonden þus þat Baptist is not worþi to declare

Cristes manhede. But as me þinkiþ hit is betture and more sewynge þis gospel to seye þat Iohn grauntiþ hym not worþi to lowse þe ordre of Crist, by whyche Crist hadde ordeynet to be patrown of cristen men, for þis ordre is a þwong to bynde mennys wille togedre. (1.343/68–74)

The highly subjective and interested interpretation of the gospel passage – Christ's 'order' must not be violated by inventing new private religions – is described as somehow 'better' and more importantly, as more faithful to ('sewynge') the text.

There are several injunctions to the effect that the Bible should not be amended: both the 'words' and the 'wit' of Holy Writ must be kept, 'for no man schulde presume to amende holy wryt, but kepe it in þe forme þat God hymself haþ 3ouen it' (11.1 68/25–7). Fundamentally positivistic in their attitude to meaning, they can acknowledge the possibility of misinterpretations without giving rise to unsurmountable anxieties. Sermon 92 points out that even the apostles went wrong: 'And so wordus þat ben wel seyde may li3tly be takon amys, siþ þe apostlus tokon amys þis word of Crist so pleynly seyd'. Yet the recognition of the facility of interpretative error is left behind quite easily: 'Lord! siþ þese wordus of Crist may be wel þus vndurstonden, what schulde meue ony man to take false wyt by hem?' (11.219/39–220/54).[29]

The only major anxiety relates to the misuse of *scientia*; for the sermons are keenly aware of the facility of intellectual abuse, originating in vanity or *curiositas*. A stock phrase is therefore: 'Muse we not . . .', 'musing' being synonymous with fallen intellectual curiosity. Sermon 120 exhorts us to leave behind 'gramarienys dou3tys' (11.310/7); the same sermon warns against idle speculation: 'Recke we not who þis man was, ne trowe we not to mannys talis þat þis was Marcial, or Iohn, or anoþer apostle' (11.310/16–18). The sermons are uneasy in their attitude towards logic. Generally dismissing it as the corrupt province of 'clerks' and 'sophisters',[30] they occasionally, and self-consciously, resort to learned grammatical or logical argument. Sermon 56 attempts to explain Christ's words to his apostles in John 15:15 ('Henceforth I call you not servants') by distinguishing between two classes of servants, servants of condition and servants of ministry, the latter category being further subdivided into servants of outward service and servants of both outward service and of privy counsels. The apostles were servants in the latter sense and not in the former: 'And by þis equiuocation may

men lyȝtly acorden Cristus lawe; for, as clerkys wyton wel ynow, con-
tradiccion is not only in wordys' (II.9/73–75).³¹ Sermon 63 seems to be
endorsing (ironically?) logical study for those who do not quite understand the intricacies of the philosophy of 'accidents': 'þese foolis muten
lerne predicamentis and ten kyndus of þingus, and þanne þei may see þer
folyes' (II.45/57–59). In Sermon 82, the fiend is shown to be trapped in
an *insolubilis*: he loses both when man is able to resist his temptations
and even when man fails to do so, for each lost soul does not add to his
glory, 'but more to his dampnacioun'; the fiend is thus 'concludede in
insolible' (II.159/151–160/161).³²

Generally, however, the sermons are critical of intellectual speculation outside strictly defined limits.³³ Theoretically – and there is of
course a huge gulf between theory and practice – all the sermons should
have been written on the model of sermons 104, 163 or 167, consisting as they do largely of translation and paraphrase with only a
minimum amount of commentary. The naked text is offered without
the apparatus of interpretative handmaidens who threaten to assume
dominium.

The characteristics of Lollard hermeneutics outlined so far – intentionality, 'common opinion', *circumstancia litterae* – feed into its overt
theory postulating an 'open' biblical text with accessible and determinate meanings. There is, however, an equally prominent but radically
different emphasis in the sermons: on the unfathomable complexity and
multivalence of the Bible. As we saw with Lollard faith in human ability
to judge of an individual's participation in *recte vivendi*, there is a basic
uncertainty in Lollard visions of scriptural meaning. The 'mysty' speech
of Christ is often pointed to (II.22/25); reference to the 'harde' parables
of Christ is frequent (II.38/51–52); there are problematic invocations
of the 'plenteous' wit of God's Word. The possibility of alternative interpretations is sometimes acknowledged implicitly ('þis story of Crist
may bytokene', I.297/20), sometimes explicitly.

> And þus eche story of myracles of Crist may be moralisyd to a good
> witt. Ne hit is no perele to varien in suche wittis, so þat men varye
> not fro trewþe ne fro good lore, for þe Holy Gost, auctour of þese
> wordis, ordeynyth men to haue alle syche wittes; and he ordeyneþ þis
> tixt to meuen hem herto. How scholde such sense ben errour in man?
> But suche wordes axen good iugement, for manye eretykes seyn þat

þei han witt of God, and ȝet hit may ben on of þe fendis eresyes. (1.319/59–66)

It should be noted how this passage attempts to forge a hermeneu-tic *aurea mediocritas* between an extreme Wycliffite position of 'literal' meanings and divine intentionality, and a traditional position of inter-pretative polysemy such as that articulated by Abelard[34] or, as we shall see in the next chapter, by Nicholas Love. But whereas Love focusses on the knowing subject's interpretative 'desire', the sermon-writer empha-sises the divine 'ordination' of men to have 'alle syche wittes'. There is moreover an important codicil which lands us firmly in the hermeneu-tic dead-end: false interpreters can always claim that they know God's meaning, when in reality they are of the devil's party.[35] The quality that the worthy interpreter should possess is that of 'good judgment', a quality left without further clarification.

Occasionally, there are passages where several interpretations of the same biblical text are offered with the implication that all are equally acceptable. On John 6:6–11:

> As philosophres seyn þese mesures of þese vesselis ben þe olde cery-monyes, þat weren bedon of God, and somme fownden of Iewis; and alle þese weren fullyd of Crist. But to anoþur wit þis architriclyn was þe manhede of Crist, for he made þis miracle by his godhede. (1.363/71–5)

This approach is of course traditional; so is the passage on the significant obscurity of biblical language:

> And so Crist telluþ in parables his wyt for manye causis: furst for men unworþie to knowen hit ben blynde by derk speche,[36] moreouer for men, þat traueylen more medfully, and bettur prenteþ þer wyt þusgate. (1.389/114–118)

Such an unpolemical acknowledgement of the 'derkness' of biblical lan-guage fits in well with an equally unproblematic espousal of the tra-ditional shell-kernel model of interpretation. 'But hit were to wyte þe moral sence of þese wordes, siþ þis curnel is more swete þan sence of þe story' (1.403/60–61), says the sermon-writer of Matthew 15:21–8, before offering an extended spiritual interpretation of the woman of Canaan as 'þe substaunce of mannys sowle' (1.403/65).

The conflict between the 'open' and 'dark' visions of scripture informs Sermon 50. Arguing for the essential unity of the Trinity on the basis of Christ's words 'All things that the Father hath are mine: therefore said I, that he [the Holy Ghost] shall take of mine, and shall shew it unto you' [John 16: 15], there is a desire to present the divine words as unenigmatic, 'open', while paradoxically acknowledging their need for elucidation:

> But siþ þis word of Crist is soþ, hit scheweþ oponly þat Crist is God; and of hym wiþ hise Fadur comeþ forþ þe Hooly Goost. þis Hooly Goost may not be maad but euere comeþ forþ of þese two, as ʒif þe schynyng of þe sonne come forþ euere of liʒt and briʒtnesse. But for þis sentence ys myche hyd fro wyt of þe comune puple, þerfore schulden preestis schapon of þe wordys of þis gospel wat myte profiʒte to his puple aftur vndurstondyng of hem. (1.451/72–79)

The passage combines Lollard emphases on an open, accessible biblical sentence with an apparently traditional, indeed reactionary adherence to a theory of pastoral rhetoric which regards the gospel as a difficult text to be 'shaped' by the priest into 'profitable' pellets for the unlearned.[37] However, this conservatism is less problematic than it seems, for the passage, though seemingly articulating a rhetorical, indeed hierarchical vision of meaning, actually relies on a concept of the 'good' interpreter as a transparent medium which merely clarifies and renders intelligible pre-existent meaning, but does not, in any real sense, constitute, create or determine such meaning. The 'priest-people' hierarchy is only apparent, for what is operative here is the notion of what Rita Copeland has called the Lollard 'horizontal classroom' in which exegete and 'pupil' work together – at least in theory – in an environment of 'hermeneutical communalism'[38] as the devoted *ancillae* of the 'open' Word of God.

The sermons' theorisations of their interpretative premises, values and practices thus refuse, perhaps inevitably, to fall into place as coherent visualisations of a new hermeneutics, clearly distinguished from the excesses and corruptions of the old. Such indeed is the informing polemic, but an examination of hermeneutic practice complicates the question of the sermons' self-understanding. Let us look at a few substantial exegetical passages. Sermon 62 discusses Christ's words in Luke 14:31–2:[39]

> Dyuerse men vndyrstonde þis tixt to dyuerse wyttis byneþe byleue, but we were wont to tellon it þat eche man schulde ben a kyng and gouerne

þe rewme of his sowle by kepyng of ten comaundements . . . þe toþur kyng wiþ twenty þowsynde, is comunly seyd þe feend, for Ioob seiþ þat he is kyng vpon alle children of pruyde . . . And ʒif þese ten þowsynde ben alle þo þat helpon Godus part, and þese twenty þowsynde alle þo þat louen dowbulnesse to helpe þe feend, it semeþ not aʒenys Godys wyt, siþ his wordys ben plenteuous. (II.39/92–40/106)

Note how the passage, beginning with an acknowledgement of hermeneutic variability (leading to some meanings being found 'beneath belief', i.e., readings which cannot be considered as part of 'express faith' but may be accepted as pious opinion), proceeds to the sermon's own interpretation, the only justification offered for the latter being a vague reference to custom – 'wont to tellen it'/'commonly said' – and a quite unconvincing gesture in the direction of circumstantial reading: Job describes the fiend as a king. At the end, one returns to a world of uncertainty, this time conceptualised positively: the Word is rich in different kinds of signification.

In Sermon 71 (II.88–93), passages from which I have already examined, the theoretical desperation of the sermons comes to the fore. There is a profound urge theoretically to defend interpretative practice, an urge that – given the fluid and polemical nature of the interpretations offered – issues in the presentation of a highly conflicted hermeneutics. Sermon 71 is based on Matt. 24, a locus classicus for apocalyptic readings. First, there is an invocation of *intentio auctoris*; we are told that Christ is 'all-witty', and therefore foretold present tribulations in Matt. 24:24: 'And heere it semeþ to monye men þat Crist spac of þis tyme in whiche þese two popis fiʒton þus togydere; for siþ Crist is al-wytty, and loueþ wel his chirche, and telluþ in Apocalipse of monye lasse perelus, why schulde he not tellon of þis, þat is so perelows?' (II.91/90–94). This is followed by an attempt at historical justification of the interpretation – 'And herfore seiþ Crist in þe same chapitre þat þer schal be þanne greet tribulacion, what maner was neuere fro þe bygynnyng of þe world til now, and schal not be aftur' (II.91/97–100); then comes a reference to the impossibility of knowing which of the two popes is worthy of damnation – it is suggested that they both are (II.91/103–92/105). Christ's 'open' law banning warfare is then cited (II.92/112–3); another reference is made to the hermeneutic opacity of the hypocrites who rule the Church (II.92/117–120).

This is followed by a passage describing how the other words in Matt. 24 can 'be applyed to þis [present] tribulacion' (II.92/130–1). The notion of 'applied' meanings is important, for it refers to the tradition of self-consciously reading *into* the Bible relevant meanings, dependent on the needs and intentions of the interpreter.[40] Though, in theory, such meanings could be thought of as intended by God in the plenitude of his knowledge, they could, in practice, constitute precisely the kind of corrupt 'glosynge' so derided by the Lollards. It is fascinating to note how the Lollard exegete, in a fashion very similar to that of Wyclif, ends by using hermeneutic techniques elsewhere strenuously disavowed.[41] The sermon we have been examining then goes on to leave other possible meanings to be found by those inspired by God, as long as their words and deeds accord; and it ends with the exhortation: 'But hold we us in byleue of which we ben certeyn' (II.93/132–7). The final capitulation almost acknowledges the sermon's own rhetoricity: 'reasons' have been marshalled to support its polemic, reasons ultimately recognised to be less than absolutely reliable and therefore obliquely dismissed.

The semantic polyvalence on which the sermon we have been reading bases its polemic elsewhere leads to an intellectual abdication. Sermon 81 on Luke 11:35–6:

> And, for þes derke wordus of Crist makon monye men to muse, men sekon dyuerse weyȝes to vndurstonde Cristus wordus... Howeuere Crist vndurstood, we byleuon þese wordus ben soþe, and ful of resoun and wyt, knowon to hem þat he wole schewe hyt. (II.153/115–122)

Such passages are not informed by any theory of reading; instead, they lay emphasis on divine inspiration. By itself, this would have been traditional and unproblematic; the difficulty, as in Wyclif, is that Lollard theory tends at the same time to valorise intellectual study, as evidenced not only in the sermons themselves, but also in such Lollard aids to study as the *Glossed Gospels*.

The key word in the 'negative' hermeneutics is 'sutil', for 'sutilte' is opposed to 'openness'. The sermons' general emphasis on the non-hierarchical intellectual accessibility of the Bible (after all, as we have seen in Chapter 3, one of the main conservative arguments against translation was that the 'lewed', unpossessed of the requisite intellectual equipment, would not understand and would therefore be led into heresy) is therefore severely qualified when it is a case of explicating 'subtle' biblical words. Sermon 86 suggests that the Bible, even in its inception, is not an unproblematically 'open' text: 'Nathanael was a wys man, and þerfore spac Crist more sutylly [John 1: 47–8], for, as Poul seiþ, we spekon wysdam among wyse men' (II.181/79–80). An anxious consciousness of biblical polysemy informs this 'sutil' vision of the Word. In Sermon 96, Matt. 2:20–3 is discussed:

> Bysyde lettre of þis gospel may men moue doutus of scole: but me þinkuþ now it is betture to touche lore of vertewys. We schal byleue þat al þe gospel, be it neuere so literal, techeþ what þing schal byfalle, and how þat men schal lyue. (II.234/38–41)

This is followed by a moral application: as Christ was pursued by the devil, so true men are persecuted now. One cannot assume that one is of God's party, but persecution is a fair symptom that one probably is. The cowardly give in to a 'false peace' with the 'men of this world' and the fiend; conversely, the absence of such apparent 'peace' 'is sygne to many þat God loueþ hym'. The sermon ends:

> Eche word of þis gospel may be toold to þis entent; but it suffisuþ to haue þe roote, and goo liȝtly to oþre wyttis. And muse we not how þis kyngdam cam from Archilaus to Eroude, for ȝif it hadde be profiȝtable, God wolde haue tolde it in his lawe. And so monye trewþus proȝfite more whil þei ben vnknowe to men þan þei schulden profiȝte knowon, as Godus lawe techeþ us. (II.235/62–67)

The passages just cited exemplify the characteristic movement of the sermons from the hermeneutics of text – here suggesting that the 'literal' includes the tropological and the anagogical, without any directive as to how these other senses are to be discerned – to the hermeneutics of salvation. For the validity of one's interpretation depends on the possibility of one's salvation. There is at the end a movement back to the text: an ambiguous reference to 'entent' (could be both authorial and/or lectoral); a positivist emphasis on getting the 'root' of a text;[42] an embarrassed, slightly awkward transition to the other (rhetorical) senses (one trips over to them 'liȝtly'); a penultimate warning against curious speculative 'musing' implying that the sermon's own interpretation has been anything but that; and a final undeveloped reference to the profitability of unknown truths. Scriptural polysemy thus constitutes an abiding theoretical crux in the sermons: it is both acknowledged and disavowed. Sermon 97, explicating the multiple 'wits' of the story of the magi's gifts, refers, unexpectedly, to the 'better' wit of the Church. A 'common-sense' interpretation of the gold (i.e. money), myrrh (i.e. ointment) and incense (i.e. fragrance to drown the stench of the stable) is followed by a more recondite reading: 'But me þinkuþ þat þe wyt is betture þat þe chirche synguþ of þis; in gold ys Cristus regalye, in incence his presthede, and in myrre his sepulture' (II.238/71–239/74). As usual, it is left unexplained why the Church's wit should be 'better' in this particular case.

Sermon 98 addresses the dangers of a strictly literalist interpretation. Peter's words from Matt. 19:27 ('Behold, we have forsaken all and followed thee') are the source of the problem here. Peter, strictly speaking, cannot be saying the truth: as a poor fisherman, he had very little, and by no means everything to forsake; moreover, he did not forsake the Trinity.

> How approueþ Crist þes false wordus of Petre? Here it semeþ to monye men þat Petre vndurstod þus, þat þei forsokon alle þingus, for alle þes worldly goodus, siþ þei heldon þer bussynesse, and þer wylle, fro þes goodis. And þis wyt mente Crist in his speche aftur to Petre. And þus bidduþ Crist, in Luc and Iohn, to forsake and hate seuene goodis, and þes wordus may serue wel to þis vndyrstondyng. (II.240/10–16)

Christ's own words in Matt.19:29 ('And everyone that hath forsaken houses, or brethren, or sisters . . . shall receive an hundredfold') give rise to similar literalist problems:

> And þanne may we telle scorne by suche asse argumentis, ȝif a man schal haue here an hundredfoold so good þing as is þis wyf, þanne he schal haue an hundred wyues. Kepe we wordus of þe gospel, and þe wit of it þerwiþ, and alle þe feendus or false men may not disproue a word þerof.[43] (II.243/85–90)

The word-wit conflict is both recognised and displaced, the *décalage* traced through the sermon being collapsed at the end.

The sermons thus vacillate between two hermeneutic systems: one postulating an 'open', anti-hierarchical and accessible text, the other acknowledging that the often obscure scriptures require 'myche special declaryng' (I.521/14–5). The sermon-writers seem to be undecided between a vision of God's Word as infinite in significance because of the unfathomable polysemy of the divine intention ('We reproue not þis wyt, for God is large in his lore', 1.550/41), and God's Word as an ultimately limited signifier whose meaning can be grasped with certainty through an understanding of the 'entent' of the Holy Ghost: 'And wolde God þat heretykes in mater of þe sacred oost kowden vndurstonde þis sutyl wordis and soþe, to þe entent of þe Holy Ghost!' (1.531/64–66).

The same indeterminacy underlies the discussion of the topos of fourfold interpretation. Sermon 19 offers a traditional and unproblematic account of the four senses of scripture (1.556/16–557/22). But this account occurs in the context of a discussion of Paul's interpretation of Abraham's two sons, one by a bondmaid, the other by a freewoman (Gal. 4:22–4) as the two covenants of Sinai and Jerusalem, and continues: 'Poul swiþ here þe secounde [allegorical] wit, and he hadde auctorite þerto' (II.557/22–3). It appears that the second, third and fourth wits require special authorisation. The sermon goes on to say that: 'Poul as a good doctour feyneþ no fable by mannys wit, but he seiþ þat it is writon in þe lawe of oure byleue' (1.557/30–1). The implication, surely, is that 'unauthorised' spiritual interpretations belong to the domain of 'mannys wit'. But who is to determine which biblical passages authorise or dictate a four-fold interpretation, and which do not?

The one general principle offered in this context suggests that 'spiritual' interpretations are called for only when reading passages from the Old Testament, the New Testament demanding a 'literal' reading. The crucial 2 Cor. 3:6 ('for the letter killeth, but the spirit giveth life'), is interpreted in such a way that it discountenances modern emphases on 'spiritual' interpretations: Paul was merely pointing to the difference between the 'figural' ceremonies of the Old Law, and the 'graceful' ceremonies of the New (1.652/38–42). The sermon-writer points to the fact that the devaluation of the letter results in practice in a glossator's corrupt paradise:

> And heere anticristis truauntis spekyn aȝen þe newe lawe, and seyen þat literal witt of it shulde neuere be takun but goostly witt; and þei feynen þis goostli witt aftir shrewed wille þat þei haue.[44] And þus þes foure sectis ben aboute to distrye literal witt of Goddis lawe; and þis shulde be þe first and þe moste bi whiche þe chirche shulde be reulid. And aȝenus þis witt anticrist argueþ many weyes: 'þat hooli writ is

fals bi þis bi many partis of holi writt, and so þer is anoþer witt þan þis
literal witt þat þou hast ȝouen, and þis is a mysti witt, þe whiche Y
wole chese to ȝyue'. And þus fayliþ autorite of hooli writt bi anticrist.
(1.652/44–653/53)

Perverse hermeneusis is seen to arrogate to itself the authority of the
Holy Ghost. 'Letter killeth' applies only to the Old Law, for with the
coming of the new dispensation, it is necessary to interpret the Hebraic
law 'goostli'. The words of the New Testament are already 'spiritual';
they have already fulfilled the figures of the Old Testament – therefore
they should be read literally.

> But Poul seyþ to þis entent *þat lettre* in þe tyme of grace þat is takun of
> þe oolde lawe, and holden þat it shulde euere laste, as it lasted for þat
> tyme, *sleeþ* men goostli; for it lettiþ men of bileue þat þei ben now nerr
> to blis þan þei weren in þe oolde lawe bi comyng of Crist in tyme of
> grace. But leeue we þes heresyes and bileue we þat many þyngis were
> bedyn to fadris of þe olde lawe in fygure of þyngis in time of grace; and
> þis figure schal be goostli knowen, for ellis literal vndirstondyng wole
> slee mennus soulis bi vnbileue. But *spiritual* vndirstondyng *quykeneþ*
> mennus soulis bi ryȝt bileue. And, ȝif þou wilt knowe þe ground to
> iuge of þes vndurstondyngis, bigynne at cristen mennus bileue, and
> trowe þat Crist haþ now lyued heere, as it was fygurid in þe oolde lawe,
> and abide it not as ȝit to come. And so eche word of þe newe lawe
> þat souneþ to uertues of Crist and to charite of his chirche schulde be
> takun aftir þe lettre. (1.653/53–68)

This is of course a perfectly conventional account of ideal interpretation, based on medieval Christian topoi about the *modus significandi*
of the Old Testament.[45] But even here, there are problems. Apart from
the fact that the discussion does not address the issue of spiritual or
apocalyptic interpretations of the New Testament, the 'ground' of our
scriptural readings is here held to be 'Christian men's belief' and the
'charite of [Christ's] chirche', which, in this instance, are treated as self-
explanatory, indeed as constituting an evident and reliable standard of
judgment independent of postlapsarian human waywardness. But such
is not always the case. Despite their attempt to postulate such categories
of the supra-mundane and yet recognisable good, the sermons often
show a striking awareness of the dangers of the postlapsarian condition:
the divine can and indeed is clouded over, distorted and made into

something other by corrupt and *powerful* human volition: '[Priests and pharisees] seyn þat Godis lawe is false, but ʒif þei gloson hit after þat þei wolen; and þus þer *gloos schulde be trowed as byleue of cristen men*, but þe tixt of Godis lawe is perelous to trowe' (1.424/16–425/19; italics mine). The sermon proceeds to point out that, for the fallen glossers, heretics are defined as those who are against them, even when such 'trew men' are only enunciating God's law:

> But God wolde þat þese [secular] lordes passedon Pilate in þis poynt and knewon þe trewþe of Godis lawe in þer modyr tonge, and haue þese two folc [priests and pharisees] suspecte for þer cursed lyuyng and huydyng of Godys lawe fro knowyng of seculeris; for by þis cautel of the feend ben manye trewe men qwenchede, for þei wolen iuge for heretykes alle þat spekon aʒeynes hem – ʒe, ʒif þei tellon Godys lawe and schewe synnes of þese two folc. (1.425/36–42)

The false interpreters and opponents of God's law are seen to be part of a corrupt political establishment which uses its worldly power to hinder a just and popular dissemination of God's law:

> And þus doon owre hyʒe preestis and oure newe religiows: þei dreedon hem þat Godis lawe schal qwikon aftur þis, and herfore þei make statutes stable as a stoon, and geton graunt of knytes to confermen hem, and þese þei marken wel wiþ witnesse of lordis, leste þat trewþe of Godis lawe hid in þe sepulchre berste owt to knowyng of comun puple. (1.426/44–50)

This sermon suggests a paradoxical recognition: the truth of God's law can and indeed often is replaced by statutes stable as a stone, so that for many, it is these statutes which in effect constitute the only law. But divine law exists independently of such fallen power and its corrupt domain, a law which the Lollards will bring back into the foreground through a correct hermeneutics independent of such mechanisms of power.

This disjunction of hermeneutics and power (i.e. there is a true hermeneutics independent of religious and political institutions) results in a very Wycliffite absence of self-reflexiveness. A general warning is sounded to those who would arrogate to themselves the priestly pre-rogatives on the assumption that they are indeed 'verrey vykares' (1.435/42–8), but there seems to be no consciousness of the possibility of extending such a caveat to comparable Lollard convictions. The absurdity of having two Popes who are perpetually contradicting each other is fully underlined (1.435/52–5; 1.609/48–61 0/51), but a similar political analysis of the Lollard-Church confrontation is avoided: 'And so þei [Popes, false 'vykerus'] myȝte not pleynliere schewen hem haue no such power þan for to bargeyne herwiþ, and boosten hem to haue such, for þanne þei ben none of hem to whom Crist ȝaf þis power' (1.435/49–52). One is very close here to an ideological *impasse*: the conviction of a direct, 'ecstatic', access to God can result only in a critique of other ideologies, not one's own. Indeed, vertical references to divine intention and divine inspiration enable the polemically very useful dismissal of any criticism directed against the Lollards themselves as inspired by the antichrist:

> þes wordis þat Poul spekiþ here [Gal. 4:1–5] ben hyȝe in trewþe and in wyt, and alle þe men in þis world konne not blame þe ton of þes. But wel I wot þat God grauntiþ to fewe men to knowe hem here; but ȝet we schulden trowe þes wordis and worschipe hem, and traueyle on hem to wyte what þes wordis menen, as men schullen wyte aftur in heuene. And for to haue mynde of þis seynt þat men passe not fro his wyt, *somme men wolon go nyȝ hise wordis by vndurstondyng þat God ȝyueþ hem; for ellis myȝten alle hise wordis be alyenyd, and al his wyt by anticrist.* (1.502/49–57; italics mine)

What is operative here is an anti-intellectual hermeneutics. The biblical words are profoundly mysterious and it is easy to be misled, but for those who have been granted divine inspiration, the obscure text becomes a transparent medium through which God's intention shines. The Lollards thus bring us back to a tradition of biblical *lectio* which devalues intellectual effort and emphasises a correct moral disposition, indeed a correct moral 'being' in relation to the sacred text for the apprehension of 'correct' meanings therof.[46] It is only occasionally, and even then, tangentially that the sermons acknowledge that such a theory of interpretation merely shifts the disputed hermeneutic locus from the 'validity' of interpretation to the 'authenticity' of inspiration without really solving any problems:

> And þus it were a muche vertu to gete aȝen owre formere fredom, and trowe no prelat in þis chyrche, but ȝif he grownde hym in Godus lawe. And þus men schulde schake awey al þe lawe þat þe pope haþ maad, and alle rewlis of þes newe ordris, but in as muche as þei ben

> growndide in þe lawe þat God haþ ȝouon. But loke þis growndyng
> disseyue þe nowt! – for yt may falle þat anticrist by hise newe lawis
> and hise byddyngus haue moo bussy seruantis to hym, þan haþ Crist
> by his lawe to serue hym for blisse of heuene. (1.503/80–89)

This is the closest that the sermons approach to addressing the interrelationship of hermeneutics and power: antichrist's servants, far out-
numbering those who serve Christ, might – with their new 'lawis and
byddyngus' – deceive one into thinking that certain interpretations are
grounded in God's law, when in 'reality' they are not.

The anti-intellectualism of the sermons results in a devaluation
of academic training,[47] and an emphasis on proper inner ordering:
'And þis mannys wyt mut be clene þat schulde knowe wel þis matere'
(II.262/88–9). The sermons therefore show a significant interest in psychology. False interpretations are the result of an inner dysfunction,
typically taking the form of a disordered will triumphing over 'reason',
or alternatively, correct 'wit'.

> And wyt wiþinne in mannys heed, þat is God hymself, mut meue
> hise owtwyttus to worche as þei schuldon . . . erþly fumes, comyng
> fro þe stomac, ben greet cause of þis sleep [of sin] . . . worchyng of
> a mannys sowle aboute suche [earthly] þingus makeþ worldly fumes
> lette a mannys resoun to knowon heuenly goodis . . . We schuldon
> wake to resown. (II.118/25–37)

When worldly concupiscent excess 'passuþ good resoun', the 'neruys
of charyte . . . faylon in [the] herte', and our eyes become blind to all
that really matters (II.138/85–9). Adam and Eve brought about the fall
by their 'rebellion to resoun' (II.230/8); and in the present day, man's
'weyward wit' and 'venymous wille' lead him astray (II.282/20–283/25).
In Sermon 144, men are exhorted to subject themselves to an inner
ordering and cleansing so that the 'power to understand' is undimmed:

> It is knowun bi Goddus lawe þat þe hed of mannus spirit is his power
> to undurstonde [interpreting Matt. 6:17], and þat shulde algatis be
> anoyntid, for it shulde be maad clene, and his entent shulde be riȝttid
> þat he haue deuocion to God . . . And he wayschiþ his soulis face
> whanne he temperiþ his soule þus to resoun, þat he . . . algatis triste
> to Goddis reward for seruys þat he doiþ to hym. (III. 56/18–57/27)

The ideal understanding is the result of a harmonious working of wit
and will: 'Ofte tymes is hering takun for hering of þe soule [referring

to John 8:43], whanne wit and wille comen togidre and conseyuen þe treuþe' (III.78/40–2).

The psychological category of 'reason' thus occupies a significant niche in Lollard theory.[48] It is associated with the correct ordering of man's *affectus*; it is also an important aspect of God's Word and correct modes of reading the scriptures. As a hermeneutic tool ('open reason'), it points towards the positivist vision of scriptural meaning as accessible and determinate. As an ideal mental category defined in terms of its Godwardness, it points instead towards the negative vision of the Word as opaque and dark, capable of being understood correctly only when the mind, through the illumination of a 'reason' quite different from rationalist common-sense, has been made subject to God. The former concept of reason informs passages such as the following: 'And þei [doctors] schuldon sauere Godus wordus, and declaron hem by resoun'(II.143/41–2); 'Here may we gederon [referring to Luke 12:32] opyn reson þat Cristus children schulde not dreedon; for ȝif God ȝyue a betture þing, he ȝyueþ al þat suweþ þerof' (II.275/53–5). The second concept is expressed in passages such as: 'ȝif [men] ben rewlude by reson, Cristus lawe is beste and ynow' (II.86/108–9); 'now þis world haþ blyndud men aȝenus þer wyt and þer resown.' (II.127/106–7).

'Reason' is thus a category both outside of the scriptural text – reason *or* holy writ can be used to persuade[49] – and inside: right reason, as an aspect of God's will, is *defined* by a proper understanding of his Word. Most often, the word is used in such a way that it spans both meanings: '[The three wise kings] lyuedon in worschipe aftur þer stat, and tauȝte þer puple Godis lawe and resoun, as þei hadden be þre men of heuene' (II.236/14–5); 'No mon þat is in byleue dreduþ of þis gospel þat ne Crist chargede þes wordis eche by resoun' (II.268/30–1). Note the ambivalence in the last passage: if God defines what 'reason' is, and if one believes in God, there is no question of doubting the 'reason' of God's Word.

The ambivalent use of the concept of 'reason' is characteristic of Lollard hermeneutics even outside the sermons. As a brief excursus, I have looked at the *Dialogue between Reson and Gabbyng*, a Lollard 'determination' preserved in MS Trinity College Dublin 245.[50] 'Reson', in the *Dialogue*, is both God (and that aspect of man which brings him closest to God), and 'rationality' (including the sense of 'rational argument'). The *Dialogue* begins with identifying Reson and Gabbyng with God and the fiend respectively: 'Reson and Gabbyng, whiche ben Crist and þe fende' (p. 689).

God as Reason delineates the proper role of secular authority: defending his law against the fiend 'bi strengþe medelid wiþ resoun' (p. 689): 'True lordis schal in charite help þise two sistris [the clergy and the laity] to lyve and mayntene hem bi wey of resoun to serve God' (p. 691). Discussing the riches of the priests of the Old Law, Reson says: 'we knowe not bi reson wheþir prestis of þe Oold Lawe, or prestis þat nowe ben dreynte in goodis weren in more synne aȝeynes truþe. For boþe synneden aȝeyns reson' (p. 703). In the above passage the first 'reason' seems to be referring to 'common-sense'; the second to 'divine reason'. Dismissing the Pope's law as irrelevant to the Christian life, Reson says: 'And so reson wiþ Goddis lawe schuld oonly be acceptid here' (p. 705). 'Reason' in this instance is obviously in a category compatible with but distinct from the divine rationality which is God and his Word. Gabbyng replies to Reson's last argument that such a stance unwarrantedly denies the importance of tradition. Reson counters by dismissing Gabbyng's words as 'not of resoun but of chidyng wiþoute witt' (p. 705). 'Reason' is thus polarised against 'witlessness'. Reson goes on to say that the words of true men are to be believed only when grounded in the faith or in 'reson of Goddis lawe' (p. 705). Everything else is a matter of opinion and not belief. And in yet another reference, 'resoun . . . or hooly writt' is identified as the only source of truth (p. 706).

The ambiguity in Lollard notions of 'reason' and its relationship to God's Word – rooted in an effective exploitation of the wide semantic range of the word 'reason'[51] – is yet another expression of the duality of Lollard thought. Lollard 'cultural theory' is informed by the same uncertainty. Gabbyng, in the *Dialogue*, points out quite pertinently that 'oolde custome of many seynts schulden be holden Goddis lawe, siþ a þousand men wolen witnesse aȝeyne a fewe critikis' (p. 705), which, as we shall see, is one of Netter's points. The constitution or otherwise of 'law' by 'custom' has of course always been one of the cruces of legal theory, and forms, quite characteristically, one of the problematic issues in Lollardy. The simpler, oppositional view makes a categorical distinction between the 'false lawes' of the Pope and the Christian faith (II.64), between God's law and 'costomys of þe feend' (II.104/102).[52]

However, this clear distinction is blurred in Sermon 70. After castigating the Pope for ordaining laws 'euene wiþ Godis lawe', the sermon informs us that 'oþre lawes men schulde not take, but as brawnchis of Godis lawe' (II.85/80–86/110). The problem remains the same as that of discerning 'grounded' readings: which laws can 'legitimately' be considered 'branches' and not 'distortions' or 'additions'? The sermon returns to the idea of a transparent interpreter who 'kunne[s] and declare[s]' God's law and shows that it is 'ynow' (II.86/116–7). The interpenetration of custom and law is recognised only in the case of cultural systems subjected to critique: for instance, we are told of the ceremonies of the Jews which 'þei kepten as þer bileue' (III.82/46–7). The sermons display a typically clear grasp of the interdependence of religious forms and the realm of the political and the economic;[53] once again, the analysis declines to draw any general conclusions about institutionalised religion per se, which would of course problematise the Lollards' own religio-political agenda. It would be no doubt foolish to expect such an extension of Lollard critiques to this agenda; what is surprising is the extent to which the critiques *are* taken, so that one can almost glimpse, just round the corner as it were, the sermons' consciousness of the polemics and politics of their own idealism.

The question becomes particularly important when one considers the sermons' extreme, and in this respect thoroughly traditional, polemics of biblical history.[54] Repeated parallels are made between the scribes and pharisees and their activities and the present day clergy, to the extent of suggesting that many of Christ's actions against the former were proleptic of his views of the latter. In Sermon 86, the fact that Christ let his apostles 'wende into þe world and lyue comun lyȝf as labrieerus' is interpreted as one of his implied condemnations of the enclosed religious:

> But here we trowon þat Crist dude þus to confounde þes cloystrerus, for Crist wyste wel þat þei schulden come to and disseyue myche of þis world, and seyeþ þat it falluþ not to hem to labure, ne dwelle owt of þer cloystre, siþ þei passon oþre men in newe signes þat þei han fownde. (II.184/160–64)

In a passage already examined, the sermon-writer suggests that the perilous last times referred to in Matt.24:24 must be prophetic of the contemporary world, as such tribulations have never been witnessed before (II.91/90–100). The 'literal' sense of Christ's actions postulated here is evidently one that develops through time: where, then, is the theoretical difference from a hermeneutic discourse which relies on ecclesiastical traditions as institutionalised expressions of an ever-developing dialogic scriptural meaning? As Ralph Hanna puts it, in his discussion of 'prophetic' readings of the Bible in the Lollard *Vae Octuplex*:

> Reading the text this way, as a Lollard, makes revelation continuous, a product of historical consciousness, yet equally of historical estrangement from the letter. Such a hermeneutic strategy thus undoes its own claims – rather than being at the origin, the adept reader can only be later, only involved in claiming that he recuperates the origin through his reading.[55]

Indeed, Bostick quotes a remarkable passage from the Preamble to the *Opus Arduum* in which the apocalyptic exegete suggests that his act of interpretation is parallel to John's original act of authorship: 'Moreover, by some hidden guidance there are many impulses that draw and push one to undertake this burden. Thus the interpreter is in much the same position as John, the author of the Apocalypse.'[56]

Where then does the Lollard exegete place himself in relation to the text he glosses? In his most idealistic theoretical formulation he is, to borrow Wyclif's image, an *ancilla*, a hand-maid, clarifying the words of her mistress, Scripture. His exegetical practice and even theory are, however, self-conflicted, and difficult to delineate satisfactorily. For the description which would seem to come closest to encapsulating the peculiar texture of the sermons ('pieces of polemic based on appropriate biblical exegesis') would be flawed. The sermons stop just short of betraying an awareness of their own rhetoric – an awareness, that is, of the intimate relationship of their highly flexible hermeneutics and the local, and universal, urgencies of their religio-political agenda. 'Polemics' implies a certain self-conscious strategy of argument, an acknowledged rhetoricity; I am not at all sure that the sermons would recognise such a description of themselves. Their intense, and fraught, theoretical awareness of themselves as exegesis coexists with an apparent refusal to confront the ideological bases informing and sustaining that exegesis. As a result, they seem to demand a deconstructive reading, for their theoretical positivism is combined, as in Wyclif, with an embeddedness in an inherited dialogic discourse with radically different premisses and implications. The sermons enact a confrontation between the discourse of persuasion, rhetoric and dialogue[57] and the discourse of 'truth', the confrontation resulting in collapse. As such, they seem to be symptomatic of late-medieval preoccupations, when the search for certitude becomes as intense as the impossibility of attaining it; hence, we may note, the repeated Gordian-knot-cutting vertical references to revelation. It is interesting to note that Jean Gerson, at around the same time, wrote a tract on the discernment of 'true' revelation, and explained his rationale: 'Dicamus praeterea quoniam non est humanitus regula generalis vel ars dabilis ad discernendum semper et infallibiliter quae verae sunt et quae falsae aut illusoriae revelationes' ('We can also say that there is for human beings no general rule or method that can be given always and infallibly to distinguish between revelations that are true and those that are false or deceptive').[58] It is also worth bearing in mind that there was a heightened interest in the fourteenth and fifteenth centuries in the interrelationship of logic (theoretically aligned to 'truth') and rhetoric (theoretically aligned to persuasion and power), and the postulation of a category of 'moral dialectic' which seeks to reconcile the logical interest in the cognitive with the rhetorical interest in the active: '[la dialectique morale] est donc d'une part une méthode de connaissance, et de l'autre un enseignement des moyens de formuler les directives d'action' ('moral dialectic is then partly a way of knowing, and partly [a way of] teaching the means of formulating the rules of action').[59] The sermons in effect try to bring about such a reconciliation: their hermeneusis is directed towards both the scriptural text and the outside world of political and religious dispute. But the result is a fragmentation of discourse rather than a unification.

Peter von Moos, in his discussion of John of Salisbury, has an illuminating passage on what he describes as John's 'dialogic model of perception', in which rhetoric and dialectic are viewed together as addressing 'den "menschlichen Faktor", die soziale, historisch relative Dimension' ('the "human factor", the social, historical relative dimension') of discourse, in which the audience or respondent is always included.[60] What we witness in the sermons is a polarisation of divine scriptural 'truth' and the human, historical dimension that their polemical exegesis addresses, and this tension between a theoretical emphasis on interpretative certitude and a practical embeddedness in rhetoric results in the rich and pervasive incoherence I have been outlining.

Sermon 68, discussing the relative importance of prayer and good works (teaching and preaching the gospel), argues as follows:

> Crist haþ ordeyned hise preesetis boþe to teche and preche his gospel, and not for to preye þus, and to be hyd in suche closettis . . . And ȝif þe feend alegghe þe salm þat Dauyd roos at mydnyȝt to confesse to his God, why schulde not we now do so? But here we axen þe feendis clerk, siþ Crist dwellud al nyȝt in his preyer, and in day taȝte þe puple . . . wy schulde not preestis now do þus? And siþ same salm seiþ, 'Lord, how I haue loued þi lawe, al þe day it is my þowt', wy schulde not we hoolde þis more, siþ it is muche betture þan to rise at mydnyt? (II.75/105–16)

The sermon goes on to compare those who rise at night to thieves: 'and so vson þese newe þeuys, þat cam in aboue þe dore'. It ends with the assertion that these thieves will not achieve salvation, however much they pray; how much more useless, therefore, are their prayers for others (II.75/124–76/130).

Such a mode of argumentation – countering one authoritative passage by another, making colourful derogatory remarks about the opposing camp – is firmly in the tradition of medieval *disputatio*. What is lacking is the sense of play that one encounters, for instance, in William Woodford's logical flytings or in Chaucer's portrait of rhetorical *disputatio* in the Wife of Bath's Prologue, which von Moos felicitously describes as 'Spielernst' ('earnest game')[61] and which Thomas Netter would later disavow as 'scholasticus ludus' ('scholastic game').[62] That is because Lollard hermeneutics and polemics, though often exploiting sceptical modes of disputation, are in their primary thrust a quest for certitude. As Reson says in the *Dialogue*: 'But it is a grete foly to trowe hem [the 'new beliefs' of the Pope and his Church] to lyȝtly, for truþe of man is litle inouȝ to be prented wiþ Goddis lawe, whi schuld man made to mannes ymage, charge his soule wiþ siche uncerteyne þingis?' (p. 706). Ultimately, the sermons suggest a positivism trapped in the dialogic; an attempt at establishing linear, direct access to 'truth' trapped in a discourse which habitually valorises what von Moos describes as 'denken in Alternativen'.[63] It is a particular irony that this entrapment should emerge with such clarity in the 'sermons': for received homiletics was happily aware of its embeddedness in rhetorical, persuasive uses of language, and a cognate exegesis.[64]

The next chapter examines a practical enactment of the traditional 'dialogic' approach to scripture, not indeed as it finds expression in disputation, but as it informs meditative *lectio*.[65] Nicholas Love's *Mirror* accepts, self-consciously, certain inherited modes of devotional reading, and deploys them against the Lollards, thereby underlining not only the hermeneutic gulf which separates this vision of valid scriptural meaning from that of the Lollards, but also the polemical, reactionary charge that traditional exegetical practices had assumed in the new heretical environment.

5

Nicholas Love and the Lollards

The Mirror of the Blessed Life of Jesus Christ was one of the most popular of
late medieval devotional and meditative texts.[1] Written in the early
fifteenth century by Nicholas Love, prior of Mount Grace Charterhouse
in Yorkshire, the work is extant in forty-nine complete or near-complete
manuscripts and is found in the form of fragments and extracts in another twelve.[2] It therefore forms, along with the Wycliffite Bible, the
Brut Chronicle and Walter Hilton's *Scale of Perfection*, one of the most
widely disseminated works in Middle English prose. The *Mirror* was a
free translation into the vernacular of a Franciscan text generally ascribed
to St. Bonaventura in the Middle Ages, the *Meditationes Vitae Christi*.[3]
The *Meditationes* itself was one of the most protean and popular of
Franciscan devotional works, extant in hundreds of Latin manuscripts
and translated over the Middle Ages into almost every major European
tongue.[4] In English, there were already partial translations extant before
Love's version appeared: the prose free translation known as *The Privity
of the Passion*;[5] the rhymed-couplet translation ascribed to Robert
Mannyng;[6] a third translation of the Passion section extant in eight
manuscripts; and four other partial translations.[7]

Nicholas Love's translation was, however, endowed with a specially
privileged status. It was licensed by Archbishop Thomas Arundel in
1410 as an official alternative to the Lollard Bible, the use of which had
been severely restricted.[8] Moreover, his certificate of approval is found
attached to nineteen copies of the text. Arundel, we are informed:

> post inspeccionem eiusdem per dies aliquot . . . proprie vocis oraculo
> ipsum in singulis commendauit & approbauit, necnon & auctoritate
> sua metropolitica, vt pote catholicum, puplice communicandum fore

decreuit & mandauit, ad fidelium edificacionem, et hereticorum siue lollardorum confutacionem.[9]

after examining it for several days . . . commended and approved it personally, and further decreed and commanded by his metropolitan authority that it rather be published universally for the edification of the faithful and the confutation of heretics or lollards.

The *Mirror* engages with Lollardy on several planes. There are passages of doctrinal polemic combating Lollard views on confession, the Eucharist, the giving of tithes, the dependence or otherwise of priestly teaching on priestly morality. Such passages are accompanied in many copies by marginal notes 'contra lollardos'. Love also adds a 'Treatise on the Sacrament' to the *Meditationes*, thereby emphasizing orthodox views on the nature of the Eucharist.[10] More interestingly, however, the *Mirror* wages a hermeneutic war on Lollard approaches to the scriptural text. Much more subtly articulated than the anti-Lollard doctrinal propaganda, Love's conservative hermeneutics is nevertheless central to the *Mirror*'s orthodox polemic. However, it is my contention that the *Mirror* is ultimately uneasy in its response to Lollardy, so that an overt rejection of Lollard assumptions and aims coexists with a complex and uncertain accommodation of certain primary hermeneutic emphases of the heresy. I argue that this element of uncertainty in Love's polemical espousal of traditional hermeneutics is reflected in the presentation of the text in most of the extant manuscripts of the *Mirror*, a presentation which subtly refashions the *Meditationes*' own theoretical assumptions regarding the interrelationship of scriptural and ecclesiastical authority, and 'correct' modes of reading the Bible.

Love's choice of the Pseudo-Bonaventuran meditations, in which traditional Franciscan spirituality finds one of its fullest and most definitive expressions,[11] was a calculated one. His translation as a whole is based on what was, in the Lollard context, a reactionary approach to scriptural Word and authority. The *Mirror* is not merely a translation of a much-venerated Franciscan devotional work, it is also – and more importantly – a mediation of the Bible characterised by its own rhetorical strategies, and it draws on a textual-political ideology entirely removed from that of the Lollards.[12] As has been pointed out by Michael Sargent, though the *Mirror* was extremely successful in 'confuting Lollard demands for an English Bible, it did not in fact answer them'.[13]

The Lollards had emphasised the importance of a precise knowledge of the exact words of Holy Writ, unadulterated by the 'cautela diaboli' introduced by ecclesiastical mediators. In theoretical terms, Wyclif himself, we may recall, had made a firm distinction between 'exposition' and 'text' in *De Veritate*: the text is the *domina* served by her *ancilla*, the exposition. Wyclif gives theoretical centrality to a concept of the Bible as a unique text, demanding from the reader a constant and significant awareness of its separate hermeneutic status. *De Veritate*, as we have seen, postulates categories of scriptural logic and form which dictate their own principles of explication to the properly equipped, devout, 'rational' reader. Such a reader is expected to attempt to understand the Bible 'literally', which in Lollard theory involves accessing the divine intention. 'Inspiration' (from the Holy Spirit) and 'open reason' form the twin exegetical positives;[14] they are necessary correctives to the human propensity to become false glossators of God's Word. A governing fear in the work of Wyclif and his followers is the possibility of 'imposing' an alien (human) hermeneutics or a fallen logic on the Bible; and an important preoccupation is the need to distinguish between the authority of God and the authority of lesser *auctours*, of however venerable a pedigree.[15]

A corollary of such an insistence on the unique and separate validity of the scriptural text is the development of an academic scholarship interested in the textual condition of the Bible, and the 'authenticity' of interpolations or interpretations sanctified by tradition. Wyclif's own inadequate and perfunctory theoretical gestures in the direction of philological studies[16] are transformed, by his followers in the practical sphere, into a profound interest in what we would now call textual criticism, and in matters of presentation of the text, evidenced not only in the Wycliffite Bible, but also in the *Glossed Gospels*, and in the Long English Sermon Cycle. Because of a genuine attempt at establishing a Bible 'somdel trewe', to quote the Prologue to the Wycliffite Bible,[17] and a firm belief that human additions to God's Word must be kept rigorously distinct from what they attempt to elucidate, the Lollards display a remarkably self-conscious interest in the presentation of texts.

The Prologue to the Wycliffite Bible is acutely aware of issues of textual authenticity. The first chapter makes an important distinction between canon and apocrypha. After listing the canonical books of the

Old Testament, the Prologue points out that 'what euer book in the olde testament is out of these fyue and twenty byfore seid, shal be set among apocrifa, that is, with outen autorite of bileue; therfore the book of Wisdom and Ecclesiastici and Judith and Tobie be not of bileue.' The canonical books, however divided, are of 'autorite of bileue, either of cristen feith.' Apocrypha, in so far as they are conducive to charity, may indeed be used for edification, but 'not to conferme the autorite of techingis of holy chirche'. Books that are not of the number of Holy Writ 'owen to be cast fer awey'. The apparent contradiction in the above is then resolved. Apocrypha fall into two main categories: books of anonymous authorship but 'open' truth, which may be used to learn virtue but not to prove issues of faith; and books the truth of which is doubted and therefore rejected. Judith falls in the first class; examples of the second are provided by 'the book of the ʒong childhed of the Sauyour, and the book of the takyng up of the body of Seynt Marye to heuen'.[18]

The Prologue is also intelligently aware of the problems inhering in the textual condition of the Latin Bible. The Psalter, for instance, differs much from its Hebrew original: 'Noo book in the eld testament is hardere to vndirstonding to vs Latyns, for oure lettre discordith mych fro the Ebreu';[19] moreover, the Church tends to ignore Jerome's translation from the Hebrew in favour of an inferior version. Many of the existing Latin versions of the Bible are corrupt, 'ful fals'. Therefore the 'comune Latyn biblis han more nede to be correctid, as many as I haue seen in my lif, þan haþ þe English bible late translatid'. Verses from the Hebrew – derived from Jerome and Lyra – are therefore set in the margins of debatable passages. The Church itself has been to blame, for 'in ful fewe bokis þe chirche rediþ þe translacioun of Ierom, as it mai be preuid bi þe propre orignals of Ierom whiche he gloside'.[20] The Prologue therefore emphasises the need for extreme circumspection in establishing a 'true' text: 'First þis symple creature hadde myche trauaile wiþ diuerse felawis and helperis to gedere manie elde biblis, and oþere doctouris and comune glosis, and to make oo Latyn bible sumdel trewe'.[21]

The interest in establishing a 'correct' biblical text leads to an equal interest in separating text from commentary. Henry Hargreaves cites a remark by the Lollard scribe of London, Lambeth Palace MS 1033: 'Here endith the prologe on Isaye, and here bigynneth the text of Isaye. With a short glose on the derke wordis; and loke eche man, that he wryte the text hool bi itself, and the glose in the margyn, ether leve it al out.'[22] Moreover, as Anne Hudson points out, 'any glossing' – in the extant manuscripts of the Wycliffite Bible – '(by double renderings or by explanatory extra words) is underlined in red so that it can quickly be perceived as such'.[23]

Equally self-consciously careful are the *Glossed Gospels*. For instance, in Cambridge, Trinity College MS B.1.38, the Prologue states:

> þe text of þe gospel is set first bi it silf. an hool sentence togider and þanne sueþ þe exposicioun in þis maner/First a sentence of a doctour declaringe þe text is set aftir þe text/and in þe ende of þat sentence. þe name of þe doctour seiynge it is set þat men wite certeynli hou feer þat doctour goiþ/and so of alle doctours and lawis aleggid in þis exposicioun. (fol. 7r)

The above passage is followed by a meticulously detailed explanation of the work's code of reference. For instance:

> whanne y seye austin here he is aleggid in hise twey bokis of þe lordis sermon in þe hil which sermon conteyneþ þe v and vi and vii chapters of matheu/whanne y seye bede in his omelie. eþer gregory in his omelie and telle not in what omeli y take þat sentence of alquyn on matheu. (fol. 7r)

What is noteworthy is that such academic precision of reference supports a work declaredly meant for the unlearned or those possessing only basic literacy: the Prologue states that it is a great work of mercy and charity to 'telle opinli þe treuþe of þe holi gospel to lewid men and sympli lettrid prestis' (fol. 7r).[24]

A similar textual consciousness informs the presentation of the text in the Long English Sermon Cycle. Anne Hudson describes in her introduction to the *English Wycliffite Sermons* how meticulously the Lollards distinguish between words of the sermon-lections and other quotations: 'The care with which the lection's words are marked off obviously reflects Lollard concern for the precise words of scripture, and for the education of the laity and clergy in the discernment of authority.'[25] Similar is the case with the Lollard revision of Richard Rolle's Commentary on the Psalter, where much attention is paid to distinguishing, by means of different scripts, between Latin biblical text, translation and commentary.[26] In a short tract on the *Ave Maria*, the Lollard author condemns even apparently minor changes to biblical texts, for, as he points out, if 'þe pope may ȝive pardoun bi addinge of þes two wordis, so may he adde oþere mo, and wiþdrawe, as him likiþ, and so turne Goddis lawe into lawe of Antecrist'.[27]

Nicholas Love's translation is very different. Arundel's reply to the Lollard emphasis on the necessity of general lay access to the exact words of Holy Writ seems to have been to endorse and circulate a work which provides anything but that, a work which offers scripture along with orthodox interpretation and commentary, anti-Lollard polemic and non-biblical devotional material in one indivisible whole. The authority that the *Mirror* upholds is that of the ecclesiastical establishment – an authority that is political, textual and hermeneutic. The *Mirror*, in many ways, endorses precisely that concept of authority which the Lollards explicitly questioned in *The Lanterne of Liȝt*:

> Here summe obiectun þat þe gospel is not of autorite but in as miche as þe chirche haþ autorised it & cannonisid it, for þei sein þat no man knowiþ suche wordes to be þe gospel, but as þe chirche haþ determyned in her determynacioun. þis conclucion semeþ to smak heresie.[28]

Against this, one may place the equally explicit affirmation of a contrary viewpoint in Arundel's *Constitutions*, which, in the course of laying down the procedure for recanting heretical teaching, states that 'truth' is, by definition, what the Church has determined it to be.[29]

As opposed to the Wycliffite insistence on scripture as a text which demands, indeed dictates, its own special and unique hermeneutics, and the associated interest in establishing a correct biblical text which must not be violated, Love's translation seeks to locate authority in a discourse outside the text, in the interpretations dictated or 'determined' by the Church. Relevant biblical 'text', in this rhetorically conscious hermeneutic, is subject to modification and transformation according to the local needs of intended purpose and audience, and according to the political and historical situation of the interpreter. The aim is the creation of a 'fructuose' – to use one of Love's favourite words – meditative text.

Love's translation therefore bases itself on a literary-political ideology which is much more self-consciously rhetorical, much less insistently textual. The biblical text is used as the occasion for an affective and rhetorical literary creativity which implicitly denies the Wycliffite disjunction of divine text and human hermeneutics. Instead, the *Mirror* in effect insists on the univocity, the continuity of the Divine Word and the human through a constant violation of what Vincent Gillespie calls 'the decorums of textual boundaries'.[30] Such violation of textual integrity, though possessing a long affective prehistory, had acquired, by the time Love was writing, a strong reactionary charge. The *Mirror* therefore begins, in a prologue added to the *Meditationes*, with a reference to the Pauline topos of 'Quecum scripta sunt ad nostram doctrinam scripta sunt', followed by a significantly polemical translation: 'þerfore to strenkeþ vs & confort vs . . . spekeþ þe Apostle þe wordes aforseid to this entent seying *þat all thynges þat ben written generaly in holi chirche ande specialy of oure lorde Jesu cryste* þey bene wryten to oure lore' (p. 9/16–20; italics mine).[31] The critical assumptions underlying this passage should be noted. There is first of all the rhetorical emphasis: 'to strenkeþ vs'; secondly, there is the unsignalled hermeneutic act which interprets Paul's 'entent' and issues in a major unsignalled interpolation into the translated passage: '[written] generaly . . . cryste'. The interpolation is of course central to Love's own rhetorical concerns: the non-scriptural devotional material in his translation must be shown to be as 'fructuose' and therefore as 'authentic' as the actual biblical passages, and the most efficient way of doing this is by citing a major scriptural authority ('þe gret doctour & holy apostle *Powle*'). The saint's waxen nose, to recall Alan of Lille's image for the flexibility of 'authorities', has been, after all, only slightly bent. The point made here is taken up later:

> Ande for þis hope & to þis entent with holi writte also bene wryten diuerse bokes and trettes of//devoute men not onelich to clerkes in latyne, but also in Englyshe to lewde men & women & hem þat bene of symple vndirstondyng. Amonge þe whiche beþ wryten deuovte meditacions of cristes lyfe more pleyne in certeyne partyes þan is expressed in the gospel of þe foure euangelistes. (p. 10/3–9)

The 'entent' of Holy Writ and other non-scriptural devotional material is held to be the same, though works belonging to the second class may be 'more pleyne' than the gospel, the implication being a certain blurring of authoritative boundaries. The Proheme continues:

> Ande as it is seide þe deuoute man & worthy clerke *Bonauentre* wrot hem to A religiouse woman in latyne þe whiche scripture ande wrytyng for þe fructuouse matere þerof steryng specialy to þe loue of Jesu ande also for þe pleyn sentence to comun vndirstondyng semeþ amonges oþere souereynly edifying to symple creatures. (p. 10/9–14)

Having underlined the rhetorical fruitfulness of, and the 'plain' edification offered by, his *auctor*, Love proceeds to defend the meditative technique of creating 'imaginations' as efficacious in 'styryng symple soules to þe loue of god'. He continues, further on in the Proheme:

> Wherfore we mowen to stiryng of deuotion ymagine & þenk diuerse wordes & dedes of him & oþer, þat we fynde not writen, so þat it be not aзeyns þe byleue, as seynt Gregory & oþer doctours seyn, *þat holi writte may be expownet & vndurstande in diuerse maneres, & to diuerse purposes.* (pp. 10/43–11/3; italics mine)

It is significant that the defence of the spiritual efficacy of non-scriptural devotional material should shade off into a defence of the flexibility of biblical interpretation – what is emphasised is the purpose of the devotional work. It is rhetorical *intentio* which determines attitudes to both text and hermeneutics; indeed, *no* real distinction is made between the two. Exposition or exegesis ultimately transforms, indeed constitutes 'fruitful' scriptural 'text'; to borrow Rita Copeland's words, 'rhetorical invention is constituted through the *modus interpretandi*.'[32]

And indeed that is inevitable, for the *Mirror* is a highly selective, affective *exposicio* of the sentence of both its immediate authority the *Meditationes* and its ultimate the Bible. What is operative is a concept of the value-laden *sententia* of Christ's life finding different linguistic-textual expressions without undergoing any essential change. Because of the unfathomable profundity of the Bible, all such rhetorical reinventions of the text – modifications, additions, expositions – are regarded as fully justifiable, though inevitably only partial renderings, partial illuminations of the divine *pagina* or the divine *vita*.[33]

In fact, Love's espousal of this traditional, monastic model of scriptural *lectio* is self-conscious and polemical. We must remember that the *Mirror* was composed, endorsed and circulated at a time when

substantial and extensive debate over the nature of religious intellection appropriate for and indeed permissible to the laity had already
taken place. Bonaventure's 'imaginative' meditative discourse, premised
as it is on a near-complete elision of the literal words of the Bible,
therefore assumes a new reactionary and polemical inflection in the
Lollard environment. Love's development of this discourse seeks implicitly to battle the biblically informed, theoretically engaged, vernacular exegetical polemics of the Lollards such as we have seen support
the English Wycliffite Sermons. And because its combative usage of the
inherited Bonaventuran devotional discourse is deliberate, Love's text
repeatedly betrays an abiding and uneasy self-consciousness of his meditative – and, by implication – scriptural methodology. This defensive
self-consciousness finds pervasive expression in the *Mirror*: vocabulary
which by this time had assumed strong Lollard resonances is insistently
and combatively deployed; an awareness, entirely alien to the *Meditationes*, of the hermeneutic values informing meditative discourse repeatedly comes to the surface; and, concomitantly, there is a heightened
emphasis on the spiritual excellences and fruitfulness of the devotional
tradition within which Love locates himself. 'Devout meditations' or
'devout imaginations' are polarised against 'express' meanings,[34] and
justified by repeated references, not all of which are derived from the
source text, to their 'fruitfulness', and their 'sweet taste'. The category of
'fruitful' encompasses both the words and deeds of Christ as recorded
in the gospels and expositions thereof by holy men and doctors. Discussing John 4:32 in a passage original to him, and sign-posted as such
by a marginal 'N', Love says:

> Miche more gostly fruyt is contenede in þis gospel, þe which whoso
> desireþ to knowe more fully he sal fynde it in þe boke of seynt Austyn
> vpon þe gospel of Jon, where he makeþ of þe processe of þis gospel a
> longe processe & clergiale ful of gostly fruite.[35] (p. 97/31–5)

The identity of scripture and expositions of scripture assumed in the
above passage is a general *datum* in the *Mirror*. Love visualises himself
as part of an authoritative and holistic tradition of Christian meaning
offering a particular kind of meditative exegesis. He therefore repeatedly
directs his readers to other exegeses: 'What þat þees þre ʒiftes offred of
þese kynges bytoken gostly & many oþere þinges þat þe gospel more
ouere telleþ at it is expownet by holy doctours is sufficiantly & fully

writen in many oþer places' (p. 45/6–9).³⁶ Discussing the episode of the
raising of Lazarus, Love says, in a passage original to him: 'þe reisyng
of Lazare principaly is comendet & souerenly is to be consideret, not
onely for þe souereyn miracle itself, bot also for many notable þinges
þat befeele in þat myracle & diuerse misteries, þe whech seynt *Austyn*
clergialy treteþ.' (p. 125/4–8). As a result, in a remarkable inversion of
hermeneutic norm, we are given the Augustinian exposition before the
letter of the story. (The related *Meditationes* passage deals only with the
story.) The conceptual unity of the Bible and its authoritative exegesis
is thus underlined.

What is of governing importance is edification, 'fruitfulness', and
to this purpose it is allowable to read the Bible selectively: 'Forþermore
leuyng many wordes of þe gospel, & takyng þat semeþ most notable
to oure edificacion' (p. 130/31–2). One of Love's favourite words
in this 'fructuose' context is 'processe', meaning both 'sequence of
events/progression' and 'purpose/goal'.³⁷ The progression of Biblical
events has as its 'in-eched' *processe* the stimulation of prayer and meditation and the giving of *ensaumples* to the devout. The pattern most often
followed by Love tends to include the citation of a Biblical passage (the
'ground'); a 'historical' reconstruction or invention based on this; a
contemplative passage, usually of heightened tone, drawing attention to
the affective potential of the invented scene and to its exemplary value;
finally a passage of prayer or homiletics. Of course, the various elements
might occur in a slightly different order, but this forms the general
pattern. A fairly typical example would be Chapter 12 in *Die Martis*:
'How þe child Jesus laft alone in Jerusalem' (p. 57/26). It begins with
the gospel story of Jesus's journey to Jerusalem with his parents when
he was twelve and his staying behind there; is followed by an affective
emphasis on Mary's sorrow ('Wherfore here we mowen haue resonably
gret compassion of þe gret anguyshe'); a pointer to the *ensaumple* offered
('here mowe we lern, what tyme tribulacion & anguysh fallen to vs not
to be . . . miche disturblet þerby'); a prayer uttered by Mary in which
the reader is expected to participate; a passage of 'historical' invention
('In þis forseid processe of Jesu what hope we þat he dide . . . ?'); more
ensaumples ('we mowe note & lerne þre notable þinges'); and finally a
piece of homiletic addressed to the religious (pp. 57–60). The various
stages of such a 'processe' are often emphasised by the standardised

marginalia occurring in many copies of the *Mirror*. For instance, in the similar rhetorical presentation of Magdalen's conversion, the marginal notes are detailed. At the beginning, there is a 'nota verba magdalene intima' to indicate Magdalen 'þenkynge as it were in þis manere'; a further 'nota' to signal the affective passage and 'the gostly fruite' to be plucked; 'notabilia' pointing to the 'grete notabilities to oure edificacione'; and finally a reference to St Bernard as the authority for the homiletic passage (pp. 90–2).

The creative *lectio* exemplified in such affective and rhetorical meditations finds an unusually explicit expression in Love's treatment of the *Ave Maria* in a passage original to him. The greeting, we are told, is 'grounded' in the gospel; therefore Love wishes to elaborate on it 'to stire þi deuocion þe more in seying of þat gretyng': 'As I conceyue þis gretyng in maner as holi chirch haþ ordeynet it to be seide, haþ fyue parties in þe which mowen be vndurstand specialy þe fyue ioyes of oure lady' (p. 28/9–11). What is remarkable about this passage is the signalling of the entirely subjective nature of the hermeneutic act about to be performed on Gabriel's words ('As I conceyue') while simultaneously suggesting that this reading of the Gospel text is somehow ratified, ordained by the larger authority of Holy Church, and by implication, God. The dubious syntax – one is never quite sure whether 'in manere' refers to Love's 'conceyuing' of the greeting or Holy Church's 'ordaining' of it – is crucial in this respect. The question of the precise authoritative status of this particular reading is thus left open. Love then proceeds to provide an exegesis of Gabriel's greeting: 'In þe first part of þis gretyng . . . þow maiȝt vndirstond', 'In þe seconde party . . . may be vndurstonde' and so on (pp. 28–9).[38] This is followed by the suggestion that the devout Christian may actually include Love's exegesis in his or her saying of the prayer: 'And if þe lust in þis gretyng specifie þe fyue ioyes with þe fyue vertues before seide, þow maiht sey þus in short wordes' (p. 29/30–1). In two variant readings of the passage which follows, Love emphasises that one need not necessarily abide by his reading, as long as the reading one provides is endowed with the proper devotional 'entent': 'Chese he that liste to rede or write this processe as hym semeth best/or in other better manere ȝif he kan/so that be it one be it othere that the ende and the entente be to the worschippe and the plesynge of oure lord Jesu and his blessed moder marye.'[39] Such passages make clear the self-consciously active role that hermeneutics assumes in the particular mode of biblical *lectio* embraced by Love.[40] In such a theoretical framework, 'exposicio', in the terms of Wyclif's image, is no longer 'ancilla textus', but has raised itself to the status of 'domina'.

The determining importance of hermeneutic/rhetorical intention is later underlined in Love's discussion of the *Pater noster* in a passage original to him:

> Bot one þinge touchyng þis praiere, soþely I trowe þat whoso wole ʒiue his entent fort sey it with deuocion & haþ an inwarde desire to þe gostly vndurstondyng þerof... shale þorh grace by processe of tyme finde so miche confort þerinne, þat þere is none oþere praiere made of man þat shal be to him so sauory & so effectuele... And so shale he fynde in his soule whan god wole ʒife his grace with gret likyng *diuerse vndurstandyng þerof most pertynent to his desire & þat oþere þan is writen in þe comune exposicion þerof.*[41] (p. 86/29–40; italics mine)

Textual meaning is here explicitly held to be dependent on readerly 'desire'. As Copeland says: 'Medieval exegesis replicates rhetoric's productive application to discourse: as the orator fitted a speech to the particular circumstances of persuasion, so in a certain sense the medieval exegete remodels a text for the particular circumstances of interpretation.'[42] Indeed, there is, in this scheme of things, no separate theoretical consciousness of 'text'; what is of importance is a continuum of 'text' – both biblical and expository – and reader, the latter composing, within the broad outlines of the former, his own variations.[43]

However, as I emphasised earlier, Love is conscious of what is, in the Lollard context, his reactionary interpretative ideology. His work, while placing itself firmly in the camp of orthodoxy, also shows an uneasy attempt at coming to terms with the theoretical Lollard location of authoritative meaning in the 'literal' sense of the exact words of scripture understood according to the intention of the Holy Spirit. This duality in Love – emphasising the hermeneutic authority of the Church, and of the devout reader operating within the Church, while acknowledging the textual authority of scripture – finds, as I will go on to show, a parallel in the presentation of the text in most of the extant manuscripts.

Love's problematic response to the way in which his source treats the Bible finds repeated, though necessarily oblique expression in the course of the *Mirror*. Being a self-conscious reader of the Gospels, he retains, often with significant modifications, the Pseudo-Bonaventuran references to suggestive omissions in the evangelical narratives. For instance, the important passage at the beginning of Caput 15, in which the Pseudo-Bonaventura explicitly questions and offers his own hypothesis about the evangelical silence in relation to Christ's youth and early manhood, is translated in full by Love, with suggestive explicatory additions. 'Nec in scripturis reperitur quod in toto isto tempore aliquid fecerit' (p. 64/6–7; p. 531) is rendered as 'we fynde noȝht expressed in scripture autentike what he dide' (p. 61/3–4), thus implying that there is the required information in the work of secondary authors. The Pseudo-Bonaventura's glancing reference to his earlier statement that nothing is affirmed which cannot be proved by the authority of sacred scripture or the doctors[44] is then drawn out in full:

> not fully affermynge in þis or oþer þat we mowe not opunly preue by holi writ or doctours apreuede bot deuoutly ymaginyng to edificacion & stiryng of deuocion, as it was seid in þe proheme of þis boke at þe begynnyng.[45] (p. 61/21–5)

The adverb 'opunly' is to be noted. It is a word which had achieved prominent currency among the Lollards, generally used, in its adjectival form, to describe a category of scriptural meaning held to be independent of the interpreting reader or institution: 'open' proofs based on the scriptures render the interpreter transparent and deny him hermeneutic agency.[46] A marginal note found in many copies, a variant of which also accompanies a related passage in the Proheme, emphasises Love's discretion: 'Nota bene pro sano intellectu' (p. 10). Indeed, as one's acquaintance with such passages deepens, one realises that Love is almost on the defensive in relation to this meditative technique of *creating* a sacred *vita* while in theory merely elucidating it. This is understandable when one recalls Lollard warnings against curious tamperings with God's Word: 'hold we us payed on þe mesure þat God hath ȝyuen vs and dreme we noht aboute newe poyntis þat þe gospel leuyth, for þis is synne of curioste þat harmeth more þan profiȝteth'.[47] Moreover, as Anne Hudson points out, classical anecdote, moral exemplum and hagiography were anathema to Lollard homiletics.[48] It is worth noting at this point that the *Mirror* itself is found associated with the lives of the saints Nicholas, Catherine and Margaret in Cambridge, Corpus Christi College MS 142; with the *Legenda Aurea* in London, British Library, MS Additional 11565; with a Middle English version of the Gospel of Nicodemus in Oxford, Bodleian Library, MS Bodley 207; and with texts such as the 'Charter of Jesus Christ', the 'Fifteen Oes' and the 'Fifteen Joys of Our Lady' in Tokyo, T. Takamiya, MS 4.

Love's unease in relation to his assumption of a traditional hermeneutic framework finds pervasive expression in his ubiquitous use of the word 'open'. As we have noted, the adjective 'open' was habitually used by the Lollards to emphasise their direct access to a divine intention informing a scriptural text which offers to its readers meanings of an unmediated clarity. I will provide a selection of the *Mirror*'s references to 'openness'; when no pseudo-Bonaventuran citations are provided, the use of the word is original to Love.

Joseph's tolerant attitude to Mary's mysterious pregnancy is 'an opun ensaumple of reproue to gelouse men' (p. 33/26); the Epiphany is the 'opune shewyng of oure lorde' (p. 42/16); in Jesus's nativity in the manger 'we mowe se opune ensaumple of perfite mekenes' (p. 45/32–3); 'pouerte and buxumnesse' are 'opunly shewed' in the life of simplicity led by Mary and Joseph (p. 49/27); the apostle 'opunly sheweþ' the necessity of humility (p. 62/21–2);[49] Jesus reproved the tempting devil 'opunly' (p. 74/20); we do not read 'opunly & fully' that Jesus began public preaching in the year following his baptism, though he probably preached in private (p. 78/29);[50] Jesus utters the oblique words 'þis day is þis scripture fulfilled in ȝoure eres', thereby 'not opunly expressyng or nemyng him self' (p. 79/16–7);[51] the 'text of þe gospel opunly telleþ' the true manner of prayer, fasting and of other virtues (p. 84/19). It would have been an 'opun foly' for the martyrs and saints to have prayed for mere bodily security; therefore the *Pater Noster* is to be understood spiritually (p. 87/35). The faith and belief of one man can help and save another, as emerges from the story of the 'palatyk man'; and 'þis is opunly aȝeynus sume heritikes þat holden þe contrarie opynion' (p. 89/22-3).[52] The gospels speak of the feeding of the multitude twice; 'in þe whiche processe takyng hede to þe wordes & þe dedes of oure lorde as þe gospel opunly telleþ we mow se to oure edificacion gostly, many gude stiringes' (p. 103/7–9). Jesus gave us an example in his 'opene reising' of the second dead body: if our sins are 'opunly knowen' we ought to do 'opune penance as holi chirch haþ ordeynet' (p. 127/41–3). In the episode of the raising of Lazarus, Jesus first tells his disciples that Lazarus sleeps. They interpret his words literally; as a result he declares 'to hem opunly, þat he spake first mistily' (p. 130/26–7). Lazarus comes out of his tomb still bound in his grave-clothes; the disciples then 'lose and unbind him'. Augustine interprets the episode spiritually; Lazarus, i.e. the sinful man, remains bound in sin until released by 'goddus ministres'. Love comments: 'In þe which we mowe se opunly a sufficient auctorite aȝeynus hem [evidently the Lollards] þat repreuene confession ordeynet by holi chirch' (p. 135/1–2).[53] Caiaphas scornfully prophesied in the council of the Pharisees that Jesus would die for the salvation of mankind: and 'so haue we here opun ensaumple þat wikked men & reprouede of god hauen sumtyme þe ȝift of prophecye' (p. 136/19–20). Jesus 'opunly declared [his] deþ' in John 12:8 (p. 139/34). He commended alms-giving 'as it is opunly shewede in þe gospell of Marke & of Luke' (p. 140/22). There are references to Jesus's 'opun' preaching (both in the sense of 'public' and 'clear'; pp. 143/25; 144/35); we are also informed that he submitted humbly to Thomas's doubts 'to þe more opun preue & certeyntye of his verrey Ressurexion' (p. 208/31–2). Miracles relating to the Eucharist are for the 'opune prefe of þe grete vertue þerof' (p. 230/7); there are more references to 'opune miracles' and 'opune prefes' in the passages which follow (pp. 235/10, 15; 236/36; 237/4).

Equally noticeable for its ubiquity in the *Mirror* is the invocation of 'reason'. The nature of the role of 'reason' in faith is of course an issue with a vast prehistory in Christian thought.[54] However, as we have already examined in relation to Wyclif and the English Wycliffite Sermons, the notion of 'reason' was put to an ambiguous and highly polemical use in Lollard hermeneutic discourse. Contemporary opponents of the Lollards noted their theoretical reliance on 'reason',[55] and Nicholas Love seems to have been no exception. The *Mirror* is, as a result, pervasively, almost obsessively, concerned either to justify its own biblical *lectio* as rational, or to defend its transcendence of 'reason'. Towards the beginning, when translating the pseudo-Bonaventuran account of the debate amongst the four daughters of God, Love introduces a new character: Resone, the Chancellor of God. It is he who reads out the divine 'determination' of the conflict (p. 16/9–16); and it is he who finally 'termyne[s] which person of þre fader & son & Holigost one god sholde become man', choosing 'soþfast wisdome þat is þe son, so þat as he felle to deþ by þe fals worde of þe feende, þat he rise aʒeyne to life by þe trew worde of gode' (p. 17/29–31). He thus devises the 'most resonable victory of þe enmy' (p. 17/31). 'Reason', here, in a fashion akin to Lollard usage, seems to stand for both 'divine reason' and human rationality.

Jesus was named thus because the word means 'saviour'; therefore 'þis name resonably is aboue al names' (p. 40/37–8). When contemplating the poverty of Mary and Joseph, 'be reson we shold be stired to compassion' (p. 49/25–6). Jesus goes with his parents to Jerusalem 'to honour & wirchipe his fadere of heuen in hese fest dayes as reson wolde' (p. 57/31–2). When Mary discovers that he has been left behind in Jerusalem, she is grief-stricken: 'Wherfore here we mowen haue resonably gret compassion of þe gret anguyshe þat our ladies soule is now inne for hir sone' (p. 58/26–8). Jesus chose simple fishermen instead of learned clerks as the 'ground' of the Church so that the worthy deeds done by them might be ascribed not to their own merits but to that of Jesus himself: 'þis he reseruede & kept to him self as it was reson' (p. 80/27–8). If we look upon the poverty and the hunger of the disciples, 'we oweþ resonably to be stirede to þe loue of pouerte' (p. 98/20–1). When the Jews try to trap Jesus into claiming godhead to be able to accuse him as a traitor to Caesar, he answers with innocent discretion: 'And forþermore when oure lord hade concludet hem in þat party by reson & auctorite of holi writte, þat þei miht not aʒeyn seye, & þei not withstandyng his resonable & meke answere, & so gudely wordes, continueden . . . in hir malice' (p. 128/32–6). Jesus chose to have supper at the house of Simon the Pharisee where Mary Magdalen had first expressed her contrition to him, because he knew that she loved that place and wished to do her joy: 'for þat one skil he chase þat place at þat tyme, specialy for Maries sake as we mowe resonably suppose' (p. 138/39–41). The monastic practice of fasting on Wednesday is defended as being 'resonably ordeinet' because Christ was (supposedly) betrayed to his enemies on a Wednesday (p. 145/17). There are four important *notabilia* about the last supper, 'of þe whech inward meditacion shal by reson stir

oure loue to oure lord Jesu' (p. 146/31–2). Jesus's 'gift' to man on this occasion – the Eucharist – should 'by reson' kindle man's soul and inflame it
to love (p. 151/43), for we must always bear in mind the 'gracious & resonable makyng & ordinance of þat blessede sacrament' (p. 152/24–5).
The phrase 'gracious & resonable ordinance' recurs later (pp. 156/15,
223/5). The disciples' grief must 'resonably' stir us to great compassion
(p. 158/16); the supreme charity of Christ is above all expressed in his
passion, which should 'resonably' inflame and burn our hearts in love
(p. 162/39). The wisdom of the clerks and 'reason' accord in supposing
that Christ must have had the 'clannest complexione þat euer was manne
or miht be' (p. 161/31). When Jesus asks for the cup to be passed from
him, God the Father explains that the redemption of mankind 'may not
be fulfilled & done so conueniently & resonably without shedyng of his
blode' (p. 165/39–41). The day of the Ascension is 'by reson' greater
and holier than any other (p. 218/22). The Pseudo-Bonaventura spec-
ulates about the food that the angels served Jesus after his long fast:
'De hoc enim scriptura non loquitur. Possumus autem hoc uictoriosum
prandium sicut uolumus ordinare' (p. 89/121–3; pp. 539–540). Love
translates: 'Here of spekeþ not holi writ, wherfore we mowe here ymag-
ine by reson & ordeyne þis worþi fest as vs likeþ, not by errour affermyng
bot deuoutly ymaginynge & supposyng' (p. 74/40–3).

Indeed, Love virtually introduces into the *Meditationes* the concept of 'resonable ymagynacioun' in relation to the Gospels.[56] The
Pseudo-Bonaventura's rhetorical question about the apostles' tears in
the episode of the raising of Lazarus (Caput 66, 'An non credis quod
et ipsi fuerint lacrimati?', p. 230/31; p. 592) is rendered as: '& as reson
telleþ þe disciples wepene' (p. 132/24). In an interpolated passage
in the course of the Thursday meditation, Love wonders what Jesus
might have done on the Wednesday preceding the Passion: 'what dide
oure lord Jesus & his blessed cumpany þat day? We fynde not writen
expresse in þe gospele . . . Me þinke it resonably to be trowede, þat he
was . . . occupiede in praiere' (p. 145/25–6). In yet another passage
original to him, Love speaks of the 'vnresonable ymaginacion' which
blinds 'gostly', making men believe that Jesus's godhead reduced the
intensity of his sufferings as man (p. 161/8–9). Again, 'we resonably
mowe suppose' the harsh words with which the torturers of Christ
upbraid him (p. 168/17). Jesus's apocryphal appearance to his mother

'may be resonably trowede' (p. 195/3); for even though 'it is not writen in any place . . . we resonably & deuoutly trowe it as it is seide before' (p. 211/4–5). After the Ascension of Jesus, we may 'resonably trowe' that all the host of heaven rejoiced in song (p. 217/20).

This emphasis on reason ties in with Love's general defensiveness in relation to the devout imagination, which 'invents' meanings (in both senses), and forms part of his response to Wycliffite insistence on 'open reason' in the interpretation of the Bible. In the passages I have examined above, 'reason' is treated positively, either as an aspect of the divine ordinance of things, or as an aspect of the ideal devotional *mentalité*. There is, however, another dimension to his response to 'reason'. In this more traditional scheme, the truths of faith transcend mere 'reason'; therefore what is called for is 'buxom' acquiescence in the formulations of Holy Church. Anything in belief that passes 'kyndly reson' must be believed as true according to the dictates of the Church (p. 22/23–5). Later, 'reson' is coupled with 'sensualite' (the *Meditationes* has a reference only to 'sensualitas', p. 49/34; p. 525) as part of the incomprehension inherent in the fallen human condition: Joseph and Mary are moved by their 'kyndly' reason and sensuality to pray God the Father to defend his son, even though they know that the latter had assumed manhood for our salvation (p. 52/40–3). In another passage, customs 'grondet vpon reson' are polarised against the biddings of God and the ordinances of the Church; though the former are acceptable, the latter are infinitely more important (p. 112/39–43). When Christ ordains the Eucharist, the disciples in their wonder 'laft alle hir kyndely reson of manne, & onely restede in trew byleue' (p. 151/33–5). Christ's ordinance of the sacrament is thus simultaneously 'reasonable' (p. 152/24), and 'aʒeynus mannus reson' (p. 153/41).

The conflict between the two visions of 'reason' informs the 'Treatise on the Sacrament' as well. There are repeated assertions of the Eucharist's transcendence of 'kyndely reson', here generally coupled with 'bodily wittes', and generally opposed to 'trewe byleue' (pp. 227–9). We are warned not to 'seke curiously in ymaginacioun of reson þe merueiles of þis worþi sacrament' – note how even the normally desirable meditative category of 'resonable ymaginacioun' is rejected here (p. 229/32–3). 'Grete clerkes' are criticised for relying upon their 'kyndely reson, & þe principales of philosophy, þat is mannus wisdame grondete only in kyndely reson of man' (p. 237/24–6). The 'disciples of Anticrist þat bene clepede Lollardes' do precisely this, relying on the false doctrine of Wyclif, 'þe whech þorh his grete clergy & kunnyng of philosophye was deceyuede in þat he ȝaf more credence//to þe doctrine of Arestotele þat stant onely in naturele reson of man' (p. 238/36–9). Aristotle, along with natural reason, teaches that accidents cannot remain without substance; therefore the 'maister of Lollardes' relying on 'naturele science' reproved and scorned the sacrament (p. 239/7–13). However, after this – one would have thought – decisive rejection of the pretensions of reason in the domain of faith, Love executes a sudden volte-face: 'In þe which [true] byleue by reson we sholde be so saddely sette þat after þe sentence of þe apostle Poule, þouh//þere came done an Angele fro heuene & tauht þe contrarye we sholde not ȝiue credence to him' (p. 239/29–32).

I have been arguing that Love's use of the concepts of 'reason' and 'open meanings' is polemical and combative, turning against the Lollards words which had assumed prominence in the 'Lollard sect vocabulary'. This becomes particularly clear in an original passage (sign-posted as such by Love's customary marginal 'N') in the course of the Wednesday meditation. The passage is described in the margin as against Lollard views of confession. Mary Magdalen's contrition is wordless; and this gives rise to the 'fals opinyon of lollardes þat shrift of mouþe is not nedeful, bot þat it sufficeþ onely in herte to be shriuen to god' (p. 92/42–4). Love offers 'an answere resonable'. Jesus was both man and God, and therefore Magdalen's inner contrition was 'opune' to him 'as is to man þe spech of mouþe, as oft siþes þe processe of þe gospel telleþ, & specialy here opunly' (p. 93/7–9). Since we do not have the God-man as our confessor, it is necessary that our contrition be expressed in words. And so Holy Church has 'resonably' ordained 'knowlech by mouþe'. Love continues:

> we haue perfite ensaumple opunly shewed in þis blessede woman þat was before so sinful Marie maudleyn in þe processe before seide of þis gospel, as it is opune ynogh touching þe first part & þe last, þat is to sey repentance & satisfaccion. & as to þe seconde þat is confession þouh we rede it not of hir by worde spekyng, for þat was no nede to him þat knewe fully hir herte. (pp. 93/39–40/1)

Love is also conscious of the Lollard emphasis on the 'literal' sense and on divine intentionality; and he is as uncertain in his response to these

Lollard positives as he is to 'reason'. On the one hand, there is an overt distrust of the letter; on the other, there is an obvious need to prove that 'gostly' readings, grounded in reason, are evidence of the *intentio auctoris* and therefore valid. In *Die veneris*, Chapter 44, there is an interpolated passage where Love discusses Jesus's momentous words 'My God! My God! why hast thou forsaken me?' The literal understanding of the words is false, says Love, and the enemies of Christ rejoiced in that falsehood. They failed to realise that these words are used by Jesus not to mean what they seem to mean but to betoken his full assumption of manhood and all its incomprehension in suffering:

> Soþely as it semeþ þer was neuer worde þat oure lorde Jesus spake þat
> ȝafe so miche boldenes to hees enemyes . . . for [þei] vndirstode it þat
> tyme bot nakedly[57] after þe letter sowneþ. Bot oure lord wolde shewe
> in to þe last ende, þat as he suffrede in body fully after þe kynde of
> man so also in his spekyng after þe infirmite of man. (p. 179/25–32)

In another passage original to Love – and this is an *ymaginacioun* – the overt meaning of the psalm *Deus laudem* is displaced by the meaning intended by Jesus when he uttered it, we are asked to imagine, on the Wednesday preceding the Passion:

> And so skilfully men mowe suppose, þat in þat praiere to þe fadere
> specialy he seide þe psalme *Deus laudem*, þat dauid seide in prophecye
> of him, & of Judas . . . bot þan moste proprely it was seide of him self,
> not desiring by þe wordes of þat psalme veniance of hese enmyes, as
> it semeþ after þe sentence of þe letter bot conformyng his wille riht-
> wisly to þe wille of þe fadere, &//propheciyng þe riȝtwise punishing
> & veniance deseruyng of hem, þat so maliciously conspirede aȝeynus
> him. (p. 145/35–43)

Once again, it is the *intentio dictatoris* which endows the words with their true meaning.

The key word in this context, as we have seen before, was 'express', used, like 'open', to denote meanings not requiring interpretation, meanings which are transparently informed by authorial intention. Speaking of Mary and Martha, the Pseudo-Bonaventura says: 'Scire autem debes quod per istas duas sorores dicunt sancti duplicem uitam intelligi, scilicet actiuam, et contemplatiuam' (p. 172/22–3; p. 570). Love translates this first: 'By þees tweyn sisteres . . . as holy men & doctoures writen ben vndurstande tweyn maner lifes of cristen men' (p. 120/2–4). This piece of traditional hermeneutics, where scriptural meaning is dictated from without by the academic and spiritual establishment, is however followed, a few pages later, by an emphasis on the 'intrinsic', 'intended' meaning of the episode of the two sisters. Discussing John 11.20 in a passage original to him, Love says:

> And so it semeþ by þees wordes, so specialy after þe letter tellyng howe þese tweyn sistres Martha & Maria, diuersely hadden hem as anentes Jesu þat þe holi euangelist *John menede gostly here* as he doþ in oþere places . . . Lo how *expressly* here also is tokened gostly what longeþ to þe contemplatife. (pp. 130/36–131/39; italics mine)

The unease with a traditional hermeneutic model which finds expression here also extends to Love's attitude to the Pseudo-Bonaventura's lavish and delighted meditative uncertainty about the details of the events recorded in the gospel. The more uncertain they are, the greater is the imaginative scope offered to the devout reader. Love generally tends to curb the meditative excesses of his source. The *Meditationes*, describing the Last Supper, points out that the gospel does not make it clear whether Christ and his disciples stood or sat at board when the Paschal Lamb was presented to them. However, the Pseudo-Bonaventura goes on, one can meditate in both ways: 'Sed attende quod dupliciter potes hic meditari: uno modo, ut sedeant, ut dixi; alio, ut stent recti' (p. 244/60–3; p. 596). Love is much more brusque: 'So þat þouh þei stoden in þat tyme, neuerles þei seten also in oþer tyme, as þe gospel telleþ in diuerse places' (p. 148/10–12). In *Die Veneris*, Love discusses the two possible ways in which Jesus might have been crucified: either he was nailed to the cross which had been erected already, or he was nailed prone on the cross before it was raised and set in the mortice on the ground. The Pseudo-Bonaventura, after giving one version, says: 'Sunt tamen qui credunt quod non hoc modo fuerit crucifixus . . . Quod si hoc magis placet, conspice' (pp. 271/44–272/48; p. 606). This fine Franciscan tentativeness is replaced in Love by an almost irritated dismissal of the issue: 'Bot wheþer so it be in one maner or in oþere soþe it is þat oure lorde Jesus was nailede harde vpon þe crosse'[58] (p. 177/37–9).

The impression produced by these slight but pervasive modifications of the pseudo-Bonaventuran passages referring to the gospel text, along with his emphasis on 'reason', suggest that Love was having to come to terms with contemporary Wycliffite criticism of the Church's 'perverse' glossings of God's Word and its emphasis on the non-canonical. Indeed, he occasionally leaves out some of the apocryphal material in his original: the pseudo-Bonaventuran Caput LXXII ('Quomodo Dominus Jesus praedixit mortem suam matri'), and references to Joseph of Arimathia and the lesser James.[59] Love's translation thus seeks to accommodate, even while implicitly rejecting, the Lollard valorisation of *sola scriptura* understood according to God's intention.

Such an impression is further strengthened by the *mise-en-page* of the *Mirror* manuscripts, which is characterised by a quite remarkable degree of uniformity for a widely-disseminated vernacular text of this period. Ian Doyle points to this:

> Most copies are on skin, of small quarto or folio size, by practised scribes, with ample colour and illumination of initials, rubrics, head-lines, etc., and the Latin notes . . . contents-table, prologue, side notes, appended treatise varying little in relative disposition, though not always all present.[60]

I have examined forty manuscripts,[61] including one that contains substantial extracts but not the whole text (Cambridge, University Library, Hh.i.11), and found thirty-five of them to be very similar in general disposition and lay-out. They include the important Cambridge, University Library, MS Additional 6578 which Sargent chooses as his base manuscript, and which might have been the very copy presented to Arundel for his approbation.[62] They provide substantial evidence that the text, marginalia and the pattern of rubrication were standardised, presumably at some early point in the process of transmission.

Such standardisation has important implications. The general uniformity of the manuscripts suggests a careful interest in the 'uncorrupted' transmission of the text. Sargent notes that 'the number of major alterations to the text of *The Mirror of the Blessed Life of Jesus Christ*, as compared to such contemporary texts as Walter Hilton's *Scale of Perfection*, William Flete's *Remedies Against Temptations*, or the works of Richard Rolle . . . is remarkably small, and the degree of textual variation on the whole is remarkably little'. He suggests that this textual uniformity – and, one may emphasise, the uniformity of presentation – arises from the *Mirror's* embeddedness in the Lollard conflict: a polemical work must after all ensure that its polemic is transmitted without change, and the Lollards were particularly careful about the transmission of their own texts.[63]

More recently, Sargent has identified what he designates as the β- and α-recensions of the *Mirror*. The former he considers to be instances of a 'pre-publication' version of Love's text, circulating before it had been examined officially, and betraying, through certain textual disruptions, an on-going process of composition and revision; the latter being a more finished, 'post-publication' version circulated after the approbation of Arundel had been obtained.[64] It is to be noted, however, that the same apparatus, in terms of marginalia and patterns of rubrication, characterises manuscripts of both recensions. This would suggest that it formed an integral part of the very conception of the *Mirror*, accompanying the text, in the terms of Sargent's analysis, in both the (as it were) 'draft' and 'final' versions.

What is even more interesting is the nature of the *mise-en-page*. Much of the marginal apparatus is devoted to the identification of cited authorities, often in scrupulous detail,[65] and the quotation of biblical passages in the Latin of which the translations are found in the body of the text. Almost all the manuscripts display the same marginalia, with relatively few variations.[66] There are a number which omit large sections, or discontinue the marginalia after a certain point, but the bits and pieces which do appear belong recognisably to the same apparatus. Among the manuscripts I have examined, this is the case with sixteen;[67] of the rest only two are without any marginalia at all (Cambridge, University Library Hh.i.11, Oxford, Bodleian Library, Bodley 634), the remaining ones displaying a full or nearly full apparatus. Thus, despite some variation, there is a general uniformity in the presentation of the text and the contents and location of the marginalia. This uniformity would suggest that the apparatus may have been authorially endorsed[68] or at least officially ratified initially[69] so that scribal transmission was relatively careful and regular.

The other major element in the presentation of the text is rubrication. There is a more or less consistent attempt at distinguishing biblical words from non-scriptural material by rubrication, underlining or, as occasionally in Oxford, Bodleian Library, Bodley 131, by using a different script. Once again, there is a degree of variation, with some manuscripts being more careful in separating biblical and non-biblical words than others. At their most rigorous, the manuscripts give the Latin biblical text in the margin in red, the vernacular translation being underlined in red in the body of the text. A variant of this pattern involves incorporating the Latin biblical citations into the body of the text in red, in which case the vernacular translations are often left unmarked.[70] Of the manuscripts I have studied, twenty-four display a more or less uniform interest in rubrication; around twelve are lax, with occasional bursts of precision,[71] and only four are without any attempt at rubrication. These are Cambridge, University Library, Hh.i.11, Glasgow, University Library, Gen. 1130, London, British Library, Additional 11565 and Additional 19901.

What is fascinating about this careful and self-conscious presentation of the text in the *Mirror* manuscripts is how substantially it differs from that of the contemporary manuscripts of the *Meditationes Vitae Christi*.[72] The *Meditationes* manuscripts from the fourteenth and fifteenth centuries occur in a vast variety of forms, from relatively lavish productions such as Cambridge, University Library, Kk.iv.23, to little pocket-books such as Oxford, Bodleian Library, Canon Liturg. 226, meant for quotidian personal meditation. However, the typical *mise-en-page*, irrespective of the quality of the manuscript, is characterised by an almost entire absence of scribal marginalia and rubrication. The text, though divided into chapters preceded by rubricated headings, is presented, within each chapter, as a solid undifferentiated mass. There is no standardised attempt at distinguishing scriptural words from the rest – even momentous utterances such as 'Consummatum est' can remain unmarked. There is no marginal citation of authorities, though there is intensive, unmarked citation within the text itself. A few manuscripts, such as London, British Library, Royal 7D. xvii underline the names of cited authorities while ignoring biblical words; and one or two, such as Oxford, Bodleian Library, Bodley 162, attempt to mark out scriptural words, though occasionally underlining what is regarded as important non-scriptural material as well. But most go for the undifferentiated presentation, the implied pattern of reading being obviously one with close affinities to the monastic *lectio*. The reader is expected, like St. Cecilia, to 'port[are] . . . in pectore' the 'Euangelium Christi' (p. 7/5–6; p. 510).

The *Mirror* manuscripts on the other hand give evidence that a great deal of thought has been devoted to the presentation of the text. I have come across only one manuscript which follows the Latin pattern with neither marginalia nor biblical rubrication: Cambridge, University Library, Hh.i.11. This manuscript, however, is a special case, since it consists of a miscellany, probably made by nuns, with extensive extracts from the *Mirror* along with extracts from *The Prickynge of Love*, *The Seven Poyntes of Trewe Love and Everlastynge Wisdome*, the Middle English *Revelations* of Elizabeth of Hungary, Flete's *Remedies against Temptations*, Walter Hilton and Anselm of Canterbury.[73] Most other *Mirror* manuscripts are very different. Authorities are marked and identified, and biblical words are distinguished from non-scriptural material. Of course, the precision with which such a distinction is made falls far short of the consistency and meticulousness one finds in Lollard manuscripts. Indeed, the very form of the *Mirror*, based as it is on an inextricable mingling of the scriptural and the non-scriptural, would make the achievement of anything like Wycliffite textual precision near-impossible. Equally interesting are the extensive marginal citations of authorities and the almost uniform omission of gospel-chapter citations in the chapter headings.[74] The pseudo-Bonaventuran manuscripts regularly provide gospel references in the capitula, and the French version by Jean Galope in Cambridge, Corpus Christi College MS 213, for instance, largely follows this pattern. So does Paris, Bibliothèque Nationale, MS Ital.115, the Italian version on which Isa Ragusa's and Rosalie Green's edition of the *Meditationes* is based.[75]

What emerges from this evidence is a certain indeterminacy in authorial and/or official attitude towards the text. The meditative thrust of its contents would seem to be in conflict with the academic, textual consciousness implied by the *ordinatio*.[76] At the same time, the relative paucity of precise references to the gospel-chapters would fit in with the transmission of the *Mirror* as an implied substitute for the gospel. As with Love's attitude towards the tradition of meditative reinvention of the gospels which supports the *Meditationes*, there seems to be a central dubiety in his attitude towards his chosen *ordinatio* and its ideological implications. In mediating to a vernacular audience a familiar text with its own, associated, modes of reading in a political context critical of received notions of text and authority, Love shows himself to be caught between two worlds: one insisting on the identity of the authority of scripture and that of the ecclesiastical establishment, the other emphasising the disjunction between the two. The tradition of the exegetical reinvention of scripture, of which the *Meditationes* forms an important part, was one which rendered unnecessary an academic presentation that pointed out textual or authoritative boundaries. In fact, the new textual consciousness extends, in Love's case, to making a distinction between his additions to the pseudo-Bonaventuran text and the original. Twenty-seven manuscripts of the *Mirror* are preceded by the following notice:

> Attende lector huius libri prout sequitur in Anglico scripti, quod vbicumque in margine ponitur litera N verba sunt translatoris siue compilatoris . . . Et quando peruenitur ad processum & verba eiusdem doctoris [Bonaventura] inseritur in margine litera B.

> Note, reader of the following book written in English, that wherever the letter 'N' is placed in the margin, the words are added by the translator or compiler . . . And when it returns to the narrative and words of that doctor, then the letter 'B' is inserted in the margin.[77] (p. 7)

But the actual realisation of this principle, at least in all the manuscripts now extant, is half-hearted, for it is only sporadically that the additions are indeed signalled by a marginal 'N'. This is in sharp contrast to the precision of (possibly) another Carthusian of the time, 'M. N.', the translator of Margarete Porete's *Le Mirouer des Simples Ames*.[78] It survives in three manuscripts, of which I have examined Cambridge, St. John's College MS C. 21.[79] M. N.'s additions take the form of distinct and separable units, which makes his task relatively simple.[80] In contrast, Love's inadequately realised, yet, given the unexceptionable nature of his source-text, unusually punctilious gesture in the direction of textual precision suggests once again that ideas about textual authority akin to those of the Lollards are being imposed upon a translation based on principles which simply refuse any such imposition. For the *Mirror* does not subscribe to any conception of textual fidelity: the alterations to the *Meditationes* are too minutely pervasive for it to be really possible to separate addition from original. It is as if one were to sit down with Chaucer's 'translacioun' of *Il Filostrato* and try to place a marginal 'C' beside each of his 'in-echings'.

The *Mirror* thus articulates a hesitant and uncertain response to the ideological implications of the modes of textual presentation favoured by the Lollards. As I have argued, this uncertainty has its roots in Love's fundamentally ambiguous conceptualisation of the nature of valid scriptural 'authority'. Thomas Netter of Walden, writing his monumental anti-Wycliffite encyclopaedia in the 1420s, is, as we shall see in the next chapter, far less ambivalent about fighting the enemy on its own ground. Extant manuscripts of the *Doctrinale Antiquitatum Fidei Catholicae Ecclesiae* such as Cambridge, University Library, Dd. viii. 16–17 or Oxford, Bodleian Library, Bodley 262 scrupulously distinguish Netter's own contributions from those of his authorities: these original passages are always prefaced by the word 'actor' in red.

Thomas Netter, however, was writing a work of reference in an academic-ecclesiastical textual environment. As such, his self-conscious interest in matters of presentation, though of heightened significance in the Lollard context, is not entirely unexpected. In contrast, the evidence of the *Mirror* manuscripts is indeed remarkable. It is tempting to suggest that the *Mirror* bears witness to orthodox recognition of an important Lollard achievement: the breaking-down of the barrier between an enclosed academic milieu with its own rules and conventions of written communication, and a wider, comparatively unlearned world of lay devotion.

6

Thomas Netter and John Wyclif: hermeneutic *confrères*?

Thomas Netter of Walden,[1] writing against Wyclif in the 1420s, shares, to one's initial surprise, in the hermeneutic world of his opponent. The peculiar high-medieval synthesis of faith, scepticism and conservative politics which informs William Woodford's theoretical tracts, the *Quattuor Determinationes*, and which is so alien to the modes of Wyclif's thought, is replaced in Netter's *Doctrinale Antiquitatum Fidei Catholicae Ecclesiae*[2] by a remarkable (though often, by virtue of their very different politics, tenuously sustained) agreement with the heresiarch on certain fundamental assumptions about the nature of Christianity. And this is perhaps not so remarkable after all: for Woodford's work assumes a secure political and academic environment which had been severely threatened by the time Netter was writing.[3] Though Netter does not, as a rule, address directly the problems raised by the conversion of Wycliffism into an extra-mural movement of popular radicalism,[4] his work is informed by an urgent consciousness of the necessity of endowing the ecclesiastical *status quo* with a firm theoretical anchorage. His is a full-scale attempt at justification, but like Wyclif's work and unlike that of Woodford, it betrays no pragmatic awareness of itself as one kind of rhetorical gesture among several. The academic, sceptical-rhetorical consciousness of the contingency of authorities and interpretations and their implicatedness in the uncertainties and mutabilities of various kinds of politics is rigorously – often uneasily – shunned by Netter: he is very much, like his opponent, arguing for determinate religious truth.

Netter was a Carmelite and Prior Provincial of the order from 1414 till 1430, when he died. He studied in Oxford, and remained in touch with the university. He participated in a number of Lollard trials, among them those of John Badby (1410), Sir John Oldcastle (1413), William Taylor (1423) and William White (1428). He attended the Council of Pisa in 1409, and most probably the Council of Constance in 1414.[5]

The *DFC* is a vast encyclopaedic work, divided into six books, of which the first four are relatively short (forming volume 1 by early convention), the final two each occupying, in many manuscripts and in the 1757–9 Venetian edition, a separate volume. Though the date of Netter's commencement of the work is uncertain, papal letters of acknowledgement show that the first volume had been completed by 1 April 1426 and the second by 8 April 1427. The third volume was completed before Netter died in November 1430.[6] The three volumes deal comprehensively with Wyclif's views of the deity and the Church (Books 1 and 11); with issues of special concern to the 'private religions' (Books III and IV); and with the sacraments and sacramentals (Books V and VI). The most extended discussion of Netter's work as a whole is the doctoral dissertation of K. S. Smith, who pays special attention to Netter's ecclesiology of 'Tradition'.[7] For the purposes of this chapter, I have focussed on those sections of the *DFC* which deal explicitly with issues of hermeneutics and textuality, though one must remember that Netter's entire discussion is informed by a vision of right *auctoritas* based on and emerging from his engagement with the interrelationship of scriptural interpretation and the Church. The passages I examine are from the Prologue, the first Article of Book 1 ('Qui est de Essentia, Potencia, & Scientia Dei'), the second Article of Book II ('Qui est de Ecclesia in Communi, de qua est fides in Symbolo'), the section entitled 'De Sacramento Eucharistiae' from Book V, and relevant discussions of the validity of images from Book VI.[8] The following discussion is therefore by no means a comprehensive one; rather, it is offered as an introduction to some of the characteristic emphases of this important fifteenth-century anti-Lollard text, emphases which, taken together, afford a fascinating insight into the impact of Wycliffite thought – in both hermeneutic and methodological terms – on contemporary intellectual orthodoxy. It will be my contention in this chapter, as I have suggested earlier in the Introduction, that Netter's *anti-*Wycliffite thought shows crucial epistemological affinities with Wyclif's own, affinities which point towards new directions in fifteenth-century intellectual *mentalités*.

An important and abiding theoretical distinction in the *DFC*, is, in fact, Wycliffite: the distinction between 'text' and 'interpretation'. For Woodford, as we have seen, such a distinction can at best be tenuous: there is no 'text', in any meaningful sense, independent of the web of interpreting individuals and institutions which constitutes hermeneutic *auctoritas*. In particular, the Bible is the product of a multitude of historical and political circumstances, and attempts at final readings of so complicated and disputed a document, the very composition of which is open to debate, must necessarily be misguided. The same consciousness underlies Woodford's ecclesiology, expressed in his refusal to postulate an idealised *ecclesia primitiva* offering frozen, static Christian values in a permanently pure and accessible form, and as such, constituting the norm against which the modern faith must be judged. Netter, on the contrary, accepts both the existence of and the normative role of the primitive church.

In the *DFC*, a firm theoretical distinction is made between the sense of sacred scripture and what he describes as 'our sense'. In his extended discussion in Book V of important eucharistic passages in the Bible, he includes a chapter entitled: 'Wycleffus quomodo abutatur scripturae verbis contra sacram Eucharistiam (How Wyclif misuses the words of scripture against the sacred Eucharist)':

> Hoc etiam unum cupio christianis omnibus esse commune, ut cum scripta divina proferimus, ea non captivemus sensibus nostris, sed eis potius nostros captivemus sensus. (II.236)

> But this one [thing] I desire to be in common to all Christians, that when we cite the divine scriptures, we do not make them captive to our senses, but rather make our senses captive to them.

A passage from Augustine's *De Genesi ad litteram*[9] is cited as authority: we should make scriptural *sentence* ours rather than attempting to prove ours scriptural. Wyclif and his followers fight not for the *sentence* of scripture but for their own:

> non pro sententia divinae Scripturae, sed pro sua dimicant, ut eam velint esse Scripturae sanctae sententiam, quae sua est, tamquam pueri dicentes: Ecce Scriptura dicit Christum esse primam literam, & ultimam Alphabeti, quia ipsemet dicit: *Ego sum alpha et omega*; & tamquam pueri exinde contendant Christum esse illud mutum, & sensibile elementum. (II.236)

> They fight not for the meaning of divine scripture, but for their own, as if they wish what is their own [meaning] to be the meaning of Holy Scripture, saying, as if [they are] children: 'See how Scripture says that Christ is the first and last letters of the alphabet, because he himself says, "I am alpha and omega"'; and, like children, from that contend Christ to be that senseless and perceptible element [in the Eucharistic bread].

Note, incidentally, the reference to the child's powers of perception, which Netter shares with Woodford. But whereas for the latter, the child's limited powers of understanding the scriptures are invoked, characteristically, as an argument against Wyclif's attempts at fixing scriptural meaning – meaning must necessarily be dependent on the reader[10] – Netter groups Wyclif along with children for reading into Holy Writ his own unwarranted meanings. The implication is of course that there are valid meanings elsewhere which do not depend on the reader. Netter sees himself as fighting not for his own *sentence* but for that of Christ and the Apostles.

Interestingly, Netter proceeds immediately to invoke intentionality as the defining criterion of meaning. Wyclif pays more attention to the material bread in Christ's words than to the bread of his flesh, which Christ above all intended to signify:

> Sic idem dicit, corpus suum esse panem mutum & sensibilem, quia dixit *Hoc est corpus meum*; retinens semper in ore suo saporem panis materialis, quem audivit Christum in manibus accepisse; sed ad panem carnis suae, quam Christus potissime intendebat, nunquam attendens. (II.236)

> Thus [Wyclif] says that [Christ's] body is senseless and perceptible bread, since Christ said, 'This is my body', retaining always in his [Wyclif's] mouth the taste of material bread, which he has heard Christ take into his hands, but never attending to the bread of his flesh which Christ above all intended [to signify].

Netter proceeds, in a very clever move, to damn Wyclif's interpretation of Christ's words (that the substance of bread remains after consecration) as not only an incomprehension of Christ's intention, but also as a violation of biblical textuality – Wyclif 'adds' the word 'natural' to the biblical text: 'Addat enim panem naturalem, dicens *Hoc est corpus & naturalis panis*, & jam falsum dicens peperit inequitatem, formavit errorem' ('For [Wyclif] adds "natural bread", saying, "This is [my] body and natural bread", and already uttering a falsehood, he has given birth to inequity and created error', II.237). Rev. 22:18 is next cited: 'If any man shall add unto these things, God shall add unto him the plagues that are written in this book'.

The implication is that some interpretations are not 'additions' to the text but are merely 'elucidations'. Only the Church interprets, or rather 'understands', *pure* – 'purely', 'clearly', 'completely', for it possesses the sense 'closer' to that of the evangel:

> Quis non videt jam Ecclesiam habere propinquiorem Evangelii sensum? Pure enim observat in consecrando, pure intelligit quod Christus dixit . . . Sancta ergo Ecclesia Catholica, et sola illa, vel membrum ejus, potest vere dicere.[11] (II.237–8)

> Who does not see now that the Church has the more faithful [nearer] sense of the Gospel? For it observes [this sense] completely in consecrating [the Host], and completely understands what Christ said . . . Therefore the Holy Catholic Church, and only it or its part, can pronounce truly [in matters of faith].

And one of the justifications of the Church's prerogative in matters of interpretation is, Netter suggests (once again invoking a principle dear to the Wycliffites), its reliance on the actual words of scripture. Indeed, when discussing the significance of the proposition 'Hoc est corpus meum', he uses the highly charged adverb 'nude',[12] thereby implicitly accepting Wyclif's emphasis on the primary importance of the biblical text shorn of its traditional interpretative apparatus:

> Sed hoc sufficit fidei Ecclesiae, quod verba Christi in Evangelio nude accepta panem denuntiant materialem in subjecto, & praecise panem; & corpus Christi verum in praedicato, nihilque aliud. (II.239)

> But this suffices to the faith of the Church, that the words of Christ in the Gospel, when taken nakedly [without any additions], point to the material bread, and specifically the bread [i.e. the bread alone], in the subject, and to the true body of Christ in the predicate, and to nothing else.

In fact, Netter repeatedly conflates two categories of 'perversion', one consisting in misinterpretation, and the other in corrupting the text. This follows from his identification of what he regards as 'correct' interpretation with the 'text' of the Bible, another point that he shares with the Wycliffites. The process perhaps needs to be explained in detail: on the one hand, a distinction is made between 'text' and 'interpretation', the implication being that some 'texts' are outside the domain of interpretation, and on the other, the categories of 'text' and 'correct interpretation' are conflated, since, it is held, 'correct interpretation' is necessarily a transparent elucidation of the text. This is precisely what Wyclif himself does in his polemic: as Hurley points out, many of *De Veritate's* allegations that the *moderni* dismiss scripture as 'falsissima et absurdissima'[13] merely imply that Wyclif's own interpretations were rejected.[14]

Netter, in a similar manner, denounces Wyclif's use of 'sit Deus omnia in omnibus' from 1 Cor. 15:28[15] to support his theory of eternal ideas. Wyclif is the worst possible interpreter, says Netter, because he simultaneously perverts the sense and corrupts the text: 'Pessimus commentator Scripturae Apostolicae, qui simul & semel pervertit sensum & corrumpit textum' ('[Wyclif is] the worst commentator on apostolic scripture, [because] he simultaneously and repeatedly perverts the sense and corrupts the text', 1.47).[16] After accusing Wyclif of 'transforming' 'scripturam Pauli in scripturam haeretici' ('the writing of Paul into the writing of a heretic'), Netter rounds off the section with the assertion that Wyclif's exposition is far from the apostolic text: 'Longe igitur est textus Apostoli ab expositione Wicleffi nostri, qui hoc exponit de Deo in ratione *principii*, quod dixit apostolus *de Deo* in ratione *finis*' ('The text of the Apostle is thus very far from the exposition of our Wyclif, who expounds in terms of the beginning what the apostle said about God in relation to the end', 1.48). Wyclif has misinterpreted what the Apostle said about the final state of the Church after resurrection by applying it to the present, and thereby 'transformed' scripture.[17] This recognition of the power of the reader to 'violate' ideal textual meanings is worthy of the author of *De Apostasia* himself.[18]

Indeed, the polarisation of 'text' and 'gloss' forms one of the fundamental theoretical (as well as ideological) assumptions in the *DFC*. Wyclif is described as the 'pessimus glossator' who interprets Grosseteste's opinion that accidents (in the Eucharist) remain by themselves, as meaning that accidents remain by themselves in the 'act of considering' of the faithful (II.497). Netter is appalled at such brazen distortion of the 'express words' of the doctor:

> Pessimus ergo glossator iste, qui arctat sensum Doctoris ad subsistentiam formarum accidentalium solum in *consideratione*, quando expressis verbis dicit eas subsistere in ipso esse.[19] (II.497)

> Therefore [Wyclif] is the worst glossator, [since he] limits the sense of the Doctor as to the subsistence of accidental forms solely to [subjective] 'consideration', when he [the Doctor] says in express words that they remain in [actual] being itself.

Netter proceeds to cite authorities against Wyclif's idiosyncratic reading of his *auctor*, and points out that Wyclif's gloss is both forced and extraneous, as well as contrary to 'all catholic writers'. For his reading to be of any value, Wyclif must show where sacred scripture speaks thus, and also demonstrate that the doctors whom he glosses maintain customarily that a thing cannot be absolutely present if not equally present in someone or other person's subjective 'consideration' (II.498–9). The discussion moves on to the relevant passage from Grosseteste, followed by an invocation of the 'prudent reader' (of the doctor): the latter will always find, somewhere in the doctor's writings, some indication of his mind, which would prove Wyclif's gloss to be false:

> Iam ergo quotiens glossam suam intulerit, inspiciat lector prudens verba Doctoris; & (non dubium) aliqua semper parte aliquid de mente Doctoris inveniet, quod glossam Wicleffi falsam esse convincet. (II.500)

> Now therefore how often [Wyclif] inflicts his [own] gloss, let the prudent reader inspect the Doctor's words [to assess]; and, without doubt, he will always find in some part [of the text] something [indicating] the Doctor's mind which will prove Wyclif's gloss to be false.

Netter is then moved to anger at Wyclif's cavalier hermeneutics in *De Apostasia*, where his 'distortions' of various *auctores* are followed by the statement (in Netter's quotation) that 'sic possunt glossari Doctores, quotquot venerint' ('Thus can the Doctors be glossed, as many as turn up').[20] Netter continues:

> Et hoc modo multo consonantius sensibus Doctorum, contra quorum glossas possunt glossae tuae seponi, quotquot venerint. Non dubium, ipsa veritas Doctoralis glosas respuit corruptrices a verbis suis, quantum mare detestatur & ejicit mortuos suos. (II.500)

And this way is much more consonant to the senses of the Doctors, against whose glosses your glosses, as they turn up, can be put aside. There is no doubt that doctoral truth itself has expelled corrupt glosses from its words, just as the sea detests and ejects its dead.

As was the case with Wyclif's image of scriptural truth as a ship, Netter's – of doctoral truth as the sea which detests and ejects its dead, i.e. corrupt glosses – seeks to locate the agency of meaning in the text. Wyclif's glosses are 'contra intentionem Philosophi' ('against the intention of the philosopher [being glossed]', as emerges if one goes back to the context, the 'integer textus' ('the whole text', II.501). Netter therefore repeatedly points to the entirely subjective and idiosyncratic nature of Wyclif's scriptural interpretations, which their author had endowed with the sanction of sacred intentionality:

> Vere in hoc ipso [divine revelation] tibi scutum formasti, sub quo satis errares impune, & hoc ipsum tu facis cum allegas Scripturas, & de sensu Spiritus Sancti, quasi tibi revelatus esset desuper, jactas inaniter. Quomodo ergo tibi definienti & erranti in materia fidei sub praetensa Scripturarum authoritate fidem vendicas, & pristinis haereticis fidem negas? (1.336)

> Indeed, you have formed your shield in this itself [i.e. in divine revelation], under which you err sufficiently with impunity; and you do the same [thing] when you cite the scriptures and boast in an inane fashion of the sense of the Holy Ghost, as if [it] would be revealed to you from above. Therefore how do you, [when you] define and err in matters of faith under the pretended authority of the scriptures, claim faith for yourself, and deny faith to the old heretics?

As Netter points out, all the ancient heretics operated in a very similar manner, invoking the assent of the Holy Ghost.[21] Moreover, Christians could easily point out that Wyclif's 'authorities' are misinterpreted and his claims to revelation a sham:

> Forsitan unum dicendo respondes, quia Scripturae eorum sunt extortae, & revelationes, illusiones sunt, & fictitiae. Sed qualiter hic probabis, aut quomodo vis fidelem inducere ut tibi credam potius sic dicenti, quam alteri deneganti? Sic enim de te dicunt Catholici, authoritates scilicet quas inducis, extortas esse, & nulla specialis revelationis certificatione suffultas. Cur & tu definis errorem circa fidem, & Praelatis denegas authoritatem definiendi pro fide? . . . Sed an

veram revelationem habueris, quomodo ego hoc sciam, ut credam? (1.336–7)

Perhaps you answer, saying, one, because their scriptures are distorted, and [their] revelations illusory and feigned. But how will you prove this, and how do you wish to persuade the faithful so that I may rather believe you saying thus, than another denying [what you say]? For the orthodox say this of you: the authorities which you present are distorted and are supported by no certificate of [any] special revelation. Why do you both define error [in matters of] faith and deny to prelates the authority to define for faith? . . . But if you were to have true revelation, how would I know this, so that I may believe?

Netter by this time has forced the debate over interpretation to one of its logical ends: each interpreter must invoke – at least in a monologic and positivistic framework of meaning – some certitudes to justify his readings, but these certitudes ('revelation' in this case) are equally open to hermeneutic variation. He therefore has to suggest a way out of this battle-ground of endlessly warring interpretations. He does so, first, by postulating, as we have already remarked, a 'text' which dictates its own 'proper' reading (shades of Wyclif again); and second, by stating that the 'true' church has access to this correct reading. The problems raised by such a formulation are twofold: the Bible is famously (or notoriously) a text full of 'slippages' from its apparently 'proper' meanings, and therefore peculiarly vulnerable to the agency of the interpreter; and second, what is the 'true church' and how are its teachings to be accessed?

It is while attempting to confront these problems that Netter's thought betrays its affinities – no less in its weaknesses than in its strengths – to that of Wyclif. We have seen how Wyclif primarily situates himself within a sciential hermeneutics (where rules for the interpretation of scripture are sought from within scripture itself), and then in effect redefines *scientia* to include all the interpretative liberties accommodated within the sapiential tradition. Netter too is ambiguous in his choice of hermeneutic framework. Like Wyclif, he shows a pronounced attraction towards *scientia*, and like Wyclif he is acutely aware of its possible pitfalls and inadequacies. However, where Wyclif conceptualises *sapientia* in individual terms – *caritas*, humility, *recte vivendi* and (therefore) inspiration – Netter centres *sapientia* in ecclesiastical interpretative traditions.[22] But there is one major problem. The hermeneutics which finds expression in 'tradition' is fundamentally dialogic, for tradition, as Wyclif recognised in his criticism of the Pope's power to dictate meaning, is an ever-developing realm of almost 'free-floating' scriptural or pseudo-scriptural signifiers assuming different meanings for different cultural and political systems. As a result, almost any opinion on any scriptural passage is likely to be contained in some one or other of its expositors; and one constructs the particular 'meaning' one wants by means of a judicious selection of authorities from the vast body of commentary literature. For a thinker such as Woodford, with his sceptical dialogic vision of meaning, 'tradition' poses no problem. For a positivist such as Netter, it does. What we witness, therefore, in Netter's conceptual tussles with 'tradition' is an attempt to render it monologic, to suggest that a unity of scriptural meaning emerges from a tradition which, in yet another Wycliffite resonance, is merely the herald, the 'praeco' of an unvitiated, indeed uninterpreted source of 'truth'.

I will begin by examining Netter's concept of the 'true church'.[23] It consists in an unbroken tradition handed down by Christ and the Apostles through the subsequent hierarchy to the present day. Individual members within this tradition may err now and then, but the tradition itself, based as it is on a superb consensus embracing the greatest and holiest of men over hundreds of years, cannot. When venturing into doubtful matters of faith, we must therefore inquire what the apostles and their successors felt, and take into account the opinion of the succession of 'approved' men after them including catholic doctors from our own time. Truth is then elicited from the concordance of their words:

> Ita nempe in dubiis fidei debemus inquirere quid senserunt Apostoli, quid successores Apostolorum, & deinceps viri probati, & usque ad haec nostra tempora Catholici Doctores, reliquerunt in scripturis; & secundum quod ipsorum verba concordant, sic elicere veritatem. (1.338)

> Certainly, in doubtful matters of faith, we must inquire what the apostles felt, [and] what their successors, and 'approved men' after them right up to the catholic doctors in our times have left in writings, and [we must] elicit the truth according to the harmony of their words.

Netter underlines the importance of consensus by citing Matt. 28:20 ('Ecce ego vobiscum sum omnibus diebus'); the testimony it provides is much more certain than that of any single person, which might be false:

> Non dixit, *tecum sum*, scilicet cum aliqua singulari persona, sed *vobis-cum sum*, cum tota Ecclesia Catholica et Apostolica, quae seduci non potest, nec seducere; & habet fidele testimonium de Christo, & novit omnia mysteria sponsi sui. Et nonne hoc certius testimonium, quod universalis spondet Ecclesia, quam quod unus aliquis forte mendax? (1.337)

> It does not say, *I am with thee*, i.e. with some single person, but *I am with you*, with the whole Catholic and Apostolic Church, which cannot be led astray, nor lead astray, and which has the faithful witness of Christ, and knows all mysteries of her spouse. And is not this a more certain witness, which the universal Church promises, than some individual perhaps deceitful?

Acts 15:28 is quoted ('visum est enim Spiritui Sancto et nobis nihil ultra imponere vobis oneris quam haec necessario') to make the case for a unity of Church and the Holy Spirit:

> non dixerunt, *visum est Spiritui Sancto, & Scripturae*, sed *Spiritui Sancto et nobis*, qui hic repraesentamus Ecclesiam; & non tamen *nobis* sine Spiritu Sancto, sed Spiritui Sancto in se, & Spiritui Sancto in nobis, in Ecclesia: qui in dubiis fidei nunquam deest Ecclesiae, promittente illi Christo, *Spiritus Sanctus docebit vos omnem veritatem.* (1.337)

> They do not say, *it seemed to the Holy Ghost and to Scripture*, but *to the Holy Ghost and to us*, who here represent the Church; and yet not *to us* without the Holy Ghost, but to the Holy Ghost in itself, and to the Holy Ghost in us, in the Church. The Holy Ghost never deserts the Church in doubtful matters of faith, Christ having promised to her: *the Holy Ghost will teach you all truth.*

The ideal of concordance, however, becomes problematic the moment it is used to counter Wyclif's potent criticism of the contemporary Church. Wyclif's point was precisely that the ecclesiastical 'concordance' of the recent past and the present was a false concordance, a corruption and perversion of the pure faith as it was preached and lived by Christ and his disciples, an agreement among the followers of Antichrist to cheat and deceive those who looked for the true light. Netter therefore has to insist that the ecclesiastical tradition as it survives is a true witness to the practices and beliefs of the primitive church. His historiography is therefore of a profound positivism, comparable to that of Wyclif. The Church is an uncorrupting witness to the first purity of the faith. The role of the witness is thus identical to that of the uninterpreting mediator. While some earlier medieval historiographies had a deep-seated and sophisticated awareness of any mediation of past events being necessarily a version among the many possible, a version based on either what is thought of as worthy of being remembered or the specific rhetorical aims of the historian,[24] both Netter and Wyclif have to postulate the possibility of an *essential* access to the past. Wyclif's point was that the present had fallen off and had to be taken back to the past; Netter's was that the past, in its essentials, survived in ecclesiastical traditions of the present.

It is fascinating to find him using the same image to describe the role of the Church in relation to the faith and the scriptures as Wyclif does to describe the role of the interpreter in relation to the text.[25] The Universal Church, we are told, is coeval with scripture and its 'institutor', Christ. Moreover, its witness is equally the object of the Christian faith as is Holy Writ itself. However, it is subject to the Bible as is the witness to the judge, evidence to truth, proclamation to definition, and herald to king:

> universalis Ecclesia catholica non est Scriptura Sacra posterior, sed coaeva ipsi, & ejus latori Christo, sicut sponsa sponso, & corpus capiti . . . Fides autem ut est Ecclesiae Catholicae, in hoc accedit fidei Scripturarum, quod non licet de ipsa dubitare, eo quod testimonium Ecclesiae Catholicae est objectum fidei Christianae, sicut est testimonium & legislatio Scripturae Canonicae. Subjicitur tamen ipsi sicut testis judici, & testimonium veritati, sicut praeconizatio definitioni, & sicut praeco Regi. (1.351)

> The universal catholic Church does not come after sacred scripture, but is coeval with it and its institutor Christ, like a wife to her husband, and a body to its head . . . But the faith of the Catholic Church is like the faith of scriptures in this that it is not permissible to doubt it, because the witness of the Catholic Church is the object of the Christian faith as is the witness and law of canonical scripture. Nevertheless it is subject to it as is the witness to the judge, and testimony to truth, proclamation to definition and herald to king.

The Church is subject to the faith of Christ and the Apostles as witnessed in the Bible – it is its 'unmediating mediator'. And though the truths of sacred scripture may be found in later works, these are by no means of the same authority, as their role is merely to expound.[26]

> Ideo, sicut hic dixit Augustinus, quamquam in posteriorum libris invenitur ipsa veritas Scripturarum, non tamen erit in eis par authoritas: ita quamvis Fides universalis Ecclesiae invenitur per Scriptura[m][27] expressa, sicut est pene tota; non tamen est ei in authoritate par, sed ei subjicitur. Et etiam quamvis in posteriorum libris etiam invenitur, non tamen sunt illi pares, sed ipsa praeponitur, *quia aliud sunt testes, aliud testimonium.* (1.351; italics mine)

> Therefore, as Augustine says here, even though the truth itself of the scriptures is found in later books, there will not, nevertheless, be in them similar authority. Thus although the faith of the universal Church is found expressed [with the sense of *expresse* latent as well?] in scripture, as [is the case] with almost the whole [of this faith], nevertheless, it is not equal in authority to it, but is subject to it. And even though it is found in later books, [these books] are not however equal to it [scripture]. Instead, [scripture] is put before them, *because witnesses are one thing, testimony another.*

This important distinction between witness and testimony – interpretation and text – is a fair pointer to Netter's certitudes. Like Wyclif, he accepts the possibility of 'accessing' the 'true' meanings of scripture and the 'original' norms and values of the *ecclesia primitiva*.

There is obviously an imminent danger here of Netter locking himself, like his opponent, in an impregnable tower, and claiming, like him, the possession of a direct line of access to the original *fons* of religion. But he avoids this by reason of his pronounced awareness of the dangers of hermeneutic subjectivism – a vice of which he repeatedly, and not entirely without justice, accuses Wyclif, and of which Wyclif himself had repeatedly accused the sophisters and the *doctores moderni*. Netter's position ultimately emerges as one relying on what may be described as 'statistical' evidence from the commentators of the first millennium. According to him, if there is any doubt over the interpretation of any matter of faith, one should collect the opinions of as many of the early patristic commentators as possible and examine where the centre of interpretative gravity lies. The faithful Christian, Netter points out, can object that 'scripturae possunt perverti, sanctorumque dicta falsari' ('the scriptures can be distorted [and] the sayings of the saints falsified', 1.356).

When interpreting scripture, therefore, we must remember Jacob's ladder and mount to the height of God's word by means of 'expositiones doctorum fidelissimas' ('the most faithful expositions of the doctors', 1.356). Among those, the early doctors are to be reverenced because, simply, they were historically closer to the origins of the faith:

> & inter eos illi sunt aptiores in materia fidei, qui Christi & Apostolorum temporibus viciniores erant, dicente Christo ad Apostolos, *vos testimonium perhibetis quia ab initio mecum estis* [John 15:27] ... Patres sequi necesse est, si velimus aliquid de mysteriis Scripturarum, aut Fidei, recte scrutari: maxime ubi quaestio mota, tam sensus, quam rationis alta transcendit. (1.357)

> and among them, they who were closer to the times of Christ and the Apostles are more suitable in matters of faith, Christ having said to the Apostles, 'And ye also shall bear witness, because ye have been with me from the beginning' ... It is necessary to follow the Fathers, if we wish to examine in the correct fashion any part of the mysteries of the scriptures, or of the Faith, most so when the question raised transcends both sense and the heights of reason.

The authority of the early commentators, though not of course equal to that of the canonical scriptures, is nevertheless of importance: 'non quod in authoritate aequentur, absit; sed sequantur: non quidem in subsidium authoritatis Canonicae, sed in admonitionem posteriorum' ('not because the [biblical books] are equalled in authority, heaven forbid; but [because] they [the early commentators] follow [the biblical books], not indeed for the protection of canonical authority, but for the instruction of those who come after', 1.358).[28]

Netter then proceeds to discuss an associated problem – that consisting in the misinterpretation not only of the scriptures but of the patristic interpreters:

> Sed interrogant studiosi fideles: *Quid ergo male peccant haeretici contra fidem, qui & scripturis & assertionibus Patrum haereses suas defendunt? Quia testimonia illa pervertunt. Sed quomodo discernenda est corruptio testium?* (1.358)

> But the studious faithful ask: 'How therefore do heretics, who defend their heresies with both the scriptures and the assertions of the Fathers, sin badly against faith?' 'Because they pervert that testimony.' 'But how is [such] corruption of witnesses to be discerned?'

The answer (such as it is): 'Primo, si Scripturae interpretatio quam invehit, contra ipsam Scripturam ibi & alibi rite intellectam, & fidem Sanctorum Patrum, sonuerit' ('First, if the interpretation of scripture which [he] brings forward were to speak against the same scripture rightly understood here and elsewhere, and [against] the faith of the Holy Fathers', 1.358). Note here how Netter begs the question he sets out to answer (one recalls the heresiarch yet again) by introducing the phrase 'rite intellectam' as self-evident. Jerome is next cited as saying that the faith should only be expounded 'secundum concordem expositionem multorum sanctorum' ('according to the harmonious exposition of many saints', 1.358).[29]

This is followed by an intriguing passage in which Netter, in the course of condemning the heretics' presumptuous attempts at corrupting the words of Christ by appealing to him directly (!), manages to convert those who have so far been *witnesses* into *judges*.

> Ecce viam Catholicorum, quam haeretici sequi contemnunt, dicentes, omnes Sanctos priores ex consuetudine peccatores . . . Et ideo solum Christum sine medio statim appellant, putantes se posse secure corrumpere verba Christi; & sic sine judice pervertunt ad libitum. (1.358)

> Behold the Catholic way, the following of which heretics condemn, saying that all earlier saints [were] hardened sinners . . . And therefore they immediately call [upon] Christ, exclusively, without any mediators [lit. medium], thinking that they will be able to corrupt the words of Christ securely. Thus without [any] judge, they pervert [Christ's words] at will.

This is one of the passages in the *DFC* where Netter comes closest to recognising that the concepts of 'witness' and 'testimony [what is being witnessed to]', of 'interpretation' and 'text' cannot be kept absolutely separated – each informs and constitutes the other.

To an extent, the insight offered (perhaps unwittingly) by this passage informs an important strand of thought in the *DFC*. This could be described as an adherence to a concept of Tradition which bears affinities to Heiko Oberman's Tradition 1, consisting in the primacy of Holy Writ and Tradition as signifying the history of scriptural interpretation.[30] In such a scheme of things, Christ's Word and the interpreting Church are wedded into unity; trying to separate the two is the equivalent of decapitating the mystical body of Christ. However, the contemporary Church gave occasion rather obviously to both heretical and orthodox questioning of this marriage. There were those, like Woodford, who did not show any profound belief that the marriage was ever an ideal one: it was and remains a make-shift contract renewed through time, incorporating over the ages various changes and compromises. And there were those like Wyclif who located the divorce somewhere around the turn of the first millennium after Christ; his followers would question whether the marriage had indeed ever taken place.[31]

Netter was in a difficult position. He was an orthodox apologist at a time when England had already witnessed more than forty years of popular and semi-popular insurgency in the name of Christ.[32] Along with the increasingly authoritarian ecclesiastical regime, there had slowly developed a recognition in educated circles that the problems Wyclif and his followers had raised were too potent to be quelled by force alone. Netter's work belongs to a group which genuinely attempts to confront the issues raised and to provide politically viable solutions with a strong intellectual and doctrinal basis.[33]

His advocacy of Tradition I is therefore uneasy. There are occasional suggestions that the Christian tradition is ever-developing, so that valid understandings of the faith are not limited to only the *ecclesia primitiva* and the major Fathers, but continue to be provided by the modern Church.[34] But the predominant thrust of the *DFC* is towards locating, like Wyclif, relevant 'Tradition' in the early Church and the Fathers, the later Church having the 'ancillary' role of transmitter and preserver. This naturally necessitates the invention of a rationale if one is not to dismiss the later Church as a falling-off from the faith. This Netter does by means of an 'organic' metaphor: the Church, like an adolescent growing into full manhood, achieved its maturity in the times of the Apostles and the early Fathers. Once mature, no further growth is possible, even though there has been no decline in power. (The uncomfortable implications of comparing the growth of the Church to that of a human being are not recognised.)

> Ecce non minor est potestas hominis in naturalibus, cum creverit ad perfectum hominem, quam cum infans fuit, & coepit crescere . . . Cum autem factus est vir, non potest, sicut Dominus dicit, adjicere ad staturam cubitum unum, immo nec pollicem. (1.346)

> Behold: the power of a man in natural things is not less when he
> grows up into a perfect man than when he was a child and began to
> grow up . . . But when he has become a [grown] man, he cannot, as
> God says, add to [his] stature one cubit, indeed not even a finger's
> [length].

The advantage of this image is that it enables Netter to tackle quite
satisfactorily the vexed question of the biblical canon. The dependence
of the formation of the canon on historical contingencies is clearly
recognised by Woodford[35] and is part of his argument in favour of
the authority of the Church as opposed to that of scripture. From the
Lollard point of view, such an argument is of course unacceptable.[36] It
is interesting to note that it is equally unacceptable to Netter. For Netter
assumes a text-interpretation, faith-witness framework of thought which
seeks to deny the construction of the former by the latter. It is here that
the comparison of the early Church to a growing man is particularly
helpful, for the known historical circumstances of the formation of the
canon can be relegated to a period of growth. Once the faith, including
the Church and the scriptures, has achieved full maturity, there can be
no question of adding to either. Stating that 'sine authoritate testificantis
Ecclesiae non potest liber aliquis esse authoritatis Canonicae' ('without
the authority of the Church as witness a book cannot be of canonical
authority', 1.346), raises the question of whether the Church can add
books to the canon (for after all the modern Church has not declined in
strength). Can the Church, 'per subauthoritatem generalis Concilii, aut
Romanae Ecclesiae confirmantis, cum jam non sit minoris potestatis,
quam olim in primordiis suis fuit' ('by the 'sub-authority' of the general
council, or of the confirming Roman Church, since it is not of any less
power now than it was formerly at its beginning') extend the canon
(1.346)?

The answer is that it cannot, for the law of Christ has attained perfection and cannot be altered: 'Non posse jam augeri librorum numerum,
quia lex Christi jam attingit ad perfectum' ('It is not possible for the
number of books now to be increased, since the law of Christ has already
attained to perfection', 1.346). Ultimately, it is the Fathers' judgment
which counts, so that the evangels of Thomas and Bartholomew cannot
now be incorporated into the canon:

Numquid possent habere authoritatem illam [i.e. canonical] per concordem definitionem Ecclesiae? Dicit quod non [referring to Jerome's interpretation of Psalm 99 (Vulgate reading)] ... Et non dubium libri non reciperentur in authoritatem Sacri Canonis, nisi qui de illis temporibus Apostolicis agerent, & tunc temporis scripti essent ... Summa vero praesumptio foret, eos libros nunc probare, quos Patres certa ratione respuerant, quos libenter recepissent, si digni fuissent. (1.347–8)

Are there any [books] which can have that [canonical] authority by the harmonious definition of the Church? [Jerome] says no ... And there is no doubt that books may not be accepted into the authority of the sacred canon, unless they dealt with those apostolic times, and were written down then at that time ... Indeed, it would be the height of presumption to approve now those books which the Fathers rejected for valid reasons, and which, if they had been worthy, they would have willingly accepted.

We thus come back to a notion of the modern Church as an uncorrupting witness to the faith established once and for all in the *ecclesia primitiva*. To say that the Church's authority is greater than that of the scriptures is like saying that Philip, who announced Jesus to Nathanael (John 1:45), was greater in authority than Jesus himself. This passage is followed by an attempt at a *reductio ad absurdum* which comes close to collapsing on itself, pointing as it does to the dependence of a theoretically transcendent faith on the institutional and other modes of its transmission:

Et si sic, dicat conformiter parentes nostros carnales, aut paedagogos, esse altiores & eminentiores Christo, quia eorum authoritate ab infanta didicimus quid de Christo sit credendum, quid sperandum. (1.349)

And if [that is the case], [then] let him say similarly that our fleshly parents or teachers are higher and more eminent than Christ, because [it is] by their authority that we have learnt from infancy what is to be believed of Christ and what is to be hoped.

John 4:39–42 is cited to clarify the Church's role: it is like that of the woman who initially announces Christ, but once her auditors hear Christ himself, they believe 'not because of thy saying: for we have heard him ourselves'.

> Sic nec sunt ingrati filii Matris Ecclesiae, qui primo propter verbum
> Ecclesiae testantis de Christo credunt, & cum crediderint, author-
> itatem, qua inducti sunt, authoritati ejus postponunt, cui credunt;
> immo authoritate ejusdem Ecclesiae hoc decretum est, omnium scil-
> icet posteriorum hominum libros, sive Ecclesiarum, authoritati Sacri
> Canonis debere submitti, quasi ad scabellum pedum ejus. (1.349)

> Nor are the sons of Mother Church thereby ungrateful, who first
> believe [in Christ] because of the word of the Church witnessing to
> him, and, when they have believed, place the authority by which they
> are led [to faith] after his authority in whom they believe. Nay rather,
> it is by the authority of the same Church that this is decreed, that the
> books of all men or Churches coming afterwards must be submitted
> to the authority of the sacred canon, like a footstool to its feet.

Once again the passage almost unconsciously begins to move from scriptural to ecclesiastical authority, for it is the Church which decrees that
later books are not to be equated in authority with sacred scripture.

The ambiguity in Netter's conceptualisation of ecclesiastical authority
becomes particularly clear in a passage I referred to earlier, where Netter
cites Wyclif's opinion that it is blasphemous to suggest that 'Deus non
sit perpendiculariter super caput uniuscujusque hominis' ('God is not
perpendicularly over the head of everyman', 1.510). Netter scornfully
asks Wyclif why he bothers to preach if indeed that were the case;
moreover, what then is the rationale for having kings or judges?:

> Quod si ita est, cur tu praedicas, ut jactitas, verbum Dei, cum Deus
> residens in coelis ad *perpendiculum*, daret aliis Christianis ad plenum,
> sine te, verbi Dei liberrimam facultatem? Cur eminent Reges in pop-
> ulo, cur judices judicant, cum Deus residens in coelis faceret ista
> optime sine eis? (1.513)

> Because if such is the situation, why do you preach the Word of
> God as you boast [that you do], since God residing in the heavens
> perpendicularly would give other Christians fully, without you, the
> most free access to the Word of God? Why do kings stand in a high
> position over the people, why do judges judge, since God residing in
> the heavens would do this best without them?

Netter goes on to point out that the divinity manifests itself 'angularly',
through hierarchy and church tradition; indeed, if God spoke through
the mouth of Elijah (1 Kings 17:1), how much more must he minister his

grace 'per os Petri et successorum ejus, & aliorum in Ecclesia sacerdotum' ('by the mouth of Peter and his successors, and of other priests in the Church', 1.513). But such is the nature of the deity, that even when he operates 'angularly', he does not decline from the perpendicular:

> . . . deus, qui in *perpendiculo* residet super homines, non declinat a *perpendiculo*, etiam cum angulum faciat: sed simul facit cum ministro angulum; & servans rectilinium,[37] incidit fidelibus, & generat gratiam . . . Ita dico ego: quidquid facit sub angulo per ministrum, ipse immediate efficit, & *perpendiculariter* influit per semetipsum. (1.513)

> God, who resides above men perpendicularly, does not decline from the perpendicular even when he makes an angle. Instead, he simultaneously makes an angle with his minister, and preserving the straight line, enters the faithful and generates grace . . . So I say: whatever he does in an angle through [his] minister[s], he himself [also] does without mediation [lit. immediately], and by himself, perpendicularly, flows into [the faithful].

The passage clarifies, with a rare geometric precision, the conflict in Netter's account of a unified Tradition: it is simultaneously vertical (in its direct link to God) and horizontal (in its constitution by the human and the historical). In the terms of my earlier analysis, this 'Tradition' attempts to be both dialogic and monologic at the same time.

There is thus in Netter's vision of ecclesiastical authority (and, as I will show next, in his hermeneutics) an important duality. On the one hand, he postulates an orthodox, 'organic', body-and-head relationship between the Church and the faith, each involved in and determining the other. On the other, he accepts the Wycliffite identification of the scriptural text as a *locus* of meanings independent of the specificities of the interpreting reader or institution, as a text which dictates its own meanings. This vision is the one I have been describing throughout this study as 'sciential', associated – for the Lollards – preeminently with Aquinas and Nicholas of Lyra, and it regards the scriptural text as an 'object' and its explication a 'science'. As M.-D. Chenu says, Aquinas starts out from the 'principe épistémologique selon lequel un savoir trouve ses règles et sa méthode dans son *objet* propre' ('epistemological principle according to which a discipline derives its rules and its methodology from the *object* itself of study').[38] In this framework of thought a dubious scriptural passage is sought to be understood primarily in terms of context (or 'circumstantia litterae'), other related or similar scriptural passages,[39] intentionality, and original meanings. It is associated with the study, or at least an awareness, of Greek and Hebrew textual criticism and with the privileging of the literal sense – in short, the philological approach. It involves the valorisation of 'reason' and a reliance on speculative modes of knowledge, particularly logic. It also involves, at least with Aquinas, a deep faith in the validity of the biblical Word and human ability to arrive at reliable meanings thereof.

The sciential approach to scripture, as we have had occasion to note before, was problematic, particularly in its logical dimension – hence, we may recall, Wyclif's attempts at a comprehensive redefinition of the discipline and its associated methodologies. Though theoretically superior to rhetoric and leading to 'truth', 'logic' had become in practice, especially in the domains of academic and legal disputation, its handmaiden. What von Moos calls the 'menschlichen Faktor' assumes paramount importance in medieval logical discourse: 'logic' becomes part of larger persuasive and polemical mechanisms. It is this polemical, indeed human, dimension of scholastic logic that Wyclif obsessively castigates as a sterile game of vanity and power, and that leads to his total redefinition of the concept. Netter self-consciously disavows this logic in his hermeneutics; when outlining his methodology towards the beginning of the *DFC*, he distances himself from what he calls 'scholastic games':

> Et quia non scholasticus ludus est, sed fidei series; Scripturas Sanctas, & post eas, Sanctorum Patrum integras; & sine furto spatiosas authoritates, cum locis librorum et capitulorum, quam certifice possum, describam. Et demum sub nomine Authoris, eorum Doctorum partes contra haeresim, quam tunc expugnare continget, eliciam. (1.6)

> And because it is not a scholastic game, but a continuity of faith, I will cite [lit. describe], as definitely as I can, without any tricks, the Holy Scriptures, and after them, the unimpaired whole [texts] of the Holy Fathers, and [other] ample authorities with [exact] book and chapter references [lit. with the places of books and chapters]. And, finally, with the name of the author, I will bring forward passages of those doctors against the heresy, which it will then be possible to demolish.

Note the sequence of Netter's thought: the disavowal of disputative games is immediately followed by a pointer to his own textually faithful methodology – authorities are always cited with full reference to *orig-inalia* (just as, we may note, they are in Wyclif). In other words, the decontextualised citation of proof-texts is here eschewed as part of a self-consciously anti- sceptical positivist philosophy of textual meaning, a philosophy polarised against scholastic frivolity. Netter continues, significantly: 'Non in vana Philosophia, & humana sapientia fundamentum ponam hujus doctrinae cum Wicleffo, sed in verbo Dei' ('I will not, like Wyclif, place the basis of this doctrine in vain philosophy and human wisdom but in the Word of God', 1.6). He returns to the subject later in a passage which rejects, in a suggestive agglomeration, the phantasms of the *ingenium* and of arguments, the orders and arrangements of reasons and arguments in 'scholastic song', and the moral flowers of allegories deployed in a subtle style. Netter himself is intent simply upon joining together the stones of scripture by means of the cement of patristic exposition.[40] The coupling of scholastic argumentation and (it is implied) irresponsible scriptural interpretations (*morales allegoriarum flores*), bears witness to Netter's extreme unease – as extreme as that of Wyclif – with the domain of *scientia* in its actual practice. But whereas Wyclif's solution is to redefine and transform *scientia*, Netter merely distances himself from what he considers unacceptable in it, while dismissing Wyclif's own redefinition, especially in so far as it relates to 'logic', as absurd.[41]

The sciential approach had a second, even more threatening flaw in relation to Christian 'truth', as Woodford recognised when he pointed out that even Christ is, strictly speaking, a limited exemplar for modern times. Given that the Bible is an ancient text produced in very different religio-cultural circumstances, the recovery of original meanings is not necessarily relevant to or supportive of the Christian faith as actually lived. The biblical text demands – such is the nature of the faith – not recovery, but recuperation. There was Augustinian precedent for this; the saint had stated clearly that provided that:

> a man draws a meaning from them [Holy Scriptures] that may be used for the building up of love, even though he does not happen upon the precise meaning which the author whom he reads intended to express in that place, his error is not pernicious, and he is wholly clear from the charge of deception.[42]

The 'recuperative' vision of theology is the one which informs the affective tradition, which foregrounds both 'les besoins et ressources du *sujet* connaissant' ('the needs and resources of the knowing *subject*'),[43] as well as the complementary, abiding interpretative authority of the Church informed by the Holy Spirit. Since divine intentionality is infinitely mysterious and infinitely good, all meanings found *caritative* are endorsed. The definition of 'charitable', assumed to be understood in Augustine, ultimately lies outside the text. The sapiential mode of theology, with its emphasis on the mysteriousness of the holy text and the consequent inevitability of the interpreter's reliance on the authority of ecclesiastical traditions, was from Augustine onwards polarised against arguments from 'reason'.[44] The *locus* of meanings is outside the text, in an ever-growing, developing, often conflicting and contradictory tradition of commentary with which the appropriately devout reader engages.

Netter's synthesis of these varying modes of scriptural knowledge is uneasy, and has as rationale the construction of an 'objective' interpretative framework. We have already noted his attempt at codifying ecclesiastical hermeneutic traditions into a conceptual unity, at suggesting that an unchanging singularity of Christian meaning deriving directly from the original meanings of Christ and the Apostles is encapsulated in the 'succession' of faith from apostolic times until the present. We have also noted his rejection of those aspects of the medieval sciential discourse which address power, rather than 'truth' – above all the sceptical, victory-oriented modes of disputation. He is, however, deeply sympathetic to the 'objective' emphases of *scientia*, a sympathy which results in important methodological consequences.

First of all, there is a genuine attempt at contextual interpretation. One of the meanings of 'text' in the medieval period was 'a verse of the Bible'.[45] Netter, while reading any one of these 'texts', shows an awareness of the larger 'text'. Not only are the immediate *circumstantia litterae* taken into account, but also similar passages elsewhere in the scriptures. There is thus a theoretical agreement with Wyclif (and of course, Aquinas and Lyra); and Netter is at pains to show how Wyclif's practice diverges from this theoretical norm, how Wyclif, like other heretics, 'transforms' scripture: 'eadem verba dicere, sed alieno sensu vestire' ('to say the same words, but invest [them] with an alien sense', II.7).

Netter engages at length with Wyclif's views of the Eucharist and the biblical readings used to support these views. I will not primarily examine here the substantive theological content of Netter's critique of Wyclif, but instead focus on his textual methodology, and the hermeneutic values implicitly upheld therein.[46] In discussing the nature of the bread in Christ's words 'Hoc est corpus meum', Netter refers to 1 Cor. 10:16–17[47] to demonstrate the non-material nature of the 'bread' Christ refers to:

> Non credo tamen ad tantum desipuit, quod hoc intelligere Apostolum crederet quod affirmat; maxime, quia idem Apostolus qui dixit, *panis quem frangimus*, de eodem statim subjunxit: *unus panis, & unum corpus multi sumus*. Ergo si corpus Christi esset panis naturalis propter primum, aeque totus chorus christianorum esset unus panis naturalis propter secundum. Non ego devio; sed haec est norma scrutandi abdicta Scripturarum per circumstancias earum ibi, vel alibi. (II.241)

> However, I do not believe that he [Wyclif] was so foolish as to believe that the apostle signifies what he [Wyclif] affirms, especially since the same apostle who said 'the bread which we break', immediately added to it 'for we being many are one bread and one body'. Therefore if the body of Christ were natural bread according to the first [passage, 1 Cor. 10:16], the whole body of Christians would, in a similar fashion, be a [piece of] natural bread according to the second [passage, 1 Cor. 10:17]. I do not err, but this is the norm of examining the scriptures rejected [by Wyclif], [i.e.], by means of their [textual] *circumstances* here or elsewhere.

However, Netter immediately proceeds to cite a passage from Augustine's commentary on Genesis where the saint states that a given scriptural passage should be studied in three possible ways. One should try to find the intention of the [human] author, and, if this is not possible, the sense which is not impeded by the 'circumstances' of scripture. If for some reason the circumstances cannot be studied properly, then the meaning prescribed by faith should be accepted.

> Ideo dixit Augustinus, *in tanta multitudine verorum intellectuum*: nam hic locus Apostoli potest habere plures sensus, secundum plures aequivocationes panis & corporis; quorum nullus fidei sanae repugnat, sed quorum quilibet exponat Apostolum, & haeresim obruat occursantem. (II.241–2)

Therefore Augustine has said, 'in such a multitude of true understandings', for this passage from the Apostle can have many senses, according to many equivocations of bread and body, of which none is incompatible with sound faith, but of which let any explain the Apostle and overwhelm attacking heresy.

Having opened the door to meanings dictated from outside the text, Netter returns to the world of context and intentionality: 'Vide, si hoc non intendit Apostolus, qui nusquam dicit panem illum esse panem, sed solum corpus' ('See if this is not what the Apostle intends, who never says that that bread is bread but [that it is] only body', II.242). Wyclif is criticised for trying to elicit from the Apostle a meaning that is simply not there: 'Multum frustrabatur spe vana Wicleffus, quando panem illum expectavit ab Apostolo' ('Wyclif was much deceived by vain hope when he required that [natural] bread from the Apostle', II.242). Augustine and Chrysostom are cited and it is pointed out that 'tam sancti et antiqui patres nec falsi sunt interpretes' ('such holy and ancient Fathers are not false interpreters', II.243). Matt. 6:11 ('panem nostrum supersubstantialem da nobis hodie') is next discussed where the word 'supersubstantial' is expounded by means of its Greek and Hebrew originals. Jerome's account of the variant Latin translations of the Greek 'epiousion' or Hebrew 'sgolla' ('praecipuum', 'egregium', 'peculiare') is summarised as an argument for the special meaning of 'supersubstantial'. This is followed by a citation of John 6:51 ('Ego sum panis vivus') as the final blow against Wyclif's attempt at confining the meaning of 'supersubstantial' to 'terrestrial' (II.247–8).

Netter returns to the issue of the supposedly eucharistic signification of Christ's words in a later passage. Wyclif's *Trialogus* is cited as stating that Christ's words – in particular his use of the verb 'esse' in 'hoc est corpus meum' – are to be understood figuratively. Wyclif's argument is based on Gen. 41:26–7 (Joseph's interpretation of the Pharaoh's dream), where the seven ears of corn and the seven fat kine are said to 'be', rather than to 'signify', seven years of plenty:

Fides Scripturae asserit, quod septem spicae, & septem boves crassae, *sunt* septem anni fertilitatis: &, ut Augustinus notat, Scriptura non dicit, quod *significant* illos septem annos, sed quod *sunt* ipsi anni, &

talem locutionem spissim in Scriptura poteris reperire. (II.5 03, italics mine)

The faith of scripture asserts that the seven ears of corn and the seven fat kine *are* the seven years of plenty, and, as Augustine notes, scripture does not say that they *signify* those seven years, but that they *are* these years, and such locution[s] you will be able to find densely [present] in scripture.

Netter criticises Wyclif's interpretative principle as contrary to the intentions of both scripture and Augustine, for there is no authority to extend figurative modes of signification to parts of scripture which must be understood 'properly'.[48] He then quotes in full the relevant Augustinian discussion of John 13:31 ('Nunc clarificatus est filius hominis'), 1 Cor. 10:4 ('petra erat Christus'), Matt. 13:38 ('bonum vero semen hii sunt filii regni') – all of these biblical passages using 'esse' instead of 'significare'. Augustine sums up: 'Sicut ergo solet loqui scriptura, res significantes, tamquam illas, quae significantur, appellans' ('Thus therefore scripture is accustomed to speak, calling the signifying things as if [they are] those which are signified'). Netter's response to this problematic passage is characteristic.[49] Instead of offering a directly 'supplementing' reading in the manner of Wyclif, he refers to two more commentaries by Augustine, on Levit. 17:14 and on the relevant passage from Gen. 41, on the principle that Augustine himself clarifies how this statement of his should be understood.[50] These Augustinian discussions are then interpreted by Netter, with some struggle, as suggesting that it would be an error to say 'panem esse corpus Christi non longe aliter, quam petram esse Christum, aut septem annos septem spicas' ('that the [manner in which] the bread is the body of Christ is not very different from [the manner in which] the rock is Christ or the seven ears of corn the seven years', II.504). The ears of corn in the Pharaoh's dream are imaginary ones; therefore they can be read figuratively. It is, however, completely misguided to 'transfer' such an obvious trope to the 'real' mystery of the Eucharist:

Postremo peterem, quo capite, qua item authoritate, transferre audes vel potes tropum septem spicarum ad unicum corpus Christi? . . . Figuram septem spicarum, & petrae, & Joannis agnovi in locis suis; in corpore Christi non novi. Aut doce per Scripturas, aut Patrum orthodoxorum sententias, quod figura septem spicarum ad corpus Christi in Eucharistia trahi debuit. (II.5 05)

Lastly I would ask, under what head, likewise by which authority, do you dare to transfer or are able to [transfer] the trope of the seven ears of corn to the unique body of Christ? . . . The figure of the seven ears, and of the rock, and of John I have [perceived] in the relevant passages [lit. in their *loci*]; I have not perceived [a figure] in the body of Christ. But teach by means of the scriptures or the teachings of the orthodox Fathers that the figure of the seven ears of corn ought to be extended to the body of Christ in the Eucharist.

A similar misunderstanding informs the thought of those who seek to use modes of behaviour portrayed in the Old Testament as justification for actions not sanctioned by the New (II.5 05). Wyclif's audacious extension of the figurative 'esse' to the eucharistic words is reprehensible: he is thereby the inventor of a figure without any authority (*sine omni authoritate repertor*) (II.5 05). John 1 :21 is then cited: though Christ called himself Elias, using a trope, John the Baptist refused to do so, reserving the power to trope to Christ. How great therefore is Wyclif's temerity, that 'praeter, immo contra authoritatem et intentionem Christi et Scripturae, inducit tropicum sacramentum' ('beyond, nay rather against the authority and intention of Christ and scripture, he introduces a tropic sacrament', II.5 06). Note the characteristic invocation of Christ's intention, followed immediately by a reference to the unity of tradition on this issue: Augustine, Hilary, Chrysostom and so on 'uno ore confirmant' ('with one mouth confirm') that Christ's words 'proprie sonant' ('signify literally', II.5 06). Ultimately, the individual cannot be allowed the freedom to decide at his own will which sections of scripture are metaphorical or figurative, as such a liberty would imply the possible collapse of Christian history itself:

Nam sicut dicit Wicleffus propria sua licentia hoc figuraliter solum dici *Hoc est corpus meum*, nullum secum ducens, nec potens adducere testem catholicum, veterem vel novellum; quis item prohibeat alium dicere ea lege loquendi Gabrielem nuncium de coelis ad Virginem, tropicum fuisse, non historicum: *Verbum caro factum est*, figura, non natura. (II.5 06)

For just as Wyclif says on his own authority that 'This is my body' is said only figuratively, taking no one with him nor being able to

adduce a catholic witness, old or new, what would prevent another
from saying, by that law of speaking, that Gabriel being sent from the
heavens to the Virgin was tropic, not historic; [and that the statement]
'The Word was made flesh' [was] a figure, not an actuality [lit. nature].

As Augustine has pointed out in *De Doctrina Christiana*, 'proper' and
'figurative' languages must not be confused; one must pay due attention both to context and to *caritas*, and not interpret as figurative that
which does not conflict with charity when read literally. Netter therefore
returns, on the authority of Augustine, to the 'circumstancia lectionis'
(II.507). Many uses of the word 'bread' in the Old Testament are indeed 'figurative', prefiguring the body of Christ; such is not the case
with Christ's own use of the word at the last supper (II.509).

The similarity between the interpretative procedures of Netter and
Wyclif should be noted. Both study the scriptural text in a theoretically
sciential framework which yet accommodates hermeneutic liberties in
practice. The difference lies in the extra-textual discourses each author
brings to bear on the text: Wyclif emphasises revelation – God's eye-
view – leading to a proper understanding of the *intentio auctoris*, while
Netter points to his own conceptualisation of a unified tradition, in
which 'sancti doctores una fide conveniunt' ('the holy doctors meet in
one faith', 1.348). It is interesting to note that of all the definitions of
the 'true' sense of scripture available to him, Netter chooses one derived
from Ambrose[51] (significantly, from a passage from his commentary
on Rom. 5:14, where Ambrose discusses heretical interpretative practices and problems of textual authenticity): 'verum sensum arbitratur
esse de litera, quando ratio literae, & historia, & authoritas observatur'
('[Ambrose] thinks that the true meaning [comes from] the letter, when
the sense of the letter, the narrative, and authority are taken into account', II.591). The ideal sense is one which is 'of the letter', when the
(intrinsic) *ratio* of the letter and the biblical narrative, and the (extrinsic)
authority (of tradition) are observed.

Netter's uneasy espousal of a sciential approach to the scriptural text
as a domain of determinate signification which can be accessed through
an engagement with the text itself, and a clear, unified, unambiguous
hermeneutic tradition is also reflected in his justification of images. It
is beyond the scope of this book adequately to address his extended

and complex defence of images; I merely want, in a brief excursus, to point to one of his suggestive emphases. One of the devotional advantages of images – for the Lollards, one of their many disadvantages – is their appeal to the 'imagination'[52] and their fruitful indeterminacy of significance, as Reginald Pecock would discuss later. Netter cites many of the standard arguments in favour of images: their usefulness for the devout memory,[53] their affective role in increasing devotion and their antiquity. He proceeds, however, to offer the 'most beautiful reason' why images are acceptable, based on John Damascene's defence of images as justified because God assumed human form:[54] the Jews were trapped in their shadows; we, on the contrary, are liberated in images, for we see Christ now in the image of the future, in lineaments more 'express' than the dull shadows of the Jews:[55]

> Pulcherrima ratio quare noster homo transeat in imaginem, & utatur imaginum ritu cum frequentia; Judaei antiqui non sic: quia Christum nunc videmus in imagine futurorum, expressius lineamenta corporis exprimente, quam umbra stolida Judaeorum, per agnum umbratilem. Christus modo noscitur in expressa imagine sui corporis naturaliter in altari . . . Status ergo Synagogae fuit in umbra, noster in imagine. Colebant ergo Judaei coecas umbras ovis & vituli, panis propositionis, & cinerum: quae omnia longe sunt a corporis expresso charactere. (III.937)

> There is a most beautiful reason why our [Christian] man should turn to images, and use the rite of images frequently, [where] the ancient Jews [could not]: because now we see Christ in the image of future [times] in portraying [him] with corporeal lineaments more expressly than the stolid shadows of the Jews [did] by means of the shadowy lamb. Christ now is known in the express image of his body naturally on the altar . . . Therefore the state of the synagogue was in shadow, ours in image[s]. The Jews therefore honoured blind shadows of sheep and calves, of the shew-bread, and of ashes: all of which are far [removed] from the express sign of [his] body.

In the context of a rebuttal of the views of the Lollard William White, Netter points out that the Wycliffites habitually object that images, as signs, have no special cause to be honoured: one might as well adore a wisp of straw, as it has the 'mark of the Trinity'.[56] Netter's reply, based on Augustine's commentary on Psalm 103:19 (Vulgate reading), is a clever development, in terms of vocabulary with strong Wycliffite resonances, of the notion of *dulia*, the reverence due to the creature, and by extension, the adoration of Christ in respect of his creature-ness, his humanity. Wyclif had pointed to 'the poison in the honeycomb . . . worshipping the sign instead of the signified' ('signum loco signati').[57] Netter states that the incarnation has rendered signs of Christ 'express', and therefore images, as express signs of him, are valid objects of *dulia*:

> Dementiam ergo notat [Augustine] Wiclevistarum, qui redarguentes cultum imaginum, quia signa sunt, arguere solent: Adora ergo modulum straminis, quia habet vestigium Trinitatis. Nec enim omne signum adoro, sed signum expressum, & evidens apud sensum, movens statim affectum ad colendum aliquid cultu sibi debito. (III.944)

> Augustine therefore notes the madness of the Wycliffites, who, rejecting the worship of images because they are signs, are accustomed to argue: 'Adore therefore a wisp of straw, since it has the mark of the Trinity'. For I do not adore every sign, but an express sign, and [one which is] evident to the sense[s], immediately moving the emotions to worship something by the reverence owed it.

What we observe here is the same principle that informs Netter's discussion of Tradition: of endowing with the appeal of 'objective', 'express' certitude a quite separate discourse, in this case one which foregrounds the interpretative and perceptual agency of the individual.

A major expression of this 'sciential' approach in the *DFC* is a heightened consciousness of the importance of textual matters, and in this respect, Netter's orthodox work offers fascinating evidence of the kind of textually critical, incipiently historicist approach to past authorities so insisted on – at least in theory – by Wyclif and the Lollards. The unabashedly and self-consciously appropriative use of the past and its writings, such as we find given ludic articulation by John of Salisbury in his Prologue to the *Policraticus*, and such as support the whole genre of florilegia, is replaced in Netter by an anxious display of textual, and contextual, fidelity. Netter therefore shows himself to be aware of the Wycliffite emphasis on exactitude of reference. Quotations must be identified, for a proper understanding of what has been quoted may necessitate a knowledge of the text in which it is embedded, and the author from whom it originates. Once again, the hermeneutic assumptions are positivistic and anti-rhetorical: one does not merely appropriate earlier *auctours*, as in legal and dialectical disputes; one actually respects their intentions and meanings. Quotations from Wyclif himself are identified meticulously (as Wyclif himself identifies others):

> Sed idcirco hunc ordinem servare propono, ut dicta ejus ex integro cum quotatione libri, & notatione capituli, sive Partis, curem sine mutatione literae, sicut ipse scripsit, inserere, & ipsum dicto suo subscribere; ut ibi plane videre possit quilibet quid erravit, & quantum. (1.23)

> But I propose therefore to preserve this order, that I would take care to insert his sayings, unchanged and whole, with references to book and chapter or section number, without any change of letter, as he himself has written, and write [his name] after his saying[s], so that anyone would be able plainly to see here how he has erred, and to what extent.

Similar is the case with citations from other authorities, as Netter is keen to ensure that the quoted texts can immediately be located.[58] This is of particular importance when citations from Wyclif are in question, as Netter does not wish to leave the Wycliffites the option to deny that opinions alleged to be Wyclif's are not in fact his.[59]

Accompanying this methodology is a pervasive awareness of the importance of making a case for the authenticity of one's sources. Such questions are naturally best settled by going back to the oldest available copies. Hence Netter's defence of the authority of a quotation from Augustine: 'Nec tamen videbit aliquis tam antiquum codicem Augustini *de verbis Domini*, quantum ego reor, cui desit praefata sententia, si dolus non adsit, vel culpa scribentis' ('However, no one will see such an old copy of Augustine's *De Verbis Domini* (as I suppose) which lacks the before mentioned saying unless [it is a matter of] fraud or scribal error', II.249).

Wyclif, in *De Apostasia*, had denied (rightly) the authenticity of the ascription of a polemical work on the Eucharist to Augustine.[60] Netter insists that the work is by Augustine, and once again, refers to the antiquity of his codex: 'Ego enim reperi, & transcripsi de vetustissimo Exemplari, scripto antiqua valde manu formata' ('For I have discovered, and transcribed, from a very old exemplar written in a very old formed hand', II.500). He further points to Augustine's stylistic amplitude in rebuttal of Wyclif's dismissal of the work as not in keeping with the saint's style:

> Soli Wiclevistae & Berengarii sectatores oblatrant, dicentes alii, quia dictamen ejus haec verba non sapiunt, nescientes tantam esse ubertatem in saliva Doctoris, ut vix inter centum volumina tres libri ejus redoleant unum stylum. (II.501)

> Only the Wycliffites and the sectators of Berengarius rail, some [of them] saying that these words do not savour of [Augustine's] style, not knowing that the variety and plenty in the stylistic range [lit. taste] of the doctor is such that scarcely three books of his among a hundred volumes emit the fragrance of one style.

What we witness here are the beginnings of what may be described as the historical criticism of past *auctores*.

Netter's pervasive consciousness of the epistemological importance of textual authenticity – by which I mean his vision of the relevance of textual matters to the establishment of 'truth' – results in an interesting exchange with Wyclif over the authority of Ambrose. Netter cites what he considers a passage from Wyclif (his reference, to *Trialogus*, Bk 4, c. 22, is in this instance incorrect) arguing for the greater worth of the words of Christ and of Apostolic Scripture in establishing the exact meaning of the Eucharistic verses as against 'verbi Doctoris apocryphi' ('the word of an apocryphal doctor'). Wyclif is here arguing against what he considers the misinterpretation of a passage from Ambrose. Netter pounces – unfairly, it must be admitted – on Wyclif's identification of Ambrose as 'apocryphal': 'improbus, stultus & acer haereticus non veretur *apocryphum* dicere: cujus nec nomen tacitum est, nec opera vilis famae, nec incerta authoritas' ('The impudent, stupid and vicious heretic is not afraid to say 'apocryphal' [about one] whose name is not hidden, whose work is not of bad reputation, [and] whose authority is not uncertain', II.484). Strictly speaking, Wyclif is of course correct: in the terms of his analysis, the 'canon' is scripture, and only scripture, and therefore Ambrose is indeed 'apocryphal'.[61] But because of the theoretical devaluation of the so-called apocrypha which Netter shares with Wyclif, he finds the term too unworthy of Ambrose. He points out that Wyclif's 'master', the heretic Berengarius, called both Jerome and

Gregory 'apocryphal'. Netter then proceeds to criticise Wyclif for having cited Ambrose, or rather a work falsely ascribed to him, in defence of his arguments elsewhere:

> Et ipse quoque Wicleffus olim laudare eum solebat, quia ubi pro parte sua videtur sibi quod faciat, in probationem suae perditionis adducit: & pro magno etiam, titulus falsi nominis Ambrosii, vel ejus discipuli authori *de divinis officiis* tribuit, quem Cancellarius Oxoniensis *Walerannum* appellat, revera contemporaneum Anselmo, virum in erroribus deprehensum. (II.485)

> And Wyclif himself was formerly accustomed to praise him too, because where for his [Wyclif's] part it seemed to him that he [Ambrose] would be of service, he [cited him/dragged him in] in proof of his perdition; and even worse, attributed to the author of *de divinis officiis*, whom the Chancellor of Oxford calls Waleran [bishop of Memburg], in reality a contemporary of Anselm and a man corrupt in errors, the pretended honour of the false name of Ambrose, or of his disciple.

Two points are to be noted about this passage: the implicit dismissal of the modes and principles according to which medieval dialectical disputation flourished – one could of course cite in support of one's argument an authority one had dismissed elsewhere – and the strong interest in 'authenticity'. Indeed, Netter seems to have undertaken substantial historical research to attempt to establish the true author of the disputed tract.[62] And it is to the same critical self- consciousness in matters of text and authority that his repeated invocation of the 'integer textus' ('whole uncorrupted text', II.501) should be traced, for the 'intentio philosophi' ('intention of the philosopher') is most lucidly and indubitably expressed there.

A similar textual ideology informs the manuscript presentation of the *DFC*. K. S. Smith points to the uniformity of presentation of the text – it was obviously copied under strict supervision, mostly Carmelite.[63] More interestingly, Netter's own remarks in the actual body of the text are kept rigorously distinct from the surrounding *auctoritates*: these original passages are always prefaced by the word 'actor' in red.[64] The cited authorities have their names in red at the beginning of each citation, even when these are very short; occasionally, the book and chapter citations are underlined in red. Wyclif is never accorded the honour of rubrication, though detailed references to his *originalia* are provided. The early printed versions preserve this *mise-en-page*,[65] though, significantly, the much later 1757–9 Venetian edition does not. This kind of textually critical ideology, with a strong interest in the discernment of authority, obviously fits in with the 'scientific' approach to the Bible and other texts. Further, Netter's highly *self-conscious* and indeed self-righteous espousal of such an approach points to the impact that Wycliffite textual scholarship and polemic over the nature of textual authority had had on contemporary orthodoxy.

We thus witness in the *DFC* a coexistence of two modes of scholarship: one postulating meanings dictated by the text; the other locating meaning in an authoritative tradition external to the text. However, this synthesis of contextual or 'intentional' interpretation with *caritative*-authoritative justifications would perhaps have been quite typical of its times – one marshalls all possible arguments when attempting to refute one's opponent – if not for one important peculiarity. Netter goes along with Wyclif in citing only (barring a few exceptions) the major early doctors.[66] As such, his hermeneusis forms an exact parallel to his ecclesiology. The early Church provides the norms against which the modern is to be judged; similarly, interpretations of the early commentators, historically nearer as they were to understanding correctly the intentions of Christ and the Apostles, provide the securest access to Holy Writ. The positivism of approach which denies that access to the 'real' norms of the early Church and the 'real' meanings of the early commentators is as problematic as to the Bible itself, results in the similarity between Netter and his opponent that we set out noticing. His defence of the modern Church as preserver and transmitter, as well as his reliance on a millennial concordance in matters of faith, shares the same fundamental weakness – a refusal to acknowledge the centrality of rhetoric and ideology, and the inevitable triumph of contemporary institutionalised hermeneutics. K. S. Smith, speaking of Netter's conciliar theory, points out that subsequent generations of theologians were confused about Netter's exact stand on certain issues, so contradictory were the implications of his pronouncements on the power of the Council vis-a-vis 'apostolic teaching';[67] the remark is equally valid of other issues tackled in the *DFC*. Smith goes on to say that Netter's goal was only a polemical defence of all institutions of the Church. I would disagree: the confusions and contradictions in Netter's work are not the product of a self-conscious rhetoric; they are the result of a genuine attempt at understanding the nature of Christian meaning in what may be described without exaggeration as an age of crisis. Hudson's phrase 'the premature reformation' is aptly descriptive of the situation in the early fifteenth century; one can sense very strongly that the time had come for a radical overhauling of all the hermeneutic and ecclesiological *idées reçues*.

Afterword: Lollardy and late-medieval intellectuality

In 1382, Bishop Buckingham of Lincoln issued an order prohibiting one William Swinderby, *hermita*, living in the Chapel of St John near Leicester, and claiming to be a priest, from preaching against the determinations of Holy Church, and initiated proceedings against him.[1] Swinderby abjured before leaving for Coventry and later for the Hereford diocese, where Bishop Trefnant examined him again in 1391. In the account of the investigation of his beliefs recorded in the register of Bishop Trefnant, there occurs a curious passage. Among various other allegations of doctrinal heterodoxy, Trefnant criticises the fallacious hermeneutics of the new sect of Lollards, of whom Swinderby is a particularly perverse representative. According to Trefnant, the Lollards read Holy Scripture in a new way,

> exponendo . . . scripturam populo ad litteram more moderno aliter quam spiritus sanctus flagitat, ubi vocabula a propriis significacionibus peregrinantur et novas divinari videntur, ubi non sunt iudicanda verba ex sensu quem faciunt sed ex sensu ex quo fiunt, ubi construccio non subjacet legibus Donati, ubi fides remota a racionis argumento.[2]

> expounding . . . scripture to the people in the modern fashion according to the letter otherwise than the Holy Ghost demands, where words are moved from their correct meaning and appear to bring in new meanings, where the words are not to be judged by the sense they make but from the sense from which they are made, where the construction is not bound by the rules of Donatus, where faith is taken far from the force of reason.[2]

The interest of this mixed bag of polemic lies less in its articulation of a coherent vision of a heterodox hermeneutics – one would be hard pressed to find one here – than in its random juxtaposition of some contemporary intellectual counters. Some of these one would expect in such a context (the criticism of the beliefs of a presumptuous cleric of uncertain low rank): the words are distorted into a sense not endorsed by the Holy Ghost, elementary rules of grammar as codified in Donatus are not followed, irrationality reigns. But there is one part of the indictment that is startling in its seeming specificity: the Lollards interpret the biblical words 'non . . . ex sensu quem faciunt sed ex sensu ex quo fiunt'. As it stands, the phrase is, to say the least, obscure. For it is a phrase with a significant intellectual prehistory (and also posterity) in scholastic discourse relating to the vexed and ever-debated questions of *virtus sermonis* and *intentio auctoris*, questions which, as we have seen, had assumed peculiar prominence in the fourteenth-century schools.[3] In one of the clearer contributions to the debate, Ockham had stated that 'frequenter sermones authentici falsi sunt in sensu quem faciunt, hoc est de virtute sermonis et proprie loquendo, et tamen veri sunt in sensu ex quo fiunt' ('authoritative words are frequently false in [terms of] the sense which they make, 'properly' speaking by 'virtue of speech', and nevertheless they are true in [terms of] the sense from which they are made').[4] The 'sense from which the words are made' is here related to authorial intention: the surface meaning, 'by virtue of speech', may be false, but the words nevertheless remain true by virtue of the informing intention.

What is fascinating about our passage from Trefnant is the invocation, in the context of the interrogation of a cleric of dubious, even contested status, described by himself as 'bot sympully lettered',[5] of an abstruse academic debate over semantics and signification. The episcopal investigation of a person of such low status, however learned, is not the kind of context where one expects such references to an abstract and complex scholastic debate. And the casual way the reference is made, among other, less abstruse indictments, suggests that this debate and its accompanying language had become, by the 1390s, almost a polemical counter, a part of the immediately available intellectual currency of the day, open to appropriation in non-academic, extra-mural heretical contexts. This, as I argued in my Introduction, is what made the impact of Lollardy so profound: it brought out of the Schools, and into the domain of the non-clerical and the vernacular, intellectual discourses of considerable complexity, sophistication and latitude, and thereby changed the always problematic ideological positioning of such discourses within contemporary culture. For the very existence of such discourses was based on a remarkable degree of academic freedom. This freedom, which medieval academia assumed and defended, was premised on its privileged and *isolating* Latinity, with its own closed circle of clerical practitioners, subject to its own institutional regulations and constraints,[6] and using its own specialised technical vocabulary and tools.[7] Jürgen Miethke, in his discussion of such freedom in the medieval university, has pointed out that the development of the *quaestio* as a methodological tool resulted in an intellectual situation where there were no forbidden questions, only forbidden answers:

> Die scholastische Questio, die seit dem 12. Jahrhundert methodisch das Vorgehen der Wissenschaft in allen Disziplinen bestimmte und jedes literarische Genus scholastischer Texte durchwirkt und durchtränkt hat, ergeht sich in freier Fragehaltung. Verbotene Fragen gibt es nicht, allenfalls verbotene Antworten.[8]

> The scholastic *quaestio*, which, since the twelfth century, determined, in methodological terms, scientific procedure in all disciplines, and which penetrated and saturated every literary genre of scholastic text, indulged in a free attitude of questioning. There were no forbidden questions; at most forbidden answers.

Such freedom becomes unsustainable when academic discourses – especially those relating to modes of biblical signification, and the construction of interpretative authority – enter an unregulated and unsupervised sphere of 'popular' intellection, where non-forbidden questions may very easily result in forbidden answers. A further complexity is introduced when this sphere of rationalist intellectual inquiry into the nature and meaning of the sources of religious certitude is conflated with an absolutist and non-discursive reliance on 'revelation'. In this respect too, Lollardy's radically popularising ideology endowed the inherited scholastic binary of 'reason' and 'revelation' – which in any case had its own internal tensions and contradictions – with a new threatening potential, that inherent in 'ecstatic dissent'. How do institutions which incorporate divine validation into their own self-legitimising visions[9] deal with identical claims on the part of those denying their legitimacy, especially when such claims are made to support the validity of an individualised, extra-institutional hermeneutics? What

Alexander Patschovsky has described as *Selbstvergottung* ('making one-self into a god')[10] plays, as we have seen in Thomas Netter's critique of Wyclif's thought, a crucial role in the re-formation of the ideological landscape of late-medieval intellectuality. The potential for an irresolvable hermeneutic deadlock, always existent in a cultural system which looks towards the interpretation of a conceptually central text as the source of most legitimising authority, takes on body and substance in a particularly *bouleversant* fashion when such a deadlock is played out in public, with a cast including those traditionally denied participation in the definition of authority.

One of Lollardy's most destabilising – and, I suggest, one of its most far-reaching – effects was therefore not just on the contemporary Church but also on contemporary academia, in particular on the University of Oxford, and, by extension, on late-medieval religio-intellectual *mentalités*. 'Effect', perhaps, is not an entirely satisfactory word, for Lollardy, as I will proceed to suggest, equally grew out of certain pre-existent and developing problems in late-medieval scholasticism. In this context, it is useful to recall Anne Hudson's emphasis on the extent to which Lollardy initially articulated many of the pressing concerns of the time, and how, at the beginning, there were grey areas in which one could not distinguish between 'heretical' and 'orthodox'.[11] Wyclif himself, we must not forget, was part of an academic establishment which was slow to condemn his radical thought.[12] It was only in the early years of the fifteenth century, with the enactment of *De Heretico Comburendo* (1401) and the *Constitutions* (1409), that the boundaries between Lollardy and orthodoxy were laid down with a greater degree of clarity – even on questions distinct from that of the nature of the Eucharist – and that official suppression of Lollardy began on an altogether different scale. By this date, a polarisation had been achieved between 'Lollardy' and 'orthodoxy', one which gave both sides of the confrontation a more definite identity. And it is this polarisation and its attendant self-definitions on either side that constitute one of Lollardy's major impacts. Whatever its fate as a religious or political group in the fifteenth century,[13] Lollardy, I argue, half won the battle of ideas. By its unprecedented achievement in converting into a radical and popular political movement what began as dissent within the Latinate academic-ecclesiastical establishment, it changed fundamentally the nature of that establishment and its traditional intellectual liberties. Scepticism and relativism do not provide the best ground from which to fight an ideological battle, and the early fifteenth century offers evidence of the erosion of a mode of self-consciously dialogic thought, and its associated methodologies, that presuppose an assumption of considerable privilege. It is perhaps possible, but entirely unlikely, that tracts such as Woodford's *Quattuor determinationes*, with their implicitly pervasive questioning of the nature of any kind of authority, would have been produced in defence of the Church or the private religions after the *Constitutions*. Nicholas Watson has underlined the far-reaching effects of Arundel's censorship laws on vernacular writing;[14] equally far-reaching, at least in intention, were the effects of his academic prohibitions. The fourth canon expresses anxiety about *verba scandalosa* [offensive words] with respect to any of the sacraments; the fifth, eighth, ninth and eleventh canons are all in some measure directed against the dangers of disputation, or against asserting, defending or proposing suspect opinions, whether within the Schools, or without. The eleventh canon specifically targets Oxford University, and those within it who proffer conclusions, propositions or opinions in matters of faith which are either against the determinations of the Church or against good customs.[15] Fifteenth-century academic thought in England in the aftermath of the Lollard heresy still remains virtually uncharted, though Jeremy Catto does outline some significant changes in Oxford theology:

> A . . . detachment from academic theology can be detected among the theologians at Oxford. Fitzralph and Wyclif had rejected the 'frogs and toads, croaking in the swamp' of vain speculation, and their sentiments were echoed throughout the fifteenth century: by Dr Thomas Gascoigne, who looked to Jerome for a model of plain biblical learning, and rejected knowledge reputed 'subtle'; by the young chancellor William Gray and his colleague Robert Fleming, who left Oxford to study theology at Cologne and then at Padua . . . by Dr John Colet, for whom it was arrogance for Aquinas to have 'defined everything'; and implicitly by Pecock . . . by Dr Chaundler at New College . . . and by the occasional scholar who threw up study to join the Carthusians or the community of priests at Syon.[16]

The fifteenth century, however, demands far more extended study than it has yet received. My own work has focussed on issues of authority and interpretation coming to the forefront in England in the course of the interaction of a body of ideas gradually coming to be defined as 'Wycliffite' and an opposing set of emphases gradually identifiable as 'orthodox'. However, much work remains to be done on the religio-intellectual hinterland of this interaction provided by a wider European intellectual context. Such a context, as I have suggested, would indicate that Lollardy was as much a symptom as a cause of larger changes taking place in late-medieval scholasticism. The tension between what I have been describing as *scientia* and *sapientia*, between 'reason' and 'revelation', especially in relation to what was increasingly seen as the pernicious reliance on inappropriate methodologies in theological studies, seems to have come to the surface in peculiarly unsettling ways in late-medieval times.[17] Not that it was ever absent; in fact, one can argue that its presence is inevitable in the institutionalised study of God. Indeed, if one takes a bird's-eye view of the history of the major European universities, especially that of Paris, over the thirteenth and fourteenth centuries, one finds a succession of condemnations of various intellectual positions, almost always accompanied by stern warnings to theologians against the dangers of committing adultery with philosophy,[18] or against those of *doctrinae sophisticae*.[19] From the second half of the fourteenth century onwards, university statutes would often expressly articulate prohibitions against the treatment of logical and philosophical matters in the context of the study of theology, including lectures on Lombard's *Sentences* as well as on the Bible.[20] By the late Middle Ages, therefore, there was a long tradition of unease with the implications, to cite again Alain Boureau's phrase which I quoted in my Introduction, of 'the radical intellectualisation of the world under the effects of Christianity'. Such intellectualisation – fostered and legitimised through institutional sanctions, and supported by the methodologies so central to scholastic endeavour – proved in the long run unsustainable. As Damasus Trapp has memorably stated:

> Freedom perishes if without responsibility: one of the reasons why the fourteenth-century theology lost its momentum. The great aspirations of its academic freedom, so breath-taking, so unequalled and unique, came to naught because one vital factor was neglected: self-control and alertness to the dangers of licence.[21]

Trapp's vision, though couched in a language of judgment and condemnation with which one need not necessarily sympathise, nevertheless
points to a fundamental truth: intellectual freedom, when unaccompa-
nied by stringent controls, can have disturbing consequences for the
legitimacy and continuing viability of the very institutions and discourses enabling such freedom. This, I suggest, is what happened in
late-medieval Europe, and accounts for the confused but acute sense of
familiarity that the student of Lollardy has when examining the religio-
intellectual culture of the times outside the compass of the English
heresy. The intellectual trajectory of Jean Gerson, for instance, culminating in a re-visioned theology based on a categorical rejection of
those whom he described as *formalizantes*, or *phantastici*, offers striking
parallels to that of Wyclif.[22] The growing late-medieval predilection
for the notion of *scientia pietatis*, defined by Zénon Kaluza as 'la conception de la théologie comme science de la piété . . . et de l'édification
spirituelle, décidément hostile à tout mélange avec la logique' ('a conception of theology as the science of piety . . . and of spiritual edification,
clearly hostile to any logical admixture')[23] bears important affinities
to one of the fundamental motivations of Lollardy. An indecisive but
tormented engagement with the nature of the 'literal sense' and its
relationship to God's intention, again so fundamental to Lollardy's raison d'être, characterises much late-medieval hermeneutic engagement
with the scriptural text.[24] Karlfried Froelich's fascinating account of
the hermeneutic discussions at the Council of Constance offers us
the same picture: an academic freedom of thought had deepened an
awareness of the ambiguity of words and interpretations (and their
consequent openness to polemical appropriation) to an extent that a
fundamental axiom – 'suspicion and scepticism have to stop at the
threshold of the Bible' – had become in practice untenable.[25] The
'strange and sometimes almost grotesque logic', to borrow Froelich's
words,[26] of a scholasticism which sought to reconcile an unrestrained
freedom of investigation and questioning with the (in theory) unques-
tionable certitude of a revealed text seems to have begun to fracture from
the mid-fourteenth century onwards, a fracture resulting in centrifugal
forces which could no longer be contained within inherited institutional
discourses.

I wish to conclude by suggesting that Lollardy, in its inception and early trajectory, needs to be placed in the context of such an 'Endstadium' – the word is Robert Kalidova's[27] – of medieval scholasticism, an 'Endstadium' which, over the course of its development into a popular heresy, and then, later, through its Hussite posterity,[28] it equally helped to define and shape. Such definition was not necessarily limited to negative responses of suppression and confinement, though certainly these did form an important part of the reaction against 'heresy'. Lollardy equally brought about a reassessment and reconfiguration – in terms both of values and methodologies – of late-medieval intellectuality. Its hermeneutic and historical positivism, as well as its interest in textual criticism, in patristics, in ecclesiastical history and in the psychology of faith, elicited responses which had their own posterity, a posterity which, though it indeed arose out of reaction, should not be dismissed as merely 'reactionary'. This posterity requires urgent scholarly attention. Its import will remain unplumbed as long as our knowledge of the learned writings of the time remains nascent and fragmentary. I would argue that such knowledge is essential to a comprehension not only of late-medieval religious and intellectual culture in England, but also of the profound developments and changes that it was to undergo over the next one hundred years. A reassessment of the historiography of 'medieval' into 'renaissance' and 'reformation' cannot be complete without a far fuller investigation of late medieval intellectual history, including the history of intellectual institutions.

Notes

Introduction

1 *De Apostasia*, ed. M. H. Dziewicki, Wyclif Society (London, 1889) p. 49/17–25. All further references to *De Apostasia* are to this edition.

2 On the history of the term 'glossing', and its catachresis from 'explication' to 'perversion', see Beryl Smalley, 'The Gospels in the Paris Schools in the Late Twelfth and Early Thirteenth Centuries: Peter the Chanter, Hugh of St. Cher, Alexander of Hales, John of La Rochelle', *Franciscan Studies* 39 (1979), 230–54, 40 (1980), 298–369 (pp. 366–8), repr. in *The Gospels in the Schools: c. 1100–c. 1280* (London, 1985); also Guy Lobrichon, 'Une nouveauté: les gloses de la Bible', in Pierre Riché and Guy Lobrichon (eds.), *Le Moyen âge et la Bible* (Paris, 1984), pp. 95–114.

3 *De Apostasia*, p. 49/22.

4 I will not invoke here the term 'nominalism', given scholarly disagreement over what it means. However, there can be no doubt that what was traditionally seen as one of the characteristics of 'nominalism' – a self-conscious disjunction of reason and faith – does point to a major late-medieval crux. The relation of Wyclif's thought to one of the abiding intellectual preoccupations of his time demands enquiries which fall outside the scope of this study. On 'nominalism', see W. J. Courtenay, 'Late Medieval Nominalism Revisited: 1972–82', *Journal of the History of Ideas* 44 (1983), 159–64; 'In Search of Nominalism: Two Centuries of Historical Debate', in Ruedi Imbach and Alfonso Maierù (eds.), *Gli studi di filosfia medievale fra otto e novecento: contributo a un bilancio storiografico* (Rome, 1991), pp. 233–51; for a somewhat cursory but stimulating account of Wyclif's thought in relation to the 'Endstadium' of medieval thought, see Robert Kalidova, 'Joannus Wyclifs Metaphysik des extremen Realismus und ihre Bedeutung im Endstadium der mittelalterlichen Philosophie', in Paul Wilpert (ed.), *Die Metaphysik im Mittelalter*, MM 2 (Berlin, 1963), 717–23; also see Neal Ward Gilbert, 'Ockham, Wyclif and the "Via Moderna"', in Albert Zimmermann (ed.), *Antiqui und Moderni: Traditionsbewußtsein und Fortschrittsbewußtsein im späten Mittelalter*, MM 9 (Berlin, 1974), pp. 85–125.

5 See Hester Goodenough Gelber, 'Logic and the Trinity: A Clash of Values in Scholastic Thought, 1300–1335', Ph.D. thesis, University of Wisconsin (1974); *Exploring the Boundaries of Reason: Three Questions on the Nature of God by Robert Holcot OP* (Toronto, 1983); Michael H. Shank, *'Unless You Believe, You Shall Not Understand': Logic, University and Society in Late Medieval Vienna* (Princeton, 1988).

6 See, preeminently, Anne Hudson, *The Premature Reformation: Wycliffite Texts and Lollard History* (Oxford, 1988), pp. 174–277.

7 *L'Ambiguïte du Livre: prince, pouvoir et peuple dans les commentaires de la Bible au moyen âge* (Paris, 1994), pp. 407–8.

8 *Ibid.*, pp. 402–3.

9 J. de Ghellinck, 'Dialectique et dogme aux xe–xiie siècles', in *Festgabe zum 60. Geburtstag Clemens Baeumker, Beiträge zur Geschichte der Philosophie des Mittelalters*, Supplementband I (Münster, 1913), pp. 79–99 (p. 81); see also his *Le Mouvement théologique du xiie siècle* (Bruges, Brussels and Paris, 1948), pp. 66 ff., 229 ff.; and Martin Grabmann, *Die Geschichte der scholastischen Methode*, 2 vols. (Freiburg im Breisgau, 1909–11), vol. ii, pp. 111–27. On Augustine's vision of the uses of dialectic, see Jean Pépin, *Saint Augustin et la dialectique* (Villanova, Pa., 1976).

10 Anthony Kenny and Jan Pinborg, 'Medieval Philosophical Literature', in *CHLMP*, pp. 1–42 (pp. 26–9).

11 See the various articles in Klaus Jacobi (ed.), *Argumentationstheorie: Scholastische Forschungen zu den logischen und semantischen Regeln korrekten Folgerns* (Leiden, New York and Cologne, 1993); and in Johannes Fried (ed.), *Dialektik und Rhetorik im früheren und hohen Mittelalter* (Munich, 1997); also Peter von Moos, *Geschichte als Topik: Das rhetorische Exemplum von der Antike zur Neuzeit und die 'historiae' im 'Policraticus' Johanns von Salisbury* (Hildesheim, Zürich and New York, 1988), pp. 188ff; von Moos, 'La retorica nel medioevo', and Alfonso Maierù, 'La dialettica', in G. Cavallo, C. Leonardi and E. Menestò (eds.), *Lo spazio letterario del medioevo: Il medioevo latino*, vol. i, tome ii (Rome, 1993), pp. 231–71, 273–94.

12 On the idea of there being two kinds of argumentation, the first sophistical, and derived from the devil, the second 'demonstrative' and derived from the Holy Ghost, see Louis Jacques Bataillon, 'De la lectio à la praedicatio: commentaires bibliques et sermons au xiiie siècle', *Revue des sciences philosophiques et théologiques* 70 (1986), 559–75 (p. 565). The second, proper kind of *disputatio* was theoretically supposed to be intermediate between devout *lectio* and committed *praedicatio*.

13 *La littérature quodlibétique de 1260 à 1320*, 2 vols., Bibliothèque Thomiste 5 & 21 (Kain, 1925 & 35), vol. i, pp. 66–7.

14 See Beryl Smalley, 'Use of the "Spiritual" Senses of Scripture in Persuasion and Argument by Scholars in the Middle Ages', *RTAM* 52 (1985), 44–63; also her 'Gospels in the Paris Schools' for debate on the issue; John W. Baldwin, *Masters, Princes and Merchants: The Social Views of Peter the Chanter and His Circle*, 2 vols. (Princeton, 1970), vol. i, pp. 88–116; and Diana Wood, '... *novo sensu sacram adulterare Scripturam*: Clement VI and the Political Use of the Bible', in Katherine Walsh and Diana Wood (eds.), *The Bible in the Medieval World: Essays in Memory of Beryl Smalley*, SCH Subsidia 4 (Oxford, 1985), pp. 237–49.

15 *La théologie au douzième siècle* (Paris, 1957), p. 351.

16 On this issue, see preeminently, Rita Copeland, *Rhetoric, Hermeneutics and Translation in the Middle Ages: Academic Traditions and Vernacular Texts* (Cambridge, 1991).

17 'The Old Rhetoric: An Aide-Mémoire', in *The Semiotic Challenge*, trans. Richard Howard (Oxford, 1988), pp. 11–94 (p. 30).

18 *De fide catholica*, PL 210.333; trans. of cited passage in A. J. Minnis and A. B. Scott with David Wallace (eds.), *Medieval Literary Theory and Criticism c.1100–c.1375: The Commentary Tradition* (Oxford, 1988), p. 323 (n. 49).

19 An extreme example of this self-consciousness is afforded by John of Salisbury in his *Policraticus* where the exegetical reinvention of past texts, whether pagan or Christian, is subjected to the most refined, ludic irony: see Peter von Moos, 'The Use of *Exempla*

in the *Policraticus* of John of Salisbury', in Michael Wilks (ed.), *The World of John of Salisbury*, SCH Subsidia 3 (Oxford, 1984), pp. 207–61 (pp. 250–54).

20 *Penser au moyen âge* (Paris, 1991), p. 155. See also Buc, *Ambiguïté*, p. 405: '"L'idéologie (...) n'admet pas en son sein la contradiction (...) [mais] tente de la résoudre par son absence"? Cette idéologie-là n'est pas médiévale' ('"Ideology does not allow for contradiction within itself, but tries to resolve it through its absence?" Such ideology is not medieval'); and Alain de Libera, 'La Logique de la discussion dans l'université médiévale', in *Figures et conflits rhétoriques*, Editions de l'Université de Bruxelles (Brussels, 1990), pp. 59–81; Alain de Libera and Irène Rosier, 'Argumentation in the Middle Ages', *Argumentation* 1 (1987), 355–64.

21 See Bernardo C. Bazàn, John W. Wippel, Gérard Fransen and Danielle Jacquart, *Les questions disputées et les questions quodlibétiques dans les facultés de théologie, de droit et de médecine*, Typologie des sources du moyen âge occidental, Fasc. 44–45 (Turnhout, 1985); P. Glorieux, 'L'enseignement au moyen âge: techniques et méthodes en usage à la Faculté de Théologie de Paris, au XIIIe siècle', *AHDLMA* 43 (1969), 65–186 (pp. 123–36); Olga Weijers, *La 'Disputatio' à la Faculté des arts de Paris (1200–1350 environ): Esquisse d'une typologie*, Studia Artistarum 2 (Turnhout, 1995); Stephen F. Brown, 'Key terms in Medieval Theological Vocabulary', in Olga Weijers (ed.), *Méthodes et instruments du travail intellectuel au moyen âge: Etudes sur le vocabulaire*, CIVICIMA 3 (Turnhout, 1990), pp. 82–96; Alfonso Maierù, *University Training in Medieval Europe*, trans. D. N. Pryds (Leiden, New York and Cologne, 1994); Damasus Trapp, 'The Portiuncula Discussion of Cremona (ca. 1380): New Light on 14th Century Disputations', *RTAM* 22 (1955), 79–94; James A. Weisheipl, 'Curriculum of the Faculty of Arts at Oxford in the Early Fourteenth Century', *Mediaeval Studies* 26 (1964), 143-85, and his 'Developments in the Arts Curriculum at Oxford in the Early Fourteenth Century', *Mediaeval Studies* 28 (1966), 151–75; J. M. Fletcher, 'Teaching and the Study of Arts at Oxford: c. 1400–c. 1520', D.Phil. thesis, University of Oxford (1961), and his 'Developments in the Faculty of Arts 1370–1520', in J. I. Catto and R. Evans (eds.), *The History of the University of Oxford II: Late-Medieval Oxford* (Oxford, 1992), pp. 315–45.

22 See Barthes, 'What we might anachronistically call the *writer* is therefore, essentially, in the Middle Ages: 1. a *transmitter*: he passes on an absolute substance which is the treasure of antiquity, the source of authority; 2. a *combiner*: he is entitled to 'break' works of the past, by a limitless analysis, and to recompose them': 'Old Rhetoric', p. 31.

23 For *adaptare*, see C. Spicq, *Esquisse d'une histoire de l'exégèse latine au moyen âge*, Bibliothèque Thomiste 26 (Paris, 1944), pp. 281–5; also see Jacques Verger, 'L'Exégèse de l'Université', in Riché and Lobrichon (eds.), *Moyen Age et la Bible*, pp. 199–232.

24 *A locus classicus* would be Abelard: see his *Theologia Christiana*, in E. M. Buytaert (ed.), *Petri Abaelardi Opera Theologica II*, CCCM 12 (Turnhout, 1969), p. 121/1552–57.

25 See Martin Irvine, 'Interpretation and the Semiotics of Allegory in Clement of Alexandria, Origen and Augustine', *Semiotica* 63 (1987), 33–79; *The Making of Textual Culture: 'Grammatica' and Literary Theory, 350–1100* (Cambridge, 1994), pp. 162–89.

26 See W. A. Pantin, *The English Church in the Fourteenth Century* (Cambridge, 1955, repr. Toronto, 1980), pp. 132–5; Beryl Smalley, 'The Bible in the Medieval Schools', in G. W. H. Lampe (ed.), *The Cambridge History of the Bible II: The West from the Fathers to the Reformation* (Cambridge, 1969), pp. 197–219 (pp. 206–9, 216–19); William J. Courtenay, 'The Bible in the Fourteenth Century: Some Observations', *Church History* 54 (1985), 176–87; on the volume of extra-biblical speculation centred round commentaries on the *Sentences*, see John E. Murdoch, 'From Social into Intellectual Factors: An Aspect of the Unitary Character of Late Medieval Learning', in J. E. Murdoch and

E. D. Sylla (eds.), *The Cultural Context of Medieval Learning* (Dordrecht and Boston, 1975), pp. 271–339 (pp. 273–80).

27 The major general studies of medieval biblical and other exegesis which form the basis of my study are Beryl Smalley, *The Study of the Bible in the Middle Ages*, 3rd edn. (Oxford, 1983); *English Friars and Antiquity in the Early Fourteenth Century* (Oxford, 1960); *The Gospels in the Schools; Studies in Medieval Thought from Abelard to Wyclif* (London, 1981); Henri de Lubac, *Exégèse médiévale: les quatres sens de l'écriture*, 2 vols. in 4 (Paris, 1959–64); Spicq, *L'Exégèse latine*; Hennig Brinkmann, *Mittelalterliche Hermeneutik* (Tübingen, 1980); Paul De Vooght, *Les sources de la doctrine chrétienne d'après des théologiens de xive siècle et du début du xve avec le texte intégral des xii premières questions de la 'Summa' inédite de Gérard de Bologne* (Bruges, 1954); Lampe (ed.), *Cambridge History of the Bible ii*; Guy Lobrichon, 'L'Esegesi biblica: storia di un genere letterario (vii–xiii secolo)', in Cavallo, Leonardi and Menestò (eds.), *Lo spazio letterario*, vol. i, tome ii, pp. 355–81.

28 'Forme di conoscenza e ideali di sapere nella cultura medievale', in M. Asztalos, J. E. Murdoch and I. Niiniluoto (eds.), *Knowledge and the Sciences in Medieval Philosophy: Proceedings of the Eighth International Congress of Medieval Philosophy*, vol. i, Acta Philosophica Fennica 48 (Helsinki, 1990), pp. 10–71 (p. 11). The major study on the subject is Ulrich Köpf, *Die Anfänge der theologischen Wissenschaftstheorie im 13. Jahrhundert* (Tübingen, 1974).

29 See Köpf, *Wissenschaftstheorie*, pp. 158–87, 227–31, 253–7.

30 *The Harvest of Medieval Theology: Gabriel Biel and Late Medieval Nominalism* (Cambridge, Mass., 1963), pp. 361–93. Important general studies of the relationship of scripture and tradition are De Vooght, *Les sources de la doctrine chrétienne*; and Hermann Schüssler, *Der Primat der Heiligen Schrift als theologisches und kanonistisches Problem im Spätmittelalter* (Wiesbaden, 1977).

31 *The Premature Reformation*, pp. 273–7.

32 'Patristique et argument de tradition au bas moyen âge', in Albert Lang, Joseph Lechner and Michael Schmaus (eds.), *Aus der Geisteswelt des Mittelalters*, BGPTM, Supplementband iii. 1. Halband (Münster, 1935), 403–26 (p. 411).

33 *Ibid.*, p. 419

34 One of the most explicit medieval statements of 'la tradition vivante' is that of Hugh of St Victor, who, in his *Didascalicon*, insists that the 'New Testament' encompasses the decrees of the Councils, the writings of the Fathers, and writings of other orthodox writers. For discussion, see Lesley Smith, 'What was the Bible in the Twelfth and Thirteenth Centuries?', in Robert E. Lerner (ed.), *Neue Richtungen in der hoch- und spätmittelalterlichen Bibelexegese* (Munich, 1996), pp. 1–15 (pp. 2–4). See also Beryl Smalley, 'Ecclesiastical Attitudes to Novelty c. 1100–c. 1250', in Derek Baker (ed.), *Church, Society and Politics*, SCH 12 (Oxford, 1975), pp. 113–31.

35 Damasus Trapp, 'Augustinian Theology of the 14th Century; Notes on Editions, Marginalia, Opinions and Book-Lore', *Augustiniana* 6 (1956), 146–274; William J. Courtenay, 'Augustinianism at Oxford in the Fourteenth Century', *Augustiniana* 30 (1980), 58–70; also his *Schools and Scholars in Fourteenth-Century England* (Princeton, 1987), pp. 307–24; Heiko Oberman and Frank A. James (eds.), *Via Augustini: Augustine in the Later Middle Ages, Renaissance and Reformation. Essays in Honour of Damasus Trapp, O.S.A.* (Leiden, New York, Copenhagen and Cologne, 1991).

36 See John M. Rist, *Augustine: Ancient Thought Baptised* (Cambridge, 1994); Brian Stock, *Augustine the Reader: Meditation, Self-Knowledge and the Ethics of Interpretation*

(Cambridge, Mass., 1996); Gerald Bonner, 'Augustine as Biblical Scholar', in P. R. Ackroyd and C. F. Evans (eds.), *The Cambridge History of the Bible 1: From the Beginnings to Jerome* (Cambridge, 1970), pp. 541–63; R. A. Markus, 'Augustine, Biographical Introduction: Christianity and Philosophy', in *CHLGEMP*, pp. 341–53.

37 *Augustine the Reader*, p. 125.

38 'And thus a man who is resting upon faith, hope and love, and who keeps a firm hold upon these, does not need the scriptures except for the purpose of instructing others. Accordingly, many live without copies of the scriptures, even in solitude, on the strength of these three graces'. *On Christian Doctrine*, trans. J. F. Shaw, in *A Select Library of the Nicene and the Post-Nicene Fathers of the Christian Church* (Grand Rapids, Michigan, 1883, repr. 1973), p. 534. All further references to *De Doctrina Christiana* are to this translation.

39 '"Always to Keep the Literal Sense in Holy Scripture Means to Kill One's Soul": The State of Biblical Hermeneutics at the Beginning of the Fifteenth Century', in E. R. Miner (ed.), *Literary Uses of Typology from the Late Middle Ages to the Present* (Princeton, 1977), pp. 20–48 (p. 42).

40 See W. J. Courtenay, *Schools and Scholars*, pp. 327ff; also his 'Theology and Theologians from Ockham to Wyclif', in Catto and Evans (eds.), *Hist. Univ. Ox.* II, pp. 1–34 (pp. 30–34); J. I. Catto, 'Wyclif and Wycliffism at Oxford 1356–1430', in Catto and Evans (eds.), *Hist. Univ. Ox.* II, pp. 175–261; J. A. Robson, *Wyclif and the Oxford Schools: The Relation of the 'Summa de Ente' to Scholastic Debates in the Later Fourteenth Century* (Cambridge, 1961).

41 *Study of the Bible*, pp. 281ff.

42 *Ibid.*, p. 308.

43 See Gilbert Dahan, 'Saint Thomas d'Aquin et la métaphore: rhétorique et herméneutique', *Medioevo* 18 (1992), 85–117; Rita Copeland, 'Rhetoric and the Politics of the Literal Sense in Medieval Literary Theory: Aquinas, Wyclif and the Lollards', in Piero Boitani and Anna Torti (eds.), *Interpretations: Medieval and Modern* (Cambridge, 1993), pp. 1–23; A. Blanche, 'Le sens littéral des Ecritures d'après saint Thomas d'Aquin', *Revue Thomiste* 14 (1906), 192–212; P. Synave, 'La doctrine de saint Thomas d'Aquin sur le sens littéral des Ecritures', *Revue biblique* 35 (1926), 40–65; De Lubac, *Exégèse médiévale*, vol. II/2, pp. 272–302; M.-D. Chenu, *Introduction à l'etude de Saint Thomas d'Aquin* (Paris, 1954), pp. 199–225.

44 Copeland, 'Politics of the Literal Sense', p. 8.

45 *Summa Theologiae*, 1.1.10 ad 3 (Blackfriars edition), 60 vols. (1964–76), vol. 1, pp. 40–41.

46 Dahan, 'Métaphore', p. 111.

47 *Ibid.*, p. 115.

48 *L'Exégèse latine*, p. 340.

49 See Minnis and Scott (eds.), *Medieval Literary Theory and Criticism*, pp. 204–6; Spicq, *L'Exégèse Latine*, pp. 335–42; for Lyra's use of the notion of the 'double literal sense' in his Apocalypse commentary, see *Nicholas of Lyra's Apocalypse Commentary*, trans. Philip D. W. Krey (Kalamazoo, Mich., 1997), pp. 18–9. For a detailed study of Lyra's Prefaces, see J. G. Kiecker, 'The Hermeneutical Principles and Exegetical Methods of Nicholas of Lyra O.F.M. (c. 1270–1349)', Ph.D. thesis, Marquette University (1978). On Lyra's exegesis, see Herman Hailperin, *Rashi and the Christian Scholars* (Pittsburgh, 1963), pp. 137–246; De Lubac, *Exégèse médiévale*, vol. II/2, pp. 344–67; and Philip D. W. Krey and Lesley Smith (eds.), *Nicholas of Lyra: The Senses of Scripture* (Leiden, Boston and Cologne, 2000).

50 The best general account of Fitzralph's career and thought is Katherine Walsh, *A Fourteenth-century Scholar and Primate: Richard Fitzralph in Oxford, Avignon and Armagh* (Oxford, 1981). See in particular pp. 36–64, 129–181; also see her 'Die Rezeption der Schriften des Richard Fitzralph (Armachanus) im lollardisch-hussistischen Milieu', in Jürgen Miethke (ed.), *Das Publikum politischer Theorie im 14. Jahrhundert* (Munich, 1992), pp. 237–53, and her 'Preaching, Pastoral Care and *Sola Scriptura* in Later Medieval Ireland: Richard Fitzralph and the Use of the Bible', in Walsh and Wood (eds.), *Bible in the Medieval World*, pp. 251–68. For a detailed discussion of Fitzralph's exegetical theory, see A. J. Minnis, '"Authorial Intention" and "Literal Sense" in the Exegetical Theories of Richard Fitzralph and John Wyclif: An Essay in the Medieval History of Biblical Hermeneutics', *Proceedings of the Royal Irish Academy* 75 C (1975), 1–31.

51 See Walsh, *Fitzralph*, p. 36.

52 *Ibid.*, p. 129.

53 *Ibid.*, p. 148.

54 *Ibid.*, p. 171.

55 *Ibid.*, p. 172.

56 Froelich, 'State of Biblical Hermeneutics', p. 20.

57 'Il faut en effet bien voir que chez tous ces auteurs le souci d'exposer le sens littéral de l'Ecriture sainte s'accompagnait cependant du refus d'un littéralisme qu'ils eussent qualifié de judaïsant . . . la définition qu'il [Aquinas] donne du "sens littéral" de l'Ecriture est en fait large et récupère une part de ce que nous aurions cru relever du sens spirituel traditionnel' ('It is necessary to see that with all these authors, the desire to explain the literal sense of Holy Scripture was nevertheless accompanied by the rejection of a literalism which they would have gone as far as to qualify as "judaising" . . . The definition which Aquinas gives to the "literal sense" of Scripture is in fact broad, and encompasses part of what we would have thought would belong to the traditional spiritual sense'): Verger, 'L'Exégèse de l'Université', p. 216. Major studies of the interaction of Jewish and Christian exegesis are Hailperin, *Rashi and the Christian Scholars*; and Gilbert Dahan, *Les Intellectuels chrétiens et les juifs au moyen âge* (Paris, 1990), which contains a full bibliography.

58 'L'Éxègese de l'Université', pp. 216–17; on the extra-textual ideology informing Lyra's own literalism, see Philippe Buc, 'Pouvoir royal et commentaires de la Bible', *Annales: économies sociétés civilisations* 44 (1989), 691–713 (pp. 704–9).

59 'Clm 27034: Unchristened Nominalism and Wycliffite Realism at Prague in 1381', *RTAM* 24 (1957), 320–60 (p. 321).

60 'Augustinian Theology', p. 149.

61 On late-medieval scepticism, see the following articles by Leonard A. Kennedy: 'Philosophical Scepticism in England in the Mid-Fourteenth Century', *Vivarium* 21 (1983), 35–57; 'Late-Fourteenth Century Philosophical Scepticism at Oxford', *Vivarium* 23 (1985), 124–51; 'A Carmelite Fourteenth-Century Theological Notebook', *Carmelus* 33 (1986), 70–102; 'Oxford Philosophers and the Existence of God, 1340–1350', *RTAM* 52 (1985), 194–208; 'Theology the Handmaiden of Logic: A *Sentence* Commentary used by Gregory of Rimini and John Hiltalingen', *Augustiniana* 33 (1983), 142–64; see also Shank, *Late Medieval Vienna*, pp. 35–56; for medieval anxiety about scepticism, see de Libera, *Penser au moyen âge*, pp. 156–68; for medieval dismissals of scepticism, see L. M. De Rijk, *La Philosophie au moyen âge* (Leiden, 1985), pp. 214–8.

62 On the universities' self-definition in terms of their intellectual liberty, see Jacques le Goff, 'Les intellectuels au moyen age', in Jacques le Goff and Béla Köpeczi (eds.),

Intellectuels français, intellectuels hongrois: XIIIe–XXe siècles (Budapest and Paris, 1985), pp. 11–22 (pp. 18–19); for the relationship of French Universities to various institutions of power, see J. Verger and C. Vulliez, 'Crises et mutations des universités françaises à la fin du moyen âge', in J. Verger (ed.), *Histoire des universités en France* (Toulouse, 1986), pp. 109–37 (pp. 113–25); see also W. J. Courtenay, 'Inquiry and Inquisition: Academic Freedom in Medieval Universities', *Church History* 58 (1989), 168–81; Ian P. Wei, 'The Self-Image of the Masters of Theology at the University of Paris in the Late Thirteenth and Early Fourteenth Centuries', *Journal of Ecclesiastical History* 46 (1995), 398–431; Astrik L. Gabriel, 'The Ideal Master of the Mediaeval University', *Catholic Historical Review* 60 (1974), 1–40; J. Leclercq, 'L'Idéal du théologien au moyen âge', *Revue des sciences religieuses* 21 (1947), 121–48; George H. Williams, *Wilderness and Paradise in Christian Thought: The Biblical Experience of the Desert in the History of Christianity and the Paradise Theme in the Theological Idea of the University* (New York, 1962), pp. 158–83; Jacques Verger, 'Teachers', in Hilde De Ridder-Symoens (ed.), *A History of the University in Europe I: Universities in the Middle Ages* (Cambridge, 1992), pp. 144–68 (pp. 161–5). The best recent study of notions of intellectual liberty in the medieval university and the institutional constraints thereon is J. M. M. H. Thijssen, *Censure and Heresy at the University of Paris 1200–1400* (Philadelphia, 1998).

63 See Nicholas Watson, 'Censorship and Cultural Change in Late Medieval England: Vernacular Theology, the Oxford Translation Debate, and Arundel's *Constitutions* of 1409', *Speculum* 70 (1995), 822–64; A. K. McHardy, '*De heretico comburendo*, 1401', in Margaret Aston and Colin Richmond (eds.), *Lollardy and the Gentry in the Later Middle Ages* (Stroud and New York, 1997), pp. 112–26.

64 See Catto, 'Wyclif and Wycliffism at Oxford', pp. 255–61.

65 Anne Hudson, 'Lollardy: The English Heresy?', in *Lollards and their Books* (London and Ronceverte, 1985), pp. 141–63.

66 'Intellectuals in the Middle Ages, 1957–95', in Miri Rubin (ed.), *The Work of Jacques le Goff and the Challenges of Medieval History* (Woodbridge, 1997), pp. 145–55.

67 *Ibid.*, p. 151.

1 John Wyclif and the truth of sacred scripture

1 *De Veritate sacrae scripturae*, ed. Rudolf Buddensieg, 3 vols., Wyclif Society (London, 1905–7). All references are to this edition and given after citations in the text.

2 See Williel R. Thomson (in part from the notes of S. Harrison Thomson), *The Latin Writings of John Wyclyf: An Annotated Catalog* (Toronto, 1983), pp. 14–15; and Anne Hudson, 'The Development of Wyclif's *Summa Theologiae*', forthcoming in Zénon Kaluza and Maria Teresa Fumagalli Beonio-Brocchieri (eds.), *John Wyclif: Logic, Politics, Theology*.

3 See Michael Hurley, '"Scriptura Sola": Wyclif and his Critics', *Traditio* 16 (1960), 275–352; G. A. Benrath, 'Traditionsbewußtsein, Schriftverständnis und Schriftprinzip bei Wyclif', in Zimmermann (ed.), *Antiqui und Moderni*, pp. 359–82.

4 The dating and process of composition of *De Veritate* admit of some uncertainty; see Thomson, *Latin Writings*, pp. 55–6; Anne Hudson, 'The Development of Wyclif's *Summa Theologiae*'; 'Cross-referencing in Wyclif's Latin Works', in Peter Biller and Barrie Dobson (eds.), *The Medieval Church: Universities, Heresy, and the Religious Life*, SCH Subsidia 11 (Oxford, 1999), pp. 193–215. However, the exact date is not of governing importance for the analysis attempted in this chapter, and I accordingly treat the work as a unity.

5 Ed. R. L. Poole (Book I) and J. Loserth (Books II and III), 3 vols., Wyclif Society (London, 1885, 1900–4).

6 On this issue, see Edith C. Tatnall, 'Church and State according to John Wyclyf', Ph.D. thesis, University of Colorado (1964); Michael Wilks, 'Predestination, Property and Power: Wyclif's Theory of Dominion and Grace', in G. J. Cuming (ed.), SCH 2 (London, 1965), pp. 220–36; '*Reformatio Regni*: Wyclif and Hus as Leaders of Religious Protest Movements', in Derek Baker (ed.), *Schism, Heresy and Religious Protest*, SCH 9 (Cambridge, 1972), pp. 109–30; Arthur Stephen McGrade, 'Somersaulting Sovereignty: A Note on Reciprocal Lordship and Servitude in Wyclif', in Diana Wood (ed.), *Church and Sovereignty c. 590- 1918: Essays in Honour of Michael Wilks*, SCH Subsidia 9 (Oxford, 1991), pp. 261–8.

7 See Joseph H. Dahmus, *The Prosecution of John Wyclyf* (New Haven, 1952), pp. 7–73; and Catto, 'Wyclif and Wycliffism at Oxford', pp. 202–8; Peter McNiven, *Heresy and Politics in the Reign of Henry IV: the Burning of John Badby* (Woodbridge, 1987), pp. 19–35.

8 See A. J. Minnis, *Medieval Theory of Authorship: Scholastic Literary Attitudes in the Later Middle Ages*, 2nd edn. (Aldershot, 1988), pp. 73–117.

9 Sections from the *Postilla* have been edited in *WBK*; also see Beryl Smalley, 'John Wyclif's *Postilla super totam Bibliam*', *Bodleian Library Record* 4 (1953), 186–205.

10 On the metaphysical background to Wyclif's identification of scripture with the mind of God, see Maarten J. F. M. Hoenen, 'Theology and Metaphysics: the Debate between John Wyclif and John Kenningham on the Principles of Reading the Scriptures', forthcoming in Kaluza and Fumagalli Beonio-Brocchieri (eds.), *John Wyclif*.

11 See R. J. Hankinson, 'Philosophy of Science', in Jonathan Barnes (ed.), *The Cambridge Companion to Aristotle* (Cambridge, 1995), pp. 109–39.

12 See R. A. Markus, 'Augustine, Biographical Introduction: Christianity and Philosophy' and 'Augustine: Reason and Illumination', in *CHLGEMP*, pp. 341–53, 362–73, for a discussion addressing the complexities in Augustine's thought on these issues. See also Stock, *Augustine the Reader*, and Maria Manuela Brito Martins, 'Le Projét herméneutique augustinien', *Augustiniana* 48 (1998), 253–86. On Wyclif's Augustinianism, see Gordon Leff, 'Wyclif and the Augustinian Tradition, with Special Reference to his *De Trinitate*', *Mediaevalia et Humanistica* NS 4 (1970), 29–39; Ian Levy, 'John Wyclif and Augustinian Realism', *Augustiniana* 48 (1998), 87–106.

13 See Paul Ricoeur, *The Rule of Metaphor: Multi-disciplinary Studies of the Creation of Meaning in Language*, trans. Robert Czerny with K. McLaughlin and J. Costello (London, 1977); Jacques Derrida, 'White Mythology: Metaphor in the Text of Philosophy', tr. F. C. T. Moore, *New Literary History* 6 (1974), 5–74; Janet Soskice, *Metaphor and Religious Language* (Oxford, 1985); also see Peter Dronke, *Dante and Medieval Latin Traditions* (Cambridge, 1986), pp. 1–31.

14 In fact, scriptural 'sense' as opposed to the mere words, is the 'real' scripture: 'sensus verborum . . . est scriptura realis', *WBK*, p. 364.

15 Ecclus 24:23, Psalm 128:3, Ecclus 24:19, Song of Solomon 2:13.

16 On Wyclif's realism, see Alessandro D. Conti, *Esistenza e verità: forme e strutture del reale in Paolo Veneto e nel pensiero filosofico del tardo medioevo* (Rome, 1996), pp. 38–40, 164–7; *Johannes Sharpe: Quaestio super universalia* (Florence, 1990), pp. 295–309; Anthony Kenny, 'The Realism of *De Universalibus*', in Anthony Kenny (ed.), *Wyclif in his Times* (Oxford, 1986), pp. 17–29; Kenny, 'Realism and Determinism in the Early Wyclif', Vilém Herold, 'Wyclifs Polemik gegen Ockhams Auffassung der platonischen Ideen und ihr Nachklang in der tschechischen hussitischen Philosophie' in Anne Hudson

and Michael Wilks (eds.), *From Ockham to Wyclif,* SCH Subsidia 5 (Oxford, 1987), pp. 165–77, 185–215; Hoenen, 'Theology and Metaphysics'.

17 'Analogy and Formal Distinction: On the Logical Basis of Wyclif's Metaphysics', *Medieval Philosophy and Theology* 6 (1997), 133–65 (p. 143).

18 *Discourse and Dominion in the Fourteenth Century: Oral Contexts of Writing in Philosophy, Politics and Poetry* (Princeton, 1995), p. 81.

19 'Logical Basis of Wyclif's Metaphysics', pp. 154–8.

20 See Paul Vincent Spade, 'The Rationale for the Theory of Essential Predication', in his Introduction to Wyclif's *On Universals*, trans. A. Kenny (Oxford, 1985), pp. xli–xliii.

21 As Conti sums up: '[T]he nucleus of [Wyclif's] metaphysics lies in his trust in the scheme *object-label* as *the* general interpretative key of every logico-epistemological problem. [He] firmly believed that language was [I would say: 'ideally ought to be'] an ordered collection of signs, each referring to one of the constitutive elements of reality, and that true (linguistic) propositions were like pictures of their inner structures or/and mutual relationships' ('Logical Basis of Wyclif's Metaphysics', p. 164).

22 On my translation of 'nomen' as 'part of speech', and on the larger scholastic background to discussions of 'equivocation', see E. J. Ashworth, 'Analogy and Equivocation in Thirteenth-Century Logic: Aquinas in Context', *Mediaeval Studies* 54 (1992), 94–135, esp. p. 104; also see her 'Equivocation and Analogy in Fourteenth Century Logic: Ockham, Burley and Buridan', in B. Mojsisch and Olaf Pluta (eds.), *Historia Philosophiae Medii Aevi: Studien zur Geschichte der Philosophie des Mittelalters* (Amsterdam, 1991), pp. 23–43; and 'Analogy, Univocation and Equivocation in Some Early Fourteenth Century Authors', in J. Marenbon (ed.), *Aristotle in Britain during the Middle Ages* (Turnhout, 1996), pp. 233–47.

23 On 'universals', see Marilyn McCord Adams, 'Universals in the Early Fourteenth Century', in *CHLMP*, pp. 411–39; also see Conti, *Esistenza e verità*, pp. 89–152.

24 'Logical Basis of Wyclif's Metaphysics', pp. 143–4, italics mine.

25 See Anthony Kenny's discussion of resemblance and universals in 'The Realism of the *De Universalibus*', p. 27. On a contrasting view of biblical metaphorical meaning which foregrounds the interrelationship of such meaning and tradition, see Soskice, *Metaphor and Religious Language*, p. 158: 'So, to explain what it means to Christians to say that God is a fountain of living water, or a vine-keeper, or a rock, or fortress, or king requires an account not merely of rocks, fountains, vines, and kings but of a whole tradition of experiences and of the literary tradition which records and interprets them.'

26 On the notion of *minor mundus*, see Ernst Stadter, 'Die Seele als "Minor mundus" und als "Regnum": Ein Beitrag zur Psychologie der mittleren Franziskanerschule', in Paul Wilpert (ed.), *Universalismus und Partikularismus im Mittelalter*, MM 5 (Berlin, 1968), pp. 56–72.

27 'De virtute sermonis' is literally 'by force of the word'. The phrase was a topical one in the fourteenth century, and seems to admit, in Wyclif, a range of rather imprecise usage, encompassing both 'surface sense of words' and 'authorially intended meaning'. For discussion of the phrase, see William J. Courtenay, 'Force of Words and Figures of Speech: The Crisis Over *Virtus Sermonis* in the Fourteenth Century', *Franciscan Studies*, NS 44 (1984), 107–28; Neal Ward Gilbert, 'Ockham, Wyclif and the "via moderna"', in Zimmermann (ed.), *Antiqui und Moderni*, pp. 85–125 (pp. 93, 100–106, esp. n. 46); Johannes M. M. H. Thijssen, 'The Crisis over Ockhamist Hermeneutic and its Semantic Background: the Methodological Significance of the Censure of December 29, 1340', in Costantino Marmo (ed.), *Vestigia, Imagines, Verba: Semiotics and Logic in Medieval*

Theological Texts (xiith–xivth Century) (Turnhout, 1997), pp. 371–92; also see Copeland, 'Politics of the Literal Sense', pp. 15–16.

28 'Expresse' is another word for 'explicitly'; on the pairs 'explicite/implicite' and 'expresse/virtute' in medieval theories of the proposition, see Gabriel Nuchelmans, *Late-Scholastic and Humanist Theories of the Proposition* (Amsterdam, Oxford and New York, 1980), pp. 22, 78, 100.

29 These *apologiae* for figurative language are elsewhere cited approvingly by Wyclif: see Poole (ed.), *De Civili Dominio i*, p. 439/23–6.

30 *De Doctrina Christiana*, Book ii, c. 6: 'Does the hearer learn anything more than when he listens to the same thought expressed in the plainest language, without the help of this figure? And yet, I don't know why, I feel greater pleasure in contemplating holy men, when I view them as the teeth of the Church' (p. 537).

31 Copeland, 'Politics of the Literal Sense', p. 12.

32 See Stephen L. Wailes, 'Why Did Jesus Use Parables: The Medieval Discussion', *Mediaevalia et Humanistica* 13 (1983), 43–64.

33 'sensus allegoricus docet mediate vel inmediate credenda, sensus anagogicus docet mediate vel inmediate speranda, sed sensus tropologicus docet mediate vel inmediate meritorie agenda. et sic correspondent per ordinem fidei, spei et caritati. illi autem, quibus placet distingwere sensum literalem secundum racionem vel partes subiectivas ab aliis, debent dicere, quod de racione sensus literalis est, quod sit sensus catholicus inmediate elicitus ex scriptura, et alii tres sensus, si inmediate eliciuntur ex scriptura, tunc sunt literales. si autem mediate, tunc sunt sensus allegoricus, tropologicus vel anagogicus, non literalis' (I.123/9–124/1). Compare with this the more straightforward statement in Wyclif's Bible Commentary that 'est . . . lex evangelica infallibilis, quia a deo immediate tradita': *WBK*, p. 99, n. 30.

34 For the wider epistemological background, see Katherine H. Tachau, *Vision and Certitude in the Age of Ockham: Optics, Epistemology and the Foundations of Semantics, 1250–1345* (Leiden, New York, Copenhagen and Cologne, 1988).

35 The citations for 'immediate' in the *MLD* include several which associate the word with direct inspired access to God: s. v. senses 2 and 3.

36 'Logic and the Trinity', pp. 19ff.

37 Wyclif's 'sensus aggregatum' may be a variation on the scholastic 'sensus per adaptationem'. This refers to the technique of finding culturally acceptable meanings in scripture even when not evidently suggested by the actual biblical words. Such 'adaptation' foregrounds the relationship between 'modum intelligendi nostrum' and the Bible: see Spicq, *Exégèse latine*, pp. 281–5.

38 On the use of the term 'questionista' to indicate a category of student at Oxford, see Olga Weijers, *Terminologie des Universités au xiie siècle* (Rome, 1987), p. 182.

39 Cf. Anne Hudson and Pamela Gradon (eds.), *English Wycliffite Sermons*, 5 vols. (Oxford, 1983–96), vol. i, p. 517/9–11; also see Wyclif's *Dialogus sive Speculum Ecclesie Militantis*, ed. Alfred W. Pollard, Wyclif Society (London, 1886), p. 29/13–17 for a variation on this theme.

40 For patristic treatments of a hermeneutic Fall, see Eric Jager, *The Tempter's Voice: Language and the Fall in Medieval Literature* (Ithaca, N.Y., 1993), esp. pp. 31–8.

41 On this topos, see de Lubac, *Exégèse médiévale*, vol. ii/2, pp. 54–58.

42 See Minnis and Scott (eds.), *Medieval Literary Theory*, p. 204.

43 Wyclif is here drawing on Nicholas of Lyra, who proposed, on the basis of the same scriptural passages, the notion of a 'duplex sensus litteralis': see Minnis and Scott

(eds.), *Medieval Literary Theory*, p. 206. On Wyclif's reading of Lyra, see *WBK, passim*; also Philip Krey, 'Many Readers but Few Followers: The Fate of Nicholas of Lyra's "Apocalypse Commentary" in the Hands of his Late-Medieval Admirers', *Church History* 64 (1995), 185–201 (pp. 195–201).

44 *WBK*, pp. 371–2.

45 *Ibid.*, p. 373.

46 On the traditional association of *pueri* with superficial textual meaning, see Suzanne Reynolds, *Medieval Reading: Grammar, Rhetoric and the Classical Text* (Cambridge, 1996), pp. 152–3.

47 To an extent, of course, such must be the ideal theoretical movement of any course of scriptural study – to go from the visible to the invisible – but it is the breathtaking celerity of Wyclif's thought which sets it apart, encompassing as it does, almost in the same gesture, fine disputes over the meaning of problematic words such as 'eros' followed by radical transitions to a supra-textual fideistic discourse. Hugh of St. Victor, for instance, is quite clear about the separate domains of these two kinds of knowledge, or rather, as he puts it, of knowledge and virtue: see Smalley, *Study of the Bible*, pp. 86–8. And Wyclif himself, in his Bible Commentary, suggests that the devout student must aim at both the instruction of the intellect in truth [*instruccio intellectus in veritate*], and the charitable information of the affectus [*informacio caritativa affectus*]: *WBK*, p. 363; also see p. 38, n. 85, for Wyclif's statement that 'contemplacio fidelium' is better than the 'modus contemplandi philosophorum'. The collapsing into each other of the separate domains of intellect and affect is absent here. On the distinct domains of the speculative and the contemplative, see de Lubac, *Exégèse médiévale*, vol. 1/2, pp. 633–43; Köpf, *Wissenschaftstheorie*, pp. 199–210.

48 On a parallel tension in Augustine between the conceptual centrality of the Bible, and the irrelevance of the sacred text to him who has attained a life of *caritas*, see Introduction (pp. 10–11).

49 For instance, Wyclif repeatedly criticises Mohammed for discouraging open debate about his scriptural laws (1.253/14–16; 1.261/14–200). The Pope is like Mohammed in similarly forbidding disputation about his *potestas* (1.262/8–17).

50 My translation of 'modum' is provisional; the word was used in a variety of technical grammatical and logical senses: see Gabriel Nuchelmans, *Theories of the Proposition: Ancient and Medieval Conceptions of the Bearers of Truth and Falsity* (Amsterdam and London, 1973), *passim*.

51 Imbach cites, among others, Humbert de Romans, Stephen of Tournai and Konrad of Megenberg, all of whom make a categorical distinction between clerk and lay in the matter of divinity: see *Laien in der Philosophie des Mittelalters: Hinweise und Anregungen zu einem vernachlässigten Thema* (Amsterdam, 1989), pp. 18, 19, 24. We shall see in chapter 3 how anti-Wycliffite polemicists such as William Butler and Thomas Palmer would stress the arcane wisdom of scripture, and its vulnerability to pernicious misreadings by the untrained and the *illiterati*.

52 Richard and Mary Rouse point out that there is a change in the notion of *auctoritas* over the twelfth and thirteenth centuries: 'In the prologue to the *Liber florum*, written in the first half of the twelfth century, it is the books, the whole works, that have *auctoritas*; by the mid-thirteenth century, *auctoritas* (used in the proper context, of course) means "extract from a whole work" – it is used in precisely the same situations where earlier centuries would have said *sententia* or *dictio*': 'Florilegia of Patristic Texts', in *Les Genres littéraires dans les sources théologiques et philosophiques médiévales*, Université Catholique de Louvain, Publications de l'Institut d'Études Médiévales, 2nd series, 5 (Louvain,

1982), pp. 165–80 (p. 173). Also see Stephan Kuttner, 'On "Auctoritas" in the Writing of Medieval Canonists: the Vocabulary of Gratian', in his *Studies in the History of Medieval Canon Law* (Aldershot, 1990), pp. 69–80 (p. 73), for Gratian's similar (and influential) use of the word.

53 The emphasis, at least in theory, on context and *originalia* when reading *auctores* was not confined to Wyclif in the Middle Ages: see J. de Ghellinck, '*Originale et Originalia*', *Bulletin du Cange* 14 (1939), 95–105; and Minnis, *Theory of Authorship*, pp. 156–9; also see Damasus Trapp on the 'historico-critical attitude' towards texts in the fourteenth century in 'Augustinian Theology of the 14th Century', pp. 146–274.

54 On the intimacy of Aristotelian logic and *scientia* in Aquinas's thought, see Scott MacDonald, 'Theory of Knowledge', in Norman Kretzmann and Eleonore Stump (eds.), *The Cambridge Companion to Aquinas* (Cambridge, 1993), pp. 160–95, esp. 162–5; as Shank puts it, 'Aristotle's syllogistic still undergirded most formal argumentation, and was virtually synonymous with natural reason itself': *Logic, University and Society in Late Medieval Vienna*, p. 58.

55 For an account of the tussle of 'rhetoric' and other disciplines, including 'logic', in medieval discussions of the hierarchy of sciences, see Rita Copeland, 'Lydgate, Hawes, and the Science of Rhetoric in the Late Middle Ages', *Modern Language Quarterly* 53 (1992), 57–82; also see P. Osmund Lewry, 'Grammar, Logic and Rhetoric 1220–1320', in J. I. Catto (ed.), *The History of the University of Oxford 1: The Early Oxford Schools* (Oxford, 1984), pp. 401–33 (pp. 431–2); and his 'Rhetoric at Paris and Oxford in the Mid-Thirteenth Century', *Rhetorica* 1 (1983), 45–63, where he points to the theoretical distinction between 'the power of words playing on the emotions' and 'intellectual judgment of truth' (p. 49). He further suggests that in the thirteenth-century universities, 'the fourth book of Boethius' *De topicis differentiis* commonly provided an occasion for considering rhetoric and its relation to logic' (p. 61).

56 Also 1.386/23: 'logica scripture sacre, que est forma verborum Cristi'.

57 See L. M. De Rijk, 'Logica Oxoniensis: an Attempt to Reconstruct a Fifteenth-century Oxford Manual of Logic', *Medioevo* 3 (1977), 121–64; Paul Vincent Spade and Gordon Anthony Wilson (eds.), *Johannis Wyclif Summa Insolubilium* (Binghampton, N.Y., 1986), pp. ix–xxiii; E. J. Ashworth, 'Les manuels de logique à l'Université d'Oxford aux xive et xve siècles', in J. Hamesse (ed.), *Manuels, programmes de cours et techniques d'enseignement dans les universités médiévales* (Louvain, 1994), pp. 351–70; also see Conti, *Esistenza et verità*; and Massimo Mugnai, 'La "expositio reduplicativarum" chez Walter Burleigh et Paulus Venetus', in Alfonso Maierù (ed.), *English Logic in Italy in the 14th and 15th Centuries* (Naples, 1982), pp. 305–320, for contemporary uses of Wyclif's logical works.

58 Quoted by Shank, *Logic, University and Society in Late Medieval Vienna*, p. 76; also see Fritz Hoffmann, 'Robert Holcot – Die Logik in der Theologie', in Paul Wilpert and W. P. Eckert (eds.), *Die Metaphysik im Mittelalter*, MM 2 (Berlin, 1963), pp. 624–39; and his *Die theologische Methode des Oxforder Dominikanlehrers Robert Holcot*, BGTPM, NS5 (Münster, 1972).

59 'Theology and Metaphysics'.

60 Note also the defence of scriptural logic in his Commentary on Luke 9:3, where he discusses apparently contradictory statements made by Christ such as John 7:16, and 14:10 ('my doctrine is not mine'). All such contradictions hide mysteries; in this particular case Christ signals that his doctrine is not his originally but that of his Father who sent him: 'quod Christus est duplicis nature secundum quarum unam fecit reverenciam patri

dicendo, quod doctrina vel sermo non fuit suus, significat illam originaliter vel autoritative, sed patris mittentis'; *WBK*, p. 362.

61 See the 'Proemium' (perhaps composed later than the actual work) to Wyclif's *De Logica I*, ed. M. H. Dziewicki, Wyclif Society (London, 1893), p. 1; also *De Veritate* 1.387/10–388/10, II.20/15–21.

62 Note that in the course of his Commentary on Luke 9:3, Wyclif appears to endorse an Aquinian theory of the 'subalternating' hierarchy of disciplines, with theology at its head: 'oportet theologum discere novo modo sciencias subalternatas, cum theologia rectificat omnes alias tamquam finis, ideo oportet quod alia sibi obediant, ut sugent sensum suum'; *WBK*, p. 365. This is a more standard view: the theologian ideally has both *scientia* and *sapientia*; and achieving the higher 'knowledge' does not imply negating the lower. In fact, scriptural logic is 'subtilissimam, brevissimam, facillimam et logice philosophorum conformissimam' (p. 363). On Aquinian 'subalternation', see M.-D. Chenu, *La théologie comme science au XIIIe siècle*, 3rd edn., Bibliothèque Thomiste 33 (Paris, 1957), pp. 71–85.

63 On the range of possible senses of 'sophistry', see Weijers, *Terminologie*, pp. 181–2.

64 *WBK*, pp. 363–4.

65 On Wyclif's approach to the relationship of reason and faith, see Leff, 'Wyclif and the Augustinian Tradition', though Leff underplays Wyclif's polemical use of 'reason'.

66 *The Trinity and the Unicity of the Intellect*, trans. Rose Emmanuella Brennan (St. Louis and London, 1946), p. 60.

67 *Summa Theologiae* Ia.1.1, in Blackfriars vol. I, pp. 8–9.

68 *Trinity and Unicity*, tr. Brennan, p. 59.

69 *Théologie comme science*, p. 90.

70 For more (positive) references to 'reason', see 1.253/23, 1.259/6, 1.271/12, 1.295/2.

71 Minnis, '"Authorial Intention" and "Literal Sense"', p. 14; also see his discussion of the five grades of scripture. On the parallelism between the five grades of scripture and the five steps of the philosophical universal in *De Universalibus*, see Gellrich, *Discourse and Dominion*, p. 91.

72 Note the irony in this passage: the problem of 'correct codices' is invoked even as it is dismissed!

73 '"Authorial Intention" and "Literal Sense"', p. 14.

74 On Jerome, see H. F. D. Sparks, 'Jerome as Biblical Scholar', in Ackroyd and Evans (eds.), *Camb. Hist. Bible I*, pp. 510–541 (pp. 526–32). On medieval textual criticism, see Raphael Loewe, 'The Medieval History of the Latin Vulgate' in Lampe (ed.), *Camb. Hist. Bible II*, pp. 102–154; also Heinrich Denifle, 'Die Handschriften der Bibel-Correctorien des 13. Jahrhunderts', in Heinrich Denifle and Franz Ehrle (eds.), *Archiv für Literatur- und Kirchen-Geschichte des Mittelalters* 4 (1888), 263–311, 470–601.

75 Note Wyclif's casual reference to this fraught nexus in medieval biblical studies. Nicholas of Lyra, preeminently, devoted much attention to the implications of textual discrepancies between the Hebrew text and the Vulgate, and one would have expected Wyclif to pay more than cursory attention to Nicholas's emphases. On Lyra's dependence on Rashi and on corrected Bibles in his exegesis, see Hailperin, *Rashi and the Christian Scholars* (Pittsburgh, 1963), pp. 137–45; on medieval discourse relating to the Hebrew text, see Dahan, *Intellectuels chrétiens*, pp. 272–85.

76 It is this aspect of Wyclif's thought which is most distant from that of his followers: the translators of the Wycliffite Bible were acutely aware of issues of textual criticism; see chapter 5 below.

77 Note that Wyclif, when outlining the moral and intellectual equipment that a true priest should possess, asks rhetorically how priesthood is possible without the key of suitable knowledge: 'quomodo, queso, fiet presbiter sine clave sciencie pertinentis?' (ii.201/21–2). In fact, the churchman can be allowed to spend time away from his cure to study in the schools (iii.39/5–7).

78 See also 1.1 01 /20–1 03/1 0.

79 Note again Wyclif's radicalism in this matter: see Imbach, *Laien in der Philosophie*, pp. 13–26 (clergy vs. laity); 71–6 (role of women).

80 'non debet cristianus fingere equivocaciones nisi pertinenter fundabiles ex scriptura' (1.28/11–12).

81 This is what Robert Lerner has described as 'ecstatic dissent': see 'Ecstatic Dissent', *Speculum* 67 (1992), 33–57.

82 'alius est modus scientiae, qui est secundum comprehensionem veritatis per humanam rationem; alius est modus scientiae secundum affectum pietatis per divinam traditionem': *Summa Theologiae*, 4 vols. in 5 (Quaracchi, 1924–48), vol. 1, pp. 8–9. For Alexander, see Elisabeth Gössmann, *Metaphysik und Heilsgeschichte: Eine theologische Untersuchung der Summa Halensis (Alexander von Hales)* (Munich, 1964), esp. pp. 19–27. The translations given here are from Minnis and Scott (eds.), *Medieval Literary Theory*, p. 214; see also the editors' discussion of the passage on p. 200.

83 See Köpf, *Wissenschaftstheorie*, pp. 158–87, 227–31, 253–7. Wyclif himself talks of the importance of abiding by the sense elicited by 'sancti doctores concorditer': *De Veritate*, 1.386/1–3.

84 I use the word 'positivist' as a convenient shorthand to indicate the following aspects of Wyclif's, and the Lollards', hermeneutics: a postulation of determinate, final and accessible textual meanings which are independent of their reception; an assumption that the ideal reader is a transparent (non)-interpreter, who mediates or even clarifies such meanings without introducing any change; and a concomitant distrust of 'glossing' or rhetoric as pertaining to a wholly evitable 'misinterpretation'.

2 *William Woodford's anti-Wycliffite hermeneutics*

1 *De Apostasia*, p. 10/20–21.

2 Related words in this context would include, as we have seen, *mediate* and *immediate*, and *fundate*, translated normally by the Lollards as 'groundid'. Reginald Pecock was later to note Wycliffite reliance on the 'express' meanings of scripture: see H. Leith Spencer, *English Preaching in the Late Middle Ages* (Oxford, 1993), pp. 136–7.

3 On Woodford, see *BRUO* 2081–2; *HLW* 819–22; Jeremy Catto, 'William Woodford O.F.M. (c.1330–c.1397)', D.Phil. thesis, University of Oxford (1969); Eric Doyle, 'William Woodford, O.F.M. (c.1330–c.1400): His Life and Works together with a Study and Edition of his "Responsiones Contra Wiclevum et Lollardos"', *Franciscan Studies* 43 (1983), 17–187.

4 *Premature Reformation*, p. 47.

5 On the *Quattuor Determinationes* (henceforth QD), see Eric Doyle: 'William Woodford on Scripture and Tradition' in I. Vàzquez (ed.), *Studio Historico-Ecclesiastica: Festgabe für L. G. Spätling* (Rome, 1977), pp. 481–504; also his 'William Woodford, O.F.M., and John Wyclif's *De Religione*', *Speculum* 52 (1977), 329–36. The tract has been edited by M. D. Dobson in an unpublished thesis (c.1932) now kept at Greyfriars, Oxford. I am much indebted to Greyfriars and Professor Anne Hudson for providing access to the thesis. All references are to this edition and given at the end of citations; I have also provided folio references to Oxford, Bodleian Library, MS Bodley 703, a compendium

of treatises relating to Wycliffism mostly by Woodford. On the *determinatio* as a form, see Weijers, *Terminologie*, pp. 404–7.

6 See Edith C. Tatnall, 'Church and State according to John Wyclyf'; also her 'John Wyclif and *Ecclesia Anglicana*', *Journal of Ecclesiastical History* 20 (1969), 19–43; William Farr, *John Wyclif as Legal Reformer* (Leiden, 1974); and Hudson, *Premature Reformation*, pp. 314–58.

7 In a memorable passage, Woodford compares human reliance on ecclesiastical or conciliar tradition to the judge's reliance on the uncertainties of evidence; the Christian who does not know that the council has erred, and has not heard those skilled in theology question the conciliar determination, must abide by it, even if it is false: 'debent catholici nullo modo scientes contrarium adherere sentencie [of the conciliar determination], sicut iudex adherere testimonio testium in iudicio, quos in nullo habet suspectos nec potest repellere, sed reputat et reputare debet esse testes veraces quamuis de facto deponant falsum' (p. 90; fol. 84v).

8 For a summary of his arguments, see Doyle, 'William Woodford on Scripture and Tradition', pp. 491–6.

9 See Minnis and Scott (eds.), *Medieval Literary Theory*, pp. 203–7.

10 *The Holy Bible ... made from the Latin Vulgate by John Wycliffe and his Followers*, ed. J. Forshall and F. Madden, 4 vols. (Oxford, 1850), vol. 1, p. 43.

11 'Quidem autem doctor venerabilis huius vniuersitatis solempnis, prout intellexi, tractans istam materiam, sumpsit contineri explicite in sacra scriptura pro omni illo quod potest deduci ex sensu historico vel litterali secundum sensum quem auctor intendit, implicite contineri in eadem pro contineri in eadem in sensu mistico, et sic potest vti terminis istis qui voluerit' (*QD* p. 174; fol. 99r).

12 See Minnis, '"Authorial Intention" and "Literal Sense"', p. 29. See also Wyclif's commentary on the Book of Revelation, where the sense primarily and principally intended by the author ('quem primo et principaliter intendit auctor') and which John meant to signify ('quem Johannes intellexit signari') is emphasised, along with the suggestion that such sense is perfectly expounded only by those to whom it is allowed by the special gift of God'(speciali dono dei'): *WBK*, p. 304.

13 'voces vel codices non esse nisi signa scripture sacre, que est spiritus sancti sciencia', *De Veritate*, 1.228/5–6; see Chapter 1 above.

14 *De Veritate*, 1.109/1–2.

15 'tamen sacra scriptura non est corrupta vel falsa sumpta sicut prius secundum textum et intencionem, in quibus a primis suis autoribus tradebatur' (*QD* p. 174; fol. 99r).

16 The fifteenth chapter of the Prologue has been edited by Anne Hudson, *Selections from English Wycliffite Writings* (Cambridge, 1978), pp. 67–72. All references to Chapter 15 are to this edition; the present citation is on p. 67.

17 For instance, there is some uncertainty in the gospels as to the exact hour of the crucifixion: '[Scriptum est] in Matheo et in Iohanne quod dominus noster hora 6a crucifixus est. Rursum scriptum est in Marcho quod hora 3a crucifixus est' (*QD* p. 93; fols 85r–v).

18 The early scribes, not having heard of Asaph, erroneously emended his name to Isaiah; Matt. 27:9 cites the prophet Jeremiah for a reference to the thirty pieces of silver when the reference should have been to Zach. 11:12; the Hebrews, after the passion of Christ, corrupted the passive form of 'occidere' in his words 'Ego occidar et ego vivere faciam' into the active 'occidam' (this on the authority of Fitzralph). All this points to the defective state of the Bible as we have it: 'Ex quibus verbis, Ieronimus patet expresse quod textus eciam euangelicus quem nos habemus, est defectuosus...' (*QD* pp. 93–4; fols 85r–v).

19 The impious errors committed by scribes and interpreters ('sacrilega facta scribarum et interpretum') have consisted in deliberate deletions and substitutions: 'Misteria et secreta predicta de libris abraserunt, legem vero aliam et propriam ibi contra preceptum domini posuerunt'. Moreover, our scriptures are most corrupt where they speak of the passion and the death of Christ, for many thought it impossible that God could die, and therefore, fearing mockery, transformed the scriptures: 'et ideo talia abraserunt et aliter mutauerunt, timentes suas scripturas a gentibus irrideri et de propriis scripturis inter se scandalum generari' (*ibid.* pp. 94–5; fol. 85v).

20 Lyra provides many instances of disagreement between our text and the Hebrew text ('multa exempla quomodo textus noster discordat a textu Ebrayco et aliquando contrariatur'), of which Woodford cites a few (*ibid.* p. 96; fols 85v–86r).

21 'Ex contentis in sacra scriptura et notorie veris, sequitur quod multa sunt notorie vera que non sunt contenta in scriptura sacra. Patet hac primo quia ad Colocenses, vltimo capitulo [Coloss. 4:16], habetur expresse quod Paulus apostolus scripsit epistolam ad Laodicenses eque sicut ad Colocenses . . . et notorium est quod illa epistola ad Laodicenses non continetur in canone biblie. Sequitur ergo ex scriptura et notoriis veris, quod aliqua sunt auctentice vera que non sunt contenta in sacra scriptura. Vnde diu post ecclesiam primitiuam, magis certum fuit epistolam ad Laodicenses fuisse epistolam Pauli apostoli quam epistolam ad Hebreos'. Woodford goes on to cite the various conflicting opinions on the authorship of Hebrews, and points out that its Pauline authorship is not certified by scripture ('quod fuerit Pauli, non est contentum in sacra scriptura'). *Ergo*, truths of lesser authority are included, and truths of greater authority may be found outside the Bible (*ibid.* pp. 59–60; fol. 79v).

22 Jude 1:14 refers to a prophecy of Enoch not part of the canon ('expresse allegatur prophecia Ennok . . . et notorium est quod liber prophecie eius sic allegatus et ex allegacione auctenticatus, non continetur in canone biblie'); 1 Mach. 16:23–24 similarly 'allegat librum sacerdocii Iohannis' not included in the canon; 1 Kings 22:39 refers to the chronicles of the kings of Israel, which, according to Lyra, were burnt and never found again; 2 Mach. 2:1, 13, 24 refer to various texts no longer extant; 1 Kings 4:33–4 refer to works by Solomon where he describes beasts, trees and herbs, works which we do not have even though they might have been useful for understanding the scriptures: 'quas descripciones non habemus quamuis essent vtiles pro intellectu scripture' (*ibid.* pp. 60–2; fol. 79v).

23 It is in this context that Woodford's apparent failure, noted by Hudson (*Premature Reformation*, p. 48), to take into account Wyclif's emphasis on scriptural *auctoritates* should be placed. For Woodford, the borderline between the 'authorities' of the scriptural and the extra-scriptural is too blurred for any such distinction to be meaningful. Too much is dependent on local and temporal factors. He points out, for instance, that the canons of the apostles were once numbered among the books of the New Testament: the apostles 'tradiderunt eciam fidelibus leges multas ad obseruandas, quas ipsi fecerunt, et que adhuc vocantur "canones apostolorum", et que tante fuere auctoritatis tempore Iohannis Damasceni, quod liber Clementis continens canones apostolorum connumeratus fuit cum libris Noui Testamenti' (p. 112; fol. 88v). Hence Woodford's citation of the 'apocryphal' as 'authoritative'. For instance, he refers to Veronica's handkerchief as a justification of images, for images are legitimised by unwritten traditions of the early Church: 'ex tradicione Christi non scriptura in biblia et ex tradicionibus ecclesie primitiue in biblia minime contentis' (p. 58; fol. 79r). Similarly, he refers to canon law and to various historical chronicles. Similar is his methodology in *De dominio civili clericorum* (1376), where he defends the Church's right to civil dominion by means of arguments

based on scripture, canon law, civil law, philosophy and natural reason. As Eric Doyle points out in the Introduction to his edition of the tract, 'this work shows him to have been a practical thinker, in no sense an idealist, and very much a protagonist of the *status quo*'. Wyclif, characteristically, answered (in chapters 18 and 19 of *De Civili Dominio III*) only those arguments derived from scripture: *De Dominio Civili Clericorum*, ed. Eric Doyle, *Archivum Franciscanum Historicum* 66 (1973), 49–109 (pp. 66–7). Also see Catto on Woodford's similar methodology in *De sacramento altaris* (1383/4): 'William Woodford, O.F.M.', p. 289; and Laurence Eldredge, 'Changing Concepts of Church Authority in the Later Fourteenth Century: Peter Ceffons of Clairvaux and William Woodford, O.F.M.', *Revue de l'Université d'Ottawa* 48 (1978), 170–78 (pp. 175–78). On the importance of unwritten tradition in late-medieval ecclesiology, see Schüssler, *Primat der heiligen Schrift*, pp. 78ff.

24 On Lollard usage of 'grounded', a word derived from the Latin 'fundatus', see Anne Hudson, 'A Lollard Sect Vocabulary?', in *Lollards and their Books*, pp. 165–80 (pp. 171–2).

25 'proposiciones scripture continue indigent interpretatione' (*QD* p. 184; fol. 100v).

26 On 'ymaginacio', see *MLD*, esp. senses 1b and 2e.

27 *De Apostasia*, pp. 19/23–4, 39/27–30, 49/17–25.

28 Introduction to *De Benedicta Incarnatione*, Wyclif Society (London, 1886), p. xxv.

29 *De Apostasia*, pp. 44/35–45/6.

30 This is almost a perfect practical enactment of the theoretical principles underlying the *ad hoc* application of 'authorities' to particular situations, depending on what one is trying to prove, in medieval legal logic. See the discussion by Peter von Moos in his study of the argumentative *exemplum*: 'Das argumentative Exemplum und die "wächserne Nase" der Autorität im Mittelalter', in W. J. Aerts and M. Gosman (eds.), *Exemplum et Similitudo: Alexander the Great and Other Heroes as Points of Reference in Medieval Literature* (Groningen, 1988), pp. 55–84 (esp. p. 66). For the contradictions in Lollard invocation of the notion of *intentio auctoris*, particularly in the context of apocalyptic or anti-fraternal readings of scripture, see Ralph Hanna III, '"Vae octuplex", Lollard socio-textual ideology, and Ricardian-Lancastrian prose translation', in Rita Copeland (ed.), *Criticism and Dissent in the Middle Ages* (Cambridge, 1996), pp. 244–63; also see Curtis V. Bostick, *The Antichrist and the Lollards: Apocalypticism in Medieval and Reformation England* (Leiden, Boston and Cologne, 1998); see further Chapter 4 below.

31 As Copeland says, 'Politics of the Literal Sense', p. 14: 'Intention is the most flexible and expedient of rhetorical concepts, adaptable and attributable in any circumstances'.

32 'Et vlterius dico, quod alique sunt auctoritates tales que possunt intelligi de illa scriptura sacra que condicionaliter dicitur 'Liber Vite', licet non de sacra scriptura secundum quod sumitur pro canone biblie in textu et sensu, in quibus a primis suis auctoribus tradebatur scripture' (*QD* pp. 176–7; fol. 99v).

33 On the hermeneutic background to the usage of the word 'proper' as indicating 'literal/grammatical' meaning, see Thijssen, 'The Crisis over Ockhamist Hermeneutic', pp. 375–7; and Zénon Kaluza, 'Les Sciences et leurs langages: Note sur le Statut du 29 Décembre 1340 et le prétendu Statut perdu contre Ockham', in Luca Bianchi (ed.), *Filosofia e teologia nel trecento: Studi in ricordo di Eugenio Randi* (Louvain, 1994), pp. 197–258 (pp. 226–35).

34 Woodford is here using the word 'term' in the technical sense of 'what is subjected to the predicate or predicated of the subject in an ordinary categorical proposition': see Paul Vincent Spade, 'The Semantics of Terms', in *CHLMP*, pp. 188–96 (p. 188).

35 Elsewhere, Woodford was more sceptical of the certainty of 'scientific' knowledge; in the course of his discussion of the Eucharist, he cited the standard sceptical instances of a stick which appears bent in water, and the colours of the dove's neck: see Catto, 'William Woodford, O.F.M', pp. 279–80. On the sciences in late medieval Oxford, see J. D. North, 'Natural Philosophy in Late Medieval Oxford', in Catto and Evans (eds.), *History of the University of Oxford II*, pp. 65–102; for a particular instance of the tussle between the desire for certitude and a sceptical critique of scientific discourse, see A. George Molland, 'Nicole Oresme and Scientific Progress', in Zimmermann (ed.), *Antiqui und Moderni*, pp. 206–22. For a comprehensive account of medieval notions of the certitude or otherwise of 'scientific' knowledge, and indeed, of the proper object of such knowledge, see Tachau, *Vision and Certitude*; a particularly clear discussion she cites is that of Adam Wodeham: 'Now the question is whether the act of scientific knowledge has as its immediate object a thing or a sign, that is, the proposition (*complexum*) in the mind or the things signified by the proposition': see p. 278.

36 See Thijssen, 'Crisis over Ockhamist Hermeneutic', pp. 375–81; Kaluza, 'Les Sciences et leurs langages', pp. 223–55; Hoenen, 'Theology and Metaphysics'.

37 Kaluza, 'Les Sciences et leurs langages', p. 227.

38 See in this context Froelich, 'State of Biblical Hermeneutics', pp. 20–48.

39 To an extent, therefore, the otherwise helpful distinction that Heiko Oberman makes between Tradition I (primacy of Holy Writ and Tradition as signifying the history of scriptural interpretation), and Tradition II (equal emphasis on unwritten or extrascriptural but nevertheless 'authoritative' sources of the faith) does not apply to Woodford. He would certainly have agreed with the validity of Tradition II, but would have argued that both the 'traditions' are implicated in each other, for the boundaries of the extrascriptural and what is to be found in the history of the interpretation of scripture are blurred, to say the least. See *Harvest of Medieval Theology*, pp. 361–93.

40 *On Christian Doctrine*, p. 538.

41 *De Apostasia*, p. 10/7–27.

42 See R. N. Swanson, *Universities, Academics and the Great Schism* (Cambridge, 1979), and Brian Tierney, *Foundations of Conciliar Theory: The Contribution of Medieval Canonists from Gratian to the Great Schism* (Cambridge, 1955; repr. 1968).

43 Note Woodford's broad cultural-historical scope; Wyclif would have dismissed this argument as entirely irrelevant. The same psychology lies behind his repeated references to the importance of extra-scriptural tradition for the proper functioning of the institutions of civil law and the universities. Extending (scornfully) Wyclif's assertion that all human traditions are to be dismissed, Woodford says that accepting such an extreme position would imply the negation of much ecclesiastical and all civil obligation: 'Sic enim oporteret omnem fidelem non obseruare canones apostolorum; sic oporteret ecclesiam non obseruare tradiciones apostolicas non descriptas in scriptura; sic oporteret iudices ciuiles non obseruare in puniendo latrones, homicidas, proditores per leges ciuiles, quas seruare, iurati sunt. Sic oporteret cancellarios uniuersitatum et procuratores semper non obseruare statuta uniuersitatum' (*QD* pp. 144–5; fol. 94r). Catto refers to Woodford's sense of 'the living experience of the Church, inseparable as it seemed from the quarrels and transgressions of civil society': 'William Woodford, O.F.M.', p. 184.

44 '[Veritates proprie ecclesiastice] non sunt proprie veritates catholice, que sunt particulares veritates particularium ecclesiarum, et non vniuersales veritates ab omnibus catholicis credende . . . Patet ergo quod multe sunt veritates proprie ecclesiastice que non sunt proprie catholice nec contente in canone biblie, quia biblia fuit completa antequam

erant ille veritates inuente, et patet quod multi catholice tenentur illis firmiter adherere sub pena peccati' (*QD* pp. 83–4; fol. 83v). See on this issue, Smalley, 'Ecclesiastical Attitudes to Novelty'; and Ludwig Hödl, 'Universale christliche Ethik und particulares kirchliches Ethos im unterschiedlichen Verständnis der scholastischen Theologie von der "perfectio evangelica"', in Wilpert (ed.), *Universalismus und Partikularismus im Mittelalter*, pp. 20–41.

45 'Verum certum potest papa cum consilio suo generali facere esse articulum fidei, loquendo proprie de fidei articulo, et tamen non potest cum concilio suo facere idem esse verum catholicum . . . [Sed] veritatem [catholicam] potest facere esse articulum fidei . . .' (*QD* p. 91; fol. 85r).

46 Wyclif's *Principium*, quoted by Beryl Smalley, 'The Bible and Eternity: John Wyclif's Dilemma', *Journal of the Warburg and Courtauld Institutes* 27 (1964), 73–89 (p. 81).

47 See in this context, Janet Coleman on Ockham's contingent vision of 'history': *Ancient and Medieval Memories: Studies in the Reconstruction of the Past* (Cambridge, 1992), p. 527.

48 For visions of the Early Church, see Glenn Olsen, 'The Idea of the *Ecclesia Primitiva* in the Writings of the Twelfth-Century Canonists', *Traditio* 25 (1969), 61–86, and Gordon Leff, 'The Apostolic Ideal in Later Medieval Ecclesiology', *Journal of Theological Studies*, NS 18 (1967), 58–82; also his 'The Making of a Myth of a True Church in the Later Middle Ages', *Journal of Medieval and Renaissance Studies* 1 (1971), 1–15.

49 See Edith Tatnall, 'John Wyclif and *Ecclesia Anglicana*'; also her 'Church and State', pp. 249–61.

50 The same point is made by Woodford in *Responsiones contra Wiclevum*; for discussion see Doyle, 'William Woodford, O.F.M.', pp. 100–101. On the notion of a progression in the faith from Judaic to Christian times, a progression compared to the change in modes of pedagogy according to the various stages of human growth and development, see Dahan, *Les intellectuels chrétiens*, p. 505.

51 'Licet ordinacio [humana] det in casu complementum ordinicioni diuine, non propter hoc est homo ordinans architector et Deus nudus artifex' (*QD* p. 151; fol. 95r). Indeed, Woodford points out that the human and the divine cannot be distinguished categorically. (Cf. the similar religious ideology underlying Nicholas Love's vision of the Word; see Chapter 5 below). Apart from the argument that the legitimising authority of the Church is always necessary ('regula euangelica [est] indiga auctorizacione ecclesie', p. 182; fol. 100r), there is the more important perception that there never was any religion without human admixture ('nec est vel fuit aliqua vmquam talis religio; nec Christus nec apostoli talem religionem seruauerunt', p. 145; fol. 94r). And if one must look for scriptural proof, there is the instance of David who extended worship by establishing new forms of devotion: 'volens ampliare cultum diuinum, constituisset multitudinem cantorum, ianitorum, vaticinorum . . . [et] scriptura recitat hoc esse factum in ampliacionem diuini cultus' (p. 152; fol. 95r). Moreover, Christ himself was not less perfect because he was born of the Virgin and not solely of God (p. 154; fol. 95v).

52 Catto also outlines the difference between Woodford's *Postilla* and that of Wyclif. The former is 'a moralising commentary', 'intent on elucidating the text for guidance on the moral law'. 'There is little sign in the *Postilla* of the historical researches which appear in the *Determinationes*'. Wyclif's *Postilla* is more interested in explicating the biblical text rather than its application to the moral sphere, 'as a book to be read, not as a work of reference'. See Catto, 'William Woodford O.F.M', pp. 85, 127, 159.

53 'oportet dampnare vitam omnium sanctorum regnum canonizatorum ab ecclesia, et aliorum sanctorum dominorum temporalium, et omnium sanctorum episcoporum qui

cum sanctis collegiis habuere dominium ciuile in communi, quod est nimis absurdum'
(*QD* p. 159; fol. 96v).

54 The questionings after all traditionally took place within the academic discourse. Note
that as late as 1411, a proctor from Oriel College, John Birch, resisted Archbishop
Arundel's dictatorship and proposed that 'the faculty of arts should be free to hold
probable opinions as in the past'. See Catto, 'Wyclif and Wycliffism at Oxford',
pp. 248–9.

55 *Geschichte als Topik*, pp. 276ff; see also Alain de Libera on the 'dimension ludique' of
argumentation in 'La Logique de la discussion', p. 63.

56 Thomas Netter of Walden, writing against Wyclif more than three decades later, in
the 1420s, recognised this scholastic predilection clearly; when outlining his methodology towards the beginning of his *Doctrinale Antiquitatum Fidei Ecclesiae Catholicae*,
he distances himself from such scholastic games: 'Et quia non scholasticus ludus est,
sed fidei series'; ed. B. Blanciotti, 3 vols. (Venice, 1757–9; repr. Farnborough, 1967),
vol. I, col. 6: see Chapter 6 below.

57 See the discussion of the *Rhetorica Ecclesiastica* in von Moos, 'Das argumentative Exemplum', pp. 63ff. and his Bibliography.

58 *Premature Reformation*, p. 48.

59 See Robson, *Wyclif and the Oxford Schools*, pp. 190–5.

60 See Beryl Smalley, 'Wyclif's *Postilla* on the Old Testament and his *Principium*', in *Oxford
Studies presented to Daniel Callus*, Oxford Historical Society NS 16 (Oxford, 1964),
pp. 253–296 (p. 291).

61 Kenny and Pinborg cite the theories of Siger of Brabant and Henry of Brussels, 'Medieval
Philosophical Literature', pp. 27–8.

62 See Chapter 3 below.

63 For instance, Wyclif's argument that divine ordinations are better than those made
by man and God is countered thus: the traitor Judas was made an apostle only by
Christ, whereas Paul and Barnabas were made apostles not just by God but also by men
('non solum a Deo sed ab hominibus ministerialiter facti sunt apostoli') (Acts 13:3).
Abiding by Wyclif's belief would then imply that the appointment of Paul and Matthew
as apostles was less perfect than that of Judas: 'Dicere ergo quod nihil ordinatum ab
homine est ita perfectum sicut a solo Deo ordinatum, est dicere quod apostolatus Pauli
vel Mathie non est ita perfectus sicut apostolatus Iude proditoris, quod est absurdum'
(*QD* p. 153; fol. 95v).

64 See Chapter 1 above. Woodford here is entirely deserving of Wyclif's condemnation
of such usages of logic in his Bible Commentary; see *WBK*, p. 363, where in the
course of a discussion of Jesus's enigmatic words in John 7:16, Wyclif criticises those
proud sophisters who are more interested in apparent contradiction rather than in the
apprehension of *sentence*, in the novelty of words rather than in the imitation of scripture
in logic or philosophy.

65 Thomas Netter, writing with the benefit of hindsight, does engage with the former; he
underlines the unreliability of 'reason' and points to the golden mean offered by the faith
of the Church between the highest authority of scripture and the lowest authority of
'reason'. Such a faith binds the wavering reason of man to the twin authority of scripture
and Church as if with the girdle of Paul: 'Humana vero ratio ut plurimum est hypocrit-
ica, veritatem simulans, cum non sit, ut probant haereticorum dogmata . . . Media ergo
est inter supremam auctoritatem Scripturae & infimam rationem fides Ecclesiae, Scripturas venerabiliter attolens & exhibens, & rationem vagam hominis ad hanc geminam
auctoritatem quasi alligans zona Pauli', *Doctrinale*, ed. Blanciotti, vol. III, col. 399.

66 'La Logique de la discussion', p. 60.

67 The relationship of antiquity and authority formed one of the major sites of dispute between Wyclif and Kenningham, the latter arguing that antiquity is no indication of truth: 'antiquitas non aucteticat'; see W. W. Shirley (ed.), *Fasciculi Zizaniorum* (Rolls Series, p. 5, quoted by Hoenen, 'Theology and Metaphysics'). As Beryl Smalley memorably said: 'Wyclif . . . killed Time but did not get rid of the corpse', 'The Bible and Eternity', p. 88. See also Robson, *Wyclif and the Oxford Schools*, pp. 155–61, 166–70.

68 Catto, 'Wyclif and Wycliffism at Oxford', p. 221.

69 'A sense of tradition implies a political consciousness, a sense of community, which Woodford found in the community of all Christians . . . [His] empirical cast of mind was not disposed to reduce the rich texture of religious life and tradition to the single idea of the Church; for him the Church was the community of all Christians, exhibiting the same diversity as he found in the secular world and in nature' (Catto, 'William Woodford, O.F.M.', p. 300). In keeping with his holistic view of Christianity, Woodford rejected, as Catto points out (p. 199), the Bonaventuran vision of his own order as having an exclusive relationship to Christ.

3 Vernacular translations of the Bible and 'authority'

1 See, generally, Tierney, *Conciliar Theory*; Walter Ullmann, *The Origins of the Great Schism: a Study in Fourteenth Century Ecclesiastical History* (London, 1948); Swanson, *Universities, Academics and the Great Schism*; for Wyclif's thought on the subject, see Tatnall, 'John Wyclif and *Ecclesia Anglicana*', and 'Church and State', pp. 43–92, 248–90; F. W. Maitland, 'Wyclif on English and Roman Law', *Law Quarterly Review* 12 (1896), 76–8.

2 See Hudson, *Premature Reformation*, pp. 238–47.

3 For the *Constitutions*, see David Wilkins (ed.), *Concilia Magnae Brittaniae et Hiberniae*, 4 vols. (London, 1737), vol. III, pp. 314–19; for discussion, see Watson, 'Censorship and Cultural Change'; McNiven, *Heresy and Politics*, pp. 114–17; Spencer, *English Preaching*, pp. 163–88.

4 On Ullerston, see *BRUO* 1928–9; *HLW*, 516–7. For the ascription to him, see Anne Hudson, 'The Debate on Bible Translation, Oxford 1401', in *Lollards and their Books*, pp. 67–84 (pp. 74–7).

5 On Butler, see *BRUO* 329; *HLW* 757. Butler's tract is edited by Margaret Deanesly from Oxford, Merton College MS. K.2.2, in *The Lollard Bible and other Medieval Biblical Versions* (Cambridge, 1920), pp. 401–18; all references are to this edition and given after citations in the text. For further information about the tract, see Deanesly, *Lollard Bible*, pp. 289–90; Hudson, *Lollards and their Books*, pp. 67, 81, 155–7.

6 On Palmer, see *BRUO* 1421–2; *HLW* 674. Palmer's tract is edited by Deanesly from Cambridge, Trinity College, MS B.15.11; see *Lollard Bible*, pp. 418–37. All references are to this edition and given after citations in the text. Deanesly accepts the 1430 manuscript attribution of the tract to Palmer; so does Professor Hudson, who has pointed out to me that the tract shows similarities in argument to a tract on images ascribed in a colophon to Palmer in Assisi, Biblioteca Communale MS 192, fols. 133–46, also preserved in acephalous form in London, British Library, MS Harley 31, fols. 182–94v.

7 'Debate on Bible Translation', p. 83.

8 *Ibid.*, pp. 75–6.

9 The only near-complete version of the tract is to be found in Vienna, Österreichische Nationalbibliothek MS 4133. All folio references are to this manuscript; I have modernised

the punctuation, and expanded conventional abbreviations silently. See *Tabulae Codicum Manuscriptorum . . . in Bibliotheca Palatina Vindobonensi*, Academia Caesarea Vindobonensis, 7 vols. (Vienna, 1864–75), vol. III (1869), p. 175.

10 For a brief summary of the tract, see Hudson, 'Debate on Bible Translation' pp. 71–4.

11 'Item illud est illicitum per quod compago corporis christi mistici dissolueretur, doctorum ordo uilesceret, et membra loca sibi indebita vsurparent. Sed hoc fortasse continerent habita translacione canonis in uulgare. Laici enim et simplices tunc docere presumerent, doctoresque contempnerent, et se de archanis fidei intromitterent. Quo habita de facili fides periclitaretur, sequereturque ruina ecclesie satis grauis. Et confirmatur ratio: si enim simplices intelligendo latinum ex hoc ut plurimum usurpant sibi docendi officium, quanto magis si biblia esset in uulgare translata' (fol. 195v col. b).

12 *St Jerome: Letters and Selected Works*, translated by W. H. Fremantle in *A Select Library of the Nicene and Post-Nicene Fathers of the Christian Church* (Oxford and New York, 1893), p. 99; *PL* 22.544.

13 The episode of Medad and Eldad was evidently one of the topoi in favour of translation; Tract 5 in Cambridge, University Library MS Ii.vi.26, a Lollard compilation of twelve tracts in English in favour of vernacular scriptures, cites the same passage from Numbers: fol. 39v. On Ii.vi.26, see Hudson, *Premature Reformation*, p. 424; and Simon Hunt, 'An Edition of Tracts in Favour of Scriptural Translation and of Some Texts connected with Lollard Vernacular Biblical Scholarship', D.Phil. Thesis, University of Oxford (1994).

14 Another topos: the parable of the talents is also cited in Tract 5, CUL Ii.vi.26, fol. 31v.

15 On the idea that catechetical instruction received at church should be retailed at home, see Vincent Gillespie, '*Doctrina and Predicacio*: The Design and Function of some Pastoral Manuals', *Leeds Studies in English*, NS 11 (1980), 36–50; also his 'The Literary Form of the Middle English Pastoral Manual with particular reference to the *Speculum Christiani* and some related texts', D.Phil. thesis, University of Oxford (1981), where he demonstrates, on the basis of manuscript evidence, 'the way in which [pastoral] manuals could become accessible to those who were literate but not in orders' (p. 128). He also points out that 'pastoral aids for the clergy [were] often strikingly reminiscent of books used in schools' (p. 52). Ullerston's remarks should be placed in the context of the contemporary argument about whether there is a difference between preaching and teaching, the former only allowable to the clergy, but the latter permitted to a wider range of people. Both sides, Lollards and orthodox, made use of this distinction or disputed it, as suited their case – for instance, Margery Baxter in the 1428–31 Norwich trials argued she was only teaching, as did Margery Kempe; the 37 *Conclusions* maintained that no useful distinction could be made. See Spencer, *English Preaching*, pp. 33–64.

16 The same passage from Augustine is cited in Tract 1, CUL Ii.vi.26, fol. 2r–v: 'ech man in his owne houshold/schuld do þe office of a bisshop. in techynge. & correcctynge of common þingis.' The tract further points out (fol. 20v) that Augustine himself was converted by his mother when everyone else failed.

17 See James Innes, *Lectures and Tractates on the Gospel according to St John*, 2 vols. (Edinburgh, 1874), vol. II, p. 161; *PL* 35.1768–9.

18 Interestingly, Tract 5 in CUL Ii.vi.26 cites the same scriptural passage in making a case, on the authority of Gregory, for lay preaching / teaching: fols. 33v–34r.

19 Note that lay people, including women, could (according to canon law) baptise in cases of extreme necessity (most commonly when a child is going to die immediately at birth), and also, though this was less frequently mentioned, *in extremis* a person could confess to a layman (presumably usually at point of unexpected death). These exceptions were

mentioned by Lollards as justification for lay ability to administer other sacraments, and hence the issue became a rather sensitive one. See Hudson, *Premature Reformation*, pp. 298–9.

20 The Lollards too came up with this disingenuous argument. Tract 2 in CUL Ii.vi.26 asserts that those who say that vernacular scriptures would give the laity the opportunity to be rebellious against the political–ecclesiastical hierarchy 'opynly sclandre god auctor of pees and his holy lawe þat euer techiþ meken[e]sse pacience and charite' (fol. 24v).

21 Tract 1 in CUL Ii.vi.26 points out that Christ taught the gospel in Hebrew, and as it was later necessary to translate into Latin and Greek, so now it is necessary to translate into English: 'Ryȝt so þe kynge of heuene wolde þat his lawe & his welle were cried and tauȝt opinly to þe pepel ... he tauȝte þe pater noster & þe gospel in ebrew. swych langage as þe iwis vseden to whom he prechid. And as neful as it was to translate þe gospel from ebrewe in to grwe & in to latyn for helpe of þe peple þat couden noon ebrwe. now it is nedful & leful to translate in to englysche for helpe of englisch peple' (fol. 6r–v).

22 For the reference to Bacon, see J. S. Brewer (ed.), *Opus Tertium*, in *Rogeri Bacon Opera Quedam Hactenus Inedita*, vol. 1 (Rolls Series, London, 1859), pp. 54–5.

23 Hudson, 'Debate on Bible Translation', pp. 79–80, points out that Ullerston quotes Wyclif's *De Potestate Pape* in his *Defensorium*; Wyclif being referred to as 'quidam doctor huius cathedre venerandus'.

24 *Ibid.*, p. 70.

25 I am much indebted to Anne Hudson for this suggestion.

26 See F. M. Powicke, *The Medieval Books of Merton College* (Oxford, 1931), p. 206; H. O. Coxe, *Catalogus Codicum MSS ... in Collegiis Aulisque Oxoniensibus*, 2 vols. (Oxford, 1852), pp. 41–3 (under Merton).

27 See *BRUO* 1824–5; *HLW* 682–4.

28 See Joy Russell-Smith, 'Walter Hilton and a Tract in Defence of the Veneration of Images', *Dominican Studies* 7 (1954), 180–214; also see *HLW* 735–6.

29 See *BRUO* 30–1; *HLW* 521–3.

30 See Beryl Smalley, 'Which William of Nottingham?', *Mediaeval and Rennaissance Studies* 3 (1954), 200–38, esp. pp. 223–5; *HLW* 795–6. The selection of *quaestiones* was probably the work of John Wykeham: see *HLW* 354.

31 See *BRUO* 662; *HLW* 242; also Simon Forde, 'Theological Sources cited by Two Canons of Repton: Philip Repyngdon and John Eyton', in Hudson and Wilks (eds.), *Ockham to Wyclif*, pp. 419–28.

32 See Michael Wilks, *The Problem of Sovereignty in the Later Middle Ages: The Papal Monarchy with Augustinus Triumphus and the Publicists* (Cambridge, 1963).

33 See *BRUO* 1957–8; *HLW* 335–6.

34 'Nam si propterea non permitteretur ewangelium scribi in anglico quia sunt multi tractatus anglicani continentes hereses et errores, a pari siue a fortiori prohiberent scripturam in latino, que per totam Christianitatem posset disseminari' (fol. 199r col. a).

35 On 'contingents' and causality, see Calvin Normore, 'Future Contingents', in *CHLMP*, pp. 358–81; William J. Courtenay, 'Covenant and Causality in Pierre d'Ailly', *Speculum* 46 (1971), 94–119; 'The Critique of Natural Causality in the Mutakallinum and Nominalism', *The Harvard Theological Review* 66 (1973), 77–94; both reprinted in his *Covenant and Causality in Medieval Thought* (London, 1984); on scepticism and causality, see Kennedy, 'Philosophical Scepticism in England in the Mid-Fourteenth Century', 35–57. Larger scale studies of these and related issues are M. J. F. M. Hoenen, *Marsilius of Inghen: Divine Knowledge in Late Medieval Thought*

(Leiden, New York and Cologne, 1993), and William J. Courtenay, *Capacity and Volition: A History of the Distinction of Absolute and Ordained Power* (Bergamo, 1990).

36 Contrast with this the persistent Lollard emphasis on scripture as an 'open' text. The word suggests that the Bible is a text 'which reads itself, a message which requires no interpretation, only a gesture'. See Ralph Hanna III, 'The Difficulty of Ricardian Prose Translation: The Case of the Lollards', *Modern Language Quarterly* 51 (1990), 319–40 (p. 336). Also see Copeland, 'Politics of the Literal Sense', pp. 19–20.

37 Courtenay, *Schools and Scholars*, p. 210.

38 *Ibid.*, p. 212; see also Courtenay, *Capacity and Volition*.

39 *De Ecclesia*, ed. J. Loserth, Wyclif Society (London, 1886), p. 350/4–11.

40 'Wyclif and Hierarchy', in Hudson and Wilks (eds.), *Ockham to Wyclif*, pp. 233–44 (p. 243).

41 *De Ecclesia*, p. 341/1–6; see also Farr, *John Wyclif as Legal Reformer*, pp. 81–138; Tatnall, 'Ecclesia Anglicana', and 'Church and State', pp. 137–73, 201–47.

42 *Laien in der Philosophie*, p. 19.

43 'Lollardy: the English Heresy?', p. 156. Tract 1 in CUL ii.vi.26 further points out that if the conservative argument that scriptural language is too difficult for the 'lewid' is accepted, then not only the laity but also large sections of the clergy must be denied the Bible: 'I seie bi þe same skyl neiþer þe lewid pepel. neiþer þe lewid men of holy chirche seculer reguler schulden haue it ne rede it in latyn' (fol. 7r). The tract proceeds to assert that apart from the 'ydiotis', there is 'anoþer manner of lewid pepel þat is lettrid', and indeed 'better þan þe prest' (fol. 8v). Men of Holy Church must be prepared to speak of 'witte and wisdom' with this latter group, and be 'redy to answer to her doutis' (fol. 9v).

44 My emendation; Deanesly reports 'de revelationibus originalibus'.

45 Imbach quotes Stephen of Tournai on the separate jurisdictions of clerk and lay: 'Civitas ecclesia; civitatis rex Christus; duo populi duo in ecclesia ordines: clericorum et laicorum; duae vitae: spiritualis et carnalis; duo principatus: sacerdotium et regnum; duplex iurisdictio: divinum ius et humanum'; *Laien in der Philosophie*, p. 19. On the emergence of the notion of the (non-clerical) 'people' in the early Middle Ages, see the short account in André Vauchez, *The Laity in the Middle Ages: Religious Beliefs and Devotional Practices*, trans. Margery J. Schneider (Notre Dame and London, 1993), pp. 39–44.

46 Nicholas Love's *Mirror of the Blessed Life of Jesus Christ*, significantly, refers to the same topos: the affective narration of Jesus's life is thought to be 'souereynly edifying to symple creatures þe whiche as childryn hauen nede to be fedde with mylke of lyȝte doctryne & not with sadde mete of grete clargye'; ed. Michael G. Sargent (New York and London, 1992), p. 10/14–16; on this topos, see Nicholas Watson, 'Conceptions of the Word: the Mother Tongue and the Incarnation of God', in Wendy Scase, Rita Copeland and David Lawton (eds.), *New Medieval Literatures* 1 (1997), 85–124 (pp. 91–8).

47 On the definition of the dissenting Lollard subject in terms of 'intellectual labour' in William Thorpe's account of his examination by Archbishop Arundel, see Rita Copeland, 'William Thorpe and His Lollard Community: Intellectual Labor and the Representation of Dissent', in David Wallace and Barbara Hanawalt (eds.), *Bodies and Disciplines: Intersections of Literature and History in Fifteenth-Century England* (Minneapolis, 1996), pp. 199–221 (pp. 200–201).

48 Note the difference in emphasis from Wyclif's discussion of parables: see Chapter 1 (pp. 32–5) above.

49 For a medieval theoretical discussion of the issue, see A. J. Minnis: 'The *Accessus* Extended: Henry of Ghent on the Transmission and Reception of Theology', in Mark D. Jordan and Kent Emery Jr (eds.), *Ad Litteram: Authoritative Texts and Their Medieval Readers* (Notre Dame, 1992), pp. 275–326 (esp. pp. 285–9); also his 'Medium and Message: Henry of Ghent on Scriptural Style', in Richard G. Newhauser and John A. Alford (eds.), *Literature and Religion in the Later Middle Ages: Philological Studies in Honor of Siegfried Wenzel* (Binghampton, N.Y., 1995), pp. 209–35.

50 'Democratic' is of course an anachronistic word to use here; less so, however, if one understands it to mean 'against institutionalised hierarchies'.

51 See *BRUO* 1389.

52 See M. R. James, *The Western Manuscripts in the Library of Trinity College, Cambridge: A Descriptive Catalogue*, 4 vols. (Cambridge, 1900–4), vol. 1, pp. 473–5.

53 See *BRUO* 504.

54 Cambridge, Trinity College MS B.15.11: Palmer's tract occupies fols. 42v–47v; it is followed by Boraston's *De Unione Ecclesiasticis Veritatis*, fols. 49r–54v. His *Mutabilitate Mundi* occupies fols. 69v–71r; also included is a legal tract by Boraston, fols. 56r–69v. Woodford's *Contra Trialogum* occupies fols. 1r–42r.

55 See *BRUO* 221; *HLW* 609–10; S. L. Forte, 'Simon of Boraston: His Life and Writings', *Archivum Fratrum Praedicatorum* 22 (1952), 321–45.

56 Palmer expresses his fear that the evil interpretations of the Lollards would lead astray the unlearned if they had vernacular scriptures, p. 425; also see p. 421 for a reference to the Lollards who believe that all truths are contained in scripture.

57 On this topos, see Copeland, *Rhetoric, Hermeneutics, and Translation*, pp. 42–55.

58 Forshall and Madden (eds.), *Holy Bible*, vol. 1, pp. 43–4.

59 'If a bird's nest chance to be before thee in the way in any tree, or on the ground, whether they be young ones, or eggs, and the dam sitting upon the young, or upon the eggs, thou shalt not take the dam with the young. But thou shalt in any wise let the dam go, and take the young to thee'.

60 Ed. Brewer, pp. 89–90.

61 For Bacon's vision of biblical and other textual corruption, see Brewer (ed.), *Opus Tertium*, pp. 92–3. On Bacon's textual consciousness, see Loewe, 'Latin Vulgate', pp. 147–51; Smalley, *Study of the Bible*, pp. 331–33.

62 For a brief account of the contemporary reception of the Latin Vulgate, see Loewe, 'Latin Vulgate', pp. 107–8.

63 'Alia causa poterat esse: quia translacio ipsorum septuaginta per laudabilem ecclesie consuetudinem, que pro lege habenda est, uel saltem legi equallet, longe ante tempora Augustini fuerat confirmata. Translacio uero Ieronimi, quamuis melior erat, qui contemporaneus erat Augustino pro tempore Augustini non tante fuerat ut uerisimiliter creditur ab ecclesia accepta. Habuit igitur beatus Augustinus tunc temporis rationabilem causam translacionem septuaginta aliis translacionibus preferendi . . . In istis temporalibus legibus quamquam de hijs homines iudicent cum eas instituunt, tamen cum fuerint institute et firmate non licebit iudici de ipsis iudicare, sed secundum ipsas. Modo uero, quia ecclesia prefert translacionem Ieronimi, ipsam pre ceteris preellegit [*sic*]; Augustinus, si modo viveret, esset cum ecclesia concorditer ellecturus' (fol. 200r col. b).

64 On the medieval sense of the mutability of law, see Charles Duggan, *Twelfth Century Decretal Collections and their Importance in English History* (London, 1963); also see Donald R. Kelley, 'Clio and the Lawyers: Forms of Historical Consciousness in Medieval Jurisprudence', *Mediaevalia et Humanistica*, NS 5 (1974), 25–49, esp. p. 34, where he points out that underlying medieval notions of legal change 'was an attitude that could

not help but subvert the uniform and universalist ideals of Roman law which even humanists took over intact: there was a sort of historical and geographical relativism demanding that human institutions should be interpreted in terms of conditions and environment as well as ideal or precept'. For a more general survey, with a bias towards the Renaissance, see Ian Maclean, *Interpretation and Meaning in the Renaissance: The Case of Law* (Cambridge, 1992).

65 Nicholas Watson interestingly suggests that there is an implied link between a lack of grammatical regulation in the vernacular and 'the unruliness of those who speak it': 'Censorship and Cultural Change', p. 844.

66 On academic usage of 'repetere', see Weijers, *Terminologie*, pp. 365–72.

67 *De Nova Praevaricantia Mandatorum*, in R. Buddensieg (ed.), *John Wiclif's Polemical Works in Latin*, 2 vols., Wyclif Society (London, 1883), vol. 1, pp. 109–50 (p. 126/4–7).

68 *English Preaching*, pp. 156–63 (p. 162).

69 The last category was one of Wyclif's and the Lollards' *bêtes noires*. Note that in the excerpt from Ullerston's tract which was rendered into English by the Lollards, the passage we have been examining is translated quite accurately, with, however, the offensive hagiographical suggestion left out: 'If . . . any prest seie he can not preche, oo remedie is, resyne he vp his benefice; anoþer remedie is, if he wol not þ[i]s, recorde he in þe woke þe nakid text of þe Soundaie Gospel þat he kunne þe groos story and tell it to his puple'. See C. F. Bühler, 'A Lollard Tract: on Translating the Bible into English', *Medium Aevum* 7 (1938), 167–83 (p. 175/166–71); also see Hudson, 'Debate on Bible Translation', pp. 68–71. On Lollard attitudes to saints, see Hudson, *Premature Reformation*, pp. 197, 302–3.

70 See Hudson, 'Debate on Bible Translation', p. 73.

71 See Hudson, 'Debate on Bible Translation', pp. 73–4. Gonville and Caius College, Cambridge, MS. 803/807 frag. 36 has the following colophon to Ullerston's (fragmentary) tract: 'Explicit tractatus Magistri Ricardi Vllerston [ ] de transla [ ]/[ ] sacre scripture in vulgare editus ab eodem Oxon' [ ] domini 1401'.

72 It is perhaps worth pointing out that Ullerston was a Fellow of the Queen's College, Oxford in 1391–2, though it is perhaps unlikely that he would have determined at such an early stage in his career: see *BRUO* 1928.

73 'Wyclif and the Vernacular' in Hudson and Wilks (eds.), *Ockham to Wyclif*, pp. 281–330 (pp. 289–90, 303).

74 See Aston, 'Wyclif and the Vernacular', pp. 304–5.

75 His knowledge of the *De Potestate Pape*, as also his *Petitiones*, points towards this; see Hudson, 'Debate on Bible Translation', pp. 79–80.

4 The English Wycliffite sermons: 'thinking in alternatives'?

1 *English Wycliffite Sermons*, ed. Hudson and Gradon, 5 vols. (Oxford, 1983–96). All references are to this edition (henceforth *EWS*), and are given after citations in the text; the numbering of the sermons follows that of the edition.

2 Introduction to *EWS* I.8–50, esp. 44–50.

3 On authorship, see *EWS* IV.20–33.

4 See Hudson's Introduction to *EWS* I.124–51.

5 See *EWS* IV.34.

6 *Premature Reformation*, pp. 197–200; also see *EWS* IV.34–6.

7 See Gradon's 'Relation of the English Cycle to Wyclif's Latin Sermons' in the Introduction to *EWS* III.xcix–cxlviii; also Hudson, 'Biblical Exegesis in Wycliffite Writings', in *John Wyclif e la tradizione degli studi biblici in Inghilterra*, Dipartimento di lingue e letterature straniere moderne: Sezione di anglistica (Genoa, 1987), pp. 61–79 (p. 71);

detailed notes comparing the English sermons with those of Wyclif are to be found in *EWS* IV and V.

8 See *EWS* IV.35.

9 I use the word 'popular' with full awareness of its possible vagueness of reference. The sermons themselves, however, do not avoid the notion of the 'people'. As one sermon puts it, the orthodox extablishment is worried that the truth of God's law will burst out to 'knowyng of comun puple': 1.426/49–50.

10 Sargent (ed.), *Mirror*, p. 9/18–20.

11 Italics in citations, unless specified as mine, follow Hudson's and Gradon's edition; they signify underlined or rubricated biblical words in the manuscripts.

12 Cf. Wyclif's own glossing of the passage in *De Veritate*: 'secundum apostolum Rom. decimo quinto quecunque scripta sunt *in scriptura divinitus inspirata*, ad nostram doctrinam scripta sunt' (1.131/15–18, italics mine).

13 Note the use of 'express'; see Chapter 2 above.

14 On the use of 'grounded', see Hudson, 'A Lollard Sect Vocabulary?', pp. 171–2.

15 A recognised academic joke: the name of Tobias's dog was a type of 'futile pedantic speculation'. See Hudson, 'Biblical Exegesis', p. 72; for references to similar remarks in Wyclif, see *EWS* V.199.

16 On the centrality of the notion of 'hypocrisy' to Wyclif's, and his followers', vision of the Church and its abuses, see Bostick, *Antichrist and the Lollards*, pp. 62ff, 99. The theme of hypocrisy and corrupt hermeneutics ties in with the problematic Lollard notion of dominion: 'true dominion' depends on the moral status of the officer imposing it. The catch, of course, is that only God can know that: see *EWS* IV.161–2; Hudson, *Premature Reformation*, pp. 359–62.

17 On the phrase 'true men', see Hudson, 'A Lollard Sect Vocabulary?', pp. 166–7; and Matti Peikola, *Congregation of the Elect: Patterns of Self-Fashioning in English Lollard Writings* (Turku, 2000), pp. 81ff.

18 See Ernst Robert Curtius, *European Literature and the Latin Middle Ages*, tr. Willard R. Trask (London, 1953), pp. 316–19; also see *De Veritate*, 1.108/12, for Wyclif's comment on the '[liber] hominis naturalis ut anima'.

19 'Sutil' was a charged Lollard word, meaning both 'obscure' and 'obfuscatory', often, though not always, used to criticise 'ungrounded' misinterpretations of the Bible by the orthodoxy. In an English Lollard tract, the phrase 'sutilte aȝenus charite' occurs to describe attempted 'groundings' of undesirable customs in scriptural 'misreadings': see *De Officio Pastorali*, in Conrad Lindberg (ed.), *English Wyclif Tracts 1–3*, Studia Anglistica Norvegica 5 (Oslo, 1991), pp. 30–81 (p. 43); also see *EWS* 1.232/12, for an accusation levelled against the modern-day 'scribes and pharises' who allege that the law of God is 'so sotyl and so holy' that only they can explicate it. William White, a Lollard burnt in 1428, spoke of the subtle language of the school of antichrist, 'subtili languagio exsecrabilis conventus Antichristi'; quoted by Bostick, *Antichrist and the Lollards*, p. 156 (n. 44). On the use of the adjective 'subtile' as a term of approbation in medieval scholastic discourse, see William J. Courtenay, 'John of Mirecourt and Gregory of Rimini on whether God can undo the Past', *RTAM* 39 (1972), 224–56 (p. 245); reprinted in *Covenant and Causality*; a Latin Wycliffite sermon speaks of the necessity of not obscuring the truth of God 'per scolasticas subtilitates': see *Premature Reformation*, p. 273.

20 Note the distrust of 'glosyng' rhetoric implicit in these words; cf. Wyclif's phrase 'cautela diaboli' in G. Lechler (ed.), *De Officio Pastorali* (Leipzig, 1863), p. 35, when describing homiletic adulteration of the Word. Contrast with this tracts on pastoral rhetoric such as

Robert of Basevorn's *Forma praedicandi*, with their firm recognition of the importance of the end that is 'coveted', though no doubt such an end is meant to be (in theory) good. Tr. Leopold Krul, in James J. Murphy (ed.), *Three Medieval Rhetorical Arts* (Berkeley and Los Angeles, 1971), pp. 111–215. Also see Spencer, *English Preaching*, pp. 78–108, 228–47.

21 This is of course to ignore all the complexities in medieval theory of scriptural authorship; see Minnis, *Medieval Theory of Authorship*, pp. 73–112.

22 Perhaps such a context would go some way towards explaining the otherwise unlikely Lollard involvement with *Oon of Foure*, a translation of Clement of Llanthony's gospel harmony, the *Unum ex Quattuor*. See Hudson, *Premature Reformation*, pp. 267–8. P. M. Smith, 'An Edition of Parts I–V of the Wycliffite Translation of Clement of Llanthony's Gospel Harmony "Unum ex Quattuor", known as *Oon of Foure*', Ph.D. thesis, University of Southhampton (1984), points out that Clement's work was based on St. Augustine's *De Consensu Evangelistarum*, which the saint wrote as a defence against heretics who emphasised contradictions in the gospels (p. xciii). Hunt, 'An Edition of Tracts', pp. 65–71, while arguing against Lollard authorship of the tract, provides evidence of the popularity of the text among Lollards.

23 This is one of Wyclif's main points: see Chapter 1 above.

24 See *MED*, senses 2, 3a, 4a, 6b: 'image', 'representation', 'symbol', 'parable', 'metaphor', 'letter of an alphabet'.

25 Indeed, it is this insistent, pervasive and overtly *theoretical* consciousness of themselves as an exegetical endeavour that most distinguishes the Wycliffite sermons from other contemporary 'orthodox' homiletic productions such as John Mirk's *Festial*. The sermons of this latter collection, possibly written with some intention of providing an antidote to Lollard scriptural interests, are emphatically and resolutely uninterested in their own theoretical premisses. See Alan J. Fletcher, 'John Mirk and the Lollards', *Medium Aevum* 56 (1987), 217–24; and Theodor Erbe (ed.), *Mirk's Festial* (EETS, 1905).

26 Von Nolcken, 'A "Certain Sameness" and Our Response to It in English Wycliffite Texts', in Newhauser and Alford (eds.), *Literature and Religion*, pp. 191–208 (197ff); Hudson, 'A Lollard Sect Vocabulary?', p. 171.

27 Hudson, *ibid.*, pp. 174–5.

28 For other Lollard iterations of the same theme, see *EWS*, v.297.

29 See in this context von Nolcken's discussion of what she calls the 'moral confidence' of the Lollards: 'A "Certain Sameness"', pp. 204–6.

30 See also II.24/80–82 (scornful reference to equivocation); II.46/100–47/107 (logical speculation against the truth of God's word).

31 Cf. Wyclif, *De Veritate*, I.9/8–10.

32 On 'insolubles', see Paul Vincent Spade, 'Insolubilia', in *CHLMP*, pp. 246–53.

33 Bostick, *Antichrist and the Lollards*, pp. 109–10, quotes the Lollard *Opus Arduum*, which contrasts the fables of the poets and 'vain philosophy' to apostolic injunction.

34 See p. 219 n. 24, and Smalley's account of the Victorines and Peter Comestor, Peter the Chanter and Stephen Langton, *Study of the Bible*, pp. 120–263 (esp. pp. 242–63).

35 This is in fact one of Netter's potent criticisms of Wyclif: how does one substantiate genuine inspiration? 'Sed an veram revelationem habueris, quomodo ego hoc sciam, ut credam?'; see *Doctrinale*, vol. I, col. 337; and further Chapter 6 below.

36 On Lollard imagery of light and darkness, see Gloria Cigman, '*Lux luceat vestra*: The Lollard Preacher as Truth and Light', *Review of English Studies*, NS 40 (1989), 479–96 (pp. 494–6).

37 See my discussion of William Butler in Chapter 3 above.

38 'Childhood, Pedagogy, and the Literal Sense: From Late Antiquity to the Lollard Heretical Classroom', in Scase, Copeland and Lawton (eds.), *New Medieval Literatures* 1 (1997), 125–56 (pp. 148, 155).

39 'Or what king, going to make war against another king, sitteth not down first and consulteth whether he be able with ten thousand to meet him that cometh against him with twenty thousand?'

40 For 'apply', see *MED*, senses 3b and 3c: 'to apply a statement as suitable or appropriate', 'to apply an allegory to a specific instance'.

41 On such 'applicative' or 'adaptive' interpretations, see Introduction, p. 219, n. 23. See *EWS* II.125/49–51, for another reference to 'vndurstondyngus' being 'applied to þe text'.

42 For 'root', see *MED*, senses 4a and 4b: 'basis', 'foundation', 'fundamental or essential part'.

43 Cf. *De Veritate*, 1.58/16–21.

44 The Lollard *Floretum* is similarly anxious about the dangers of spiritual interpretation; see Bostick, *Antichrist and the Lollards*, p. 197. On the *Floretum*, see Anne Hudson, 'A Lollard Compilation and the Dissemination of Wycliffite Thought', in *Lollards and their Books*, pp. 13–29.

45 See Anna Sapir Abulafia, 'Jewish Carnality in Twelfth-Century Renaissance Thought', in Diana Wood (ed.), *Christianity and Judaism*, SCH 29 (Oxford, 1992), pp. 59–75; also Venicio Marcolino, *Das Alte Testament in der Heilsgeschichte*, BGPTM, NS 2 (Münster, 1970), pp. 83–122.

46 See Chapter 1 for Wyclif's reliance on inspiration and *sapientia*. Hudson's discussion of Lollardy's hostility to learning (*Premature Reformation*, pp. 224–7) needs to be extended; much of the criticism is indeed directed towards contemporary academic abuses, but there is also this other, more fundamental, hermeneutic anti-intellectualism in Lollardy. See Cigman's discussion of a Lollard sermon on the theme 'scientia inflat': 'Lollard Preacher', p. 487; and Bostick's account of the heretic Walter Brut who maintained that God typically communicates through visions, prophecies and mysteries to 'peccatoribus, et laycis, ydiotis': *Antichrist and the Lollards*, p. 149.

47 Sermon 74 points out that Peter, who had 'prerogatif' before the other disciples, had no 'speculatif kunnyng' ('of gemetrie, ne of oþre sciensis') but 'practik, put in dede, how men schulden lyue by Godus lawe' (II.109/76–9); note also the Lollard devaluation of academic expertise in Lindberg (ed.), *De Officio Pastorali*, pp. 50–1.

48 For further uses of the notion of 'reason' in Lollard writings, see Fiona Somerset, *Clerical Discourse and Lay Audience in Late Medieval England* (Cambridge, 1998), pp. 180–3.

49 'preestus schilde not fiȝte, but meue men by resoun and Godus lawe to trewþe' (II.112/21–2); '[the principles of papal election] may not be growndud in resoun, ne in Godus lawe' (II.188/63–4); '[The new orders] can neiþur teche by reson, ne by beleue, þat [their patrons] ben seyntus in heuene' (II.225/112–3). Note that opponents of Lollardy, when referring contemptuously to their emphasis on reason, generally signify this version. Hudson quotes Oxford, Bodleian Library, MS Laud misc. 706, fol. 106v: 'they [Lollards] presume so meche of hor owne witte þat hom semes what article of oure feythe may noȝt clereliche be conseyuet be hor kyndeliche resoun, it owe to be anuwet and set aside': *Premature Reformation*, p. 220 (n. 249); Thomas Netter too chooses to identify Wycliffite 'reason' with 'rationality', see Chapter 2, p. 236, n. 65.

50 Edited by A. Butrym as *A Dialogue between Christ and Satan*, in 'An Edition, with Commentary, of the Wyclifite Tracts contained in Trinity College Dublin C.V.6',

Ph.D. thesis, Rutgers University (1971), pp. 689–709. All references are to this edition and given after citations in the text.

51 See John A. Alford, 'The Idea of Reason in *Piers Plowman*', in E. D. Kennedy, R. Waldron and J. S. Wittig (eds.), *Medieval English Studies Presented to George Kane* (Cambridge, 1988), pp. 199–215.

52 Also see Bostick's discussion of the *Opus Arduum*'s similar polarisation of canon law and *lex Christi: Antichrist and the Lollards*, pp. 102–113.

53 See II.163/71–5: 'popus wolon haue þe furste fruytus for beneficis þat þei ȝyuon, and byschopus an hundred schyllyngus for halwyng of o chyrche, and lordus wolon haue long seruyse for o chirche þat þei ȝyuen, and þis is worþ ȝer by ȝeer muche rent or muche money'; II.197/113–4: 'þe feend techeþ hise clerkus to seke aftur feynede answerus. And þei seyn, furst, þat by þis dowyng þei ben in quyete and in pees, and so þey serue God betture'; also see the disparaging comment of Tract 7 in CUL MS Ii.vi.26: 'þe farisees weren men of religion þat maden to hem custommys and kepten hem as for lawe', in Hudson (ed.), *Selections*, p. 109.

54 On Wyclif's, and the Lollards', apocalyptic thought, see Penn R. Szittya, *The Antifraternal Tradition in Medieval Literature* (Princeton, 1986), esp. pp. 152–82; Bostick, *Antichrist and the Lollards*; Alexander Patschovsky, '"Antichrist" bei Wyclif', Anne Hudson, 'Lollardy and Eschatology' in Alexander Patschovsky and František Šmahel (eds.), *Eschatologie und Hussitismus*, *Historica*, Series Nova, Suppl. 1 (Prague, 1996), 83–98, 99–113. For a more general theoretical discussion of the appropriative use of 'history' in constructing arguments, see von Moos, *Geschichte als Topik*, pp. 208ff; also his 'The Use of *Exempla* in the *Policraticus* of John of Salisbury', pp. 207–61.

55 'Ricardian-Lancastrian Prose translation', p. 252.

56 *Antichrist and the Lollards*, p. 50.

57 One may recall Roland Barthes again: '*Dialectica* is an art of living discourse, of dialogue. There is nothing Platonic about such dialogue, there is no question of a subjection on principle of the beloved to the master; dialogue here is aggressive, its stake is a victory which is not predetermined: it is a battle of syllogisms, Aristotle staged by two partners. Hence *Dialectica* is finally identified with an exercise, a mode of exposition, a ceremony, a game, *disputatio* (which might be called: a colloquy of opponents)': 'The Old Rhetoric', p. 39.

58 *De distinctione verarum revelationum a falsis*, in Palémon Glorieux (ed.), *Oeuvres Complètes*, 10 vols. (Tournai, 1960–73), vol. III (1962), pp. 36–56 (p. 37); trans. Brian Patrick McGuire, *Jean Gerson: Early Works* (New York and Mahwah, 1998), pp. 334–64 (p. 335); also see *De probatione spirituum*, in Glorieux, vol. IX (1973), pp. 177–85.

59 Jerzy B. Korolec, 'Jean Buridan et Jean de Jandun et la relation entre la Rhétorique et la Dialectique', in Wolfgang Kluxen et al. (eds.), *Sprache und Erkenntnis im Mittelalter*, 2 vols., MM 13 (Berlin, 1981), vol. II, pp. 622–627 (p. 623). Korolec further points out (p. 627) that Jean Buridan and Jean de Jandun were not isolated in this vision of the duality of logic; Jean Gerson shared a similar point of view.

60 *Geschichte als Topik*, p. 246.

61 Von Moos, *ibid.*, pp. 276–286. As the Wife says: 'For myn entente nys but for to pleye', in L. D. Benson (ed.), *The Riverside Chaucer* (Oxford, 1988), p.107/192.

62 See Chapter 2, p. 236, n. 56; see also Chapter 6 below.

63 Von Moos, *Geschichte als Topik*, pp. 238ff.

64 See James J. Murphy, *Rhetoric in the Middle Ages: A History of Rhetorical Theory from St. Augustine to the Renaissance* (Berkeley and Los Angeles, 1974), esp. pp. 292ff. Murphy

discusses one of the earlier preaching manuals, the *Liber quo ordine sermo fieri debeat*, by Guibert, later Abbot of Nogent, who treats preaching and multiple interpretations of scripture as a natural conjunction (pp. 301–3). Also see his discussions of Alexander of Ashby, who exhorts the preacher to present 'charming allegories' ('dulce exponere allegoriam'); Thomas of Salisbury (on preaching as a kind of rhetoric); Richard of Thetford, who classes 'spiritual' interpretations under modes of 'amplification'; Jean de la Rochelle, who identified the tropological and anagogical senses as the most effective for preaching, and so on. Murphy points out that the standard feature of the vast numbers of *artes praedicandi* is an emphasis on the four senses of interpretation and the use of *exempla* (p. 341). The Lollards successfully avoided the latter, but remained – inevitably – indebted to rhetorical uses of the former.

65 My coupling together of these apparently removed discourses is not fanciful: both are based on selective, and self-consciously 'interpretative' readings of scripture. It is interesting to note that the compiler of the *Pharetra*, a Franciscan *florilegium* written before 1261, and extant in over two hundred manuscripts, visualised his work as being of particular utility to meditation, preaching and disputation: 'ordinavi, ut quae ad meditationem, praedicationem, disputationem ibidem essent utilia, levius reperirentur'; see Rouse and Rouse, 'Florilegia of Patristic Texts', p. 175.

5 Nicholas Love and the Lollards

1 *The Mirror of the Blessed Life of Jesus Christ*, ed. Michael G. Sargent (New York and London, 1992). All references, unless otherwise specified, are to this edition and are given after citations in the text. Italics in quotations, unless specified as mine, are editorial and signify rubrication or underlining in the manuscripts.

2 For a brief descriptive catalogue of the extant manuscripts, see Sargent (ed.), *Mirror*, pp. lxxii–lxxxvi.

3 The *Meditationes* is printed as *Ioannis de Cavlibus Meditaciones vite Christi*, ed. M. Stallings-Taney, *CCCM* 153 (Turnhout, 1997); also in A. C. Peltier (ed.), *S. Bonaventurae Opera Omnia*, 15 vols. (Paris, 1864–71), vol. XII (1868), pp. 509–630; I have provided references to both editions after citations in the text. For its possible composition by John de Caulibus, a Franciscan friar from San Gemignano, see Sargent (ed.), *Mirror*, pp. xv–xvi; and M. Deanesly, 'The Gospel Harmony of John de Caulibus, or S. Bonaventura', in C. L. Kingsford (ed.), *Collectanea Franciscana II*, British Society of Franciscan Studies 10 (Manchester, 1922), 10–19. On dating, see Sarah McNamer, 'Further Evidence for the Date of the Pseudo-Bonaventuran *Meditationes Vitae Christi*', *Franciscan Studies* 50 (1990), 235–61. On the interrelationship of the *Meditationes* and the *Mirror*, see Sargent (ed.), *Mirror*, pp. xxx–xliv.

4 See Michael G. Sargent, 'Bonaventura English: A Survey of the Middle English Prose Translations of Early Franciscan Literature', in J. Hogg (ed.), *Spätmittelalterliche geistliche Literatur in der Nationalsprache*, 2 vols., Analecta Cartusiana 106 (Salzburg, 1983–4), vol. II, pp. 145–76 (pp. 149–51); also Sargent (ed.), *Mirror*, pp. xix–xx.

5 Carl Horstman (ed.), *Yorkshire Writers: Richard Rolle of Hampole, an English Father of the Church, and His Followers*, 2 vols. (London, 1895–96), vol. I, pp. 198–218.

6 J. Meadows Cowper (ed.), *Meditations on the Supper of our Lord, and the Hours of the Passion by Cardinal John Bonaventura. Drawn into English Verse by Robert Mannyng of Brunne*, EETS OS 60 (1875).

7 See Elizabeth Salter: *Nicholas Love's 'Myrrour of the Blessed Lyf of Jesu Christ'*, Analecta Cartusiana 10 (Salzburg, 1974); Sargent, 'Bonaventura English', p. 151.

8 The seventh of the Constitutions of Archbishop Arundel forbade the translation or the reading of the Bible in English without special permission from the ecclesiastical authorities. See Wilkins (ed.), *Concilia*, vol. III, p. 317.

9 For the complete text of the Memorandum, see Sargent (ed.), *Mirror*, p. 7/10–22; trans. by Sargent, p. xiv. In Cambridge, Trinity College MS B.15.16, there is an attempt to create a vernacular equivalent of this passage by placing, in isolation at the end of the manuscript (fol. 134r), both the Latin *memorandum* and the last few lines of Love's text which come before the treatise on the sacrament and on which Arundel's mandate is a variation: 'And for als miche . . . lollardes & heritykes' (p. 223/1–9).

10 See Sargent (ed.), *Mirror*, pp. xliv–lviii.

11 On the *Meditationes* and the associated devotional tradition in which the *Mirror* may be located, see Salter, *Nicholas Love's 'Myrrour'*, pp. 39–118; I. R. Johnson, 'The Late-Medieval Theory and Practice of Translation with special reference to some Middle English Lives of Christ', Ph.D. thesis, University of Bristol (1990); and Sargent (ed.), *Mirror*, pp. ix–xx.

12 It is interesting to note how often the *Meditationes* is associated with established power-structures: Love's version received official archepiscopal endorsement; Cambridge, Corpus Christi College MS 213, Jean Galope's translation, was dedicated to the 'tres hault, tres fort, et tres victorieux prince Henri quint' (fol. 1r), a second copy being presented to the Duke of Exeter; another French adaptation was completed for Jean, duc de Berry in 1380; and M. Deanesly refers to a Spanish translation made by the Franciscan bishop, Francis Ximenes: 'Gospel Harmony', p. 12. The *Mirror* too would have a significant upper-class readership; see Kathleen L. Scott, 'The Illustration and Decoration of Manuscripts of Nicholas Love's *Mirror of the Blessed Life of Jesus Christ*', in Shoichi Oguro, Richard Beadle and Michael G. Sargent (eds.), *Nicholas Love: Waseda 1995* (Cambridge, 1997), pp. 61–86.

13 Sargent, 'Bonaventura English', p. 154.

14 For Wycliffite discussion of the hermeneutic roles of 'inspiration' and 'reason', see Chapters 1 and 4 above; also see Forshall and Madden (eds.), *Holy Bible*, vol. I, pp. 3, 29, 30, 43.

15 See *De Veritate* 1.391/2–10; the Prologue to the Wycliffite Bible points out that: 'þe princis of þe chirche þat weren þerinne ben þe postlis, þat hadden autorite to writen holi writ, for bi þat same þat þe apostlis writiden here scripturis bi autorite, and confermyng of þe Holi Gost, it is holi scripture and feiþ of cristene men, and þis dignite haþ no man aftir hem, be he neuere so holi, neuere so kunnyng, as Ierom witnessiþ on þat vers [Psalm 87.6, Vulgate reading]': in Hudson (ed.), *Selections*, p. 67.

16 See chapter 1, pp. 54–9; we may recall that *De Veritate* argued in favour of corrected texts (1.195/1–3).

17 Hudson (ed.), *Selections*, p. 67.

18 Forshall and Madden (eds.), *Holy Bible*, vol. I, pp. 1–2.

19 *Ibid.*, p. 38.

20 Hudson (ed.), *Selections*, p. 69; note the emphasis on 'origynals', on the importance of going back to Jerome's 'propre' text, uncorrupted, it is implied, by subsequent mediators. High medieval usage of the word in the sense of 'l'oeuvre complète d'un écrivain, par opposition aux gloses et aux extraits' ('the complete work of an author, as opposed to glosses and extracts'), fits in well with the Wycliffite emphasis on authorial intention and context: de Ghellinck, '*Originale et Originalia*', p. 104.

21 Hudson (ed.), *Selections*, p. 67. Contrast with this textual anxiety what Beryl Smalley describes as the 'either-or system' of 'textual criticism', where alternative readings were

accepted according to differing exegetical imperatives. Smalley cites Stephen Langton, 'the greatest Biblical scholar of the later twelfth century', 'famous for his emendations and . . . frequently cited in thirteenth century *correctoria*'. Langton 'delights in collecting alternatives. A reading which bears clear signs of corruption may be useful to him afterwards, for the spiritual exposition; Langton joyfully adds it to his list'. While discusssing Zach. 1:21, he sets out one reading, then adds: 'That is the text given by Jerome and the Lombard, but the other reading accords better with the tropology': *Study of the Bible*, pp. 220–21. The circumstances of textual transmission of scripture are here creatively utilised so that Holy Writ is not only expounded but constituted according to hermeneutic purpose.

22 'The Wycliffite Versions', in Lampe (ed.), *Cambridge History of the Bible* II, pp. 387–415 (p. 413).

23 *Premature Reformation*, p. 198.

24 Similar prologues and epilogues, insisting on the necessity of distinguishing text and exposition, and emphasising the importance of specificity of reference, are to be found in Oxford, Bodleian Library, MSS Bodley 143, Bodley 243, Laud Misc. 235; London, British Library, MSS Additional 41175, Additional 28026; Cambridge, Fitzwilliam Museum, MS McClean 133. See H. Hargreaves, 'Popularising Biblical Scholarship: the Role of the Wycliffite *Glossed Gospels*' in W. Lourdaux and D. Verhelst (eds.), *The Bible and Medieval Culture*, ed. W. Lourdaux and D. Verhelst (Louvain, 1979), pp. 171–89; Hunt, 'An Edition of Tracts', pp. 56–65, 181–88; Copeland, 'Childhood, Pedagogy and the Literal Sense', pp. 151–56.

25 1.134–51 (p. 135).

26 For instance, in Oxford, Bodleian Library, MS Hatton 12 (original Rolle commentary), Latin texts occur in red in a very large script; the unrubricated translation and commentary form one undifferentiated whole. In another Bodleian Rolle Psalter, MS Bodley 467, sporadic attempts at distinguishing translation and commentary through a difference in script towards the beginning of the manuscript soon give way to an undifferentiated presentation, to the extent that there is often no distinction made between the Latin text and the rest. By contrast, the Lollard revision in Bodleian Library, MS Bodley 877 meticulously underlines the translation in red. In MS Bodley 288, another Lollard revision, the visual hierarchy is further emphasised with Latin text in dark textura, translation underlined in red and commentary unrubricated. See Hudson, *Premature Reformation*, pp. 259–64; and Michael P. Kuczynski, 'Rolle among the Reformers: Orthodoxy and Heterodoxy in Wycliffite Copies of Richard Rolle's *English Psalter*', in William F. Pollard and Robert Boenig (eds.), *Mysticism and Spirituality in Medieval England* (Cambridge, 1997), pp. 177–202.

27 T. Arnold (ed.), *Select English Works of John Wyclif*, 3 vols. (Oxford, 1869–71), vol. III, p. 112.

28 Ed. L. M. Swinburn, EETS OS 151 (1917), p. 31.

29 See the fourth Constitution in Wilkins (ed.), *Concilia*, vol. III, p. 316, col. II. Cf. Love: 'And þerfor when þou herest any sich þinge in byleue þat passeþ þi kyndly reson, trowe soþfastly þat it is soþ as holy chirch techeþ & go no ferþer' (p. 22/23–5). Later he replaces the *Meditationes*' exhortation not to seek 'nouas deuociones et amicicias' (p. 85/39; p. 538) with 'Seke not by curiosite newe knowleches & frendeshipes' (p. 72/21).

30 '*Lukynge in haly bukes: Lectio* in some Late Medieval Spiritual Miscellanies', in Hogg (ed.), *Spätmittelalterliche geistliche Literatur*, vol. II, pp. 1–27 (p. 23).

31 On this Pauline topos in medieval homiletic discourse, see Spencer, *English Preaching*, pp. 78 ff.

32 *Rhetoric, Hermeneutics, and Translation*, p. 166. She traces the origins of these ideas to Augustine's *De Doctrina Christiana*, in which *inventio* is defined as a 'method of discovering those things that are to be understood' (pp. 154–5). The two senses of the word 'invenire' – 'to invent' (the province of 'ymaginacioun'/rhetoric); and 'to find' (the province of exegesis/hermeneutics) coalesce.

33 Indeed, the unfathomable profundity of Christ's life is presented as the rationale for calling the text a 'mirror': p. 11/10–19. On the mirror-image in medieval literature, see Anna Torti, *The Glass of Form: Mirroring Structures from Chaucer to Skelton* (Cambridge, 1991).

34 'And so what tyme or in what place in þis boke is writen þat þus dide or þus spake oure lorde Jesus . . . & it mowe not be preuet by holi writ or grondet in expresse seyinges of holy doctours it sal be taken none oþerwyes þan as a deuoute meditacion' (p. 11/5–9). The original reads: 'si id per Scripturam non possit probari, non aliter accipias quam deuota meditacio exigit' (p. 10/100–1; p. 511).

35 Also see p. 33/31: original reference to the 'fructuose' doctrine offered by Joseph and Mary; p. 84/13: 'longe sermone & full of fruyte' for 'pulcherrimus . . . et copiosus' (p. 101/7; p. 544); p. 85/34: the 'gostly fruite & swete tast' of the *Pater Noster* (original passage); p. 146/38: Christ's 'noble and fructuose sermon' where the Pseudo-Bonaventura has 'pulcherimi sermonis' (p. 243/16; p. 596); p. 163/1: another original reference to his 'fructuose sermone'; p. 206/20–1: 'whoso haþ any deuocion & gostly tast' for the source-text's 'si aliquid deuocionis habes' (p. 314/30–1; p. 621); pp. 207/5 & 210/10: more original references to 'gostly sauour' and 'gostly tast'.

36 Also see p. 83/30–2: 'Anoþere vnderstandyng is in þees wordes þe which doctours comunly tellen, & þerfore we passe ouer þat, at þis tyme'; p. 117/34–5: 'þis proces aftur þe exposition of seynt Gregory & oþer doctours is ful dredeful to al cristiene men.'

37 Senses 1a and 1e in *MED*.

38 Note that the form 'is/may be/ought to be understood' is on occasion used by Love to translate the pseudo-Bonaventuran 'adaptari'. Referring to Christ's first miracle in turning water into wine, Love says: 'by þe whech is vndurstonde also þe gostly bridale of holy chirch' (p. 43/10–11). His source-text runs: 'quod eciam ad Ecclesiam et spirituales nupcias potest adaptari' (p. 40/22–3; p. 522). On 'adapted' senses of scripture, see Introduction, p. 219, n. 23.

39 The textual authority of this passage is, however, problematic; see M. G. Sargent, 'Versions of the Life of Christ: Nicholas Love's *Mirror* and Related Works', *Poetica* 42 (1995), 39–70 (pp. 61–2). It is printed in L. F. Powell (ed.), *The Mirrour of the Blessed Lyf of Jesu Christ* (Oxford, 1908), p. 36.

40 Note that in Oxford, University College MS 123, the *Mirror* is followed by a tract on prayer (fols. 74v–75v) in which devotional *entent* is all-important: the tract teaches how to moralise the various parts of one's bed into holy meditations. The entire compilation seems to be a self-conscious one, for the tract on prayer is followed by a polemical defence of the sacraments as being 'grounded' in the Gospel. 'Heretics' are criticised for being 'ful of wordis not vnderstandynge þe gospel' (fol. 76r).

41 On the medieval conceptualisation of the *Pater Noster* as the most complete and significant prayer, see Gillespie, 'Middle English Pastoral Manual', pp. 128–39.

42 Copeland, *Rhetoric, Hermeneutics, and Translation*, p. 64; see also James Simpson, 'Desire and the Scriptural Text: Will as Reader in *Piers Plowman*', in Copeland (ed.), *Criticism and Dissent*, pp. 215–43.

43 See in this context Jean Leclercq on the textual freedom underlying medieval devotional *lectio*, particularly in the context of prayer: 'Traductions de la Bible et spiritualité médiévale', in Lourdaux and Verhelst (eds.), *Bible and Medieval Culture*, pp. 263–77

(p. 271). Also see the section on prayers in Victor Leroquais, *Les livres d'heures manuscrits de la Bibliothèque Nationale*, 3 vols. (Paris, 1927–43), vol. I, pp. xxix–xxxii. Note in this context Lollard dismissals of prayers other than those biblically sanctioned: Hudson, *Premature Reformation*, pp. 310–13. The interrelationship of prayer and rhetoric emerges clearly in *Netter, Doctrinale*, vol. III, cols. 109–11: Wyclif says that 'homine vivente juste, Deus propter suam iustitiam dabit illi quod rationabiliter postulaverit'; and Netter, in reply, cites Jerome – God does indeed know the substance of our prayers, but as narration, not as petition. Matt. 26:39 is also cited: Christ uttered prayers other than the *Pater Noster*. Also see Jacques Dubois, 'Comment les moines du Moyen Age chantaient et goûtaient les Saintes Ecritures', in Riché and Lobrichon (eds.), *Bible au Moyen Age*, pp. 261–98, on transformative uses of the Bible.

44 'Et cum hac modificacione que tibi affermo per auctoritatem sacrae scripturae uel doctorum sacrorum non probantur, ut eciam in principio tibi dixi.' (p. 65/20–2; p. 531)

45 There is an abiding unease in the *Mirror* with the meditative predilection for 'imaginations'. Love repeatedly introduces cautious explications or caveats beyond the ones provided by his source: 'þe which processe sal be taken as in liknes & onlich as a manere of parable & deuoute ymaginacion' (p. 18/1–2); 'beware þat þou erre not in imaginacion of god' (p. 22/7); 'we shole here more specialy gedere in oure entent, & make vs by ymaginacion, as þei we were present in bodily conuersacion' (p. 128/6–8); 'Nowe go we vp by deuout contemplacion to oure lorde Jesu beholdyng in ymaginacion of heuenly þinges by likenes of erþely þinges' (p. 216/30–2). On Love's use of the phrase 'devout imagination', see Richard Beadle, '"Devoute ymaginacioun" and the Dramatic Sense in Love's *Mirror* and the N-Town Plays', in Oguro, Beadle and Sargent (eds.), *Nicholas Love: Waseda 1995*, pp. 1–17 (esp. pp. 9–12).

46 See Chapter 4 above; also see Forshall and Madden (eds.), *Holy Bible*, vol. I, p. 2, where the New Testament is declared to be 'of ful autorite, and opyn to vndirstonding of simple men', and p. 43, for the necessity of 'open' grounding of spiritual readings.

47 *EWS*, 1.241/38–40.

48 *Premature Reformation*, pp. 269–70.

49 In this instance, the word is based on the *Meditationes*' 'manifeste ostendit' (p. 66/57; p. 531).

50 The Pseudo-Bonaventure merely has: 'Non enim per totum annum sequentem predicacionis dicitur publice assumpsisse' (p. 93/34–5; p. 541).

51 The *Meditationes* has 'humiliter se incipit manifestare' (p. 94/51; p. 541).

52 The *Meditationes* reads: 'quod est contra quosdam hereticos maledictos' (p. 106/32–3; p. 545).

53 It is interesting to note that the Lollards read the same Augustinian interpretation as suggesting that 'it is an open blasfemye þat prestis forȝyuen þis sin in God, but ȝyue God forȝyue it first': *EWS* III.144/99–101. Michael G. Sargent, 'An Audience with the Archbishop: Devotional Literature and Ecclesiastical Politics in Late Medieval England' (forthcoming), draws attention to this passage.

54 See John F. Wippel, *Mediaeval Reactions to the Encounter Between Faith and Reason* (Milwaukee, 1995).

55 See Chapter 4, p. 245, n. 49.

56 On the interrelationship of 'reason' and 'imagination' in various hierarchies or syntheses of psychological categories in relation to faith, if not specifically to scriptural *lectio*, see A. J. Minnis, 'Affection and Imagination in "The Cloud of Unknowing" and Hilton's "Scale of Perfection"', *Traditio* 39 (1983), 323–366; also his 'Langland's Ymaginatif and Late-Medieval Theories of Imagination', *Comparative Criticism* 3 (1981), 71–103; also

James Simpson, *Sciences and the Self in Medieval Poetry: Alan of Lille's 'Anticlaudianus' and John Gower's 'Confessio Amantis'* (Cambridge, 1995), esp. pp. 252–71. In particular, Minnis ('Affection and Imagination', pp. 328–9) cites Richard of St Victor's *Benjamin major*, where Richard describes the six stages of mental ascent to God: (i) 'imaginative', (ii) 'in imagination but according to reason', (iii) 'in reason according to imagination', (iv) 'rational', (v) 'beyond reason but compatible with it' and (vi) above, beyond, even against reason. Love's psychological theory is by no means as sophisticated, but he may have inherited some of the terminology from Richard through Walter Hilton, whose work he did know (see *Mirror*, p. 124/31–43), and who emphasised the need for the strict control of the vagrant imagination by the intellect.

57 Note the use of 'nakedly'. The preeminent value of the 'naked text' and the 'literal sense' of the Gospel was an important part of Lollard biblical theory; Love's critical reference to the misleading nature of the 'naked' sense of the letter therefore assumes a polemical charge here.

58 The anonymous author of the *Speculum Devotorum*, a translation of Ludolf of Saxony's *Speculum Vitae Christi*, is more indulgent. It discusses the two versions, attributing one to St Bridget, and states that both are fruitful: 'wherefore I wole telle ʒow too manyrys, whyche of hem maye beste styre ʒow to deuocyon that takyth': ed. James Hogg, Analecta Cartusiana 12 (Salzburg, 1973), p. 266.

59 'How þat oure lorde aperede to Joseph of Arimathye as telleþ þe gospell of Nichodeme, & also to þe lasse James as seynt Jerom witnesseþ; I passe ouer for litel fruite of hem' (p. 202/4–6).

60 A. I. Doyle, 'A Survey of the Origins and Circulation of Theological Writings in English in the Fourteenth, Fifteenth and Sixteenth Centuries', Ph.D. thesis, University of Cambridge (1953), 2 vols., vol. 1, p. 143n. See also his 'Reflections on Some Manuscripts of Nicholas Love's *Myrrour of the Blessed Lyf of Jesu Christ*', *Leeds Studies in English* NS 14 (1983), 82–93. On the manuscripts, see the articles in Oguro, Beadle and Sargent (eds.), *Nicholas Love: Waseda 1995*; and the various articles by Michael Sargent cited in this chapter.

61 The manuscripts I have examined are: Cambridge, Corpus Christi College 142 & 143; Cambridge, Fitzwilliam Museum McClean 127; Cambridge, Trinity College B.15.16 & B.15.32; Cambridge, University Library, Additional 6578, Additional 6686, Ll.iv.3, Mm.v.15, Hh.i.11; Edinburgh, National Library of Scotland, Advocates' Library 18.1.7; Glasgow, University Library, Gen. 1130; Glasgow, Hunterian Library, T.3.15; London, British Library, Additional 11565, Additional 19901, Additional 21006, Additional 30031, Arundel 112, Arundel 364, Royal 18C. x; Manchester, Chetham's Library, 6690; Manchester, John Rylands Library, Eng. 94, Eng. 98, Eng. 413; New York, Pierpont Morgan Library, 226 & 648; Oxford, Bodleian Library, Bodley 131, Bodley 207, Bodley 634, Hatton 31, e Museo 35, Rawlinson A. 387B; Oxford, Brasenose College e. ix; Oxford, University College 123; Oxford, Wadham College 5; Tokyo, T. Takamiya, 4, 8, 20 & 63; Tokyo, Waseda University Library, NE 3691.

62 At the time of Arundel's approbation, the manuscript belonged to Mount Grace Charterhouse, of which Love was Prior. See Sargent (ed.), *Mirror*, p. lxxiii.

63 Sargent (ed.), *Mirror*, p. cvi. See also Anne Hudson, 'Some Aspects of Lollard Book Production', in *Lollards and their Books*, pp. 181–91; also her *Premature Reformation*, pp. 228–77.

64 See his 'Versions of the Life of Christ', especially pp. 51–62; also his 'The Textual Affiliations of the Waseda Manuscript of Nicholas Love's *Mirror of the Blessed Life of Jesus Christ*', in Oguro, Beadle and Sargent (eds.), *Nicholas Love: Waseda 1995*, pp. 175–274.

65 See in particular *Mirror*, ed. Sargent, pp. 9, 10, 14, 38, 63, 72, 83, 84, 100, 101, 106, 109, 111, 116, 121, 127, 238.

66 Among the manuscripts I have examined, Cambridge, Fitzwilliam Museum McClean 127 adds substantially new marginalia, consisting in two vernacular notes (fol. 2r & fol. 3r), and a number of Latin paraphrases of the vernacular text. However, this manuscript seems to have been perceived as problematic, since the text is extensively corrected in a contemporary hand. On the variations in the marginal apparatus, see Sargent, 'An Audience with the Archbishop', esp. n. 59, where he states that 'the overall shape of the apparatus of α and ß . . . remains comparable'.

67 Cambridge, Corpus Christi 142 & 143; Cambridge, Trinity B.15.32; Cambridge, University Library, Ll.iv.3 & Mm.v.15; London, British Library, Arundel 364; Manchester, John Rylands, Eng. 94 & Eng. 98; New York, Pierpont Morgan 648; Oxford, Bodleian Library, Bodley 131 & Hatton 31; Oxford, University 123; Oxford, Wadham 5; Tokyo, Takamiya 4 & 20; Tokyo, Waseda NE 3691.

68 For a discussion of the debate on the 'authority' of the marginal apparatus, see Sargent (ed.), *Mirror*, pp. cx–cxi; and Sargent's various articles cited in this chapter, *passim*. It should be pointed out that Cambridge, University Library, Additional 6578, the textually important copy, contains a full marginal apparatus.

69 On the Carthusian interest in textual uniformity, see Michael G. Sargent, 'The Problem of Uniformity in Carthusian Book-Production from the *Opus Pacis* to the *Tertia Compilatio Statutorum*', in Richard Beadle and A. J. Piper (eds.), *New Science out of Old Books: Studies in Manuscripts and Early Printed Books in Honour of A. I. Doyle* (Aldershot, 1995), pp. 122–41; also his *James Grenehalgh as Textual Critic*, Analecta Cartusiana 85 (Salzburg, 1984), pp. 15–55; for recent work on the production of *Mirror* manuscripts, see, apart from Sargent's articles, Scott, 'The Illustration and Decoration of Manuscripts of Nicholas Love's *Mirror*'.

70 On this feature, see Sargent, 'Textual Affiliations', pp. 182–5.

71 Manuscripts with uncertain rubrication are: Cambridge, Fitzwilliam Museum McClean 127; Cambridge, Trinity B.15.32; Cambridge, University Library, Ll.iv.3 & Mm.v.15; London, British Library, Arundel 364; Manchester, John Rylands Eng. 94 & Eng. 413; Manchester, Chetham's 6690; Oxford, Bodleian Library, Bodley 131; Tokyo, Takamiya 4 & 20; Tokyo, Waseda NE 3691.

72 Manuscripts examined include: Cambridge, St. John's College, D. 8; Cambridge, University Library, Additional 6315, Hh.iii.13, Kk.iv.23; London, British Library, Royal 7A. i, Royal 7D. xvii; Oxford, Bodleian Library, Bodley 162, Bodley 529, Canon Liturg. 226.

73 For discussions of Hh.i.11, see N. Chadwick and E. Colledge, '*Remedies against Temptations*: The Third English Version of William Flete', *Archivio italiano per la storia della pietà*, 5 (1968), 201–40 (pp. 206–8), and Alexandra Barratt, 'The Revelations of Saint Elizabeth of Hungary: Problems of Attribution', *The Library*, Series 6, 14 (1992), 1–11 (pp. 3–4); for discussion of the substantial female readership of the *Mirror*, see Carol M. Meale, '"oft siþis with grete deuotion I þought what I miȝt do pleysyng to god": The Early Ownership and Readership of Love's *Mirror*, with Special Reference to its Female Audience', in Oguro, Beadle and Sargent (eds.), *Nicholas Love: Waseda 1995*, pp. 19–46.

74 There is an erratic handful of specific references to the Bible; see Sargent (ed.), *Mirror*, pp. 9, 74, 79, 80, 108, 114, 126, 127, 128, 140, 198, 199, 210, 238. A few chapter-headings towards the end carry gospel references (Chapters 53, 54, 58, 59, 60).

75 *Meditations on the Life of Christ: An Illustrated Manuscript of the Fourteenth Century* (Princeton, 1961).

76 On the notion of *ordinatio*, see M. B. Parkes, 'The Influence of the Concepts of *Ordinatio* and *Compilatio* on the Development of the Book', in J. J. G. Alexander and M. T. Gibson (eds.), *Medieval Learning and Literature: Essays Presented to R. W. Hunt* (Oxford, 1976), pp. 115–40; repr. in *Scribes, Scripts and Readers: Studies in the Communication, Presentation and Dissemination of Medieval Texts* (London and Rio Grande, 1991), pp. 35–70; but see also R. H. and M. A. Rouse, '*Ordinatio and Compilatio* Revisited', in Jordan and Emery (eds.), *Ad Litteram*, pp. 113–34.

77 Trans. by Sargent, in *Mirror*, p. xxx.

78 Ed. R. Guarnieri in 'Il movimento del libero spirito', *Archivio italiano per la storia della pietà*, 4 (1965), 351–708 (pp. 513–635).

79 See '"The Mirror of Simple Souls": a Middle English Translation', ed. M. Doiron, *Archivio italiano per la storia della pietà*, 5 (1968), 241–355; there follows an Appendix by E. Colledge and R. Guarnieri on the glosses by M.N. (pp. 356–82). See also Doiron's 'The Middle English Translation of *Le Mirouer des Simples Ames*' in A. Ampe (ed.), *Dr L. Reypens Album*, Studien en Tekstuitgaven van *Ons Geestelijk Erf* 16 (Antwerp, 1964), pp. 131–52.

80 M.N. inserted his own comments because problematic passages in the original had been misinterpreted. It is at least possible, though Alexandra Barratt queries such a possibility, that M.N. was also aware of Margarete Porete's condemnation as a heretic, which would provide a further reason for his care in distinguishing addition from original: see the Appendix by Colledge and Guarnieri, and Alexandra Barratt (ed.), *Women's Writing in Middle English* (London and New York, 1992), pp. 61–3. In any case, the extreme unconventionality of Porete's text (and also the fact that it was by a woman) would make circumspection advisable, especially if the translation were made in the fifteenth century in England.

6 Thomas Netter and John Wyclif: hermeneutic confrères?

1 On Netter, see *BRUO* 1343–4; *HLW* 671–2; K. S. Smith, 'The Ecclesiology of Controversy: Scripture, Tradition and Church in the Theology of Thomas Netter of Walden', Ph.D. thesis, Cornell University (1983); and D. J. Dubois, 'Thomas Netter of Walden, O.C. (c. 1372–1430)', B.Litt. thesis, University of Oxford (1978).

2 *Doctrinale Antiquitatum Fidei Ecclesiae Catholicae*, ed. B. Blanciotti, 3 vols. (Venice, 1757–9; repr. Farnborough, 1967). All references are to this edition and will occur by volume and column number after each citation. Italics in citations, unless specified as mine, are editorial. (Henceforth *DFC*).

3 It is unsurprising, therefore, that Netter's references to his predecessor in anti-Wycliffite polemic should be infrequent. See Hudson, *Premature Reformation*, p. 50, n. 231. On academic life in England in the early fifteenth century, see Jeremy Catto, 'Theology after Wycliffism', in Catto and Evans (eds.), *History of the University of Oxford II*, pp. 263–80; Katherine Walsh, 'Die englische Universität nach Wyclif: Von geistiger Kreativität zur Beamtenausbildung?', in Alexander Patschovsky and Horst Rabe (eds.), *Die Universität in Alteuropa* (Constance, 1994), pp. 85–110.

4 There are isolated references to a woman who celebrated mass (I.296, II.71, 185); and to semi-popular Lollards (I.362, 637; III.146, 232ff., 342, 412, 455, 601, 630, 695, 763, 844, 901, 967).

5 Hudson, *Premature Reformation*, pp. 50–1; also see K. S. Smith, 'An English Conciliarist?: Thomas Netter of Walden at the Councils of Pisa and Constance' in J. R. Sweeney and S. Chodorow (eds.), *Popes, Teachers and Canon Law in the Middle Ages* (Ithaca, N.Y., 1989), pp. 290–9.

6 Hudson, *Premature Reformation*, p. 51; see also Margaret Harvey, 'The Diffusion of the *Doctrinale* of Thomas Netter of Walden in the Fifteenth and Sixteenth Centuries', in L. Smith and B. Ward (eds.), *Intellectual Life in the Middle Ages: Essays Presented to Margaret Gibson* (London and Rio Grande, 1992), pp. 281–94 (pp. 281–2).

7 Also see Schüssler, *Primat der heiligen Schrift*, pp. 88–91, 150–54; Hurley, 'Wyclif and his Critics', pp. 329–33.

8 Books III and IV are only tangentially relevant to my concerns; as Hudson points out, they are 'a justificatory history of the various orders of monks and friars, with only a few comments on specifically Wycliffite objections to them'. She suggests that these two books might have been written first, 'before Netter conceived of the possibility of writing a comprehensive attack on Wyclif and his followers': *Premature Reformation*, pp. 51–2.

9 *PL*, 34.260; also ed. Joseph Zycha, *Corpus Scriptorum Ecclesiasticorum Latinorum* 28 (Prague, Vienna and Leipzig, 1894), p. 27/13–20.

10 See Chapter 2 above, p. 73.

11 Compare William Butler's much balder formulation of the exclusive hermeneutic competence of the Church: 'Non est ergo politicum ut quicunque, ubicunque, quantumcunque voluerit se det ferventi studio scripturarum'; see Chapter III above, p. 94.

12 On the fight between the Lollards and the Church over the right to preach the 'naked text' of the gospel, see Spencer, *English Preaching*, pp. 163–201, 245–7.

13 See, for instance, *De Veritate*, 1.1 48/7–15.

14 'John Wyclif and his Critics', p. 294, n. 67.

15 'And when all things shall be subdued unto him, then shall the Son also himself be subject unto him that put all things under him, that God may be all in all.'

16 Not that Netter is unaware of what we would understand by 'textual corruption'; see below.

17 'Loquitur ista de statu finali post resureccionem, & non de statu praesentis Ecclesiae...O quam pueriliter est hoc fundamentum Scripturae ad conversiones Wiclevisticas & praesumptum & extortum! Quis unquam doctus interpres, ante istum, ibi nidum reperit idearum? Quis sic futurum in praesens, conjunctivum in indicativum, Scripturam Pauli in scripturam haeretici, transformavit impune?' (1.47). Netter's criticism of Wyclif's philosophy of eternal ideas in this passage is discussed by Robson, *Wyclif and the Oxford Schools*, pp. 234–5. Note Netter's refusal to accept Wyclif's 'global' view of scripture as one singular signifier embodying the same transcendent truth in all its parts; instead, he stresses the varying significances of different passages.

18 Also see II.8–9, where Wyclif is accused of making a false witness of the divine text, as well as the sayings of the fathers: 'quomodo formidaret haereticus iste falsificare dictum Augustini, quando non timet falsum testem facere textum Dei?' Netter then proceeds to cite 2 Thess. 2:2, where Paul warns the Thessalonians not to be troubled 'by letter as from us'. 'Ecce isti falsi prophetae loquebantur sermonem Dei, sed non *vere*. Similiter pseudoapostoli deceperunt populum tempore sancti Pauli, dicentes: *ita dicit Paulus*; & sub nomine Pauli scribentes epistolas...Notanter monuit Paulus fideles, ne cito moverentur *a sensu nostro*, id est *Apostolico*; quia sensus est interpres verbi, quem quandiu homo retinet, in verbis falli non poterit. Quid igitur ideo mirarentur fideles, quod haereticus iste verba Canonum, vel Conciliorum corrupta producat, vel ad sensum omnino a condentibus alienum?' Note the conflation of 'corruption' and forgery with 'misinterpretation': the passage suggests that the Pauline pseudoapostles' invention of fake letters from Paul is an act comparable to the 'misreading' of scripture. In both cases, 'alien senses' are sought to be endowed with apostolic authority.

19 We should note that the passage from *De Apostasia* (p. 64/3–7) discussed here is one of Wyclif's 'supplementing' readings, instances of which we have examined in Chapter 1, pp. 33–4, 61.

20 See *De Apostasia*, p. 65/4–6.

21 'Nullis adhuc haereticis defuit Scripturarum authoritas: vix ullis non ficta revelatio Sancti Spiritus in suffragium sui dogmatis venenati' (1.335). Netter is historically quite correct: see de Lubac, *Exégèse médiévale*, vol. II/2, pp. 99–113; Lerner, 'Ecstatic Dissent'.

22 Indeed, Netter's awareness that individual 'inspiration' is not a helpful hermeneutic principle ('scripta authoritas non certificat sine concordi intellectu Ecclesiae; nec revelatio sine testae', 1.339) leads to the assertion that God's power is mediated to man not 'perpendicularly', but 'angularly', through ecclesiastical hierarchy and tradition (1.513–14).

23 Smith, 'Ecclesiology', pp. 168–75, outlines the main characteristics of this Church: 'unity' (in Christ's mystical body) finding expression in the individual's sacramental participation in Christ, 'catholicity', in that it covers the whole world and for all time (heresies are therefore readily identifiable in being confined spatially and temporally), and 'apostolicity' (in its historical origins, its teaching and its hierarchical succession).

24 See Janet Coleman, *Ancient and Medieval Memories*, pp. 274–324; also John O. Ward, 'Some Principles of Rhetorical Historiography in the Twelfth Century', in Ernst Breisach (ed.), *Classical Rhetoric and Medieval Historiography*, (Kalamazoo, Michigan, 1985), pp. 103–65.

25 'exposicio quidem non est scriptura sacra, sed eius preco vel ancilla', *De Veritate*, 1.386/15–16; see Chapter 1, p. 63.

26 Netter also points out that the ancient Nicene Council merely 'declared' and did not 'create' the article of consubstantiality, the point once again being that the Church is a witness, a transparent interpreter, never an insitutor or creator of faith (1.353).

27 I have emended Netter's 'scripturas' to 'scripturam', as he treats the 'scriptures' as a singular in the rest of the sentence.

28 The distinction is similar to the one Woodford makes between precept and counsel (see Chapter 2 above, p. 82), and which Netter himself makes between 'catholic' and other articles of faith (1.353). Also see Smith, 'Ecclesiology', pp. 189–95.

29 Note how consistently Netter seeks to underplay the implications of conflict within the body of patristic commentary: this would not fit in well with his vision of a tradition marked above all by *consensus*. On other medieval engagement with this particular problem, see Abelard's *Sic et Non*; for discussion, see Jean Jolivet, *Arts du langage et théologie chez Abélard*, Études de philosophie médiévale 57 (Paris, 1969), pp. 238–51.

30 *Harvest of Medieval Theology*, pp. 361–93. See introduction above, p. 220, n. 30.

31 See Hudson, *Premature Reformation*, p. 141, on Thomas Bikenore, and p. 274, on John Skylan, both heretics who held that even the four major Fathers were not to be trusted.

32 See Steven Justice, *Writing and Rebellion: England in 1381* (Berkeley and Los Angeles, 1994), pp. 67–101; Hudson, *Premature Reformation*, pp. 60–119, '*Peculiaris regis clericus*: Wyclif and the Issue of Authority', in Martin Gosman, Arjo Vanderjagt and Jan Veenstra (eds.), *The Growth of Authority in the Medieval West* (Groningen, 1999), pp. 63–81; Margaret Aston, 'Lollardy and Sedition, 1381–1431', in *Lollards and Reformers*, pp. 1–47; Michael Wilks, '*Reformatio Regni*: Wyclif and Hus as Leaders of Religious Protest Movements'.

33 See Catto, 'Wyclif and Wycliffism at Oxford', pp. 255–261.

34 On Netter's comments on the dogmatic power of councils, see Smith, 'An English Conciliarist?', pp. 290–9; also his 'Ecclesiology', pp. 203–4, on Netter's implication that oral transmission of the faith continues 'usque in sempiternum'.

35 In this he is very close to the insights afforded by modern scholarship; see R. M. Grant, 'The New Testament Canon' in Ackroyd and Evans (eds.), *The Cambridge History of the Bible I*, pp. 284–308.

36 See, for instance, *Lanterne of Liȝt*, ed. Swinburn, p. 31.

37 I have emended Blanciotti's 'recticlinium' to 'rectilinium'.

38 *Théologie comme science*, p. 42.

39 Cf. Aquinas's famous assertion that nothing necessary for the faith is contained under the spiritual sense that is not openly conveyed through the literal sense elsewhere. See *Summa Theologiae*, 1a.1.10, in Blackfriars vol. 1, pp. 38–9.

40 'Alii supervestiant argumentorum, & ingeniorum imagines: alii scolastico carmine rationum ordines; alii morales allegoriarum flores, & rosulas subtili stylo distinguant. Mihi nihil aliud vacat, nisi lapides simplice Scripturarum, cum coemento veteris expositionis Sanctorum Patrum adjungere' (1.25).

41 Netter's critique of Wyclif's 'logic' is treated succinctly by Robson, *Wyclif and the Oxford Schools*, pp. 231–40. It is worth noting here Netter's identification of Wyclif's 'logic' as the standard-bearer of his metaphysics (1.33–4).

42 *De Doctrina Christiana*, Book 1, c. 36 (p. 533).

43 Chenu, *Théologie comme science*, p. 42.

44 Netter cites Augustine's preference for 'authority' as opposed to 'reason'; see the chapter entitled 'In rationis penetralibus fidem constituunt haeretici', III.399–400. For another reference to the Augustinian emphasis on 'authority' rather than 'reason', see I.2; Netter also points out that in matters of faith, rational investigation is secondary, I.23; and that faith goes beyond the limits of human reason, II.285. See Köpf, *Wissenschaftstheorie*, pp. 253–7.

45 *MED*, sense 1a.

46 On the Eucharistic aspect of the Wycliffite controversy, see Maurice Keen, 'Wyclif, the Bible and Transubstantiation', in Kenny (ed.), *Wyclif in his Times*, pp. 1–16; J. I. Catto, 'Wyclif and the Cult of the Eucharist', in Walsh and Wood (eds.), *Bible in the Medieval World*, pp. 269–86; Heather Phillips, 'John Wyclif and the Optics of the Eucharist', in Hudson and Wilks (eds.), *Ockham to Wyclif*, pp. 245–58; W. J. Hankey, '*Magis . . . pro nostra scientia*: John Wyclif, his Mediaeval Predecessors and Reformed Successors, and a Pseudo-Augustinian Eucharistic Decretal', *Augustiniana* 45 (1995), 213–45; also Alain de Libera and Irène Rosier-Catach, 'L'Analyse Scotiste de la formule de la consécration eucharistique', Paul J. J. M. Bakker, '*Hoc est corpus meum*: L'Analyse de la formule de consécration chez des théologiens du XIVe et du XVe siècles', in Marmo (ed.), *Vestigia, Imagines, Verba*, pp. 171–202, 427–51 and the Bibliography therein.

47 'The bread which we break, is it not the communion of the body of Christ? For we being many are one bread, and one body: for we are all partakers of that one bread.'

48 'Primus error ejus in hac parte est, quod contra leges Scripturae sacrae extendit locutionem figuratam, ut propriam: & sine authoritate figuram transfert in locum proprii. Nec hoc intendebat unquam Augustinus, nec Scriptura' (II.503).

49 On the genuine ambiguity in Augustine's discussion of the Eucharistic verse, see Hankey, 'Pseudo-Augustinian Eucharistic Decretal', pp. 228–30.

50 'Quomodo autem debeat haec sententia Augustini moderari, ipse nos doceat. Alibi forte possumus nos instrui, qualiter in hoc dicto se cupit intelligi' (II.503).

51 See *PL*, XVII.96. The Ambrose passage runs: 'Hoc autem verum arbitror: quando et ratio et historia et auctoritas observatur.'

52 See Margaret Aston, 'Lollards and Images' in her *Lollards and Reformers*, pp. 135–92 (pp. 181–87, esp. pp. 186–7): '[Pecock's] exploration of the traditional role of ecclesiastical images (as instruction and aids to devotion and recollection) led him into psychology. He showed how 'laymen's books' far exceeded their instructional role, and were deeply enriching to religious experience . . . He had a grasp of essentials, combined with a sense of the range of human experience attached to the ecclesiastical arts'. See also Hans von Campenhausen, 'The Theological Problem of Images in the Early Church', in his *Tradition and Life in the Church: Essays and Lectures in Church History*, trans. A. V. Littledale (London, 1968) pp. 171–200 (p. 186), where he points out that the use of images was, from the beginning, and indeed in its classical Greek context, related to the 'question of applying the allegorical principle of interpretation to the world as a whole'.

53 See Mary Carruthers, *The Book of Memory: A Study of Memory in Medieval Culture* (Cambridge, 1990), pp. 221–9.

54 See von Campenhausen, 'Images in the Early Church', pp. 193 ff.

55 On the issue of Judaism and images in medieval polemic, see Dahan, *Intellectuels chrétiens*, pp. 500–1.

56 This rather obscure remark perhaps needs to be placed in the context of White's assertion that 'trees growing in a wood are of greater virtue and vigour, and bear a clearer likeness and image of God, than stone or dead wood carved to the likeness of man': see Aston, 'Lollards and Images', p. 152 (n. 62). Wyclif himself spoke against any representation of the Trinity: see J. Loserth and F. D. Matthew (eds.), *De Divinis Mandatis*, Wyclif Society (London, 1922), p. 156/21–8, cited by Aston, 'Lollards and Images', p. 139.

57 See Aston, *ibid.*, p. 141; see Loserth and Matthew (eds.), *De Divinis Mandatis*, p. 157/30–34.

58 'Ego enim quoslibet Authores induxerim, ad libros, et capitula (si habeant) aut portiones minutas, ut statim possint inveniri, describam.' (I.2).

59 'Nusquam enim verba ejus sine ipso interseram: semper errorem ejus cum remissione libri & fracturae praefigam in superliminari Capituli, ne (ut solent haeretici fingere) in odium ejus imputatum illi dicant, quod ipse non dixit, non docuit, non probavit. Textus sermonis proprii, & stylus insulsus suum declarabunt authorem.' (I.2).

60 *De Apostasia*, p. 83/12–17.

61 Medieval Latin usage of the word encompassed both the senses 'uncanonical' and 'unauthentic' or 'spurious': see *MLD*, senses 1a and 1b.

62 On the uncertainty surrounding the authorship of *De Divinis Officiis*, and Netter's interest in the issue and the research he undertook to establish the authorship of the tract, see Anne Hudson, 'A Wycliffite Scholar of the Early Fifteenth Century', in Walsh and Wood (eds.), *Bible in the Medieval World*, pp. 301–15 (pp. 309–12).

63 Smith suggests that the MSS were the products of a scriptorium, probably located at one of the Carmelite houses: 'Ecclesiology', pp. 275–7; see also Harvey, 'Diffusion of the *Doctrinale*'. K. L. Scott, *Later Gothic Manuscripts 1390–1490*, 2 vols. (London, 1996), vol. I, pp. 27–8, vol. II, pp. 187–9, also agrees that 'the exceptional number of manuscripts signed by Carmelite scribes and the grouping of manuscripts through decorative work . . . are persuasive factors that much of the copying was done in two or three Carmelite houses'.

64 The MSS I have examined are: Oxford, Bodleian Library, MSS Bodley 261 & 262; Oxford, Lincoln College, MS Lat. 106; Oxford, Magdalen College, MSS 153 & 157; Cambridge, University Library, MSS Dd.viii.16–17. Compare the presentation of the

text in Love's *Mirror*, another work responding to Wycliffite criticism of authority; see Chapter 5 above. Also see Minnis, *Medieval Theory of Authorship*, pp. 152–9, especially p. 157, where Minnis cites Vincent of Beauvais' preference for the word *actor* (as opposed to *auctor*) when introducing opinions of his own or of the modern doctors.

65 Jodocus Badius Ascensius, the famous Parisian printer, brought out the work over 1521–32, as did the Venetian Giovanni Battista de Rossi (Rubeo) in 1571: see Harvey, 'Diffusion of the *Doctrinale*', pp. 285–8.

66 Smith points out that Netter's main sources are early patristic: Irenaeus, the Pseudo-Dionysius, Jerome and Augustine: 'Ecclesiology', p. 186. Hudson says that Netter's range of authorities is much smaller than that of Woodford, Bernard being 'the latest authority to be cited with any frequency; canon law and its commentators are mentioned seldom': *Premature Reformation*, pp. 52–3. Dubois points out that over sixty Fathers of the Church, and over three hundred of their theological and exegetical works, are cited, and that Netter 'in all likelihood . . . cited the great majority of his patristic sources directly from the *originalia*': 'Thomas Netter of Walden', pp. 58, 70. On the larger late antique and early medieval background to the reliance on the authority of the Fathers, see Edward M. Peters, 'Transgressing the Limits Set by the Fathers: Authority and Impious Exegesis in Medieval Thought', in Scott L. Waugh and Peter D. Diehl (eds.), *Christendom and Its Discontents: Exclusion, Persecution and Rebellion 1000–1500* (Cambridge, 1996), pp. 338–62; Schüssler, *Primat der heiligen Schrift*, pp. 36–7.

67 Smith, 'An English Conciliarist?', p. 298.

Afterword: Lollardy and late-medieval intellectuality

1 Hudson, *Premature Reformation*, pp. 74–6; also Henry Ansgar Kelly, 'Lollard Inquisitions: Due and Undue Process', in Alberto Ferreiro (ed.), *The Devil, Heresy and Witchcraft in the Middle Ages* (Leiden, Boston and Cologne, 1998), pp. 279–303 (pp. 279–85).

2 See W. W. Capes (ed.), *Registrum Johannis Trefnant, episcopi Herefordensis 1389–1404* (London, 1916), p. 232. Part of this passage is discussed and translated by Anne Hudson, '"*Laicus litteratus*": The Paradox of Lollardy', in Peter Biller and Anne Hudson (eds.), *Heresy and Literacy 1000–1530* (Cambridge, 1994), pp. 222–36 (pp. 229–30).

3 See Chapter 1, p. 225 n. 27.

4 Ockham's *Summa logicae*, ed. P. Boehner, G. Gál and S. Brown (St Bonaventure, N.Y., 1974), p. 264; quoted by Thijssen, 'Crisis Over Ockhamist Hermeneutic', p. 377. Thijssen's paper gives a succinct account of the controversies over *virtus sermonis*. The distinction also received much attention in the course of the hermeneutic debates at the Council of Constance: see Froehlich, 'State of Biblical Hermeneutics', p. 36.

5 Swinderby also articulated his distaste for 'sophisms', Capes (ed.), *Registrum*, pp. 262–3 ('I can no sophymes, ne I kepe not to use hem, gif al I couthe, for the wise man saythe that God hatith sophystical wordes'), though, as Hudson points out, Swinderby, given his acquaintance with canon law and the Bible, must have been fairly erudite: '"*Laicus litteratus*"', p. 227.

6 On this issue, see, preeminently, Thijssen, *Censure and Heresy*, esp. pp. 1–39.

7 Maarten Hoenen points out how university documents from the late Middle Ages 'reveal an increasing concern that the highly developed theories of logic and philosophical analysis might create misunderstandings when used by those who were not skilled or had no education or ability to apply them correctly – for example young students or people outside the university': 'Theology and Metaphysics'.

8 'Bildungsstand und Freiheitsforderung (12. bis 14. Jahrhundert)', in Johannes Fried (ed.), *Die abendländische Freiheit vom 10. zum 14. Jahrhundert: Der*

Wirkungszusammenhang von Idee und Wirklichkeit im europäischen Vergleich (Sigmaringen, 1991), pp. 221–47 (p. 236).

9 On medieval universities' interest in mythologising their foundation and history, often in divine or quasi-divine terms: see Williams, *Theological Idea of the University*, pp. 158–83; Astrik L. Gabriel, '*Translatio studii*: Spurious Dates of Foundation of Some Early Universities', in *Fälschungen im Mittelalter: Internationale Kongreß der Monumenta Germaniae Historica (München, 16–19 September 1986)*, 6 vols. (Hanover, 1988), vol. I, pp. 601–26.

10 'Freiheit der Ketzer', in Fried (ed.), *Abendländische Freiheit*, pp. 265–80 (p. 274).

11 *Premature Reformation*, pp. 390ff. As Nicholas Watson has emphasised, 'Lollardy began life as a powerful expression of reformist tendencies *inside* the Church, whose status as a heresy was achieved as much by reactionary shifts within the definition of orthodoxy as by its own growing extremism': 'Censorship and Cultural Change', p. 826; also see J. A. F. Thomson, 'Orthodox Religion and the Origins of Lollardy', *History* 74 (1989), 39–55.

12 A recent account of the details of Wyclif's interaction with Oxford at the time of the issuance of the papal bulls against him is given by Henry Ansgar Kelly, 'Trial Procedures Against Wyclif and Wycliffites in England and at the Council of Constance', *Huntington Library Quarterly* 61 (1998), 1–28 (esp. pp. 4–10).

13 Hudson, *Premature Reformation*, pp. 446ff; also John A. F. Thomson, *The Later Lollards 1414–1520* (Oxford, 1965).

14 'Censorship and Cultural Change'; but for a critique of some details of Watson's reading of the *Constitutions*, see Kelly, 'Lollard Inquisitions', p. 288.

15 See Wilkins (ed.), *Concilia*, vol. III., pp. 316–18.

16 'Theology After Wycliffism', p. 265.

17 As Palèmon Glorieux has stated, 'La rèforme de la théologie était à l'ordre du jour à la fin du XIVe siècle' ('The reform of theology was the order of the day at the end of the fourteenth century'): 'Le Chancelier Gerson et la réforme de l'enseignement', in E. Callistus (ed.), *Mélanges offerts à Etienne Gilson* (Toronto, 1959), pp. 285–98 (p. 285).

18 This formulation is Pope Gregory IX's, in a letter addressed to the regent masters of theology at Paris in 1228. For a brief history of this and subsequent condemnations, see Monika Asztalos, 'The Faculty of Theology', in De Ridder-Symoens (ed.), *History of the University in Europe*, pp. 409–41, pp. 421ff.

19 The phrase is from a letter from Clement VI addressed to the masters and students in Paris in 1346: see Asztalos, *ibid.*, p. 432.

20 See Asztalos on the statutes of the Universities of Paris, Bologna, Toulouse and Vienna: *ibid.*, p. 434.

21 '"Moderns" and "Modernists" in MS Fribourg Cordeliers 26', *Augustinianum* 5 (1965), 241–70 (p. 270).

22 On Gerson, see, among others, Zénon Kaluza, *Les Querelles doctrinales à Paris: Nominalistes et réalistes aux confins du XIVe et du XVe siècles* (Bergamo, 1988), pp. 35–86; Mark Stephen Burrows, *Jean Gerson and 'De Consolatione Theologiae' (1418): The Consolation of a Biblical and Reforming Theology for a Disordered Age* (Tübingen, 1991); also Wolfgang Hübener, 'Der theologisch-philosophische Konservativismus des Jean Gerson', in Zimmermann (ed.), *Antiqui et Moderni*, pp. 171–200, and Glorieux, 'Le Chancelier Gerson'.

23 'Bulletin d'histoire des doctrines médiévales', *Revue des sciences philosophiques et théologiques* 79 (1995), 113–59 (pp. 150–1).

24 See Alastair Minnis, 'Fifteenth-Century Versions of Thomistic Literalism: Girolamo Savonarola and Alfonso de Madrigal', in Lerner (ed.), *Spätmittelalterlichen Bibelexegese*, pp. 163–80.

25 'State of Biblical Hermeneutics', p. 38.

26 *Ibid.*, p. 38.

27 'Wyclifs Metaphysik des extremen Realismus', p. 717.

28 On Hussitism, its relationship to Wyclif, and its contemporary impact on thinkers such as Gerson, see the various publications of scholars such as Vilém Herold, Zénon Kaluza and František Šmahel. Also see Anne Hudson, 'From Oxford to Prague: The Writings of John Wyclif and His English Followers in Bohemia', *The Slavonic and East European Review* 75 (1997), 642–57.

Bibliography

In the following Bibliography, 'Primary Sources' lists only those manuscripts and primary texts which are cited in the book; 'Secondary Sources' lists cited works and other scholarship broadly relevant to the issues discussed.

PRIMARY SOURCES

Manuscripts

After each manuscript citation the text concerned is identified in brackets.

Assisi

Biblioteca Communale 192 (Tract on images ascribed to Palmer)

Cambridge

Corpus Christi College 142 (Love)
Corpus Christi College 143 (Love)
Corpus Christi College 213 (Jean Galope's translation of *Meditationes vitae christi*)
Fitzwilliam Museum McClean 127 (Love)
Fitzwilliam Museum McClean 133 (Glossed Gospels)
Gonville and Caius College, 803/807, frag. 36 (ascription to Ullerston)
St. John's College C. 21 (Margarete Porete)
St. John's College D. 8 (*Meditationes vitae christi*)
Trinity College B.1.38 (Glossed Gospels)
Trinity College B.15.11 (Palmer's Determination)
Trinity College B.15.16 (Love)
Trinity College B.15.32 (Love)
University Library, Additional 6315 (*Meditationes vitae christi*)
University Library, Additional 6578 (Love)
University Library, Additional 6686 (Love)
University Library, Dd.viii.16 (Netter)
University Library, Dd.viii.17 (Netter)
University Library, Hh.i.11 (Miscellany; Love)

Bibliography

University Library, Hh.iii.13 (*Meditationes vitae christi*)
University Library, Ii.vi.26 (Lollard vernacular tracts in favour of biblical translation)
University Library, Kk.iv.23 (*Meditationes vitae christi*)
University Library, Ll.iv.3 (Love)
University Library, Mm.v.15 (Love)

Dublin

Trinity College 245 (C.V.6) (*Dialogue between Reson and Gabbyng*)

Edinburgh

National Library of Scotland, Advocates' Library, 18.1.7 (Love)

Glasgow

University Library, Gen. 1130 (Love)
Glasgow University, Hunterian Library T.3.15 (Love)

London

British Library, Additional 11565 (Love)
British Library, Additional 19901 (Love)
British Library, Additional 21006 (Love)
British Library, Additional 28026 (Glossed Gospels)
British Library, Additional 30031 (Love)
British Library, Additional 41175 (Glossed Gospels)
British Library, Arundel 112 (Love)
British Library, Arundel 364 (Love)
British Library, Harley 31 (Palmer's tract on images)
British Library, Royal 7A. i (*Meditationes vitae christi*)
British Library, Royal 7D. xvii (*Meditationes vitae christi*)
British Library, Royal 18C. x (Love)
Lambeth Palace 1033 (Wycliffite Bible)

Manchester

Chetham's Library, 6690 (Love)
John Rylands Library, Eng. 94 (Love)
John Rylands Library, Eng. 98 (Love)
John Rylands Library, Eng. 413 (Love)

New York

Pierpont Morgan Library, 226 (Love)
Pierpont Morgan Library, 648 (Love)

Bibliography

Oxford

Bodleian Library, Bodley 131 (Love)
Bodleian Library, Bodley 143 (Glossed Gospels)
Bodleian Library, Bodley 162 (*Meditationes vitae christi*)
Bodleian Library, Bodley 207 (Love)
Bodleian Library, Bodley 243 (Glossed Gospels)
Bodleian Library, Bodley 261 (Netter)
Bodleian Library, Bodley 262 (Netter)
Bodleian Library, Bodley 288 (Lollard Rolle Psalter)
Bodleian Library, Bodley 467 (Rolle Psalter)
Bodleian Library, Bodley 529 (*Meditationes vitae christi*)
Bodleian Library, Bodley 634 (Love)
Bodleian Library, Bodley 703 (Woodford)
Bodleian Library, Bodley 877 (Lollard Rolle Psalter)
Bodleian Library, Canon Liturg. 226 (*Meditationes vitae christi*)
Bodleian Library, Hatton 12 (Rolle Psalter)
Bodleian Library, Hatton 31 (Love)
Bodleian Library, Laud Misc. 235 (Glossed Gospels)
Bodleian Library, Laud Misc. 706 (macaronic sermons)
Bodleian Library, e Museo 35 (Love)
Bodleian Library, Rawlinson A. 387B (Love)
Brasenose College e. ix (Love)
Lincoln College, Lat. 106 (Netter)
Magdalen College 153 (Netter)
Magdalen College 157 (Netter)
Merton College K.2.2 (Butler's Determination)
University College 123 (Love)
Wadham College 5 (Love)

Paris

Bibliothèque Nationale, Ital. 115 (Italian translation of *Meditationes vitae christi*)

Tokyo

Prof. T. Takamiya 4 (Love)
Prof. T. Takamiya 8 (Love)
Prof. T. Takamiya 20 (Love)
Prof. T. Takamiya 63 (Love)
Waseda University Library, NE 3691 (Love)

Vienna

Österreichische Nationalbibliothek 4133 (Ullerston's Determination)

Bibliography

Other primary sources

Abelard, Peter: *Theologia Christiana*, in E. M. Buytaert (ed.), *Petri Abaelardi Opera Theologica II, CCCM* 12 (Turnhout, 1969)

Alan of Lille: *De Fide Catholica*, in *Alani de Insulis... Opera Omnia*, in *PL* 210. 305–430

Alexander of Hales: *Summa Theologiae*, 4 vols. in 5 (Quaracchi, 1924–48)

Aquinas, Thomas: *The Trinity and the Unicity of the Intellect*, trans. Rose Emmanuella Brennan (St Louis and London, 1946)

Summa Theologiae, 60 vols., Blackfriars edn. (London, 1964–76)

Arnold, Thomas (ed.): *Select English Works of John Wyclif*, 3 vols. (Oxford, 1869–71)

Augustine, St: *De Doctrina Christiana*, trans. as *On Christian Doctrine* by J. F. Shaw, in *A Select Library of the Nicene and Post-Nicene Fathers of the Christian Church* (Grand Rapids, Michigan, 1883, repr. 1973)

Lectures and Tractates on the Gospel according to St John, trans. James Innes, 2 vols. (Edinburgh, 1874)

Super Genesim ad litteram, ed. Joseph Zycha, *Corpus Scriptorum Ecclesiasticorum Latinorum* 28 (Prague, Vienna and Leipzig, 1894)

Bacon, Roger: *Opus Tertium*, in J. S. Brewer (ed.), *Rogeri Bacon Opera Quedam Hactenus Inedita* (Rolls Series, London, 1859)

Barratt, Alexandra (ed.): *Women's Writing in Middle English* (London and New York, 1992)

Bonaventura: see Pseudo-Bonaventura

Bühler, C. F. (ed.): 'A Lollard Tract: On Translating the Bible into English', *Medium Aevum* 7 (1938), 167–83

Butler, William: 'Contra translacionem anglicanam', ed. Margaret Deanesly in *The Lollard Bible and other Medieval Biblical Versions* (Cambridge, 1920), pp. 401–18

Butrym, A. (ed.): 'A Dialogue between Christ and Satan' [or 'Dialogue betwen Reson and Gabbyng'] in 'An Edition, with Commentary, of the Wyclifite Tracts contained in Trinity College Dublin C.V.6', Ph. D. thesis, Rutgers University (1971), pp. 689–709

Capes, W. W. (ed.): *Registrum Johannis Trefnant, episcopi Herefordensis 1389–1404* (London, 1916)

Chaucer, Geoffrey: *The Riverside Chaucer*, ed. L. D. Benson (Oxford, 1988)

Cowper, J. Meadows (ed.): *Meditations on the Supper of our Lord, and the Hours of the Passion by Cardinal John Bonaventura. Drawn into English Verse by Robert Mannyng of Brunne*, EETS OS 60 (1875)

Doiron, M. (ed.): '"The Mirror of Simple Souls": A Middle English Translation', *Archivio italiano per la storia della pietà* 5 (1968), 241–355; followed by an Appendix by E. Colledge and R. Guarnieri, pp. 356–82

Fasciculi Zizaniorum, ed. W. W. Shirley (Rolls Series, 1858)

Forshall, J. and F. Madden (eds.): *The Holy Bible... made from the Latin Vulgate by John Wycliffe and his Followers*, 4 vols. (Oxford 1850)

Gascoigne, Thomas: *Loci e Libro Veritatum*, ed. James E. Thorold Rogers (Oxford, 1881)

Bibliography

Gerson, Jean: *De distinctione verarum revelationum a falsis*, in Palémon Glorieux (ed.), *Oeuvres Complètes*, 10 vols. (Tournai, 1962–73), vol. III (1962), pp. 36–56

De probatione spirituum, in Glorieux (ed.), *Oeuvres Complètes*, vol. IX (1973), pp. 177–85

Jean Gerson: Early Works, trans. Brian Patrick McGuire (New York and Mahwah, 1998)

Hogg, James (ed.): *The Speculum Devotorum of an Anonymous Carthusian of Sheen*, 2 vols., Analecta Cartusiana 12 (Salzburg, 1973)

Horstman, Carl (ed.): *Yorkshire Writers: Richard Rolle of Hampole, an English Father of the Church, and his Followers*, 2 vols. (London, 1895–6)

Hudson, Anne (ed.): *Selections from English Wycliffite Writings* (Cambridge, 1978)

Hudson, Anne, and Pamela Gradon (eds.): *English Wycliffite Sermons*, 5 vols. (Oxford, 1983–96)

Jerome, St: *Letters and Selected Works*, trans. W. H. Fremantle, in *A Select Library of the Nicene and Post-Nicene Fathers of the Christian Church* (Oxford and New York, 1893)

Lindberg, Conrad (ed.): *De Officio Pastorali*, in *English Wyclif Tracts 1–3*, Studia Anglistica Norvegica 5 (Oslo, 1991), pp. 30–81

Love, Nicholas: *The Mirror of the Blessed Life of Jesus Christ*, ed. Michael G. Sargent (New York and London, 1992)

The Mirrour of the Blessed Lyf of Jesu Christ, ed. L. F. Powell (Oxford, 1908)

Lyra, Nicholas of: *Nicholas of Lyra's Apocalypse Commentary*, ed. and trans. Philip D. W. Krey (Kalamazoo, Mich., 1997)

Minnis, A. J., and A. B. Scott, with David Wallace (eds.): *Medieval Literary Theory and Criticism c.1100–c.1375: The Commentary-Tradition* (Oxford, 1988)

Mirk, John: *Mirk's Festial*, ed. Theodor Erbe (EETS ES 96, 1905)

Netter, Thomas, of Walden: *Doctrinale Antiquitatum Fidei Ecclesiae Catholicae*, 3 vols., ed. B. Blanciotti (Venice, 1757–9; repr. Farnborough, 1967)

Doctrinale Antiquitatum Fidei Ecclesiae Catholicae, ed. Jodocus Badius Ascensius (Paris, 1521–32)

Doctrinale Antiquitatum Fidei Ecclesiae Catholicae, ed. Giovanni Battista de Rossi (Venice, 1571)

Ockham, William of: *Summa Logicae*, ed. P. Boehner, G. Gál and S. Brown (St Bonaventure, N.Y., 1974)

Palmer, Thomas: 'De translacione sacrae scripturae in linguam anglicanam', ed. Margaret Deanesly in *The Lollard Bible*, pp. 418–37

Pseudo-Bonaventura: *Meditationes Vitae Christi*, in A. C. Peltier (ed.), *S. Bonaventurae Opera Omnia*, 15 vols. (Paris, 1864–71), vol. XII (1868), pp. 509–630

Ioannis de Cavlibus Meditaciones vite Christi, ed. M. Stallings-Taney, CCCM 153 (Turnhout, 1997)

Ragusa, Isa and Rosalie B. Green (eds. and trans.): *Meditations on the Life of Christ: An Illustrated Manuscript of the Fourteenth Century* (Princeton, 1961)

Robert of Basevorn: *Forma Praedicandi*, trans. Leopold Krul, in James J. Murphy (ed.), *Three Medieval Rhetorical Arts* (Berkeley and Los Angeles, 1971), pp. 111–215

Bibliography

Smith, P. M. (ed.): 'An Edition of Parts I–v of the Wycliffite Translation of Clement of Llanthony's Gospel Harmony "Unum ex Quattuor" known as *Oon of Foure*', Ph.D. thesis, University of Southampton (1984)

Swinburn, L. M. (ed.): *The Lanterne of Liȝt* (EETS OS 151, 1917)

Wilkins, David (ed.): *Concilia Magnae Brittaniae et Hiberniae*, 4 vols. (London, 1737)

Woodford, William: *Quattuor Determinationes in Materia de Religione*, ed. M. D. Dobson (unpublished thesis, [Oxford, c.1932])

De Dominio Civili Clericorum, ed. Eric Doyle, *Archivum Franciscanum Historicum* 66 (1973), 49–109

Wyclif, John: *De Apostasia*, ed. M. H. Dziewicki, Wyclif Society (London, 1889)

De Benedicta Incarnatione, ed. Edward Harris, Wyclif Society (London, 1886)

De Civili Dominio, ed. R. L. Poole (Book I), Wyclif Society (London, 1885); and J. Loserth (Books II and III), 3 vols., Wyclif Society (London, 1900–4)

Dialogus sive Speculum Ecclesie Militantis, ed. Alfred W. Pollard, Wyclif Society (London, 1886)

De Divinis Mandatis, ed. J. Loserth and F. D. Matthew, Wyclif Society (London, 1922)

De Ecclesia, ed. J. Loserth, Wyclif Society (London, 1886)

De Gradibus Cleri, in J. Loserth (ed.), *Opera Minora*, Wyclif Society (London, 1913), pp. 140–4

De Logica I, ed. M. H. Dziewicki, Wyclif Society (London, 1893)

De Nova Praevaricantia Mandatorum, in Rudolf Buddensieg (ed.), *John Wiclif's Polemical Works in Latin*, 2 vols., Wyclif Society (London, 1883), vol. I, pp. 116–150

De Officio Pastorali, ed. G. Lechler (Leipzig, 1863)

Johannis Wyclif Summa Insolubilium, ed. Paul Vincent Spade and G. A. Wilson (Binghampton, N.Y., 1986)

On Universals (Tractatus de Universalibus), trans. Anthony Kenny (Oxford, 1985)

De Veritate Sacrae Scripturae, ed. Rudolf Buddensieg, 3 vols., Wyclif Society (London, 1905–7)

SECONDARY SOURCES

Abulafia, Anna Sapir: 'Jewish Carnality in Twelfth-Century Renaissance Thought', in Diana Wood (ed.), *Christianity and Judaism*, SCH 29 (Oxford, 1992), pp. 59–75

Ackroyd, P. R. and C. F. Evans (eds.): *The Cambridge History of the Bible I: From the Beginnings to Jerome* (Cambridge, 1970)

Alford, John A.: 'The Idea of Reason in *Piers Plowman*', in E. D. Kennedy, R. Waldron and J. S. Wittig (eds.), *Medieval English Studies Presented to George Kane* (Cambridge, 1988), pp. 199–215

Allen, Judson Boyce: *The Friar as Critic: Literary Attitudes in the Later Middle Ages* (Nashville, 1971)

Armstrong, A. H. (ed.): *The Cambridge History of Later Greek and Early Medieval Philosophy* (Cambridge, 1967)

Ashworth, E. J.: 'Equivocation and Analogy in Fourteenth Century Logic: Ockham, Burley and Buridan', in B. Mojsisch and Olaf Pluta (eds.), *Historia Philosophiae Medii Aevi: Studien zur Geschichte der Philosophie des Mittelalters* (Amsterdam, 1991), pp. 23–43

'Analogy and Equivocation in Thirteenth-Century Logic: Aquinas in Context', *Mediaeval Studies* 54 (1992), 94–135

'Les Manuels de logique à l'Université d'Oxford aux xive et xve siècles', in Hamesse (ed.), *Manuels, programmes de cours*, pp. 351–70

'Analogy, Univocation and Equivocation in Some Early Fourteenth Century Authors', in J. Marenbon (ed.), *Aristotle in Britain during the Middle Ages* (Turnhout, 1996), pp. 233–47

Aston, Margaret: *Thomas Arundel: A Study of Church Life in the Reign of Richard II* (Oxford, 1967)

Lollards and Reformers: Images and Literacy in Late Medieval Religion (London, 1984)

'Lollards and Images', in Aston, *Lollards and Reformers*, pp. 135–92

'Lollardy and Sedition, 1381–1431', in Aston, *Lollards and Reformers*, pp. 1–47

'Wyclif and the Vernacular', in Hudson and Wilks (eds.), *Ockham to Wyclif*, pp. 281–330

'Bishops and Heresy: The Defence of the Faith', in Margaret Aston, *Faith and Fire: Popular and Unpopular Religion 1350–1600* (London and Rio Grande, 1993), pp. 73–93

Asztalos, Monika: 'The Faculty of Theology', in De Ridder-Symoens (ed.), *History of the University in Europe*, pp. 409–41

Bakker, Paul J. J. M.: '*Hoc est corpus meum*: L'Analyse de la formule de consécration chez des théologiens du xive et du xve siècles', in Marmo (ed.), *Vestigia, Imagines, Verba*, pp. 427–51

Baldwin, John W.: *Masters, Princes and Merchants: The Social Views of Peter the Chanter and His Circle*, 2 vols. (Princeton, 1970)

Barratt, Alexandra: 'The Revelations of Saint Elizabeth of Hungary: Problems of Attribution', *The Library*, Series 6, 14 (1992), 1–11

Barthes, Roland: 'The Old Rhetoric: An Aide-Mémoire', in Roland Barthes, *The Semiotic Challenge*, trans. R. Howard (Oxford, 1988), pp. 11–94

Baswell, Christopher: *Virgil in Medieval England: Figuring the 'Aeneid' from the Twelfth Century to Chaucer* (Cambridge, 1995)

Bataillon, Louis Jacques: 'De la lectio à la praedicatio: commentaires bibliques et sermons au xiiie siècle', *Revue des sciences philosophiques et théologiques* 70 (1986), 559–75

Bazàn, Bernardo C., and John W. Wippel, Gérard Fransen, and Danielle Jacquart: *Les questions disputées et les questions quodlibétiques dans les facultés de théologie, de droit et de médecine*, Typologie des sources du moyen âge occidental, Fasc. 44–45 (Turnhout, 1985)

Beadle, Richard: '"Devoute ymaginacioun" and the Dramatic Sense in Love's *Mirror* and the N-Town Plays', in Oguro, Beadle and Sargent (eds.), *Nicholas Love: Waseda*, pp. 1–17

Bibliography

Benrath, Gustav Adolf: *Wyclifs Bibelkommentar* (Berlin, 1966)

'Traditionsbewußtsein, Schriftverständnis und Schriftprinzip bei Wyclif', in Zimmermann (ed.), *Antiqui und Moderni*, pp. 359–82

Biller, Peter, and Anne Hudson (eds.): *Heresy and Literacy, 1000–1530* (Cambridge, 1994)

Blamires, Alcuin: 'The Wife of Bath and Lollardy', *Medium Aevum* 58 (1989), 224–42

Blanche, A.: 'Le Sens littéral des Ecritures d'après saint Thomas d'Aquin', *Revue Thomiste* 14 (1906), 192–212

Bonner, Gerald: 'Augustine as Biblical Scholar', in Ackroyd and Evans (eds.), *Cambridge History of the Bible I*, pp. 541–63

Bostick, Curtis V.: *The Antichrist and the Lollards: Apocalypticism in Medieval and Reformation England* (Leiden, Boston and Cologne, 1998)

Boureau, Alain: 'Intellectuals in the Middle Ages, 1957–75', in Miri Rubin (ed.), *The Work of Jacques le Goff and the Challenges of Medieval History* (Woodbridge, 1997), pp. 145–55

Brinkmann, Hennig: *Mittelalterliche Hermeneutik* (Tübingen, 1980)

Brito Martins, Maria Manuela: 'Le Projét herméneutique augustinien', *Augustiniana* 48 (1998), 253–86

Brown, Stephen F.: 'Key Terms in Medieval Theological Vocabulary', in Olga Weijers (ed.), *Méthodes et instruments du travail intellectuel au moyen âge: Etudes sur le vocabulaire*, CIVICIMA 3 (Turnhout, 1990), pp. 82–96

Bruns, Gerald L.: *Inventions: Writing, Textuality and Understanding in Literary History* (New Haven, 1982)

Buc, Philippe: 'Pouvoir royal et commentaires de la Bible', *Annales: économies sociétés civilisations* 44 (1989), 691–713

L'Ambiguïté du Livre: prince, pouvoir et peuple dans les commentaires de la Bible au moyen âge (Paris, 1994)

Buridant, C.: 'Translatio medievalis: Théorie et pratique de la traduction médiévale', *Travaux de linguistique et de littérature* 21 (1983), 81–136

Burrows, Mark Stephen: *Jean Gerson and 'De Consolatione Theologiae' (1418): The Consolation of a Biblical and Reforming Theology for a Disordered Age* (Tübingen, 1991)

Campenhausen, Hans von: 'The Theological Problem of Images in the Early Church', in Hans von Campenhausen, *Tradition and Life in the Church: Essays and Lectures in Church History*, trans. A. V. Littledale (London, 1968), pp. 171–200

Carruthers, Mary: *The Book of Memory: A Study of Memory in Medieval Culture* (Cambridge, 1990)

Catto, J. I.: 'William Woodford O.F.M (c.1330–c.1397)', D.Phil. thesis, University of Oxford (1969)

'Wyclif and the Cult of the Eucharist', in Walsh and Wood (eds.), *Bible in the Medieval World*, pp. 269–86

'Some English Manuscripts of Wyclif's Latin Works', in Hudson and Wilks (eds.), *Ockham to Wyclif*, pp. 353–9

'Wyclif and Wycliffism at Oxford 1356–1430', in Catto and Evans (eds.), *History of the University of Oxford II*, pp. 175–261

Bibliography

'Theology after Wycliffism', in Catto and Evans (eds.), *History of the University of Oxford* II, pp. 263–80

Catto, J. I., and Ralph Evans (eds.): *The History of the University of Oxford* II: *Late Medieval Oxford* (Oxford, 1992)

Cavallo, G, and C. Leonardi and E. Menestò (eds.): *Lo spazio letterario del medioevo: Il medioevo latino*, vol. I, tome II (Rome, 1993)

Chadwick, N., and E. Colledge: '*Remedies Against Temptations*: The Third English Version of William Flete', *Archivio italiano per la storia della pietà* 5 (1968), 201–40

Chenu, M.-D.: 'Auctor, actor, autor', *Bulletin du Cange* 2 (1927), 81–86
Introduction à l'étude de Saint Thomas d'Aquin (Paris, 1954)
La Théologie comme science au XIIIe siècle, 3rd edn., Bibliothèque Thomiste 33 (Paris, 1957)
La Théologie au douzième siècle (Paris, 1957)

Cigman, Gloria: '*Lux luceat vestra*: The Lollard Preacher as Truth and Light', *Review of English Studies*, NS 40 (1989), 479–96

Coleman, Janet: *Ancient and Medieval Memories: Studies in the Reconstruction of the Past* (Cambridge, 1992)

Colish, Marcia L.: *The Mirror of Language: A Study in the Medieval Theory of Knowledge* (revised edn., Lincoln and London, 1983)

Conti, Alessandro D.: *Johannes Sharpe: Questio super universalia* (Florence, 1990)
'Logica intensionale e metafisica dell'essenza in John Wyclif', *Bulletino dell'Istituto Storico Italiano per il Medioevo e Archivio Muratoriano* 99 (1993), 159–219
Esistenza e verità: forme e strutture del reale in Paolo Veneto e nel pensiero filosofico del tardo medioevo (Rome, 1996)
'Analogy and Formal Distinction: On the Logical Basis of Wyclif's Metaphysics', *Medieval Philosophy and Theology* 6 (1997), 133–65

Cooper, Helen: 'Generic Variations on the Theme of Poetic and Civil Authority', in P. Boitani and A. Torti (eds.), *Poetics: Theory and Practice in Medieval English Literature* (Woodbridge, 1991), pp. 83–103

Copeland, Rita: *Rhetoric, Hermeneutics and Translation in the Middle Ages: Academic Traditions and Vernacular Texts* (Cambridge, 1991)
'Lydgate, Hawes, and the Science of Rhetoric in the Late Middle Ages', *Modern Language Quarterly* 53 (1992), 57–82
'Rhetoric and the Politics of the Literal Sense in Medieval Literary Theory: Aquinas, Wyclif and the Lollards', in P. Boitani and A. Torti (eds.), *Interpretation: Medieval and Modern* (Cambridge, 1993), pp. 1–23
(ed.): *Criticism and Dissent in the Middle Ages* (Cambridge, 1996)
'William Thorpe and His Lollard Community: Intellectual Labor and the Representation of Dissent', in David Wallace and Barbara Hanawalt (eds.), *Bodies and Disciplines: Intersections of Literature and History in Fifteenth-Century England* (Minneapolis, 1996), pp. 199–221
'Childhood, Pedagogy and the Literal Sense: From Late Antiquity to the Lollard Heretical Classroom', in Wendy Scase, Rita Copeland and David Lawton (eds.), *New Medieval Literatures* 1 (1997), 125–56

Copeland, Rita, and S. Melville: 'Allegory and Allegoresis, Rhetoric and Hermeneutics',
  Exemplaria 3 (1991), 159–87
Courtenay, William J.: 'Covenant and Causality in Pierre d'Ailly', *Speculum* 46 (1971),
  94–119
  'John of Mirecourt and Gregory of Rimini on Whether God Can Undo the Past',
  RTAM 39 (1972), 224–56
  'The Critique of Natural Causality in the Mutakallinum and Nominalism', *The
  Harvard Theological Review* 66 (1973), 77–94
  'Nominalism and Late Medieval Religion', in Trinkaus (ed.), *Pursuit of Holiness*,
  pp. 26–59
  'Augustinianism at Oxford in the Fourteenth Century', *Augustiniana* 30 (1980),
  58–70
  'Late Medieval Nominalism Revisited: 1972–82', *Journal of the History of Ideas* 44
  (1983), 159–64
  'Force of words and Figures of Speech: The Crisis over *Virtus Sermonis* in the Four-
  teenth Century', *Franciscan Studies* 44 (1984), 107–28
  Covenant and Causality in Medieval Thought (London, 1984)
  'The Bible in the Fourteenth Century: Some Observations', *Church History* 54
  (1985), 176–87
  Schools and Scholars in Fourteenth-Century England (Princeton, 1987)
  'Inquiry and Inquisition: Academic Freedom in Medieval Universities', *Church His-
  tory* 58 (1989), 168–81
  Capacity and Volition: A History of the Distinction of Absolute and Ordained Power
  (Bergamo, 1990)
  'In Search of Nominalism: Two Centuries of Historical Debate', in Ruedi Imbach
  and Alfonso Maierù (eds.), *Gli studi di filosofia medievale fra otto e novecento:
  contributo a un bilancio storiografico* (Rome, 1991), pp. 233–51
  'Theology and Theologians from Ockham to Wyclif', in Catto and Evans (eds.),
  History of the University of Oxford ii, pp. 1–34
  'Programs of Study and Genres of Scholastic Theological Production in the Four-
  teenth Century', in Hamesse (ed.), *Manuels, programmes de cours*, pp. 325–50
Coxe, Henry Octavius: *Catalogus Codicum MSS . . . in Collegiis Aulisque Oxoniensibus*,
  2 vols. (Oxford, 1852)
Curtius, Ernst Robert: *European Literature and the Latin Middle Ages*, trans. Willard
  R. Trask (London, 1953)
Dahan, Gilbert: *Les Intellectuels chrétiens et les juifs au moyen âge* (Paris, 1990)
  'Saint Thomas d'Aquin et la métaphore: rhétorique et herméneutique', *Medioevo* 18
  (1992), 85–117
Dahmus, Joseph H.: *The Prosecution of John Wyclyf* (New Haven, 1952)
De Rijk, L. M.: 'Logica Oxoniensis: an Attempt to Reconstruct a Fifteenth-Century
  Oxford Manual of Logic', *Medioevo* 3 (1977), 121–64
  La Philosophie au moyen âge (Leiden, 1985)
Deanesly, Margaret: *The Lollard Bible and Other Medieval Biblical Versions* (Cambridge,
  1920)

Bibliography

'The Gospel Harmony of John de Caulibus, or S. Bonaventura', in C. L. Kingsford (ed.), *Collectanea Franciscana II*, British Society of Franciscan Studies 10 (Manchester, 1922), pp. 10–19

Denifle, Heinrich: 'Die Handschriften der Bibel-Correctorien des 13. Jahrhunderts', in Heinrich Denifle and Franz Ehrle (eds.), *Archiv für Literatur- und Kirchen-Geschichte des Mittelalters* 4 (1888), 263–311, 470–601

Derrida, Jacques: 'White Mythology: Metaphor in the Text of Philosophy', trans. F. C. T. Moore, *New Literary History* 6 (1974), 5–74

Doiron, M.: 'The Middle English Translation of *Le Mirouer des Simples Ames*', in A. Ampe (ed.), *Dr L. Reypens Album*, Studien en Tekstuitgaven van *Ons Geestelijk Erf* 16 (Antwerp, 1964), pp. 131–52

Doyle, A. I.: 'A Survey of the Origins and Circulation of Theological writings in English in the Fourteenth, Fifteenth and Sixteenth Centuries', 2 vols., Ph.D. thesis, University of Cambridge (1953)

'Reflections on some Manuscripts of Nicholas Love's *Myrrour of the Blessed Lyf of Jesu Christ*', *Leeds Studies in English*, NS 14 (1983), 82–93

Doyle, Eric: 'William Woodford on Scripture and Tradition', in I. Vazquez (ed.), *Studio Historico-Ecclesiastica: Festgabe für L. G. Spätling* (Rome, 1977), pp. 481–504

'William Woodford, O.F.M., and John Wyclif's *De Religione*', *Speculum* 52 (1977), 329–36

'William Woodford, O.F.M. (c. 1330–c. 1400): His Life and Works together with a Study and Edition of his "Responsiones Contra Wiclevum et Lollardos"', *Franciscan Studies* 43 (1983), 17–187

Dronke, Peter: *Fabula: Explorations into the Uses of Myth in Medieval Platonism* (Leiden, 1974)

'Integumenta Virgilii', in *Lectures médiévales de Virgile*, Collection de l'école française de Rome (Rome, 1985), pp. 313–29

Dante and Medieval Latin Traditions (Cambridge, 1986)

Dubois, D. J.: 'Thomas Netter of Walden, O.C. (c. 1372–1430)', B.Litt. thesis, University of Oxford (1978)

Dubois, Jacques: 'Comment les moines du Moyen Age chantaient et goûtaient les Saintes Ecritures', in Riché and Lobrichon (eds.), *Moyen age et la Bible*, pp. 261–98

Duffy, Eamon: *The Stripping of the Altars: Traditional Religion in England 1400–1580* (New Haven, 1992)

Duggan, Charles: *Twelfth Century Decretal Collections and their Importance in English History* (London, 1963)

Eldredge, Lawrence: 'Changing Concepts of Church Authority in the Later Fourteenth Century: Peter Ceffons of Clairvaux and William Woodford, O.F.M.', *Revue de l'Université d'Ottawa* 48 (1978), 170–8

Emden, A. B.: *A Biographical Register of the University of Oxford to AD 1500*, 3 vols. (Oxford, 1957–9)

Evans, G. R.: *Old Arts and New Theology: The Beginnings of Theology as an Academic Discipline* (Oxford, 1980)

Bibliography

The Language and Logic of the Bible: The Road to Reformation (Cambridge, 1985)

'Wyclif's *Logic* and Wyclif's Exegesis; the Context', in Walsh and Wood (eds.), *Bible in the Medieval World*, pp. 287–300

'Wyclif on Literal and Metaphorical', in Hudson and Wilks (eds.), *Ockham to Wyclif*, pp. 259–66

Problems of Authority in the Reformation Debates (Cambridge, 1992)

Philosophy and Theology in the Middle Ages (London, 1993)

Farr, William: *John Wyclif as Legal Reformer* (Leiden, 1974)

Fletcher, Alan J.: 'John Mirk and the Lollards', *Medium Aevum* 56 (1987), 217–24

Fletcher, J. M.: 'Teaching and the Study of Arts at Oxford: c. 1400–c. 1520', D.Phil. thesis, University of Oxford (1961)

'Developments in the Faculty of Arts 1370–1520', in Catto and Evans (eds.), *History of the University of Oxford* II, pp. 315–45

Forde, Simon: 'Theological Sources cited by Two Canons of Repton: Philip Repyngdon and John Eyton', in Hudson and Wilks (eds.), *Ockham to Wyclif*, pp. 419–28

Forte, S. L: 'Simon of Boraston: His Life and Writings', *Archivum Fratrum Praedicatorum* 22 (1952), 321–45

Fried, Johannes (ed.): *Die abendländische Freiheit vom 10. zum 14. Jahrhundert: Der Wirkungszussamenhang von Idee und Wirklichkeit im europäischen Vergleich* (Sigmaringen, 1991)

(ed.): *Dialektik und Rhetorik im früheren und hohen Mittelalter* (Munich, 1997)

Froelich, Karlfried: '"Always to Keep the Literal Sense in Holy Scripture Means to Kill One's Soul": The State of Biblical Hermeneutics at the Beginning of the Fifteenth Century', in E. R. Miner (ed.), *Literary Uses of Typology from the Late Middle Ages to the Present* (Princeton, 1977), pp. 20–48

Fumagalli Beonio-Brocchieri, M. T., and Zénon Kaluza (eds.): *John Wyclif: Logic, Politics, Theology* (Milan, forthcoming)

Furnish, S.: 'The *Ordinatio* of Huntington Library, MS HM 149: An East Anglian Manuscript of Nicholas Love's *Mirrour*', *Manuscripta* 34 (1990), 50–65

Gabriel, Astrik L.: 'The Ideal Master of the Mediaeval University', *Catholic Historical Review* 60 (1974), 1–40

'*Translatio studii*: Spurious Dates of Foundation of Some Early Universities', in *Fälschungen im Mittelalter: Internationale Kongreß der Monumenta Germaniae Historica (München, 16–19 September 1986)*, 6 vols. (Hanover, 1988), vol. I, pp. 601–26

Gelber, Hester Goodenough, 'Logic and the Trinity: A Clash of Values in Scholastic Thought, 1300–1335', Ph.D. thesis, University of Wisconsin (1974)

Exploring the Boundaries of Reason: Three Questions on the Nature of God by Robert Holcot OP (Toronto, 1983)

Gellrich, Jesse M.: *Discourse and Dominion in the Fourteenth Century: Oral Contexts of Writing in Philosophy, Politics and Poetry* (Princeton, 1995)

Ghellinck, J. de: 'Dialectique et dogme aux xe-xiie siècles', in *Festgabe zum 60. Geburtstag Clemens Baeumker*, Beiträge zur Geschichte der Philosophie des Mittelalters, Supplementband 1 (Münster, 1913), pp. 79–99

Bibliography

'Patristique et argument de tradition au bas moyen âge', in Albert Lang, Joseph Lechner and Michael Schmaus (eds.), *Aus der Geisteswelt des Mittelalters*, BGPTM, Supplementband III. I. Halband (Münster, 1935), pp. 403–26

'*Originale* et *Originalia*', *Bulletin du Cange* 14 (1939), 95–105

Le Mouvement théologique du XIIe siècle (Bruges, Brussels and Paris, 1948)

Gilbert, Neal Ward: 'Ockham, Wyclif and the "Via Moderna"', in Zimmermann (ed.), *Antiqui und Moderni*, pp. 85–125

Gillespie, Vincent: '*Doctrina* and *Predicacio*: The Design and Function of some Pastoral Manuals', *Leeds Studies in English*, NS 11 (1980), 36–50

'The Literary Form of the Middle English Pastoral Manual with particular reference to the *Speculum Christiani* and some related texts', D.Phil. thesis, University of Oxford (1981)

'*Lukynge in haly bukes*: *Lectio* in some Late Medieval Spiritual Miscellanies', in Hogg (ed.), *Spätmittelalterliche geistliche Literatur*, vol. II, pp. 1–27

'Vernacular Books of Religion', in Griffiths and Pearsall (eds.), *Book Production and Publishing in Britain*, pp. 317–44

Glorieux, Palémon: *La littérature quodlibétique de 1260 à 1320*, 2 vols., Bibliothèque Thomiste 5 & 21 (Kain, 1925–35)

'Le Chancelier Gerson et la réforme de l'enseignement', in E. Callistus (ed.), *Mélanges offerts à Etienne Gilson* (Toronto, 1959), pp. 285–98

'L'Enseignement au moyen âge: techniques et méthodes en usage à la Faculté de Théologie de Paris', *AHDLMA* 43 (1969), 65–186

Goff, Jacques le: 'Les intellectuels au moyen âge', in Jacques le Goff and Béla Köpeczi (eds.), *Intellectuels français, intellectuels hongrois: XIIe–XXe siècles* (Budapest and Paris, 1985), pp. 11–22

Gössmann, Elisabeth: *Metaphysik und Heilsgeschichte: Eine theologische Untersuchung der Summa Halensis (Alexander von Hales)* (Munich, 1964)

Grabmann, Martin: *Die Geschichte der scholastischen Methode*, 2 vols. (Freiburg im Breisgau, 1909–11)

Gradon, Pamela: 'Relation of the English cycle to Wyclif's Latin Sermons,' in the introduction to *English Wycliffite Sermons*, vol. III, pp. xcix–cxlviii

Grant, R. M.: 'The New Testament Canon', in Ackroyd and Evans (eds.), *Cambridge History of the Bible I*, pp. 284–308

Gregory, Tullio: 'Forme di conoscenza e ideali di sapere nella cultura medievale', in M. Asztalos, J. E. Murdoch and I. Niiniluoto (eds.), *Knowledge and the Sciences in Medieval Philosophy: Proceedings of the Eighth International Congress of Medieval Philosophy*, vol. I, Acta Philosophica Fennica 48 (Helsinki, 1990), pp. 10–71

Griffiths, Jeremy and Derek Pearsall (eds.): *Book Production and Publishing in Britain 1375–1475* (Cambridge, 1989)

Guarnieri, R.: 'Il movimento del libero spirito', *Archivio italiano per la storia della pietà* 4 (1965), 351–708

Gwynn, Aubrey: *The English Austin Friars in the Time of Wyclif* (London, 1940)

Hailperin, Herman: *Rashi and the Christian Scholars* (Pittsburgh, 1963)

275

Bibliography

Hamesse, J. (ed.): *Manuels, programmes de cours et techniques d'enseignement dans les universités médiévales* (Louvain, 1994)

Hankey, W. J.: 'Magis...pro nostra scientia: John Wyclif, his Mediaeval Predecessors and Reformed Successors, and a Pseudo-Augustinian Eucharistic Decretal', *Augustiniana* 45 (1995), 213–45

Hankinson, R. J.: 'Philosophy of Science', in Jonathan Barnes (ed.), *The Cambridge Companion to Aristotle* (Cambridge, 1995), pp. 109–39

Hanna III, Ralph: 'Compilatio and the Wife of Bath: Latin Backgrounds, Ricardian Texts', in A. J. Minnis (ed.), *Latin and Vernacular: Studies in Late Medieval Texts and Manuscripts* (Cambridge, 1989), pp. 1–11

'The Difficulty of Ricardian Prose Translation: The Case of the Lollards', *Modern Language Quarterly* 51 (1990), 319–40

'Vae Octuplex, Lollard Socio-Textual Ideology, and Ricardian-Lancastrian Prose Translation', in Copeland (ed.), *Criticism and Dissent*, pp. 244–63

Hargreaves, Henry: 'The Marginal Glosses to the Wycliffite New Testament', *Studia Neophilologica* 33 (1961), 285–300

'The Wycliffite Versions', in Lampe (ed.), *Cambridge History of the Bible* II, pp. 387–415

'Popularising Biblical Scholarship: The Role of the Wycliffite *Glossed Gospels*', in Lourdaux and Verhelst (eds.), *Bible and Medieval Culture*, pp. 171–89

Harvey, E. Ruth: *The Inward Wits: Psychological Theory in the Middle Ages and the Renaissance* (London, 1975)

Harvey, Margaret M.: 'Lollardy and the Great Schism: Some Contemporary Perceptions', in Hudson and Wilks (eds.), *Ockham to Wyclif*, pp. 385–96

'The Diffusion of the *Doctrinale* of Thomas Netter of Walden in the Fifteenth and Sixteenth Centuries', in L. Smith and B. Ward (eds.), *Intellectual Life in the Middle Ages: Essays Presented to Margaret Gibson* (London and Rio Grande, 1992), pp. 281–94

Hasenohr, Geneviève: 'Religious reading amongst the laity in France in the fifteenth century', in Biller and Hudson (eds.), *Heresy and Literacy*, pp. 204–21

Herold, Vilém: 'Wyclifs Polemik gegen Ockhams Auffassung der platonischen Ideen und ihr Nachklang in der tschechischen hussitischen Philosophie', in Hudson and Wilks (eds.), *Ockham to Wyclif*, pp. 185–215

Hödl, Ludwig: 'Universale christliche Ethik und particulares kirchliches Ethos im unterschiedlichen Verständnis der scholastischen Theologie von der "perfectio evangelica"', in Wilpert (ed.), *Universalismus und Particularismus*, pp. 20–41

Hoenen, Maarten J. F. M.: *Marsilius of Inghen: Divine Knowledge in Late Medieval Thought* (Leiden, New York and Cologne, 1993)

'Theology and Metaphysics: the Debate between John Wyclif and John Kenningham on the Principles of Reading the Scriptures', forthcoming in Kaluza and Fumagalli Beonio-Brocchieri (eds.), *John Wyclif*

Hoffmann, Fritz: 'Robert Holcot – Die Logik in der Theologie', in Wilpert (ed.), *Metaphysik im Mittelalter*, pp. 624–39

Bibliography

Die theologische Methode des Oxforder Dominikanlehrers Robert Holcot, BGPTM, NS 5 (Münster, 1972)

Hogg, James (ed.): *Spätmittelalterliche geistliche Literatur in der Nationalsprache*, 2 vols., Analecta Cartusiana 106 (Salzburg, 1983–4)

Hübener, Wolfgang: 'Der theologisch-philosophische Konservativismus des Jean Gerson', in Zimmermann (ed.), *Antiqui und Moderni*, pp. 171–200

Hudson, Anne: 'A Wycliffite Scholar of the Early Fifteenth Century', in Walsh and Wood (eds.), *Bible in the Medieval World*, pp. 301–15

Lollards and their Books (London and Ronceverte, 1985)

'A Lollard Compilation and the Dissemination of Wycliffite Thought', in Hudson, *Lollards and their Books*, pp. 13–29

'The Debate on Bible Translation, Oxford 1401', in Hudson, *Lollards and their Books*, pp. 67–84

'Lollardy: The English Heresy?', in Hudson, *Lollards and their Books*, pp. 141–63

'A Lollard Sect Vocabulary?', in Hudson, *Lollards and their Books*, pp. 165–80

'Some Aspects of Lollard Book Production', in Hudson, *Lollards and their Books*, pp. 181–91

'Wycliffism in Oxford 1381–1411', in Kenny (ed.), *Wyclif in his Times*, pp. 67–84

'Wyclif and the English Language', in Kenny (ed.), *Wyclif in his Times*, pp. 85–103

'Biblical Exegesis in Wycliffite writings', in *John Wyclif e la tradizione degli studi biblici in Inghilterra*, Dipartimento di lingue e letterature straniere moderne: Sezione di anglistica (Genoa, 1987), pp. 61–79

The Premature Reformation: Wycliffite Texts and Lollard History (Oxford, 1988)

'William Thorpe and the Question of Authority', in G. R. Evans (ed.), *Christian Authority: Essays in Honour of Henry Chadwick* (Oxford, 1988), pp. 127–37

'Lollard Book Production', in Griffiths and Pearsall (eds.), *Book Production and Publishing in Britain*, pp. 125–42

'The Mouse in the Pyx: Popular Heresy and the Eucharist', *Trivium* 26 (1991), 40–53

'The King and Erring Clergy: A Wycliffite Contribution', in Wood (ed.), *Church and Sovereignty*, pp. 269–78

'"Laicus litteratus": the paradox of Lollardy', in Biller and Hudson (eds.), *Heresy and Literacy*, pp. 222–36

'Lollardy and Eschatology', in Patschovsky and Šmahel (eds.), *Eschatologie*, pp. 99–113

'From Oxford to Prague: The Writings of John Wyclif and his English Followers in Bohemia', *The Slavonic and East European Review* 75 (1997), 642–57

'Cross-referencing in Wyclif's Latin Works', in Peter Biller and Barrie Dobson (eds.), *The Medieval Church: Universities, Heresy and the Religious Life*, SCH Subsidia 11 (Oxford, 1999), pp. 193–215

'*Peculiaris regis clericus*: Wyclif and the Issue of Authority', in Martin Gosman, Arjo Vanderjagt and Jan Veenstra (eds.), *The Growth of Authority in the Medieval West* (Groningen, 1999), pp. 63–81

'The Development of Wyclif's *Summa Theologiae*', forthcoming in Kaluza and Fumagalli Beonio-Brocchieri (eds.), *John Wyclif*

Hudson, Anne, and Michael Wilks (eds.): *From Ockham to Wyclif*, SCH Subsidia 5 (Oxford, 1987)

Hunt, Simon: 'An Edition of Tracts in Favour of Scriptural Translation and of Some Texts Connected with Lollard Vernacular Biblical Scholarship', D.Phil. thesis, University of Oxford (1994)

Hurley, Michael: '"Scriptura Sola": Wyclif and his Critics', *Traditio* 16 (1960), 275–352

Hurnard, N. D.: 'Studies in Intellectual Life in England from the Middle of the Fifteenth Century till the Time of Colet', D.Phil. thesis, University of Oxford (1935)

Imbach, Ruedi: *Laien in der Philosophie des Mittelalters: Hinweise und Anregungen zu einem vernachlässigten Thema* (Amsterdam, 1989)

Irvine, Martin: 'Interpretation and the Semiotics of Allegory in Clement of Alexandria, Origen and Augustine', *Semiotica* 63 (1987), 33–79

   The Making of Textual Culture: 'Grammatica' and Literary Theory, 350–1100 (Cambridge, 1994)

Jacobi, Klaus (ed.): *Argumentationstheorie: Scholastische Forschungen zu den logischen und semantischen Regeln korrekten Folgerns* (Leiden, New York and Cologne, 1993)

Jager, Eric: *The Tempter's Voice: Language and the Fall in Medieval Literature* (Ithaca, N.Y., 1993)

James, M. R.: *The Western Manuscripts in the Library of Trinity College, Cambridge: A Descriptive Catalogue*, 4 vols. (Cambridge, 1900–4)

Jardine, Lisa and Anthony Grafton: *From Humanism to the Humanities: Education and the Liberal Arts in Fifteenth- and Sixteenth-Century Europe* (London, 1986)

Jeauneau, Édouard: 'L'usage de la notion d'integumentum à travers les gloses de Guillaume de Conches', *AHDLMA* 24 (1958), 35–100

Jeffrey, David Lyle: *Chaucer and Scriptural Tradition* (Ottawa, 1984)

Johnson, I. R.: 'The Late-Medieval Theory and Practice of Translation with special reference to some Middle English Lives of Christ', Ph.D. thesis, University of Bristol (1990)

Jolivet, Jean: *Arts du langage et théologie chez Abélard* (Paris, 1969)

Jones, W. R.: 'Lollards and Images: The Defence of Religious Art in Later Medieval England', *Journal of the History of Ideas* 34 (1973), 27–50

Jordan, Mark D., and Kent Emery, Jr. (eds.): *Ad Litteram: Authoritative Texts and Their Medieval Readers* (Notre Dame, 1992),

Justice, Steven: *Writing and Rebellion: England in 1381* (Berkeley, Los Angeles and London, 1994)

Kalidova, Robert: 'Joannus Wyclifs Metaphysik des extremen Realismus und ihre Bedeutung im Endstadium der mittelalterlichen Philosophie', in Wilpert (ed.), *Metaphysik im Mittelalter*, pp. 717–23

Kaluza, Zénon: *Les Querelles doctrinales à Paris: Nominalistes et réalistes aux confins du xive et du xve siècles* (Bergamo, 1988)

Bibliography

'Les Sciences et leurs langages: Note sur le Statut du 29 Décembre 1340 et le prétendu Statut perdu contre Ockham', in Luca Bianchi (ed.), *Filosofia e teologia nel trecento: Studi in ricordo di Eugenio Randi* (Louvain, 1994), pp. 197–258

'Bulletin d'histoire des doctrines médiévales', *Revue des sciences philosophiques et théologiques* 79 (1995), 113–59

Keen, Maurice: 'Wyclif, the Bible and Transubstantiation', in Kenny (ed.), *Wyclif in his Times*, pp. 1–16

Kelley, Donald R.: 'Clio and the Lawyers: Forms of Historical Consciousness in Medieval Jurisprudence', *Mediaevalia et Humanistica*, NS 5 (1974), 25–49

Kelly, Henry Ansgar: 'Lollard Inquisitions: Due and Undue Process', in Alberto Ferreiro (ed.), *The Devil, Heresy and Witchcraft in the Middle Ages* (Leiden, Boston and Cologne, 1998), pp. 279–303

'Trial Procedures Against Wyclif and Wycliffites in England and at the Council of Constance', *Huntington Library Quarterly* 61 (1998), 1–28

Kennedy, Leonard A.: 'Philosophical Scepticism in England in the Mid-Fourteenth Century', *Vivarium* 21 (1983), 35–57

'Theology the Handmaiden of Logic: A *Sentence* Commentary used by Gregory of Rimini and John Hiltalingen', *Augustiniana* 33 (1983), 142–64

'Late-Fourteenth Century Philosophical Scepticism at Oxford', *Vivarium* 23 (1985), 124–51

'Oxford Philosophers and the Existence of God, 1340–1350', *RTAM* 52 (1985), 194–208

'A Carmelite Fourteenth-Century Theological Notebook', *Carmelus* 33 (1986), 70–102

Kenny, Anthony: *Wyclif* (Oxford, 1985)

(ed.): *Wyclif in his Times* (Oxford, 1986)

'The Realism of the *De Universalibus*', in Kenny (ed.), *Wyclif in his Times*, pp. 17–29

'Realism and Determinism in the Early Wyclif', in Hudson and Wilks (eds.), *Ockham to Wyclif*, pp. 165–77

Kenny, Anthony and Jan Pinborg: 'Medieval Philosophical Literature' in Kretzmann, Kenny and Pinborg (eds.), *CHLMP*, pp. 1–42

Kiecker, J. G.: 'The Hermeneutical Principles and Exegetical Methods of Nicholas of Lyra O.F.M. (c. 1270–1349)', Ph.D. thesis, Marquette University (1978)

Köpf, Ulrich: *Die Anfänge der theologischen Wissenschaftstheorie im 13. Jahrhundert* (Tübingen, 1974)

Korolec, Jerzy B.: 'Jean Buridan et Jean de Jandun et la relation entre la Rhétorique et la Dialectique', in Wolfgang Kluxen et al. (eds.), *Sprache und Erkenntnis im Mittelalter*, 2 vols., MM 13 (Berlin, 1981), vol. II, pp. 622–27

Kretzmann, Norman: 'Continua, Indivisibles, and Change in Wyclif's Logic of Scripture', in Kenny (ed.), *Wyclif in his Times*, pp. 31–63

Kretzmann, Norman and Anthony Kenny and Jan Pinborg (eds.): *The Cambridge History of Later Medieval Philosophy* (Cambridge, 1982)

Bibliography

Krey, Philip: 'Many Readers but Few Followers: The Fate of Nicholas of Lyra's "Apocalypse Commentary" in the Hands of his Late-Medieval Admirers', *Church History* 64 (1995), 185–201

Krey, Philip, and Lesley Smith (eds.): *Nicholas of Lyra: The Senses of Scripture* (Leiden, Boston and Cologne, 2000)

Kuczynski, Michael P.: 'Rolle Among the Reformers: Orthodoxy and Heterodoxy in Wycliffite Copies of Richard Rolle's *English Psalter*', in William F. Pollard and Robert Boenig (eds.), *Mysticism and Spirituality in Medieval England* (Cambridge, 1997), pp. 177–202

Kuttner, Stephan: 'On "Auctoritas" in the Writing of Medieval Canonists: the Vocabulary of Gratian', in Stephan Kuttner, *Studies in the History of Medieval Canon Law* (Aldershot, 1990), pp. 69–80

Lambert, Malcolm: *Medieval Heresy: Popular Movements from the Gregorian Reform to the Reformation*, 2nd edn. (Oxford, 1992)

Lampe, G. W. H. (ed.): *The Cambridge History of the Bible II: The West from the Fathers to the Reformation* (Cambridge, 1969)

Leclercq, Jean: 'L'Idéal du théologien au moyen âge', *Revue des sciences religieuses* 21 (1947), 121–48

The Love of Learning and the Desire for God, trans. C. Misrahi (New York, 1961)

'Traductions de la Bible et spiritualité médiévale', in Lourdaux and Verhelst (eds.), *Bible and Medieval Culture*, pp. 263–77

Leff, Gordon: 'The Apostolic Ideal in Later Medieval Ecclesiology', *Journal of Theological Studies* NS 18 (1967), 58–82

'Wyclif and the Augustinian Tradition, with Special Reference to his *De Trinitate*', *Mediaevalia et Humanistica* NS 4 (1970), 29–39

'The Making of a Myth of a True Church in the Later Middle Ages', *Journal of Mediaeval and Renaissance Studies* 1 (1971), 1–15

'The Place of Metaphysics in Wyclif's Theology', in Hudson and Wilks (eds.), *Ockham to Wyclif*, pp. 217–32

Lerner, Robert: 'Ecstatic Dissent', *Speculum* 67 (1992), 33–57

(ed.): *Neue Richtungen in der hoch- und spätmittelalterlichen Bibelexegese* (Munich, 1996)

Leroquais, Victor: *Les livres d'heures manuscrits de la Bibliothèque Nationale*, 3 vols. and Supplement (Paris, 1927–43)

Levy, Ian: 'John Wyclif and Augustinian Realism', *Augustiniana* 48 (1998), 87–106

Lewry, P. Osmund: 'Rhetoric at Paris and Oxford in the Mid-Thirteenth Century', *Rhetorica* 1 (1983), 45–63

'Grammar, Logic and Rhetoric 1220–1320', in J. I. Catto (ed.), *The History of the University of Oxford I: The Early Oxford Schools* (Oxford, 1984), pp. 401–33

Libera, Alain de: 'La Logique de la discussion dans l'université médiévale', in *Figures et conflits rhétoriques*, Editions de l'Université de Bruxelles (Brussels, 1990), pp. 59–81

Penser au moyen âge (Paris, 1991)

Bibliography

La Querelle des universaux: De Platon à la fin du moyen âge (Paris, 1996)

Libera, Alain de, and Irène Rosier: 'Argumentation in the Middle Ages', *Argumentation* 1 (1987), 355–64

Libera, Alain de, and Irène Rosier-Catach: 'L'Analyse Scotiste de la formule de la consécration eucharistique', in Marmo (ed.), *Vestigia, Imagines, Verba*, pp. 171–202

Lobrichon, Guy: 'Une nouveauté: les gloses de la Bible', in Riché and Lobrichon (eds.), *Moyen Age et la Bible*, pp. 95–114

'L'Esegesi biblica: storia di un genere letterario (VII–XIII secolo)', in Cavallo, Leonardi and Menestò (eds.), *Lo spazio letterario*, pp. 355–81

Loewe, Raphael: 'The Medieval History of the Latin Vulgate', in Lampe (ed.), *Cambridge History of the Bible II*, pp. 102–54

Lourdaux, W. and D. Verhelst (eds.): *The Bible and Medieval Culture* (Louvain, 1979)

Lubac, Henri de: *Exégèse médiévale: les quatre sens de l'écriture*, 2 vols. in 4 (Paris, 1959–64)

Luscombe, David: 'Wyclif and Hierarchy', in Hudson and Wilks (eds.), *Ockham to Wyclif*, pp. 233–44

MacDonald, Scott: 'Theory of Knowledge', in Norman Kretzmann and Eleonore Stump (eds.), *The Cambridge Companion to Aquinas* (Cambridge, 1993), pp. 160–95

Maclean, Ian: *Interpretation and Meaning in the Renaissance: The Case of Law* (Cambridge, 1992)

Maierù, Alfonso: 'La dialettica', in Cavallo, Leonardi and Menestò (eds.), *Lo spazio letterario*, pp. 273–94

University Training in Medieval Europe, trans. D. N. Pryds (Leiden, New York and Cologne, 1994)

Maitland, F. W.: 'Wyclif on English and Roman Law', *Law Quarterly Review* 12 (1896), 76–8

Marcolino, Venicio: *Das Alte Testament in der Heilsgeschichte*, BGPTM, NS 2 (Münster, 1970)

Marenbon, John: *Later Medieval Philosophy (1150–1350)* (London, 1987; repr. 1993)

Markus, R. A.: 'Augustine, Biographical Introduction: Christianity and Philosophy', in Armstrong (ed.), *CHLGEMP*, pp. 341–53

'Augustine: Reason and Illumination', in Armstrong (ed.), *CHLGEMP*, pp. 362–73

Marmo, Costantino (ed.): *Vestigia, Imagines, Verba: Semiotics and Logic in Medieval Theological Texts (XIIth–XIVth Century)* (Turnhout, 1997)

McCord Adams, Marilyn: 'Universals in the Early Fourteenth Century', in Kretzmann, Kenny and Pinborg (eds.), *CHLMP*, pp. 411–39

McFarlane, K.B.: *John Wycliffe and the Beginnings of English Nonconformity* (London, 1952)

McGrade, Arthur Stephen: 'Somersaulting Sovereignty: A Note on Reciprocal Lordship and Servitude in Wyclif', in Wood (ed.), *Church and Sovereignty*, pp. 261–68

McHardy, A.K.: 'The Dissemination of Wyclif's Ideas', in Hudson and Wilks (eds.), *Ockham to Wyclif*, pp. 361–68

Bibliography

'*De heretico comburendo*, 1401', in Margaret Aston and Colin Richmond (eds.), *Lollardy and the Gentry in the Later Middle Ages* (Stroud and New York, 1997), pp. 112–26

McNamer, Sarah: 'Further Evidence for the Date of the Pseudo-Bonaventuran *Meditationes Vitae Christi*', *Franciscan Studies* 50 (1990), 235–61

McNiven, Peter: *Heresy and Politics in the Reign of Henry IV: the Burning of John Badby* (Woodbridge, 1987)

Meale, Carol M.: '"oft siþis with grete deuotion I þought what I miȝt do plesynge to god": The Early Ownership and Readership of Love's *Mirror*, with Special Reference to its Female Audience', in Oguro, Beadle and Sargent (eds.), *Nicholas Love: Waseda*, pp. 19–46

Miethke, Jürgen: 'Bildungsstand und Freiheitsforderung (12. bis 14. Jahrhundert)' in Fried (ed.), *Abendländische Freiheit*, pp. 221–47

Minnis, A. J.: '"Authorial Intention" and "Literal Sense" in the Exegetical Theories of Richard Fitzralph and John Wyclif: An Essay in the Medieval History of Biblical Hermeneutics', *Proceedings of the Royal Irish Academy* 75 C (1975), 1–31

'Langland's Ymaginatif and Late-Medieval Theories of Imagination', *Comparative Criticism* 3 (1981), 71–103

'Affection and Imagination in "The Cloud of Unknowing" and Hilton's "Scale of Perfection"', *Traditio* 39 (1983), 323–66

Medieval Theory of Authorship: Scholastic Literary Attitudes in the Later Middle Ages, 2nd edn. (Aldershot, 1988)

'The *Accessus* Extended: Henry of Ghent on the Transmission and Reception of Theology', in Jordan and Emery (eds.), *Ad litteram*, pp. 275–326

'Medium and Message: Henry of Ghent on Scriptural Style', in Newhauser and Alford (eds.), *Literature and Religion*, pp. 209–35

'Fifteenth-Century Versions of Thomistic Literalism: Girolamo Savonarola and Alfonso de Madrigal', in Lerner (ed.), *Spätmittelalterlichen Bibelexegese*, pp. 163–80

Molland, A. George: 'Nicole Oresme and Scientific Progress', in Zimmermann (ed.), *Antiqui und Moderni*, pp. 206–20

Moos, Peter von: 'The Use of *Exempla* in the *Policraticus* of John of Salisbury', in Michael Wilks (ed.), *The World of John of Salisbury*, SCH Subsidia 3 (Oxford, 1984), pp. 207–61

'Das argumentative Exemplum und die "wächserne Nase" der Autorität im Mittelalter', in W. J. Aerts and M. Gosman (eds.), *Exemplum et Similitudo: Alexander the Great and Other Heroes as Points of Reference in Medieval Literature* (Groningen, 1988), pp. 55–84

Geschichte als Topik: Das rhetorische Exemplum von der Antike zur Neuzeit und die 'historiae' im 'Policraticus' Johanns von Salisbury (Hildesheim, Zurich and New York, 1988)

'La retorica nel medioevo', in Cavallo, Leonardi and Menestò (eds.), *Lo spazio letterario*, pp. 231–71

Mueller, Ivan J.: 'A "Lost" *Summa* of John Wyclif', in Hudson and Wilks (eds.), *Ockham to Wyclif*, pp. 179–83

Bibliography

Mugnai, Massimo: 'La "expositio reduplicativarum" chez Walter Burleigh et Paulus Venetus', in Alfonso Maierù (ed.), *English Logic in Italy in the 14th and 15th Centuries* (Naples, 1982), pp. 305–20

Murdoch, John E.: 'From Social into Intellectual Factors: An Aspect of the Unitary Character of Late Medieval Learning', in J. E. Murdoch and E. D. Sylla (eds.), *The Cultural Context of Medieval Learning* (Dordrecht and Boston, 1975), pp. 271–339

Murphy, James J.: *Rhetoric in the Middle Ages: A History of Rhetorical Theory from St. Augustine to the Renaissance* (Berkeley and Los Angeles, 1974)

Newhauser, Richard G., and John A. Alford (eds.): *Literature and Religion in the Later Middle Ages: Philological Studies in Honor of Siegfried Wenzel* (Binghampton, N.Y., 1995)

Nolcken, Christina von: 'A "Certain Sameness" and our Response to It in English Wycliffite Texts', in Newhauser and Alford (eds.), *Literature and Religion*, pp. 191–208

Normore, Calvin: 'Future Contingents', in Kretzmann, Kenny and Pinborg (eds.), *CHLMP*, pp. 358–81

North, J. D.: 'Natural Philosophy in Late Medieval Oxford', in Catto and Evans (eds.), *History of the University of Oxford* II, pp. 65–102

Nuchelmans, Gabriel: *Theories of the Proposition: Ancient and Medieval Conceptions of the Bearers of Truth and Falsity* (Amsterdam and London, 1973)
    Late-Scholastic and Humanist Theories of the Proposition (Amsterdam, Oxford and New York, 1980)

Oberman, Heiko: *The Harvest of Medieval Theology: Gabriel Biel and Late Medieval Nominalism* (Cambridge, Mass., 1963)

Oberman, Heiko, and Frank A. James (eds.): *Via Augustini: Augustine in the Later Middle Ages, Renaissance and Reformation. Essays in Honour of Damasus Trapp, O.S.A.* (Leiden, New York, Copenhagen and Cologne, 1991)

Oguro, Shoichi and Richard Beadle and Michael G. Sargent (eds.): *Nicholas Love: Waseda 1995* (Cambridge, 1997)

Olsen, Glenn: 'The Idea of the *Ecclesia Primitiva* in the Writings of the Twelfth-Century Canonists', *Traditio* 25 (1969), 61–86

Ozment, Steven: 'Mysticism, Nominalism and Dissent', in Trinkaus (ed.), *Pursuit of Holiness*, pp. 67–92

Pantin, W. A.: *The English Church in the Fourteenth Century* (Cambridge, 1955)

Parkes, Malcolm: 'The Influence of the Concepts of *Ordinatio* and *Compilatio* on the Development of the Book', in J. J. G. Alexander and M. T. Gibson (eds.), *Medieval Learning and Literature: Essays Presented to Richard William Hunt* (Oxford, 1976), pp. 115–141
    Scribes, Scripts and Readers: Studies in the Communication, Presentation and Dissemination of Medieval Texts (London and Rio Grande, 1991)

Patschovsky, Alexander: 'Freiheit der Ketzer', in Fried (ed.), *Abendländische Freiheit*, pp. 265–80
    '"Antichrist" bei Wyclif', in Patschovsky and Šmahel (eds.), *Eschatologie*, pp. 83–98

Patschovsky, Alexander, and František Šmahel (eds.): *Eschatologie und Hussitismus, Historica*, Series Nova, Suppl. 1 (Prague, 1996)

Peikola, Matti: *Congregation of the Elect: Patterns of Self-Fashioning in English Lollard Writings* (Turku, 2000)

Pépin, Jean: *Saint Augustin et la dialectique* (Villanova, Pa., 1976)

Peters, Edward M.: 'Transgressing the Limits Set by the Fathers: Authority and Impious Exegesis in Medieval Thought', in Scott L. Waugh and Peter D. Diehl (eds.), *Christendom and Its Discontents: Exclusion, Persecution and Rebellion 1000–1500* (Cambridge, 1996), pp. 338–62

Phillips, Heather: 'John Wyclif and the Optics of the Eucharist', in Hudson and Wilks (eds.), *Ockham to Wyclif*, pp. 245–58

Press, Gerald: 'The Subject and Structure of Augustine's *De doctrina christiana*', *Augustinian Studies* 11 (1980), 99–124

Powicke, F. M.: *The Medieval Books of Merton College* (Oxford, 1931)

Pronger, Winifred A.: 'Thomas Gascoigne [Part] 1', *English Historical Review* 53 (1938), 606–26

'Thomas Gascoigne [Part] 11', *English Historical Review* 54 (1939), 20–37

Reynolds, Suzanne: *Medieval Reading: Grammar, Rhetoric and the Classical Text* (Cambridge, 1996)

Richards, M. J. B.: 'Translation, Borrowing and Original Composition in Medieval Poetry: Studies in the *Metamorphoses*, the *Ovide Moralisé* and *The Book of the Duchess*', Ph.D. thesis, University of Cambridge (1982)

Riché, Pierre: '*Divina pagina, ratio* et *auctoritas* dans la théologie carolingienne', *Settimane di studio del centro italiano di studi sull'alto medioevo* 27 (1981), 719–63

Riché, Pierre and Guy Lobrichon (eds.): *Le Moyen Age et la Bible* (Paris, 1984)

Ricoeur, Paul: *The Rule of Metaphor: Multi-Disciplinary Studies of the Creation of Meaning in Language*, trans. Robert Czerny with Kathleen McLaughlin and John Costello (London, 1977)

Ridder-Symoens, Hilde De (ed.): *A History of the University in Europe* 1: *Universities in the Middle Ages* (Cambridge, 1992)

Rist, John M.: *Augustine: Ancient Thought Baptised* (Cambridge, 1994)

Robson, J. A.: *Wyclif and the Oxford Schools: The Relation of the 'Summa de Ente' to Scholastic Debates in the Later Fourteenth Century* (Cambridge, 1961)

Rouse, Richard H. and Mary A.: *Preachers, Florilegia and Sermons: Studies on the 'Manipulus Florum' of Thomas of Ireland* (Toronto, 1979)

'Florilegia of Patristic Texts', in *Les genres littéraires dans les sources théologiques et philosophiques médiévales*, Université Catholique de Louvain, Publications de l'Institut d'Études Médiévales, 2nd series, 5 (1982), pp. 165–80

'The Franciscans and Books: Lollard Accusations and the Franciscan Response', in Hudson and Wilks (eds.), *Ockham to Wyclif*, pp. 369–84

'*Ordinatio* and *Compilatio* Revisited', in Jordan and Emery (eds.), *Ad litteram*, pp. 113–35

Russell-Smith, Joy: 'Walter Hilton and a Tract in Defence of the Veneration of Images', *Dominican Studies* 7 (1954), 180–214

Bibliography

Salter, Elizabeth: *Nicholas Love's 'Myrrour of the Blessed Lyf of Jesu Christ'*, Analecta Cartusiana 10 (Salzburg, 1974)

'The Manuscripts of Nicholas Love's *Myrrour of the Blessed Lyf of Jesu Christ* and Related Texts', in A. S. G. Edwards and Derek Pearsall (eds.), *Middle English Prose: Essays on Bibliographical Problems* (New York, 1981), pp. 115–27

Sargent, M. G.: 'The Transmission by the English Carthusians of Some Late Medieval Spiritual Writings', *Journal of Ecclesiastical History* 27 (1976), 225–40

'Bonaventura English: A Survey of the Middle English Prose Translations of Early Franciscan Literature', in Hogg (ed.), *Spätmittelalterliche geistliche Literatur*, vol. II, pp. 145–76

James Grenehalgh as Textual Critic, Analecta Cartusiana 85 (Salzburg, 1984)

'The Problem of Uniformity in Carthusian Book-Production from the *Opus Pacis* to the *Tertia Compilatio Statutorum*', in Richard Beadle and A. J. Piper (eds.), *New Science out of Old Books: Studies in Manuscripts and Early Printed Books in Honour of A. I. Doyle* (Aldershot, 1995), pp. 122–41

'Versions of the Life of Christ: Nicholas Love's *Mirror* and Related Works', *Poetica* 42 (1995), 39–70

'The Textual Affiliations of the Waseda Manuscript of Nicholas Love's *Mirror of the Blessed Life of Jesus Christ*', in Oguro, Beadle and Sargent (eds.), *Nicholas Love: Waseda*, pp. 175–274

'An Audience with the Archbishop: Devotional Literature and Ecclesiastical Politics in Late Medieval England' (forthcoming)

Scanlon, Larry: *Narrative, Authority and Power: The Medieval Exemplum and the Chaucerian Tradition* (Cambridge, 1994)

Schüssler, Hermann: *Der Primat der Heiligen Schrift als theologisches und kanonistisches Problem im Spätmittelalter* (Wiesbaden, 1977)

Schwarz, W.: 'The Meaning of *Fidus Interpres* in Medieval Translation', *Journal of Theological Studies* 45 (1944), 73–8

Scott, Kathleen L.: *Later Gothic Manuscripts 1390–1490*, 2 vols. (London, 1996)

'The Illustration and Decoration of Manuscripts of Nicholas Love's *Mirror of the Blessed Life of Jesus Christ*', in Oguro, Beadle and Sargent (eds.), *Nicholas Love: Waseda*, pp. 61–86

Shank, Michael H.: *'Unless You Believe, You Shall Not Understand': Logic, University, and Society in Late Medieval Vienna* (Princeton, 1988)

Sharpe, Richard: *A Handlist of the Latin Writers of Great Britain and Ireland before 1540* (Turnhout, 1997)

Simonetta, Stefano: 'John Wyclif Between Utopia and Plan', in Sophie Wlodek (ed.), *Société et église: textes et discussions dans les universités d'Europe centrale pendant le moyen âge tardif* (Turnhout, 1995), pp. 65–76

Simpson, James: 'From Reason to Affective Knowledge: Modes of Thought and Poetic Form in *Piers Plowman*', *Medium Aevum* 55 (1986), 1–23

Sciences and the Self in Medieval Poetry: Alan of Lille's 'Anticlaudianus' and John Gower's 'Confessio Amantis' (Cambridge, 1995)

'Desire and the Scriptural Text: Will as Reader in *Piers Plowman*', in Copeland (ed.), *Criticism and Dissent*, pp. 215–43

Smalley, Beryl: 'John Wyclif's *Postilla super totam Bibliam*', *Bodleian Library Record* 4 (1953), 186–205

'Which William of Nottingham?', *Mediaeval and Renaissance Studies* 3 (1954), 200–238

English Friars and Antiquity in the Early Fourteenth Century (Oxford, 1960)

'Problems of Exegesis in the Fourteenth Century', in Wilpert (ed.), *Antike und Orient*, pp. 266–74

'The Bible and Eternity: John Wyclif's Dilemma', *Journal of the Warburg and Courtauld Institutes* 27 (1964), 73–89

'Wyclif's *Postilla* on the Old Testament and his *Principium*', in *Oxford Studies presented to Daniel Callus*, Oxford Historical Society, NS 16 (Oxford, 1964), pp. 253–96

'The Bible in the Medieval Schools', in Lampe (ed.), *Cambridge History of the Bible II*, pp. 197–219

'Ecclesiastical Attitudes to Novelty c. 1100 – c. 1250', in Derek Baker (ed.), *Church, Society and Politics*, SCH 12 (Oxford, 1975), pp. 113–31

'The Gospels in the Paris Schools in the Late Twelfth and Early Thirteenth Centuries: Peter the Chanter, Hugh of St Cher, Alexander of Hales, John of La Rochelle', *Franciscan Studies* 39 (1979), 230–54; 40 (1980), 298–369

Studies in Medieval Thought from Abelard to Wyclif (London, 1981)

The Study of the Bible in the Middle Ages, 3rd edn. (Oxford, 1983)

'Use of the "Spiritual" Senses of Scripture in Persuasion and Argument by Scholars in the Middle Ages', *RTAM* 52 (1985), 44–63

The Gospels in the Schools: c. 1100 – c. 1280 (London, 1985)

Smith, K. S.: 'The Ecclesiology of Controversy: Scripture, Tradition and Church in the Theology of Thomas Netter of Walden', Ph.D. thesis, Cornell University (1983)

'An English Conciliarist? Thomas Netter of Walden at the Councils of Pisa and Constance', in J. R. Sweeney and S. Chodorow (eds.), *Popes, Teachers and Canon Law in the Middle Ages* (Ithaca, N.Y., 1989), pp. 290–9

Smith, Lesley: 'What was the Bible in the Twelfth and Thirteenth Centuries?', in Lerner (ed.), *Spätmittelalterliche Bibelexegese*, pp. 1–15

Somerset, Fiona: *Clerical Discourse and Lay Audience in Late Medieval England* (Cambridge, 1998)

Soskice, Janet Martin: *Metaphor and Religious Language* (Oxford, 1985)

Spade, Paul Vincent: 'Insolubilia' in Kretzmann, Kenny and Pinborg (eds.), *CHLMP*, pp. 246–53

'The Semantics of Terms' in Kretzmann, Kenny and Pinborg (eds.), *CHLMP*, pp. 188–96

Sparks, H. F. D.: 'Jerome as Biblical Scholar', in Ackroyd and Evans (eds.), *Cambridge History of the Bible I*, pp. 510–41

Spencer, H. Leith: *English Preaching in the Late Middle Ages* (Oxford, 1993)

Bibliography

Spicq, C.: *Esquisse d'une histoire de l'exégèse latine au moyen âge*, Bibliothèque Thomiste 26 (Paris, 1944)

Stadter, Ernst: 'Die Seele als "Minor Mundus" und als "Regnum": Ein Beitrag zur Psychologie der mittleren Franziskanerschule', in Wilpert (ed.), *Universalismus und Partikularismus*, pp. 56–72

Stock, Brian: *Augustine the Reader: Meditation, Self-Knowledge and the Ethics of Interpretation* (Cambridge, Mass., 1996)

Swanson, R. N.: *Universities, Academics and the Great Schism* (Cambridge, 1979)

Sydow, Jürgen: 'Gedanken über die Auctoritas in der Kanonistik des frühen 13.Jahrhunderts (bis 1234)' in Wilpert (ed.), *Antike und Orient*, pp. 253–65

Synave, P.: 'La Doctrine de saint Thomas d'Aquin sur le sens littéral des Ecritures', *Revue Biblique* 35 (1926), 40–65

Szittya, Penn R.: *The Antifraternal Tradition in Medieval Literature* (Princeton, 1986)

Tabulae Codicum Manuscriptorum . . . in Biblioteca Palatina Vindobonensi, Academia Caesarea Vindobonenesis, 7 vols. (Vienna, 1864–75), vol. III (1869)

Tachau, Katherine H.: *Vision and Certitude in the Age of Ockham: Optics, Epistemology and the Foundations of Semantics, 1250–1345* (Leiden, New York, Copenhagen and Cologne, 1988)

Tatnall, Edith C.: 'Church and State according to John Wyclyf', Ph.D. thesis, University of Colorado (1964)

'John Wyclif and *Ecclesia Anglicana*', *Journal of Ecclesiastical History* 20 (1969), 19–43

'The Condemnation of John Wyclif at the Council of Constance', in G. J. Cuming and Derek Baker (eds.), *Councils and Assemblies*, SCH 7 (Cambridge, 1971), pp. 209–18

Thijssen, J. M. M. H.: 'The Crisis over Ockhamist Hermeneutic and its Semantic Background: the Methodological Significance of the Censure of December 29, 1340', in Marmo (ed.), *Vestigia, Imagines, Verba*, pp. 371–92

Censure and Heresy at the University of Paris 1200–1400 (Philadelphia, 1998)

Thomson, J. A. F.: *The Later Lollards 1414–1520* (Oxford, 1965)

'Orthodox Religion and the Origins of Lollardy', *History* 74 (1989), 39–55

Thomson, Williel R.: *The Latin Writings of John Wyclyf: An Annotated Catalog* (Toronto, 1983)

Tierney, Brian: *Foundations of Conciliar Theory: The Contribution of the Medieval Canonists from Gratian to the Great Schism* (Cambridge, 1955, repr. 1968)

Torti, Anna: *The Glass of Form: Mirroring Structures from Chaucer to Skelton* (Cambridge, 1991)

Trapp, Damasus: 'The Portiuncula Discussion of Cremona (ca. 1380): New Light on 14th Century Disputations', *RTAM* 22 (1955), 79–94

'Augustinian Theology of the 14th Century; Notes on Editions, Marginalia, Opinions and Book-Lore', *Augustiniana* 6 (1956), 146–274

'Clm 27034: Unchristened Nominalism and Wycliffite Realism at Prague in 1381', *RTAM* 24 (1957), 320–60

Bibliography

' "Moderns" and "Modernists" in MS Fribourg Cordeliers 26', *Augustinianum* 5 (1965), 241–70

Trinkaus, Charles (ed.): *The Pursuit of Holiness in Late Medieval and Renaissance Religion* (Leiden, 1974)

Ullmann, Walter: *The Origins of the Great Schism: A Study in Fourteenth Century Ecclesiastical History* (London, 1948)

Vauchez, André: *The Laity in the Middle Ages: Religious Beliefs and Devotional Practices*, trans. Margery J. Schneider (Notre Dame and London, 1993)

Verger, Jacques: 'L'exégèse de l'Université', in Riché and Lobrichon (eds.), *Moyen Age et la Bible*, pp. 199–232

'Teachers', in De Ridder-Symoens (ed.), *History of the University in Europe*, pp. 144–68

Verger, Jacques and C. Vulliez, 'Crises et mutations des universités françaises à la fin du moyen âge', in J. Verger (ed.), *Histoire des universités en France* (Toulouse, 1986), pp. 109–37

Vooght, Paul De: *Les Sources de la doctrine chrétienne d'après des théologiens de xive siècle et du début du xve avec le texte intégral des xii premières questions de la 'Summa' inédite de Gérard de Bologne* (Bruges, 1954)

Wailes, Stephen L.: 'Why Did Jesus Use Parables: The Medieval Discussion', *Mediaevalia et Humanistica* 13 (1983), 43–64

Walsh, Katherine: *A Fourteenth-century Scholar and Primate: Richard Fitzralph in Oxford, Avignon and Armagh* (Oxford, 1981)

'Preaching, Pastoral Care and *Sola Scriptura* in Later Medieval Ireland: Richard Fitzralph and the Use of the Bible', in Walsh and Wood (eds.), *Bible in the Medieval World*, pp. 251–68

'Die Rezeption der Schriften des Richard Fitzralph (Armachanus) im lollardisch-hussistischen Milieu', in Jürgen Miethke (ed.), *Das Publikum politischer Theorie im 14. Jahrhundert* (Munich, 1992), pp. 237–53

'Die englische Universität nach Wyclif: Von geistiger Kreativität zur Beamtenausbildung?', in Alexander Patschovsky and Horst Rabe (eds.), *Die Universität in Alteuropa* (Constance, 1994), pp. 85–110

Walsh, Katherine, and Diana Wood (eds.): *The Bible in the Medieval World: Essays in Memory of Beryl Smalley*, SCH Subsidia 4 (Oxford, 1985)

Ward, John O.: 'Some Principles of Rhetorical Historiography in the Twelfth Century', in Ernst Breisach (ed.), *Classical Rhetoric and Medieval Historiography* (Kalamazoo, Michigan, 1985), pp. 103–65

Watson, Nicholas: 'Censorship and Cultural Change in Late Medieval England: Vernacular Theology, the Oxford Translation Debate, and Arundel's *Constitutions* of 1409', *Speculum* 70 (1995), 822–64

'Conceptions of the Word: the Mother Tongue and the Incarnation of God', in Wendy Scase, Rita Copeland and David Lawton (eds.), *New Medieval Literatures* 1 (1997), 85–124

Wei, Ian P.: 'The Self-Image of the Masters of Theology at the University of Paris in the Late Thirteenth and Early Fourteenth Centuries', *Journal of Ecclesiastical History* 46 (1995), 398–431

Bibliography

Weijers, Olga: *Terminologie des Universités au xiiie siècle* (Rome, 1987)

   La 'Disputatio' à la Faculté des arts de Paris (1200–1350 environ): Esquisse d'une typologie, Studia Artistarum 2 (Turnhout, 1995)

Weisheipl, James A.: 'Curriculum of the Faculty of Arts at Oxford in the Early Fourteenth Century', *Mediaeval Studies* 26 (1964), 143–85

   'Developments in the Arts Curriculum at Oxford in the Early Fourteenth Century', *Mediaeval Studies* 28 (1966), 151–75

Wilks, Michael: *The Problem of Sovereignty in the Later Middle Ages: The Papal Monarchy with Augustinus Triumphus and the Publicists* (Cambridge, 1963)

   'Predestination, Property and Power: Wyclif's Theory of Dominion and Grace', in G. J. Cuming (ed.), SCH 2 (London, 1965), pp. 220–36

   'Reformatio Regni: Wyclif and Hus as Leaders of Religious Protest Movements', in Derek Baker (ed.), *Schism, Heresy and Religious Protest*, SCH 9 (Cambridge, 1972), pp. 109–30

   'Wyclif and the Great Persecution', in Michael Wilks (ed.), *Prophecy and Eschatology*, SCH Subsidia 10 (Oxford, 1994), pp. 39–63

   Wyclif: Political Ideas and Practice, Papers by Michael Wilks, ed. Anne Hudson (Oxford, 2000)

Williams, George H.: *Wilderness and Paradise in Christian Thought: The Biblical Experience of the Desert in the History of Christianity and the Paradise Theme in the Theological Idea of the University* (New York, 1962)

Wilpert, Paul (ed.): *Antike und Orient im Mittelalter*, MM 1 (Berlin, 1962)

   (ed.): *Die Metaphysik im Mittelalter*, MM 2 (Berlin, 1963)

   (ed.): *Universalismus und Partikularismus im Mittelalter*, MM 5 (Berlin, 1968)

Wippel, John F.: *Mediaeval Reactions to the Encounter Between Faith and Reason* (Milwaukee, 1995)

Wood, Diana: '... *novo sensu sacram adulterare Scripturam*: Clement VI and the Political Use of the Bible', in Walsh and Wood (eds.), *Bible in the Medieval World*, pp. 237–49

   (ed.): *Church and Sovereignty c. 590–1918: Essays in Honour of Michael Wilks*, SCH Subsidia 9 (Oxford, 1991)

Workman, H.B.: *John Wyclif: a Study of the English Medieval Church*, 2 vols. (Oxford, 1926)

Zimmermann, Albert (ed.): *Antiqui und Moderni: Traditionsbewußtsein und Fortschrittsbewußtsein im späten Mittelalter*, MM 9 (Berlin, 1974)

Index of names and titles

General index

CAMBRIDGE STUDIES IN MEDIEVAL LITERATURE